*The Heretic of Cacheu*

# THE HERETIC OF CACHEU

*Crispina Peres and the Struggle over Life in Seventeenth-Century West Africa*

TOBY GREEN

The University of Chicago Press

The University of Chicago Press, Chicago 60637
© 2025 by Toby Green
All rights reserved. No part of this book may be used or reproduced in any manner whatsoever without written permission, except in the case of brief quotations in critical articles and reviews. For more information, contact the University of Chicago Press, 1427 E. 60th St., Chicago, IL 60637.
The moral right of the author has been asserted.
No part of this book may be used or reproduced in any manner for the purpose of training artificial intelligence technologies or systems.
Published 2025
Printed in the United States of America

34  33  32  31  30  29  28  27  26  25    1  2  3  4  5

ISBN-13: 978-0-226-84476-3 (cloth)
ISBN-13: 978-0-226-84477-0 (ebook)
DOI: https://doi.org/10.7208/chicago/9780226844770.001.0001

First published in Great Britain in 2025 as *The Heretic of Cacheu: Struggles over Life in a Seventeenth-Century West African Port* by Allen Lane, part of the Penguin Random House group of companies.

Library of Congress Control Number: 2025932537

♾ This paper meets the requirements of ANSI/NISO Z39.48-1992 (Permanence of Paper).

Authorized Representative for EU General Product Safety Regulation (GPSR) queries: **Easy Access System Europe**—Mustamäe tee 50, 10621 Tallinn, Estonia, gpsr.requests@easproject.com
Any other queries: https://press.uchicago.edu/press/contact.html

This book is dedicated to the friends from Guinea-Bissau, Senegal and The Gambia whom I have been privileged to make over the years.

It is especially for Buba, Mama, Yahya, Mohammed and Fátima; for Baba and Hassoum; for Abdoulie, Assan, Bala and Daniel; for Alaji, Djenaba, Marém, Ndaye, Alfa and Boubacar; and for Carlos, Carmen and José.

The critique of Western humanism is not a mere historical account of what happened – the book of atrocities. It is also the mourning of what was lost, in a way that does not dwell in the trauma, in a way that allows the survivor to escape the curse of repetition, to put the debris together again

Achille Mbembe, *Necropolitics*

# Contents

| | |
|---|---|
| *List of Illustrations* | xi |
| *Acknowledgements* | xv |
| *Characters* | xxi |
| *Peoples of the Cacheu Region in the Seventeenth Century* | xxv |
| *Glossary* | xxvii |
| *Maps* | xxix |
| Introduction | 1 |
| 1. Crispina and Jorge | 25 |
| 2. Women and Power in Cacheu | 52 |
| 3. Cacheu: The Setting | 77 |
| 4. Cacheu in Regional and Global Context | 104 |
| 5. Religion, Politics and Power | 133 |
| 6. Slavery and Human Trafficking | 162 |
| 7. Work | 192 |
| 8. Entertainment and Gossip | 212 |
| 9. Time and Space | 236 |
| 10. Living, Healing and Dying in Cacheu | 253 |
| Conclusion | 275 |
| *Bibliography* | 283 |
| *Notes* | 297 |
| *Index* | 323 |

# List of Illustrations

*Picture credits are given in parentheses.*

p. 16   The fortress of Cacheu. (Nammarci, published under a creative commons licence: https://commons.wikimedia.org/wiki/File:Cacheu_statues_in_fortress.jpg)

p. 19   Our Lady of the Rosary, Cidade Velha. (Toby Green)

p. 38   Map of Cartagena, seventeenth century. (Available from Bridgeman: https://www.bridgemanimages.com/en/blaeu/cartagena-in-colombia-from-the-atlas-of-w-blaeu-seventeenth-century/engraving/asset/4730348)

p. 43   A *bolon* in northern Guinea-Bissau. (Toby Green)

p. 53   *Signare* from St Louis, Senegal. (From Jacques Grasset de Saint Sauveur, *Costumes civils actuels de tous les peuples connus* (1788); public domain)

p. 72   Postcard of the river at Farim, 1910. (Smithsonian: https://edan.si.edu/slideshow/viewer/?eadrefid=EEPA.1985-014_ref7044)

p. 74   Pepel cloth from the early twentieth century. (Lisbon, Museu de Etnologia: http://matriznet.dgpc.pt/MatrizNet/Objectos/ObjectosConsultar.aspx?IdReg=82845)

p. 76   Rice bushels, Guinea-Bissau. (Toby Green)

p. 89   A fence bordering a vegetable garden, Bijagós islands. (Toby Green)

p. 98   Olifant. Ivory, carved. Sierra Leone, c.1500–1550. (Lisbon, Museu Nacional de Arte Antiga (inv. no. 988 Div))

## List of Illustrations

p. 99 — Ivory pyx from Sierra Leone. (Walters Art Museum, licensed under a Creative Commons-Attribution ShareAlike 3.0 unported license: https://commons.wikimedia.org/wiki/File:Sierra_Leonian_-_Ivory_Pyx_with_Scenes_from_the_Passion_of_Christ_-_Walters_71108_-_View_F.jpg)

pp. 106–7 — French map of the Casamance river and Bijagós islands, 1767. (Archives Nationales d'Outre Mer, Aix-en-Provence, France. Public domain: https://recherche-anom.culture.gouv.fr/ark:/61561/1169640.1169641/daogrp/0/2)

p. 111 — Kola nuts as a wedding gift. (Azekhoria Benjamin, under creative commons licence: https://commons.wikimedia.org/wiki/File:Kolanuts.jpeg)

p. 113 — *Lumo*, Bula, Guinea-Bissau. (Toby Green)

p. 115 — Canoe on Orangozinho island, Bijagós. (Toby Green)

p. 116 — French map of Bolama island, Bissau, 1718. (Archives Nationales d'Outre Mer, Aix-en-Provence, France. Public domain: https://recherche-anom.culture.gouv.fr/ark:/61561/78781.1169637/daogrp/0/1)

pp. 124–5 — Ribeira Grande, Cabo Verde, 1655. Detail from the Atlas of Leonardo de Ferrari. (Public domain: https://commons.wikimedia.org/wiki/File:Pormenor_da_Planta_de_la_Ciudade_Cape_Verde_(1).jpg)

p. 136 — Manjako religious shrine, Jeta island, Bijagós. (Toby Green)

p. 139 — James Island Fort, The Gambia. (From Francis Moore's *Travels into the inlands of Africa*, 1738. Public domain: https://commons.wikimedia.org/wiki/File:Sketch_of_James_Island,_Gambia.png)

p. 144 — A *kapok* or silk-cotton tree, Bijagós islands. (Toby Green)

p. 150 — The restored Franciscan monastery in Cidade Velha (Ribeira Grande). (Toby Green)

p. 158 — Termite mound, Bijagós islands. (Toby Green)

*List of Illustrations*

p. 177     Silver '*daalder*'. (Public domain: https://commons.wikimedia.org/wiki/File:1601_Amsterdam_daalder_8_reales_British_Museum.jpg)

p. 183     Map of the Bijagó islands, 1767. (Archives Nationales d'Outre-Mer, Aix-en-Provence, France, 17 DFC C 55, XIV, carton 76, ark:/61561/78634.2071219. Public domain)

p. 198     Vertical loom, from today's Nigeria. 1910. (Public domain: https://commons.wikimedia.org/wiki/File:Studies_in_primitive_looms_(1918)_(14597768459).jpg)

p. 222     Playing cards from *c.*1650. (Public domain: https://commons.wikimedia.org/wiki/File:Pierre_Barbey_-_Playing_cards.TIF)

p. 224     *Warri* board. (The Horniman: https://www.horniman.ac.uk/object/14.3.66/1)

# Acknowledgements

All books are collaborative endeavours. I have learnt so much from so many people over the years, without which this one could never exist. It's hard to thank everyone who I would like to, and I apologize to everyone who the imprints of the passing years on my memory mean that I may have omitted.

I am more than usually indebted to my many friends and colleagues in Guinea-Bissau, Casamance and The Gambia, who have helped me to conduct research and taken me to key locations. In Guinea-Bissau Alaji Mamadou Ndiaye first took me to Cacheu, in 1995, and four years later introduced me to his friend Ibrahima Mansaly, teacher at Goudomp-3 school in the Casamance, who taught me a great deal about the history of Kaabu. Carmen Neto introduced me to the Guinean community in London and taught me much about her country throughout the 2000s. Later, it was a great (and fun!) privilege to work with Manecas Costa, who gave me different perspectives on Cacheu and its cultural heritage when we met in 2015 and again a couple of years later. Over the years, Carlos Cardoso has been a wonderful friend and colleague, who has materially transformed the ways in which I understand Guinea-Bissau and its peoples. And the same is even more true of José Lingna Nafafé, whose enduring friendship and faith in me has been one of the blessings of my life and career.

In The Gambia, Hassoum Ceesay has been more than a colleague: debater-king, fellow wordsmith and friend, he ensured that I was able to visit Bintang and Kaur and gain a sense of what those historic settlements may have been like several centuries ago. Baba Ceesay and Bala Saho first helped me to initiate my working relationships in The Gambia and have always been committed to the work that we shared in. I owe more than I can say to Buba

## Acknowledgements

and Mama Saho, and to many other dear friends: Sainey Baldeh, Abdoulie Jabang, Oussainou Sanneh and Assan Sarr. I Nimbara.

The journey towards writing this book began first with all these Senegambian friends, but was then kickstarted with the intervention of two generous colleagues in Britain. In 2010, Malyn Newitt suggested to Filipa Ribeiro da Silva and me that we should consider working on an edition of Crispina Peres's Inquisition trial for the British Academy's sources on African history series (www.fonteshistoriaeafricanae.co.uk). We began work with our colleague in Lisbon Philip Havik, and many years later were able to publish our collective edition of her trial, which forms the groundwork and basis for so much of the discussion that follows. The companionable years during which we worked together on this project informed me immensely about the many contexts of Crispina Peres's trial – I owe a great deal to Filipa and Philip: thank you both, *camaradas*.

A few years after this, Linda Newson very generously passed over to me her own photostats and accompanying CD-Roms of the account books of Manoel Bautista Pérez, impounded by the Inquisition in Lima in the late 1630s. Though I later made my own archival visits to Lima, where I was able to consult some of this material directly, this vast bundle of paper became absolutely essential when I combed through it again as I tried to conceive how a book like this might be written. It was typical of Linda's generosity to consider that the material might be helpful in some way.

Whatever perspectives I am able to bring to all this material emerged as well through the influence of the careful and transformative scholarship of many people. Great thanks and debts are owed to Boubacar Barry (especially for the concept of 'Greater Senegambia' without which this book would not have been conceived in its present form); Philip Havik for his immense archival research and pioneering studies of the history of gender, and then providing a detailed and invaluable critique of inconsistencies and mis-steps in the text as I prepared the proofs, for which I am immensely grateful; Walter Hawthorne for work on the Balanta and the history of Guinea-Bissau; José Lingna Nafafé for his pathfinding work on

## Acknowledgements

African–European relations in today's Guinea-Bissau (and so very much else besides); Carlos Lopes for the early historicization of Kaabu; Thiago Mota for his transformative recent work on the history of Islam in Senegambia; Peter Mark and José da Silva Horta for their work on the New Christian diaspora and art history; and Vanicléia da Silva Santos for her work on the Crispina Peres trial and on the *bolsas de Mandinga*.

For many years I have worked with the British Academy on their committee for publishing sources for African history. I am thankful to Geetha Nair, James Rivington and Portia Taylor in the Publications team for shepherding the edition of Crispina Peres' trial to publication in 2021, and to Ken Emond and Emma Deakins for their support over the years. I also thank the Academy for kindly giving permission for material from the trial edition to be reproduced in this book: © The British Academy 2021. Material reproduced by permission from *African Voices from the Inquisition, Vol. 1: The Trial of Crispina Peres of Cacheu, Guinea-Bissau (1646–1668)*, ed. Toby Green, Philip J. Havik and F. Ribeiro da Silva (2021), London: Oxford University Press.

Once I had developed over the years the relevant materials and perspectives, James Pullen helped me to work out the original idea. Meanwhile, I have been very lucky to work with the same editorial team of Simon Winder at Allen Lane and the University of Chicago Press on this book as on my earlier book *A Fistful of Shells*. When he first saw the idea Simon was immediately supportive and has been an immense editor, always understanding both the book's potential and how to bring out its ideas; at Chicago, Dylan Montanari has also been hugely helpful in putting the book through its final paces. I know how lucky I am to have worked with them both on developing this to fruition, and I am also very grateful to David Watson for a very thorough and clean copyedit of the draft text.

I also owe much to those at King's College, London, who have supported unstintingly my research into this important but neglected topic over the years. The book was written during research leave granted by the College, and couldn't have been done without it.

*Acknowledgements*

Successive heads of department have always supported the work I have done in both West Africa and the UK. I want also especially to thank my colleagues in professional services who have made all manner of complex arrangements feasible: Faida Begum, Juliette Boyd, Amy Hart, Dot Pearce and Ania Stawarska have all helped me to arrange aspects of my work without which this book could not exist. My deep and sincere thanks to them all.

The sustained research and thought which made me able to write this work came first of all during the time when I had been awarded a Philip Leverhulme Prize in History. However, then the book itself was delayed in a number of ways by the Covid-19 pandemic. Putting it finally together then came at a difficult point in my own life. I am so grateful to those who shared their own strength with me and thereby gave me the capacity to complete it, in particular: Olutayo Adesina, Samuel Adu-Gyamfi, Nat Barstow, David Bell, Muriel Blaive, Aleida Mendes Borges, Pedrito Cambrão, Oliver Davis, Érika Melek Delgado, Richard Drayton, Thomas Fazi, Bob Fowke, Sunetra Gupta, Daniel Hadas, Mike Jackson, Sinan John-Richards, Laurent Mucchielli, Reginald Oduor, Wellington Oyibo, Juliette Rouchier, Daniel Spiller, Sundararaman Thiagarajan, Ellen Townsend, Fernandes Wanda, Anjuli Webster and Reva Yunus.

I owe a particular debt to two dear friends and colleagues, Ana Lúcia Araujo and José Lingna Nafafé. They each read a complete draft of this book before anyone else and helped to shape the final version. Ana Lúcia provided all kinds of support in the writing of this book, making wonderful suggestions for illustrations and translation issues: her humane and brilliant knowledge of this period in history has been vital in helping me to reshape it into its current form, and her friendship has been essential in helping me to work on it at all. José and I meanwhile talked over many aspects of the manuscript and the hidden traces it revealed of the distant past of his country of birth – and also the sadness of writing such a book at a time when Guinea-Bissau has been suffering an enormous socioeconomic and political crisis driven by global forces, as in the past: José helped me to see traces of the religious

## Acknowledgements

and cultural worlds of Guinea-Bissau's past in the text in a materially different light, and also gave me confidence that I was on the right track.

Above and beyond all of these deeply heartfelt debts of gratitude, I am nothing without my much-beloved family: Emily, Lily and Flora. It was a joy to be able to travel with them in 2023 to these places which mean so much to me, and for them also to meet so many of the people from whom I have learnt so much. Above all else, their love and laughter ensured that I could finish this book.

# Characters

CRISPINA PERES: the richest and most powerful trader in Cacheu in the 1660s, married to two former captain-generals of the town. Of mixed African-European heritage.

JORGE GONÇALVES FRANCES: son of Álvaro, a New Christian trader who had been penanced by the Inquisition of Évora in 1594; himself a former captain-general of Cacheu and majordomo of the church of St Anthony; married to Crispina. Of mixed African-European heritage.

AMBROSIO GOMES: major commercial rival of Crispina and Jorge; one of the plotters in the Inquisition trial of Crispina.

ANDRÉ DE FARO: Capuchin missionary and author of a memorial about evangelization in Senegambia from the late 1660s; scribe in the trial of Crispina.

ANTÓNIO DA FONSECA DE ORNELAS: new captain-general of Cacheu at the time of Crispina's trial, and a major enemy of Crispina and Jorge.

ANTONIO VAZ DE PONTES: priest of Cacheu despatched by the Caboverdean governor to trade for him in Senegambia; a major slave trafficker in his own right, and a wealthy businessman as well as priest, often found in the house of his lover in Vila Quente.

BIBIANA VAZ: rose to become the most powerful trader in Cacheu by the 1680s and imprisoned the captain-general of Cacheu in her home in Farim for eighteen months; married to Ambrósio Gomes and also one of the chief plotters in Crispina's trial.

BONIFACIA: enslaved household servant of Crispina; deeply involved with her offerings to the *chinas* in an attempt to preserve the health of her child; raised with the close involvement of Sebastião Rodrigues Barraza, who then fell in love with her; died before Crispina's trial.

## Characters

DIOGO FURTADO DE MENDONÇA: Archdeacon of Cabo Verde who instigated the Inquisitorial trial of the priest Luis Rodrigues.

DOMINGOS DE AREDAS: godson and apprentice of Jorge; ransomed by Jorge from enslavement by the king of Sará; became an enemy of Crispina over a row involving *chinas* and then moved to live with Ambrosio Gomes and Bibiana Vaz; one of the main accusers in Crispina's trial.

FRANCISCO LEMOS COELHO: trader and enemy of Jorge over a street-fight with one of his relatives; author of one of the most detailed accounts to survive of life in Senegambia in the 1660s.

GASPAR VOGADO: official religious visitor of Cacheu; major administrator of the town, responsible for defences and rebuilding the church in the 1650s; one of the key instigators of Crispina's trial.

JOÃO BAUTISTA PÉREZ: New Christian trader from Montemor-o-Novo in Alentejo; spent several years living in Cacheu in the 1610s and had four children there; account books provide some of the most detailed evidence on life in Cacheu; brother of Manoel; died in 1617.

JOÃO NUNES CASTANHO: Jorge's brother-in-law; envious of the wealth of his relative, one of the main conspirators in Crispina's trial.

LEONOR FERREIRA: cotton-spinner and trader from Ribeira Grande in Cabo Verde; merchant who came to trade in Farim and Cacheu in 1655, where she knew Luis Rodrigues.

LUIS RODRIGUES: priest and drunkard; canon of the Cathedral of Ribeira Grande and priest of Farim c.1655; arrested by the Inquisition for soliciting women in the confession and deported to Lisbon; acquitted and returned to Cabo Verde, where he began the process of fomenting Crispina's trial.

MANOEL DE ALMEIDA: sergeant-major of Cabo Verde, who accompanied Crispina to Lisbon and handed her over to the Inquisitors there; acted as Crispina's interpreter in the trial; eventually became captain-general of Cacheu.

MANOEL BAUTISTA PEREZ: New Christian trader in Cacheu in the 1610s, who moved to Lima and became the richest trader there;

arrested by the Inquisition suspected of heresy in 1636; executed in the auto-da-fé of Lima in 1639; the legal dealings over his credit and debts produced some of the most detailed evidence we have on seventeenth-century Cacheu.

MARIA MENDES: cotton-spinner in Cacheu; born in Ribeira Grande, probably in the 1590s; aunt of the public scribe in Cacheu; known as having some of the best contacts with the *djabakós*.

NATALIA MENDES: herbalist living in Vila Quente, often called upon to provide cures by people in Cacheu; married to the barber-surgeon known as Frique-Fraque.

PAULO DE LORDELLO: president of the Franciscan monastery of Ribeira Grande at the time of Luis Rodrigues's trial; agitator for Inquisitorial investigations; official charged with leading the investigations leading to Crispina's arrest.

SEBASTIÃO RODRIGUES BARRAZA: household slave of Crispina and Jorge, often despatched outside the town on household errands; claimed to be related to the nobility of Casamance; apparently a Muslim, though also an inveterate drunkard.

# *Peoples of the Cacheu Region in the Seventeenth Century*

BAINUNK: most oral histories agree that they were among the oldest inhabitants of today's Casamance and Guinea-Bissau; Bugendo and Guinguim were Bainunk settlements. Under demographic and political pressure in the seventeenth century, their numbers and significance declined precipitously, and there are very few Bainunk left today.

BALANTA: in the seventeenth century found especially in the region of northern Guinea-Bissau, between Cacheu and Farim, and also south of here. Famous warriors who resisted trading and dealing with Europeans. In the nineteenth century many Balanta also migrated to the south of today's Guinea-Bissau, to become then the largest ethnic group in the country until recent years.

BIJAGÓS: people who live in the archipelago of small islands off the west coast of the mainland; said to have moved there to escape the invading armies of the Mali empire in the thirteenth century; famed warriors.

CABOVERDEANS: generally mixed-heritage people often found in Senegambia; born in the Cabo Verde archipelago of islands some 300 miles off the African coast north of Dakar in today's Senegal. Some Caboverdeans came as imperial emissaries in Church, trade and administration; others as captives of some of these people; and others as independent traders wanting to re-establish themselves in the West African homelands whence they or their ancestors had come enslaved to Cabo Verde in the sixteenth century.

JOLOF: large polity and people found north of the Gambia river; little involved in Cacheu in the seventeenth century, although some Cacheu traders did do business in Jolof lands.

## Peoples of the Cacheu Region in the Seventeenth Century

FLOUP: people who lived in the lands between Cacheu and the Atlantic Ocean, growing in importance in the seventeenth century; famous for frequency of attacks on Atlantic slave trading ships; known today as the Jola.

FULANI: cattle-herders and scholars of Islam found across West Africa from Kano to Senegambia; migrated in a large group in the late fifteenth century to the Fuuta Jaalò mountains of today's Guinea-Conakry under Koli Tenguela; involved in raiding captives for the transatlantic slave trade.

JAKHANKÉ: Sufi Islamic scholars and teachers whose centre in the seventeenth century was at Sutucó on the Gambia river; frequent traders across Senegambia and purveyors of amulets. Said to have originated from Dia, in the Middle Niger valley, perhaps the oldest urban settlement in that region (c.500 BCE).

MANDINGA: ethnic group found in Kaabu and across Casamance and Gambia; linked to the Malinké of today's Guinea-Conakry and to the Mande of the Mali empire.

NALÚ: rice-growers living in small-scale communities in the south of today's Guinea-Bissau and north of today's Guinea-Conakry.

PEPEL: major ethnic group living around Cacheu in the seventeenth century and in the *bolons* round and about, as well as in the nearby kingdom of Mata de Putame. Later subdivided into closely related groups today known as the Manjako (most focused around Cacheu and the coast), Mancaigne (around Bula) and Pepel.

SAPI: name given by the Portuguese to peoples living around Sierra Leone, some way south of Cacheu, and famous as ivory carvers; following invasions from Mane peoples in the 1560s, some moved to live in and around Cacheu.

# Glossary

*aguardente*: rum brought from the Americas.

*alcaide*: mayor or chief official of town in Senegambia, deriving from the Portuguese; in Mandinga the word is today Alkalú.

*alúas*: wooden tablets on which children practise writing Arabic verses from the Qu'ran. Still often used today.

*arroba*: a standard measure equivalent to 32 lbs or 15 kilograms.

*auto-da-fé*: public Inquisitorial procession in an urban centre, in which penitents carried candles before them before receiving their punishment; in the seventeenth century, cases of burning or garrotting were comparatively rare.

*barafulas*: white-and-blue cloth woven in the Cabo Verde islands and highly prized in Senegambia.

*bolon*: creek.

*boticário*: apothecary/pharmacist.

*cantareiras*: fixed benches for sitting in the kitchen.

*Carreira da Índia*: sea route of the Portuguese empire from Lisbon to Goa; a fleet undertook this annually once in each direction, a journey of eight months.

*chinas*: shrines of Senegambian religions; a name given by outsiders both to the religious setting in which offerings were made and to the apparel involved in these offerings, such as the pots which could be kept in the home with various special liquids.

*combete*: storehouse.

*compadre*: godfather; co-godparents were known as *compadres*.

*criado/a*: servant.

*djabakós*: healer or seer drawing on Senegambian religious practice to prescribe cures or offerings to be made.

*farim*: ruler of one of the Mandinga kingdoms of southern Senegambia.

*fazenda/fazendeiro*: plantation(-owner).

## Glossary

*gan*: extended family network.
*godenho*: measure of kola nuts.
*griot*: praise-singer.
*gris-gris*: amulet.
*grumetes*: apprentices of major traffickers, often involved in regional trade in Senegambia, where they would undertake tasks for their mentor/master's household.
*iran*: spirit-snakes with special magical properties in Senegambian belief-systems.
*kapok*: silk-cotton trees.
*Kristón*: mixed-heritage Catholics living in the port towns of today's Senegambia, acting as intermediaries for Atlantic traders.
*lumo*: rotational weekly market.
*mato*: bush; also used in colonial documents to indicate areas outside imperial control (i.e. most places).
*New Christians*: descendants of Jews who had been forcibly converted to Christianity in Portugal in 1497, or whose ancestors had chosen to convert rather than to leave Spain in 1492. New Christians held a wide range of beliefs: some were devout Catholics, others were crypto-Jews, others were more or less atheists.
*nyantio*: aristocratic warriors of the kingdom of Kaabu.
*parda*: of mixed heritage.
*praça*: fortified imperial redoubt (such as Cacheu).
*regateiras*: women trading at markets.
*signares*: mixed-heritage women who became powerful traders in the port-towns of West Africa between Senegal and Sierra Leone.
*sobrado*: house with two storeys.
*tabanka*: names for fortified villages in Senegambia, still the word for village in Guinea-Bissau today.
*tchon*: land belonging to a people or to a *gan* (extended kinship network).

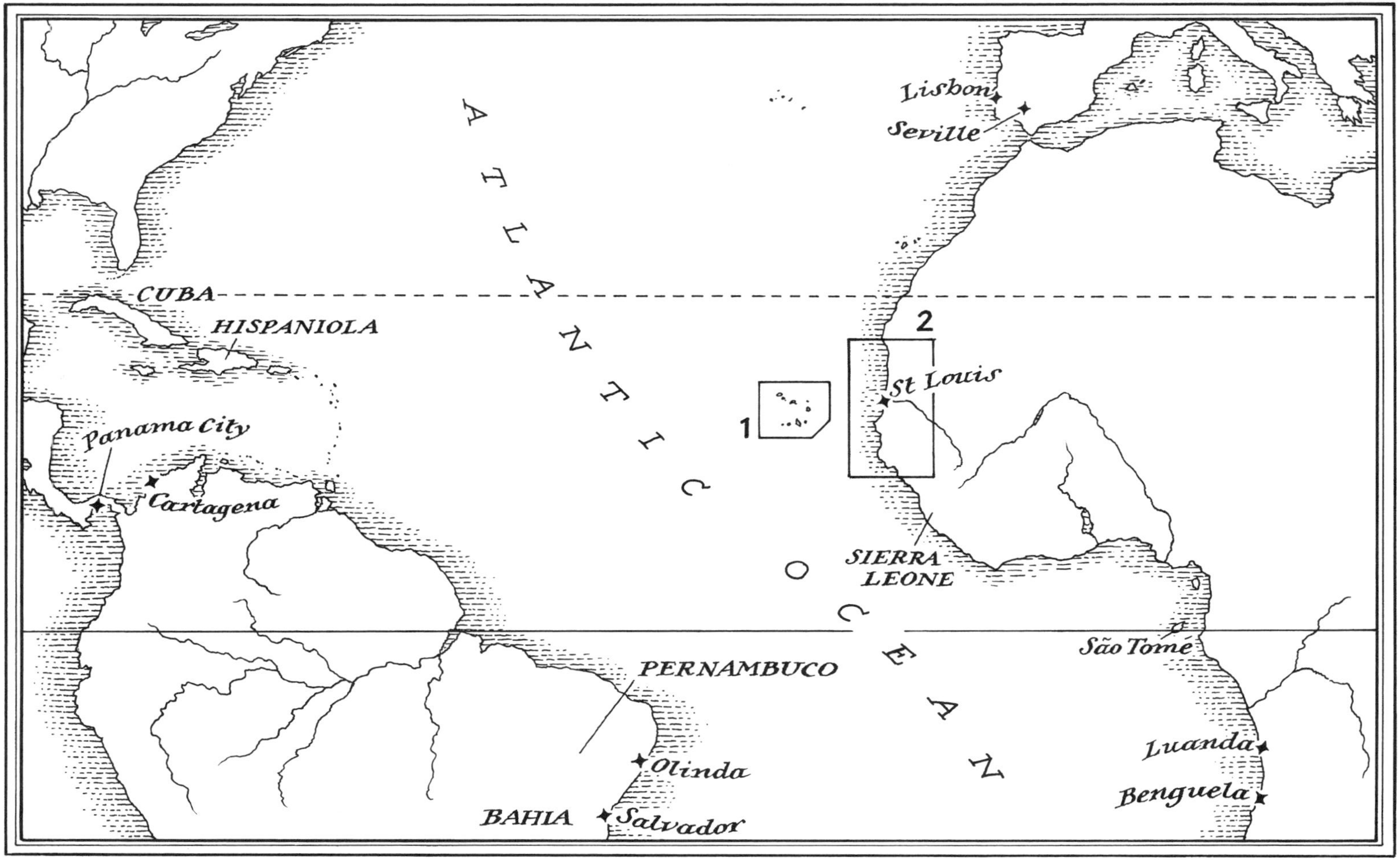

Lisbon
Seville
ATLANTIC OCEAN
CUBA
HISPANIOLA
2
St Louis
1
Panama City
Cartagena
SIERRA LEONE
São Tomé
PERNAMBUCO
Olinda
BAHIA
Salvador
Luanda
Benguela

CABO VERDE
1
2
Santo Antão
São Vicente
São Nicolau
Sal
Boa Vista
San Tiago
Fogo
Maio
Ribeira Grande
Brava
MAURITANIA
R. Senegal
FUUTA TOORO
St Louis
SENEGAL
Gorée
Arrecife/Rufisque
Joal
James Island
Kaur
GAMBIA
Cassão
Barra
Kantora
KOMBO
R. Gambia
Sanguedogu
R. Casamance
Bintang
Bichangor
Farim
Bugendo
R. São Domingos
Cacheu
Baoula
KAABU
Guinguim
Geba
Bissau
Bijago Islands
GUINEA
R. Nunez
GUINEA-BISSAU
SIERRA LEONE
Gower

## *Introduction*

Towards the middle of 1652, Jorge Mesquita de Castelbranco arrived as the new governor of Santiago, largest among the islands of the Cabo Verde archipelago and around 300 miles west of the African coastline. Castelbranco was an 'impoverished nobleman' who had been offered this position, which the officials of the Portuguese Colonial Overseas Council probably saw as something of a sinecure. The focus of empire had long moved on from Cabo Verde to Angola and Brazil, where the Portuguese were immersed in a decades-long conflict with the Dutch for control of the South Atlantic. However, Castelbranco saw things differently: being a colonial governor was still an opportunity to rebuild the family fortune, given that Santiago island had long been at the centre of the region's traffic in enslaved Africans, linking the port of Cacheu in today's Guinea-Bissau with the Atlantic world.[1]

As soon as he arrived, Castelbranco made his mark. When a wine-trader arrived from the island of Madeira, further north in the Atlantic Ocean, he imprisoned him for causing him 'offence'. Vicente Gomes, the Madeira wine-trader, had accused Castelbranco of lying and acting dishonestly when he had tried to stop him from doing business with the sweet wines still famous today, and then essential in Cabo Verde for the Catholic Communion ritual as well as for other, more dissolute, purposes. By the time of the petition, in late June, Gomes had been fuming in prison for a month: Santiago's community was small, everyone knew everyone, and he couldn't be released without the governor's approval.[2]

But meanwhile, Gomes's business partner was busy. Manoel Henriques, the scribe of the royal estate, had a side-hustle as an intermediary in the wine business. He had been selling Gomes's wine to the traders of Ribeira Grande, the capital city of the island.

## The Heretic of Cacheu

Several witnesses came forward to describe how he had placed wine in their houses for them to sell. All of them were women: Beatriz Jorge, who was thirty years old, Maria Manuel (thirty-four), Maria de Socorro (forty-seven) and Francisca Peres (thirty). In other words, and as the historian Nwando Achebe puts it, while the men paraded around harbouring enmities, sowing political chaos and proclaiming their own self-righteousness in lengthy and tedious epistles, 'women owned the marketplace' in this West African island town.[3]

Political factionalism was already rife in Santiago when Castelbranco appeared in 1652. A deposition from 1655 described how he had arrived to find that the previous governor, Pedro Semedo Cardoso, had imprisoned the judge and purveyor of the Royal Estate Manoel Paez de Aragão 'because of the great hatred and enmity that there was between them'. Cardoso had replaced Aragão with Francisco Alvares Liste as judge. The deposition went on that he had done this since both of them supported the faction led by the African inhabitants of the island, descendants of enslaved captives who had escaped to live in the high mountains of the interior in Santa Catarina, the region around what is today the town of Assomada. In fact, at that time, 'the inhabitants of the island who had been born there were mutinying, saying that they were going to come down to the city and kill all the whites there, and saying publicly that the Black man should be governor.'[4]

Thus, while women owned Ribeira Grande's marketplace, African women and men ran the island beyond it. Into this complex political world blundered Jorge Mesquita de Castelbranco, this minor Portuguese nobleman who had fallen on hard times, someone who held stereotyped and outdated views of what this world was like. As colonial governor, shouldn't he be able to do as he pleased and treat the place as his own plaything to profit from as he wished? Wasn't he automatically in charge?

But, like history itself, things weren't anything like as simple as he had imagined: by early November 1653, less than eighteen months after he had arrived, Castelbranco had been thrown into jail in the fortress of St Philip, whose restored walls and cannon still

*Introduction*

command the cliff overlooking Ribeira Grande in today's country of Cabo Verde.⁵

This book offers an account of daily life in the seventeenth-century West African port town of Cacheu. It does so through the lens of the life story of the richest trader in the town by the early 1660s, a woman called Crispina Peres. Peres was arrested for trial by the Portuguese Inquisition in 1665 and deported to Lisbon to the Inquisitorial jail. She is the 'heretic' of this book's title. And yet, while Peres was arrested for the crime of heresy, many readers may conclude by the end of the book that her real crime was that her power challenged that of the growing Portuguese empire – that her real 'heresy' was a different sort of power, and a different way of understanding the world.

Through the lives of Peres and her family, friends and enemies, this book takes us into the worlds of the women and men who lived between around 1615 and 1670 in Cacheu, in today's Guinea-Bissau,* then the major West African slave-trading port linked to the colonial world of Santiago island in Cabo Verde. We find out who the people of the town were; how they interacted with the regional and global networks that they were part of; what it was that moved them, angered them or made them afraid; how they made money; and how they enjoyed themselves, and loved, lived and died. Crispina Peres's life is the continuity which shapes the book as a whole, though at times it is set aside to engage with a broader and more holistic portrait of this seventeenth-century West African port town. In tracing these emotional, economic and social histories, I have tried to allow the lives of the people involved to emerge as in a tapestry. At times the ten chapters cover similar topics, but they always do so from a range of different perspectives. Through the slow layering-up of these different perspectives, a picture takes

---

* Hereafter, for the sake of convenience, I will refer to the general region of today's country as 'Guinea-Bissau' – although, of course, the nation state did not exist until 1974.

shape which aims to offer an overall understanding of daily life there. This structure also allows the book to embody one of its central arguments, which is that people in seventeenth-century West Africa did not operate through our current linear approach to time. Instead, they experienced the world and the passing of time in a way that was more cyclical: indeed, the rise of a linear view of time was connected to the rise of the empires of the Atlantic world.

A number of other histories of West African port cities have been written for this period, yet all the same this narrative has an unusual level of emotional detail about daily life almost 400 years ago. We are able to reconstruct these feelings because of a type of historical source that had not been drawn on by historians of West Africa until the last twenty years: the records of the Portuguese and Spanish Inquisitions. These institutions were responsible for imposing and overseeing the 'purity of the faith' not only in Spain and Portugal, but also in their colonies. While the enforcement of this policy was very sporadic in places such as today's Angola and Guinea-Bissau, in the middle of the seventeenth century two lengthy Inquisition trials were held involving West Africans. The first began in 1657, and was brought against the philandering, drunkard canon Luis Rodrigues, of the cathedral of the island of Santiago. Rodrigues was arrested in Cabo Verde for soliciting women in the act of confession and deported to the Inquisitorial jail in Lisbon in March 1658. But there, in spite of a strong range of evidence, he was pardoned.[6]

A vengeful man, Rodrigues returned to Cabo Verde in 1661 determined to get his own back on his enemies. In 1655, two years before being arrested, Rodrigues had been sent from Cabo Verde to be the parish priest of the town of Farim in Guinea-Bissau, some distance up the São Domingos river from Cacheu. There he had caused many scandals. In one sermon he had claimed that he had been given powers by the Pope to exculpate any incestual relations. He was widely accused of sleeping with any woman he found attractive, making them go to his house for confession, where he received them in breeches and a shirt lying on his bed in a special building he had assigned for this purpose. He had then embarked on an affair with a married woman whose husband had wanted to kill him, forcing him to flee Farim for Cacheu by night in the boat of someone who felt sorry for him.[7]

In spite of all this – and of the numerous accusations against him in the Cabo Verde islands as well – Rodrigues preferred to blame his enemies for his arrest and trial by the Inquisition, rather than to consider his own faults. He was a human being, warts and all. And so, on his return to West Africa from Lisbon, he set about getting his own back. Rodrigues soon drew on his political contacts to fulminate the papers leading to the second trial, which came to a head in the early months of 1665. This was the trial that was brought against Crispina Peres. Peres was married to the former captain-general of Cacheu, Jorge Gonçalves Frances, someone who in his own trial Rodrigues had declared to be his sworn enemy. After Rodrigues began the proceedings, Peres's other enemies in the town took charge, and she was eventually arrested on the charge of witchcraft. Following three years of interrogations in Lisbon, Crispina Peres was processed in an auto-da-fé there, where she was given a mild penance – as was often the case with Inquisitorial judgements by this time – returning to Cacheu in June 1668.[8]

These two trials offer remarkable social histories of a small town and its hinterlands in seventeenth-century West Africa, with the type of detail which was long assumed by historians to apply only to the worlds of Europe. While biographical histories exist for Angola in the seventeenth century, this is the first such book to be written in this era for West Africa. Those interested in this history are extremely fortunate to have these records today, since they are the only cases of their kind which have survived. They were produced at a particular point of Senegambia's history, as part of the imperial competition then growing across the world. But for the rest of its long active history, the Portuguese Inquisition did next to nothing in West Africa: by and large, its main interests in the empire were in Brazil and in Goa (where they had formed a tribunal in 1560).[9]

What is more, alongside these 1,000 folios of documents, there is a further bundle of 1,000 or so more pages of Inquisition sources.

These documents predate these trials by forty years and are housed in the National Archive of Peru in Lima. There, in the 1630s, the Portuguese slave trafficker Manoel Bautista Pérez was arrested by the Inquisition of Lima. Bautista Pérez was the richest man in the city, and his account books dating back almost twenty years were soon impounded by the Inquisition as his creditors petitioned for the debts which they claimed he owed them. Some of these account books relate to the time that he and his brother João spent as slave traffickers in Cacheu in the 1610s. João had died in Cacheu in 1617, and Manoel had come to the Americas shortly afterwards, where he grew rich. Two decades later, the account books of profit, loss and despair linked to their actions in West Africa and then South America were impounded, as the Inquisition sought to assess the size of Manoel's property.[10]

Taken all together, what has endured from that traumatic period of world history is a remarkable collection of documents of over 2,000 folios that offer the chance to reconstruct many aspects of daily life that were long assumed lost. The use of Inquisition documents to provide hitherto unparalleled social histories of medieval and early modern Europe was a feature of history-writing of the 1970s. Books such as *Montaillou* by the French historian Emmanuel Le Roy Ladurie and *The Cheese and the Worms* by Italian historian Carlo Ginzburg became widely read; and more recently the historian James Sweet used an Inquisition trial to explore the life history of Domingos Álvares, an enslaved African from today's Benin living in Brazil in the 1730s. These books collectively transformed the ability to understand the fine-grained detail, the textures and the feelings which made up human lives so long ago. In so doing, they challenged the view of history as one performed and enacted by male elites: the kings, noblemen and merchants who so often line the pages of history books.[11]

One thing which these documents also offered these historians was the opportunity to undercut stereotypes about static, unchanging communities in the past. In *Montaillou*, Ladurie takes us into the social worlds of this remote Pyrenean redoubt. In doing so, he also shows how mobile many of those who lived there were: the priests who came and went from more important towns nearby such as Aix-les-Thermes and Foix, and the herders who lived an itinerant life of transhumance in the Pyrenees with their flocks, coming and going according to the dictates of pasture, and developing emotional connections along the way.

The long-ignored survival of these documents from Cacheu means that the same kind of detailed insights are also possible for West Africa from a long-ago time. As in Montaillou, people who lived in Cacheu travelled a great deal in the wider Senegambian region in which the town is situated, and so this book offers a picture not only of daily life in this town but also of the worlds around it. What is more, one of the main protagonists of this history – Crispina Peres – was not only female but was also the most powerful merchant in the town. Here is a West African woman's life-story, bringing her daily life to us in a different way and from a much earlier period than before, across the painful chasm of time that separates us from this past.[12]

Beneath the measured script produced by the ecclesiastical scribes of these Inquisitorial trials lies a traumatic history. Some readers will wonder how far sources produced by Iberian Church institutions and their male apparatchiks can ever faithfully represent the social and emotional worlds of Senegambians from the seventeenth century. There are many layers of trauma to unpick – more than ever could be framed within a single book, or by a single historian.

Most significantly, there is the collective trauma still so widely felt today, through the globalized assault and grief which was produced by the traffic in enslaved persons. These records all exist, in some way or another, because of the transatlantic slave trade. In the first half of the seventeenth century, Cacheu was at the centre of this traffic in this part of West Africa. It had taken over that dubious mantle from the island of Santiago, Cabo Verde, which had been the fulcrum of the traffic in the sixteenth century. Entering into this book, readers will see just how far greed, violence and trauma connected to this world were workaday aspects of daily life in Cacheu. The documents force us to confront the reality of how easy it is for human beings to justify their involvement in appalling acts.[13]

Moreover, some readers may feel confused by some of the details here. If Cacheu was a centre of this cruel business, how come Senegambians were able to walk freely about the town? Didn't they fear being seized and transported out to one of the waiting ships? Of course, many of them did, as will become clear in this book – especially those who worked as servants in the homes of the main human traffickers. However, these are also questions that hark back to an earlier Western assumption that in this era Africa and slavery are somehow synonymous – that there is nothing more about daily life in West Africa that is worth remarking on.

People in Cacheu knew well that most of the captives in the traffic came from elsewhere, seized through warfare and transported by canoe or by sea to the town. The Caboverdean trader and official André Alvares d'Almada described in 1591 how the rivers of Guinea-Bissau were roamed by 'thieves, who are known locally as *gampisas*. They are like bandits, and do nothing else, stealing slaves [i.e. raiding and seizing them], and bringing them to sell to the ships.' Besides raids like this conducted from the rivers, as we will see later, the Bijagó islanders who lived in the archipelago offshore were (in)famous for conducting military raids on villages, destroying them and seizing those left behind as captives for enslavement. Alongside war captives and raiding victims, criminals, those accused of witchcraft, and debtors were also sometimes sold into Atlantic enslavement.[14]

All of this represented a new and disturbing historical dynamic. Incessant labour demands from the New World mines and plantations were transforming existing West African institutions of dependence and labour into the cruel horror of chattel slavery. Demand stoked supply. The best defence against enslavement for coastal communities in Greater Senegambia* was trade, which could provide access to

---

* The region between the Senegal river (the border between today's Mauritania and Senegal) in the north and Sierra Leone in the south.

weapons for defence and also make the Atlantic traffickers reliant on them for local trading networks. Thus, many of the people who lived in Cacheu were secure as they made a decent living through work and trade. Moreover, the Portuguese had stopped trying to raid West Africa for slaves very early in their travels down the coast, by the 1460s, since they had often found themselves outmanoeuvred militarily. Their gunpowder went damp and was useless in the rainy season, and this was for them a new environment. Instead they trusted to their demand stoking these wars fought elsewhere by the Bijagó and others to produce their captives, as we will see later in the book; and moreover they were utterly dependent on the people of Cacheu to meet their material wants, and on the people in the surrounding villages to supply them with provisions and grain stores both for the town and with which to feed enslaved captives on the 'Middle Passage'.[15]

All this can begin to explain just a small part of both the trauma and the contours of slavery that emerge in this book. Cacheu was a town which relied economically on the transatlantic traffic. The haunting echoes of this inhumane business were ever-present, from the cries of slave branding in the trading houses to the disturbing presence of captives being marched in irons through the streets to and from the port and the eerie sight of the slave ships themselves, floating out in the harbour, their lanterns bobbing up and down in the night. And yet, as human beings so often will try to ignore the cruelties and inhumanity right in front of their noses, so slavery was only one part of daily life in Cacheu – just as it forms therefore only one part of this book. This institution formed a workaday reality whose cruelty many tried to forget, forgetting also the risk for some of the household enslaved that they too might unexpectedly be seized and transported as just so much human property. Outside the households of the slave traffickers people knew that this happened rarely to people like them in the town, because of the Portuguese dependence on the residents and on the surrounding villages for the basic necessities of daily life.

Beyond this historic and enduring trauma of enslavement, there is also that of the chief protagonist herself. Crispina Peres, the

*The Heretic of Cacheu*

dynamic trader of Bainunk and Portuguese heritage, was at the pinnacle of her social and economic power in Cacheu when her enemies conspired against her, drawing on the Inquisition to bring her down. Her political and kinship links with Bainunk and Pepel kings near to Cacheu, and to other parts of the region, could not protect her. She spent three years in the Inquisitorial jail, and for one entire year she appears to have been left in the cell without any word from the judges – before being summoned before them so that their interrogations could begin again. Her life, and her marriage, were destroyed: Crispina Peres's personal pain is thus etched on many of the pages of this book.

Moreover, the very existence of these documents offers a signal perspective on this history. For why did the Inquisition decide to launch into two such lengthy (and costly) proceedings in the middle of the seventeenth century? This was part of the growing geopolitical competition which characterized Atlantic trade – and the traffic in enslaved Africans – in this period. For it was in the 1640s and the 1650s that the Dutch and the English entered this business wholesale, and that their competition began to be felt keenly by the Portuguese. Religious competition was also growing with the increasing presence in Greater Senegambia of itinerant Muslim clerics known as the Jakhanké, of French missionaries, and Spanish Capuchins arriving in the 1640s in the Cacheu and Sierra Leone regions.[16]

As it turned out, the Portuguese Inquisition would be suspended for seven years by the Vatican just a decade later, in 1674, but at the time these Inquisition trials were an attempt to assert Portuguese primacy in this colonial struggle. This was in various ways a struggle over life (and of lives): it was a struggle over the power to conscript labour, to determine worldviews and value systems in a global setting, a struggle over meaning and the authority to ascribe knowledge and to heal disease. It was also, of course, a struggle over the life of Crispina Peres herself, whose trial today thus stands as a marker for the increase in demand for enslaved Africans, the signal role that demand had in accelerating the traffic and the consequent intensification of that historical tragedy from this period onwards.[17]

*Introduction*

In this way, we are reminded of how violent and anti-historical the stereotype of Africa was, as it emerged in Europe in the writings of figures such as Hegel and Adam Smith from the late eighteenth century. Far from Africa standing 'outside history', Cacheu was deeply connected to locations around the world, ranging from Cartagena in today's Colombia and Salvador da Bahía in north-eastern Brazil, to Amsterdam, Seville and Lisbon, to Istanbul in the Ottoman empire, and to textile producers in Gujarat, India. These globalized links were connected with this growing demand for and traffic in enslaved persons: for, without being a global space in the early modern world, Cacheu – and so many other parts of Africa – could not confront us today, through these documentary traces, with the violence and complexity of this painful past.

There are many further layers of trauma which emerge from these texts. There is the way in which the concentration of economic and political power over the early modern and modern periods aggravated inequalities of all kinds. This emerges so starkly in the terse formulae of these documents, as white male priests interrogated witnesses, only then to belittle them in their discussions afterwards – the chief ground given for Luis Rodrigues's pardon by the Inquisitors of Lisbon in 1661 was that the principal witnesses against him, who were of course Black women, 'did not have the necessary qualities to proceed to his imprisonment since he is a Canon'.[18]

Then there is the social violence implicit in the way in which the Inquisitorial interrogations were carried out. Not only was all the evidence written down by male scribes as they themselves decided, but it was filtered through a layer of translation. Most of the key witnesses were West Africans who did not speak Portuguese and had their testimonies rendered by male interpreters. In the case where interrogations were conducted in the vernacular West African coastal Kriolu language, it was the scribes themselves who would then translate and interpret the questions and answers as they saw fit in the trial documents. So there is no sense in which what emerged here can be described as an unfiltered African voice.

These main sources used for writing this book thus pose questions more than they provide answers. How can documents produced as part of the power-grab of white colonial men be a reliable source of evidence to reconstruct this past, of a West African port town? And if they are going to be used, in what ways can readers – and this writer – guard against consciously or unconsciously reproducing the stereotypes which they sought to enforce?

Fortunately, many have pondered these very questions in recent years and developed techniques to address them. The historian Vanicléia Silva Santos also looked at the trial of Crispina Peres in her article on the circulation of the amulets known as 'Mandinga pouches' (*bolsas de Mandinga*) across much of the Atlantic world in the seventeenth and eighteenth centuries. As sources, these Inquisitorial texts are far from neutral. On the other hand, as Santos suggests, historians can read between the lines of what was intended in the texts to excavate its silences and the real social context which they represent: 'the historian's task is to read beneath the Inquisitor's stereotyped discourse to uncover the faith, values, and habits of the accused'.[19]

A good example of how to do this is the reading of the Inquisitorial judgement of Luis Rodrigues just discussed. The Inquisitors did not openly declare that the 'qualities' of the witnesses were insufficient to find Rodrigues guilty of heresy *because* they were Black women. However, in placing their perceived low-status qualities against the high status of the accused, a white male canon, the silence of the source on this point begins to speak loudly. The explicit social context which formed this judgement emerges with force – and so the historian has also to excavate the social and cultural worlds which helped to produce the document. This investigation offers the chance of a conversation across history: the Inquisition trials and impounded account books offer a precious window onto the intricacies of daily life, but without at the same time also using oral histories, historical linguistics and other sources to gain a sense of the wider daily life in Cacheu and the surrounding region, we cannot understand the Inquisition trials themselves.

The history that emerges from all this is one rarely told; and one which, before working with Philip Havik and Filipa Ribeiro da Silva

## Introduction

on Crispina's case, it had not occurred to me to try. As all readers know, we live in a world which is becoming ever more unequal. With the wealth and power of elites growing disproportionately as never before, sources from the distant past which can undercut the idea of 'history' as an inevitable unfolding of the history of elites are more important than ever. The social history of daily life can present a different approach to social relations and to power – and thereby remind us of the many different ways in which societies can organize and have organized themselves over time.[20]

By looking closely at details which have mostly been forgotten, this book offers several challenges to conventional ideas about economic and social change in world history. The first is linked to economics. One of the major theories of modern liberal economics is called 'institutional economics'. This holds that it is through building strong institutions that economic growth is achieved. Much of the attention paid by economists to low-income countries therefore goes into studying and promoting the building of the said institutions. However, in this book we see that it really depends on who is building them. The Inquisition was as strong a state institution as existed in the early modern Atlantic world: however, in this case, far from leading to economic stability, its power was imposed in order to stifle the entrepreneurialism and economic power of a West African woman. In other words, strong institutions building economic foundations need to be home-grown.

A second challenge comes towards the history of gender and equality. Recent changes in the way that the topic is understood by some in the West are seen by them as symbolic of modern progress. However, the Crispina Peres trial, and the lives of the many women related to her that we can glimpse through its pages and the other sources considered here, show us how mistaken it is to assume that history always proceeds inexorably towards perceived goods. In the context of women's history in Africa, historians have shown that women held more or less equal power in many of the continent's societies in ancient precolonial times, maintaining control over key aspects of political and social life, and that strong aspects of this culture persisted for thousands of years up to the dawn of colonialism.[21]

In this book, we see clearly how the power now associated with the modern state delivered an all-out attack on female agency and economic empowerment in this West African context. As capital became concentrated and its power grew, European empires – alongside the conservative Salafi Islamic reform movement that followed in the eighteenth century – certainly did not always promote gender equity. As this book shows us, they generally did the reverse, so that women in the seventeenth century like Crispina Peres could be far more powerful than is often imagined in the present. Moreover, West Africa was not alone in this dynamic since many European port cities also experienced mass male migrations by sea in this century, leaving disproportionately large populations of women who often thus controlled important aspects of the contours of daily life. In the end this study of Crispina Peres's life therefore reveals the shortcomings of simplified approaches to the history of gender in the past and present, and also suggests ways in which the strength of women in the West African past may have influenced more recent dynamics, including the role of women in Guinea-Bissau's wars of independence (1963–74).[22]

Third and finally, the details in this book present a concerted challenge to the ways in which history has usually been written in the West. For the writing of 'world history' has generally excluded Africa, and included Africans mainly through the lens of enslavement in the diaspora. In this book, we see how the multi-layered connections of Cacheu, on so many different levels, answer back. These granular details challenge not only the approach of the traditional Western historical discourse to Africa, but also challenge the nature of that discourse as a whole. This is not least because, as we see in the last chapters of the book, these details also reveal how the process of objectivity associated with the subject of history in the West was the other side of the coin of the colonial assault on Africa and Africans. The standardization of time and space through lines of longitude and claims to universal time were a core part of the scientific revolution in the seventeenth and eighteenth centuries – but as we see here, they

## Introduction

were also essential to the intensification of imperial cycles of demand and extraction.[23]

Another challenge to that language of history comes in the book's focus on spirituality and healing as a core driver of change in Cacheu. African societies are deeply religious, and yet all too often historical narratives about the continent focus on material forces as the driving motive of history. This suits Western paradigms of history, but it is certainly an approach that is foreign to almost everyone in Africa. As we will see in this book, it is impossible to consider the complex histories of the African past without grasping the centrality of spiritual approaches to life, and what this may have meant to the core actors in the historical past.

In considering these documents, therefore, there is much to surprise us about the historical process and how it has usually been written down. We don't only receive challenging perspectives on the interactions of West African men and women, the sorrowful place of slavery and empire in this history, the importance of spirituality and healing in social life, and the way in which one small town in West Africa was globally connected. We are also introduced in a unique way to the interior emotional worlds of this time and place.

Just as there are emotional underpinnings to these documents, so this is a book that has its own emotional meanings for me in writing it.

Over thirty years, I visited many times almost all the locations in which this book's histories took place. I have been to Cacheu itself on several occasions. I first visited in 1995, travelling with a Senegalese friend in the back of a pick-up from the neighbouring town of Canchungo, heartland to Guinea-Bissau's Manjako community. Cacheu was a famous town, but during the colonial era the rise of motorized transport turned it into a backwater. The road from Canchungo passes just a handful of villages, most of which are off the road – something often the case in Guinea-Bissau, where villages moved into the bush (*mato*) to escape the violence of colonialism and then the independence war. Today it sweeps into the town, down towards the wide, brown waters of the river, past the remnants of the old two-storey (*sobrado*) administrative buildings of colonial times. Down by the river is the jetty, and a recently raised memorial to the port's history of slavery. Opposite this is a museum dedicated to this history, quite recently created. By the waterfront there are some fishing canoes, and the shells of the warehouses that used to store the staple cash crop of groundnuts during the modern era of Portuguese colonialism in the twentieth century. Behind the road which follows along the waterfront, tracks dive off into the trees next to the town, where the compounds inhabited by today's community can be easily seen.

Cacheu is a far quieter place now than it was in the years on which this book concentrates. The main remnant of the old slave-trafficking times is found in the ruined fort by the riverside, with broken statues of now-dethroned Portuguese colonial 'heroes' littering the yard, and the fort's peeling whitewashed walls sealed off from the town itself by a gate. On one of my later visits, an

The fortress of Cacheu.

## Introduction

enterprising person appeared from the compounds beside the fort with a key to the padlock, which he had placed on the gate so as to charge an entry fee to visitors. Then, from the far wall of the fort backing on to the São Domingos river, I looked out at its still waters, which in the seventeenth century were busy with dugout canoes plying to the town markets, and across to the north bank of the river lined with a seemingly thick wall of mangroves, whence the creek then ran north to the markets at the Bainunk town of Bugendo.

In the seventeenth century Cacheu was not as isolated as it feels today. Boats of one kind and another arrived constantly. There were the dugout canoes which connected the town with nearby communities, as well as in the rainy season to the Gambia river through the creeks of Casamance in today's southern Senegal. These vessels unloaded rice and millet, bolts of cloth and also enslaved Africans on the waterfront. There they came upon the Atlantic vessels which then linked the town to the city of Ribeira Grande on Santiago island in Cabo Verde, and also across the Atlantic ocean to ports such as Cartagena in today's Colombia.

Ribeira Grande in Cabo Verde – the home of Governor Jorge Mesquita de Castelbranco in the 1650s – was nominally the colonial capital on which Cacheu then 'depended'. These two settlements were deeply intertwined, separated as they were by hundreds of miles of ocean waters. Cacheu residents traded with the people there, and were related by marriage to them. All of the colonial and religious officials who were despatched to Cacheu were sent from there. At the same time, most of the Africans who lived in Ribeira Grande or who had escaped to the highlands of Santiago had come from Cacheu and its environs. While in the sixteenth century Cabo Verde's connections with West Africa included areas of today's Senegal north of the Gambia river, by the period on which this book focuses the links were all with Cacheu.[24]

Ribeira Grande's site on Santiago was chosen because of the spring of fresh water which came down the steep-sided valley from which it takes its name. Cabo Verde is an arid archipelago, a slab of the Sahara in the Atlantic Ocean. Water sources are scarce on most of the islands. This deep cleft in the mesa gave life not only to the town, and to its business, but also to fruit and vegetable gardens which can still be found in the valley today, a green oasis criss-crossed by irrigation channels and small stone-lined reservoirs which wait patiently, all the year round, for the sporadic bursts of rainfall which give the whole island life. If you climb up the valley sides, you will then be confronted with a view of an unforgiving brown desert which runs for fifteen or twenty miles to the base of the crest of mountains in the middle of the island – where those captives who escaped enslavement in the sixteenth and seventeenth centuries formed their own communities in Santa Catarina, having fled across the desert from this Atlantic port.

Rather like Cacheu, Ribeira Grande is something of an empty shell today. The capital moved centuries ago about ten miles along the coast to Praia – capital city of today's Cabo Verde – where the harbour is both wider and better protected. Ribeira Grande was left with memories in stone and became known as 'the old city': Cidade Velha. Here were left the ruins of the fortress on the hillside, of the Franciscan monastery some way inland and halfway up the hillside, of early cemeteries and of the church of the Brotherhood of the Rosary with its gravestones embedded in the cobbled floor.\* Over the past twenty years, restoration projects have worked on many of these remains in Cidade Velha, giving a sense of what some might have been like when recently built, in the years during which the events of this book take shape.

However, none of this had interested many people outside the town until the last two decades, when UNESCO and the islands' historians and archaeologists became involved in these projects. Until then, the narrow bay, rocky shoreline and compact lattice of streets between the valley walls had been more or less abandoned, like this difficult and complex history, to fall into desuetude.[25]

While Cacheu depended in imperial theory on Ribeira Grande,

---

\* The Catholic brotherhood for free Black men in the Portuguese empire.

*Introduction*

The church of Our Lady of the Rosary, Cidade Velha, built in 1609.

in practical terms it was far more dependent on the communities that surrounded it. Cacheu was not some sort of isolated redoubt. It could not survive through force imposed on its neighbours, but only by dialogue. Supplies of munitions and gunpowder were poor. In the rainy season the powder got damp anyway. Numerically, the imperial settlers were vastly outnumbered. Those who survived could only do so by intermarrying, and through developing close kinship, commercial and political ties with West African peoples. As we will see in this book, they depended particularly on their West African hosts for access to healers, and the knowledge of palliative herbs which they possessed. And these healers came to Cacheu along the creeks and rivers that linked the town to the wider region.

Those creeks and rivers were the roads of the past. It's hard though to imagine anyone except drug dealers using them today to ship goods across the borders of three modern nation states (Guinea-Bissau – Senegal – The Gambia). But when the rains teem down, from May to September, the water level rises so much that whole new route maps are created. In the seventeenth century, a creek about ten miles upstream from Cacheu cut through past the town of Guinguim to Ziguinchor in Casamance (Bichangor in the seventeenth-century documents). From there, the Casamance river cuts deep into today's Senegal, and then rainy-season creeks link it to the Bintang *bolon* (creek) one of the main southern tributaries of the Gambia river. From there, Cacheu's traffickers could travel hundreds of miles east, past Cassão\* and Kaur to Kantora,† where trans-Saharan traders also visited and the Atlantic and Saharan networks met.[26]

In time, I got to know many of these places too. In 2023, I worked with colleagues in The Gambia's National Centre of Arts and Culture, delivering workshops to secondary school teachers around the country. The programme of four workshops began in a school on the edges of Bintang, today a quiet and very small town on the banks of the *bolon*. This tributary is so wide – at least 300 metres – that it is hard not to believe that you are standing on the banks of the Gambia river itself. It is lined with thick mangroves and has such a majestic sweep of water that it is easy to see how busy a waterway it must have been. Meanwhile, many of the inhabitants of the town tell how they often find remnants of the trading past: blue-and-white Portuguese tiles beneath the foundations of their houses, and in one village not far away an old abandoned cross.

Our workshop programme then ended at a school graduation ceremony in Kaur. Here the ways in which roads have reshaped the geographies of the past are even clearer. While Bintang is bypassed by the main road about five miles south from the *bolon*, and has declined in significance as a result, Kaur has simply transplanted itself a couple of miles inland from its old centre by the river to the site of the road

---

\* Near today's town of Kuntaur.
† Near today's town of Basse Santa Su, the easternmost and second city of The Gambia.

on the north bank. The riverside where the old town used to be concentrated is now a backwater, reached by a track through rice-fields, and home of a small ferry which crosses to the south bank of the Gambia river on demand. Though the new town remains a thriving market crossroads, just a few miles from the Senegalese border, it still lacks the activity of former centuries; for it was of Kaur that the Cacheu trader Francisco de Lemos Coelho wrote in 1669, 'this is the biggest town on the Gambia river . . . full of merchants'.[27]

In this way, and for decades, I was lucky enough to enter what felt like a constant dialogue between the present and those distant sources that I kept on disinterring. I developed a reasonable grasp of the Kriol and Wolof languages, learning the ways in which they too were archives of past human interactions. I learnt that many aspects of the past remained in barely disturbed ruins which archaeologists had yet to disinter: in masonry half-submerged by sand near to the Bintang jetty, and for the more distant megalithic past in the standing stones found near to quarries in the hinterlands around Kaur at Wassu. I wrote a history of the Inquisition, and co-edited a translation of the trial of Crispina Peres and a book on Guinea-Bissau. Through all those years, I gradually discovered that the most detailed sources that I could disinter were right in front of me: Inquisition records that came from southern Senegambia itself.[28]

It didn't take long for the new governor, Jorge Mesquita de Castelbranco, to become unpopular. While he claimed that he had thrown Vicente Gomes into prison for his lack of respect, the Santiago islanders had a different story to tell.

By April 1653, less than a year after he had arrived, the islanders produced their own account of the new governor's manner of proceeding. In his first months of office, he had 'dealt solely with the aim of amassing property every single day, impeding the daily business transactions of the islanders, who were forced to sell him their goods for much less than they were worth'. The argument with Gomes stemmed from Castelbranco's attempt to create a wine cartel: Castelbranco wanted to stop all other wine vendors and had thrown Gomes in jail since he had arrived from Madeira wanting to undercut Castelbranco's price by half.[29]

Indeed, where Castelbranco's greed was concerned, this was just the tip of the iceberg. Even though the islanders' main business was in 'sending goods to trade in Guinea [Senegambia, through Cacheu]', he had blocked their business completely so that only he was allowed to do this. When a French ship had arrived to sell fish, he had forced its crew to sell only to him. Several times he had arrested his enemies, too, and forced them to pay large fines to be released. And when a Spanish slave trafficker who had come from Havana wanted to buy fourteen captive Africans who had been brought by ship over 2,500 miles from the island of São Tomé, in the Gulf of Guinea, Castelbranco had blocked him and insisted on buying the trafficked enslaved himself.[30]

If all this sounds to some readers like exaggeration on the part of his enemies, the rancour which this new governor produced lived long in the memory. Eight years after he had been thrown into prison and stripped of his office, 121 islanders of Santiago signed a letter bemoaning the legacy of his ruinous rule. His actions had been so pernicious that they had 'forced people who were tired of his abuses to leave the city and go and live in the hills (as many did)'. He had made many business people go bankrupt through blocking their trade with passing ships. Such had been his ways of dealing with people that 'he seemed more like an enemy than a governor'.[31]

Some 370 years later, what sticks in the mind is the sense of enormous factionalism and rivalries rending these communities. Cabo Verde was living through a period of political tumult, in which everything seemed up for grabs. It was also living through a process of what was, from a macro-economic perspective, decline. The major routes of the transatlantic traffic were moving south, to today's Angola, Benin and Nigeria, and across to the port of Salvador in Brazil, to Barbados and Jamaica. Cabo Verde's elites were no longer in prime position to maximize this traffic. As the big merchants moved on in the hunt for profits, those who remained fought for their share of what was left.

This factionalism spilled over into the parts of West Africa which

*Introduction*

form the core of this book. As we have just seen, the main economic business of the islanders of Santiago was in sending goods to trade in the Cacheu region. That was why the Portuguese colonial edifice sought to control as far as possible the social and religious lives of its commercial enclaves there, like Cacheu and Farim. That was why the cathedral chapter of Cabo Verde nominated priests like Canon Luis Rodrigues to go and work in Farim, more than 100 miles inland up the São Domingos river from Cacheu. And all this was how and why the rancour and infighting of the islands spilt over first into the Inquisitorial trial of Rodrigues, and then into that of Crispina Peres of Cacheu.

These interrelationships of Cacheu and Ribeira Grande are something we will see in more detail later in the book. They are spelt out quite clearly in the pages of these trials. During the ecclesiastical visit to Cacheu made by Luis Rodrigues after his pardon by the Lisbon Inquisition, one of his first inquiries was into cases of alleged sodomy – a crime of heresy punished by the Inquisition – against the priest Antonio Vaz de Pontes of Cacheu. But this was hardly a neutral move, since in his own Inquisition trial Rodrigues had declared that the then-governor of Cabo Verde, Pero Ferraz Barreto – who had masterminded his arrest by the Inquisition and deportation to Lisbon – was his sworn enemy and had sent the priest Vaz de Pontes to trade in Cacheu on his behalf in place of Rodrigues.[32]

Over time, these colonial rivalries born of greed, lust, hatred and fear – of dying of fever, of attack by African revolutionaries or European pirates, of the gathering chaos of the world around them – all grew, all of it. Those men with access to colonial law sedimented their worldview and rivalries in long screeds of angry text, compacted onto rare and expensive strips of paper, despatched by ships which had as much chance of sinking as of making it to their destination in Lisbon or Brazil. Read now, many of these texts seem like talking therapies, getting anger off your chest so as all the better to pursue your war of attrition with your implacable foe. And while settlers threw about threats all the time – of the king, the army,

African maroons – few people mentioned the Inquisition. By the 1650s, not a single case had led to the deportation of someone from West Africa to Lisbon for trial. What did Inquisitors care about the way in which their mixed-heritage colonists used West African healers to eke out their lives, long before the rise of Western medicine as another offshoot of colonial power?

It seemed unlikely that that remote institution would barge into this world and seek to disrupt it. And yet, that world was changing very fast. The European imperial powers were at war with one another for influence in both Africa and the Americas, and their institutions were an important part of the game. If the Lisbon Inquisitors could exert control somewhere like Cacheu or Ribeira Grande, if they could get these tedious texts to determine reality, then they could generate the fear that is the other side of the coin of respect – and which became part and parcel of the accumulation and expropriation of property in colonial history.

So it was that the Inquisition rumbled into action, producing the many pages of these trials. And then, after all the actors therein had themselves passed on, amnesia sedimented over the layers of forgotten pages in the archives of Portugal. Products of their conflicted time and place, these documents were literally forgotten for centuries. The dead were allowed their rest, until in the late 1990s historians seeking new ways into thinking about the West African past found that these texts could still speak over the aeons of time and emotion that separate that past from this present.

The human relations which for so long were lost now re-emerge. Today they speak newly of that lost world – and of the passage of time, the objectification and the development of new perspectives which characterize the process of turning trauma into history.

I.

## *Crispina and Jorge*

'the said Crispina Peres by means of diabolic arts of witchcraft, keeps her husband in her house, with infirmities, so that he cannot leave and make voyages, by always having him at home; and [not] looking at other women'

This history begins with the people whose lives it describes. From Crispina Peres's Inquisition trial we know enough about her and her husband, Jorge Gonçalves Frances, as well as about their household, to understand something of the beliefs and motivations of these individuals who lived so long ago in Cacheu. This was at that time the most important Atlantic trading town in Senegambia, but that did not make it very big. There were a handful of colonial buildings and a few large trading houses belonging to families like Crispina and Jorge's. In this part of the town, at any one time, there may have been anything up to 1,000 people, while in the larger neighbourhoods of Vila Quente and Rua Santo António that number could have been multiplied by two or three. This town was in other words a colonial enclave, less than a century old, though the Portuguese presence in the whole Senegambian region itself dated back more than 200 years.

Cacheu was a town which depended entirely on its surrounding region. In this African Atlantic commercial centre, Crispina was the most powerful trader, someone whose wealth was such a catch that during her life she was married to not one but two captain-majors of the town. Meantime, Jorge's father had been one of Cacheu's most influential Atlantic traffickers of the first decades of the seventeenth century, with connections to Cartagena in Colombia, Lisbon, Amsterdam and Seville. Both Crispina and Jorge were of mixed heritage, with Portuguese fathers and West African mothers. Between them, they had the connections in Cacheu, in its Senegambian hinterland and in the Iberian empires, which allowed them to dominate the business of the town. This was why they were both so hated there.[1]

In the early 1660s, this hatred was channelled into this kangaroo-court Inquisition trial fomented against Crispina – in which she was accused of being a 'heretic' for practising the very same rituals as almost everyone else in Cacheu, as we will see later in more detail. The trial itself took many years to develop, and all the hearings were scrupulously annotated by scribes appointed by Friar Paulo de Lordello, the president of the Franciscan monastery in Ribeira Grande, Santiago island. After strenuous lobbying, Lordello had been appointed commissary of the Lisbon Inquisition in Cabo Verde and the adjacent coast of West Africa, and always chose his fellow Franciscan friars to be the scribes. Lordello had his own motivations, not least no doubt the hope that successful pursuit of heretics might lead to advancement in the Church – as had been the case with the Inquisitor Jacques Fournier, who as Bishop of Pamiers had pursued the Cathars in Montaillou from 1318 to 1325 and had then been elected Pope Benedict XII in 1334.

In January 1661, Lordello began to receive denunciations – at first in Ribeira Grande – as to the 'witchcraft' practised by Crispina Peres. This was a term which referred generally to African religious practice, which could be labelled by Inquisitors as heresy when practised by baptized Catholics. Later that year, Lordello sailed to Cacheu to conduct further investigations, receiving depositions from Crispina's enemies in the house of the canon António Fernandes Ximenes, and later in the hospice of the Franciscans in the town. Lordello sent these papers forthwith to the Inquisitors in Lisbon, itself a slow process, and in 1662 they ordered further investigations to be made. Lordello received more depositions from Crispina's enemies

## Crispina and Jorge

in Cacheu in 1663, which were also sent to Lisbon. On 10 January 1664, the Inquisitors of Lisbon issued a decree ordering Lordello to proceed with the arrest of Crispina, which inevitably took many months to reach his hands in West Africa. Her arrest finally happened in late January or early February 1665. Two months later, she was taken by ship to Cabo Verde, and thence to Lisbon. Here her trial would take a further three years before it concluded.[2]

Who were the individuals at the heart of this trial, Crispina and Jorge? Who were their parents, their relatives, their friends and their enemies, and how does understanding this help to make sense of their experiences? Beginning this book through their life-stories takes us right into this world which now seems so remote, while in the chapters which follow the town itself and its surroundings will emerge in greater detail. Just as Cacheu cannot be looked at in isolation from the many places to which it was connected, so Crispina and Jorge lived in a busy social whirl. Their lives make fuller sense when we know something of the people they dealt with, and we know enough of their circle to give a sense of it.

Theirs was a household that was always full of cousins, relatives by marriage and siblings passing through and staying for extended visits. These kin arrived in Cacheu from the islands of Cabo Verde and nearby towns such as Farim and Geba. They came for business, taking advantage of a good place to stop in the house of their successful relatives. The Peres/Frances household was always busy with them, and with the comings and goings of their own slaves and servants, many of whom are mentioned by name in the trial documents, and whose lives and experiences will also form a major part of this book. Households such as theirs could therefore be made up of up to thirty or forty people at times.

Busy as it was, full of kin and business partners and of the couple's enslaved captives, servants, children and young business protégés, this household was rife with familiar human emotions: envy, greed and rivalry, as well as love, desire and sorrow. Many of their kin envied the couple their success and gave evidence against Crispina to Lordello and the scribes conducting the Inquisition trial

## The Heretic of Cacheu

in Cacheu – as did some of their enslaved household servants. None of these undercurrents came as news to her, as she showed in her own evidence to the Inquisitors.

One of the most haunting aspects of the Inquisitorial judicial procedure was its secrecy, as accused people were never told the identities of their accusers. Instead, they were asked to imagine what might have been said about them, and by whom, and then were given the chance to attempt to disqualify the evidence of those they deemed their enemies. Crispina did this when she made her own accusations in her interrogation, in March 1665. Towards the end of a very long list of enemies (and potential accusers), she said:

> I also suspect the two brothers-in-law of my husband, residents on the island of Santiago, who are busy sailing on the island of Santiago route, one of them Captain João Nunes Castanho and the other António Mendes Fragoso, as they complained that my husband did not give them a lot of money and would not get along with them because of me; they never talked to me and hated me as is public and notorious . . . they always said many bad [things] about me; saying that I had kept their brother-in-law [i.e. her husband Jorge] in bed with witchcraft.[3]

She had missed nothing. Nunes Castanho was married to Jorge's sister in Santiago and declared in the trial that she had refused to allow one of her slaves called Eiria to confess to the priest when she had been ill, and that she had kept a pot over her own bed in which 'they told him that she had witchcraft in there, and diabolical things'. Moreover, he had clearly gone about Cacheu spreading gossip just as Crispina had said, since many people came forward to say that he had told them all about her alleged heresy. Or, as Jorge put it in his own evidence, 'João Nunes Castanho, and António Mendes Fragoso, my brothers-in-law, also developed hatred, because they are poor, and often came to this settlement from Cabo Verde in the hope that I would make them rich.'[4]

## Crispina and Jorge

When it came to the enslaved persons of the household, Crispina also showed a clear understanding of the hatred that underlay her daily interactions with them. Though the life of a household slave in Cacheu was much preferable to that of the life of plantation enslavement in the Americas, the terrible fear of being sold into Atlantic trafficking hung over their lives. The hatred was mutual, and as far as she was concerned none of their testimonies should be allowed to stand in the trial that was being brought against her:

> My slaves are also sworn enemies of mine and of my husband because I push them hard to work and punish them so that they work for me, which is common [practice] . . . they hated [me] a lot, especially a slave called Sebastião Rodrigues Barraza . . . a Muslim who knew [how] to read and write; and was not of great service [because he was] a heavy drinker; who I punished because he did not keep good account of certain things I assigned to him, as he was continuously drunk.[5]

Again, she was on the mark. Rodrigues Barraza was a talkative witness in the trial, giving voluminous evidence of her alleged religious infractions. This was a house where little was secret and where a culture of gossip ensured that little remained hidden for long. The household of the richest and most powerful traders of Cacheu was a place rife with envy, with people out to get one back and try to get at least a finger on the main prize.

It's therefore clear from reading through these traces of that past that greed shaped a number of aspects of daily life in this Atlantic slave-trafficking town of seventeenth-century West Africa. Yet while this was catalysed by the demand of the Atlantic empires of Spain and Portugal, and of their wastrel traders who washed up in the region, Cacheu remained very much a Senegambian space. Crispina and Jorge may both have had Portuguese fathers, and been of mixed heritage, but neither of them had ever left West Africa before Peres was deported from Cacheu in April

1665 and eventually hauled before the Inquisitors of Lisbon late that year.[6]

On 16 November 1665, Crispina Peres requested an audience at the Holy Tribunal of the Inquisition of Lisbon. The Inquisitors asked if she had come to confess her faults 'for the discharge of her conscience', but Crispina said instead that she had asked for a hearing 'in order to ask them to send her to her husband, and that she did indeed wish to confess her faults but did not know what they were'. Marooned 2,000 miles away from home and those she loved, she had decided to play the game just in order to get this nightmare to end.[7]

Once in front of the Inquisitors, Crispina was required to proceed through the various stages of the tedious Inquisitorial formulae. She was asked about her background, her life history, her grandparents and her religious upbringing. She described this in detail, through her interpreter Captain Manoel de Almeida, 'a resident of this city [of Lisbon] among the orchards by the old well', who had previously been sergeant-major in Santiago, Cabo Verde. The enormity of the injustice wrapped up in this judicial procedure is best understood when we realize that Almeida had personally been charged with bringing Peres in chains from West Africa to Lisbon, before then being deputed by the Inquisitors to act as interpreter in her trial; and the way in which this was just part of imperial career progression for Almeida is shown by the fact that, even before Crispina's trial had concluded, in 1667, he was appointed as captain-general of Cacheu, where he died two years later.[8]

In this interrogation, Crispina provided a clear account of her origins and relationships, one which is also supported by other evidence. When she was arrested she was around fifty years old, which puts her year of birth near to 1615. Her father, Rodrigo, had come from the Azores islands to settle in West Africa, while her mother, Domingas Pessoa, was of the Bainunk people, born on the Nunez river in the north of today's Guinea-Conakry. It seems that Domingas and Rodrigo had met in the port of Geba, on the Geba river

## Crispina and Jorge

some distance south-east of Cacheu, where Domingas had also been baptized a Christian. Geba was a busy trading port, linked to the Kaabu empire, but Cacheu had the more powerful Atlantic connections. So the couple had moved to the town, where Crispina had been born. Her father was still alive in 1658, then a trader in Farim, but appears to have died shortly after this.[9]

Crispina knew quite a lot about her Bainunk family, especially on her maternal grandmother's side. Her mother Domingas's own mother had been called Florença Pessoa, and had been baptized as a Christian quite late in life. Florença had lived with her husband in the town of Guinguim, not far from Cacheu on the creek that flowed north to Casamance. However, though speaking warmly of her grandmother, Crispina declared complete ignorance of her Portuguese grandparents on her father's side, stating just that they were dead and that 'she knew nothing whatsoever of their names, professions, origins and statuses'. Rodrigo Peres was, it appears, a man of few words (and also, most likely, continually absent on trading voyages from the home where she was brought up). Another possibility is that Rodrigo's family had been New Christians, descendants of those Portuguese Jews forced to convert to Christianity by Manoel I's royal decree of 1497. Some New Christians had come from Portugal to West Africa to escape the Inquisition – just as others had gone to Amsterdam, Brazil and parts of the Ottoman empire. If Crispina knew this to be related to Rodrigo's origins, revealing this information would make the Inquisitors more likely to suspect her of heresy.[10]

In her life history, Crispina said that Christianity had been an important part of her upbringing. She was baptized in her parents' home in Cacheu and anointed at the church there. She said that Rodrigo had taught her Christian doctrine 'as soon as she had reached the age of reason', and that from the age of nine onwards she had gone into churches wherever she had found them, knowing the Our Father, Ave Maria and Salve Regina prayers by heart. Finally, she told the Inquisitors that her life had been a mobile one: although she had never left Africa before this forced visit to Lisbon,

## The Heretic of Cacheu

she had 'been in Geba and on the River Nunez, in Sierra Leone, and in Recife [now called Rufisque, just south of today's Dakar,* in Senegal] and in Cacheu'.[11]

This terse summary of her life conceals a whole human universe, which it will take the rest of this book to explore. Three strands can be picked out to begin with, as a way of getting our bearings. The first is that the social world of Crispina's community in West Africa was ordered by women, not men. Crispina knew nothing of her father's life and background, and nothing of that of her mother's father either. It was her own mother, Domingas, and her grandmother Florença, who had shaped her outlook with their stories, and with the knowledge they had given her of their Bainunk roots and wider family. Women ran households in this community, just as Crispina ran hers: and this is a theme we will come across very often in this book.

Secondly, this was not some static and immovable world of disconnected peoples or 'tribes'. Crispina had ranged widely across West Africa, from the area near Dakar in the north to Sierra Leone in the south, via most of the spaces in between. She felt at home not only in Cacheu, but in the whole region. Moreover, her grandparents had done the same: born in the creeks near Cacheu, in Guinguim in northern Guinea-Bissau, they had at some point moved 200 miles south to the Nunez river, where Crispina's mother had been born. These communities constantly mixed across linguistic, religious and ethnic boundaries – which were never so sharply defined as later historians and anthropologists would claim. Again, and as with the issue of gender, this irrepressible mobility is a theme of this book which we will come across in many guises.[12]

Third, there is the question of religion. Crispina makes clear that Christianity was an important aspect of her life. She knew the names of her godparents at baptism, and the places where her mother and her maternal grandparents had been baptized too. She could recite

---

* Hereafter, just 'Dakar' – I will follow this convention for other places mentioned in this book.

the main Christian prayers. And yet, when she described her wanderings around West Africa, she said that 'she had always talked and dealt with all different types of people, both heathens [*gentios*]\* and Christians, although she had more dealings with heathens'. First and foremost, Peres was a Senegambian, and there were very few Christians in Senegambia; as her husband Jorge put it in his own testimony in her trial '[Cacheu] consists of fifteen or twenty Roman [Catholic] residents, and so many heathens that they become uncountable'. Naturally, Crispina's dealings with her Bainunk kin, with the Pepel and Floup peoples near Cacheu, with the Mandinga of The Gambia and the Jolof and Serèer further north, required her to be multilingual and to have an open approach to religion.[13]

The strength of her Senegambian identity is made plainest in the trial with the account of her arrest in Cacheu in 1665. As Antonio de Barros Bezerra – the colonial officer in charge of the arrest – put it of her husband, 'after [she was arrested], the Black heathens rioted, and the said Captain Jorge Gonçalves Frances sent [someone] to appease them'. Jorge retreated from Cacheu with many of his enslaved household servants, apparently to prevent a more widespread uprising. According to Barros Bezerra, Jorge had written to him 'that I should not understand his departure to the *mato* [bush]† as a sign of his rebellion, which it was not; it was rather because he was embarrassed and [he did not want] to see his wife board [the ship]'.[14]

When Crispina left Cacheu after her arrest, she was therefore leaving behind everything that she knew and loved. This was a place where tempers ran high between relatives and between rivals in love, and also where these loyalties clashed. This was the world that she knew. Her own relatives lived and traded in Cacheu and Farim.

---

\* By this she meant, for Portuguese ears, Senegambians who were not Christians: I will use this translation of 'heathens' in the book for the purposes of brevity, though obviously it is imperfect.
† *Mato* is generally translated as 'bush', though here it also signifies an area outside 'ordered' colonial control.

Her husband's relatives called by constantly. Often, tensions boiled over just as they did on the day she was arrested, and the people of Cacheu threatened to riot. Jorge himself described what had happened in their house one day, when his nephew had gone against his will in trying to marry Crispina's widowed daughter who lived in the house: 'one night his nephew came with armed people [to take her away from his house] . . . and the said young woman climbed on a wall of his house and left without being noticed.' The clamour of the dispute meant that she had been able to slip away into the streets, out into the darkness, where her powerful mother and stepfather were no longer in control of her destiny.[15]

Yet while Crispina was tantamount to the first lady of Cacheu, her feeling for her land ran far beyond this small town. The Nunez river area, where her mother Domingas had been born and which she had got to know well, was famous for its terrible storms during the rainy season. It was also had the largest number of elephants of anywhere in the region. According to one Portuguese priest, André de Faro, who would also be a scribe in Crispina's trial, there were so many elephants here that hunters killed at least one per day; and those Africans who hunted elephants were usually also 'sorcerers, their bodies covered with amulets'. The elephants were killed with poisoned arrows; and so strong was the poison that, when they were hit, they took just eight or ten paces before collapsing. People could strip an elephant of skin and flesh in an hour, and then grill it for its meat.[16]

Religious practice and daily life were thus completely mixed together in Crispina's experience of the world. Hunters such as these wore amulets to protect themselves from the powerful spiritual forces which so often tried to disturb the world; and hunters had long been vital across West Africa in establishing new political orders. Then in the early seventeenth century the Jesuits had established a mission in Cabo Verde, and new waves of Capuchin missionaries followed in the 1640s and 1650s. The Catholic Church had arrived with its own methods of spiritual and political ordering, and she had grown used to these too. The two lived side by side in daily life, just as the spiritual existed side by side with the necessities of political and material life. It was this reality which came face to face with the monolithic worldview of the Inquisition and the machinations of the Portuguese empire, as her enemies gathered around her in the first years of the 1660s.[17]

Like Crispina Peres, Jorge Gonçalves Frances was also born in Cacheu. One of the clearest accounts that we have of his life is from a royal petition that he sent to the Portuguese Overseas (Colonial) Council dated 5 May 1664, in which he asked to be given a pension and the habit of the *Ordem de Cristo*, so that he could move from Cacheu to Geba for the next six years. The *Ordem de Cristo* had originated with the Knights Templar during the Crusades, but by the seventeenth century it had become synonymous with riches and power in the era of the Portuguese 'discoveries': thus, in this letter, Jorge outlined the many services that he had provided to the Portuguese crown in its colonial business in West Africa.

Jorge was probably born around 1620, which made him about five years younger than Crispina. He declared that he had been born in Cacheu, and that in the 1630s he had begun to serve the empire as a soldier and then as an infantry captain, at sea and on land in West Africa. In 1645, he had sailed in his own ship to the Senegambian coast near to today's Dakar, to the ports of Joal and Rufisque, to prevent the Spanish from trading there during the civil war between Spain and Portugal that had followed the breakaway of Portugal in 1640 and the acclamation of the new Portuguese king from the House of Bragança, John IV.* This war had major consequences for the transatlantic traffic, since until then the Portuguese had been

---

* The war broke out in 1640, and continued until 1668. This had followed the 'united monarchy' of 1580–1640, when Portugal and Spain had been ruled by the same Habsburg kings. Portugal's revolt in 1640, and the installation of John IV, led to eventual independence; in retaliation, Spain barred Portuguese ships from trading in its colonies, a division between 'Spanish' America and the 'Portuguese' trade in Africa that went back to the Treaty of Tordesillas of 1497.

the suppliers of African captives to the Spanish colonies, where now that all stopped. In this aftermath, Jorge had sailed to the island of Gorée, which was to become a major site in the slave traffic from Senegambia to the Americas (and is a powerful site of memory to this day), where he prevented the Dutch from completing the fortress that they were building there. He had then seized a Spanish ship going to trade for enslaved Africans further south in Bissau and had conducted several further battles against Spanish slave-traffickers desperate to find captive Africans for their colonies in the Americas now that they were at war with the Portuguese, who had previously provided them. Jorge had then moved back to Cacheu, where he had later been made captain-major of the town like his father Álvaro had been before him.[18]

Jorge clearly made this request to move to Geba in 1664 because of the Inquisition. He wanted to move the household to a provincial backwater to escape the looming threat of the investigations which would lead to his wife's arrest the following year. And in the trial itself, the absurdity of many of the denunciations made in it about his household become clear. For not only had Jorge been a loyal military servant of the Portuguese empire, but he was also clearly a good Christian. He had twice served as majordomo (head steward) of the church of Our Lady of Victory, the oldest church in Cacheu, while he had also been the majordomo of the new church of St Anthony for eighteen years, donating the cost of making one of its three doors and helping source lime and stones for its construction. A good Christian, and a good soldier and imperial administrator, he hardly seemed to be a good candidate for someone said to be married to a witchcraft-practising heretic.[19]

Yet there was a different, hidden side to the background of this loyal Catholic servant of the Portuguese empire. For, while he was reputed in the trial documents to be of 'Old Christian' (not Jewish) ancestry, this was a lie. His father, Álvaro, had been tried and penanced by the Inquisition for 'Judaizing' before fleeing to West Africa. Born in the small town of Cabeça de Vide, in the Alentejo region of Portugal, in January 1571, Álvaro had been processed in the auto-da-fé in Évora in 1594. Arriving in the region of Cacheu by 1610 at the latest, he had quickly become an important figure in the town. By the 1630s he was captain-general – as Jorge would be after him – but was also reputed to be trading with the enemies of the Portuguese (probably including the French, hence the sobriquet 'Frances'). Arrested and thrown into jail on the Cabo Verde islands, he rapidly engineered an escape on a passing ship said to be taking salt from Sesimbra to Brazil, making his getaway with the help of signs made by lanterns which allowed him to flee by night. He died in Cacheu in 1641.[20]

Álvaro's life story shows that there was a different side to his own son Jorge's life – one that Jorge so successfully managed to hide in Cacheu that his neighbours thought him beyond reproach as a Christian, and the Inquisitorial officials did not even rake this up in its interrogations of his wife. And so, while there is no evidence that Jorge ever left West Africa, there was a more global, cosmopolitan side to his family. Jorge's son Diogo Barraça Castanho was a resident of Seville in Spain. His brother-in-law Manoel Álvarez Prieto was Álvaro's agent for the slave traffic in Cartagena, Colombia. Álvaro himself passed through Cartagena in 1629 and 1630 with his own caravel of trafficked Africans, where he no doubt lived with his son-in-law Alvarez Prieto, who had married his daughter Ana in Lisbon two years before. Jorge, on the other hand, felt most comfortable in West Africa. He was Cacheu born and raised: his mother had been an African (though we do not know her name), and he called his daughter with Crispina Peres Ohanbú (meaning 'on the back' in Pepel). He was multilingual in Senegambian languages, and so was successfully able to negotiate a pause in fighting with the Pepel kings after they rioted following his wife Crispina's arrest. His life was between two worlds: the Senegambian one he knew, and the persecuted one from which he had escaped, something of which he was vividly aware since his brother-in-law Manoel Álvarez Prieto was arrested by the Inquisition of Cartagena on suspicion of 'Judaizing' and died in jail prior to the public auto-da-fé of 1638.[21]

Crispina and Jorge thus were two trunks of the same tree. Both

*The Heretic of Cacheu*

Cartagena, seventeenth century.

had Portuguese fathers and African mothers. Both were connected to distant places in the Portuguese empire that they never saw. In spite of their Portuguese and Atlantic connections, both saw themselves firmly as Senegambians, baptized their children with indigenous names and did their best to forget their origins in the Portuguese empire – either in Crispina's case because her father did the forgetting for her, or in Jorge's because connection to the New Christians were dangerous and could threaten everything that he had (the Inquisition had seized all of Álvaro's goods when he was penanced in Évora in 1594, and all of Manuel Álvarez Prieto's when he died in their Cartagena jail cell). Thus both Crispina and Jorge were at the same time Senegambians and loyal Catholic subjects of empire deeply implicated in the traffic in enslaved Africans.

## Crispina and Jorge

In spite of these points in common, and the sense of a shared endeavour, their marriage faced many headwinds. Not only did Jorge's relatives feel envious of their success and so spread malicious gossip, but Jorge was not a healthy man. He was constantly bedridden, and, as he put it himself in his testimony, 'it is public and notorious that [I have] been sick and lying in bed for the past seven years, because of [my] sins . . . suffering infinite pain in all the joints of [my] body.' Indeed, one of the main accusations against Crispina was that she 'had kept her husband bedridden through the art of witchcraft, and when she was arrested he got up out of bed and felt better'.[22]

The official religious visitor of Guinea, Dr Gaspar Vogado, was one of the main instigators of Crispina's trial. He summarized the rumour which circulated around Cacheu as to her malign use of the arts of magic for her own ends, to defeat the jealousy she felt in Jorge's roving eye. For, according to this gossip, Jorge was kept in bed through magic in order to prevent his infidelities:

> it is widely known . . . among the heathens, that the said Crispina Peres by means of diabolic arts of witchcraft, keeps her husband in her house, with infirmities, so that he cannot leave and make voyages, by always having him at home; and [not] looking at other women.[23]

As in any marriage, there were tensions which could boil over. One witness described how Jorge had become so angry with Crispina once, seven years before – for slaughtering a goat on the helm of his ship to grant a successful voyage through this offering – that he had 'wanted to stab her with a knife and had lots of quarrels with her [about this]'. As well as this religious dispute – between the more orthodox Catholic Jorge and Crispina's mixed approach to religion – Crispina was jealous of Jorge, it seems. His relatives created tension, as did the desire of her children by her first marriage to marry against the couple's will.[24]

With all this evidence of discord, it would be easy to suggest that this was a hot-tempered union destined for rancour. Yet in reality it was just a marriage with ups and downs, like any other. For the trial also suggests that Crispina and Jorge really loved each other. As one witness against Crispina's alleged witchcraft used to keep her husband in bed also declared, 'he saw the said Crispina Peres in tears at night and during the day when her husband was in pain.'[25]

Cacheu was a place where illness was commonplace, as we will see throughout this book. The ability to cure loved ones, and the indefatigable search for treatments, was one way in which people in the town could show one another their love. People do not want their loved ones to suffer pain and can go to great lengths to prevent it. In Cacheu, this meant drawing on the skills of the *djabakós*, the healers whose knowledge of local herbs and their properties was essential. Even Inquisitorial officials such as the Franciscan friar Paulo de Lordello acknowledged that 'it was [the *djabakós*'] intention to cure him [Jorge] with natural herbs, and not witchcraft'. Nevertheless, this dependence on Senegambian healers was one which could easily be turned against you by your enemies in the context of the Inquisition.[26]

Cacheu was a town where workaday hatreds could easily prosper, alongside nascent cut-throat capitalism. If the envy of relatives was as bad as it got, that could perhaps have been contained. However, dislike and discord cut much deeper than that. Though most of the captives trafficked away into the Atlantic came from some distance away, slavery was widespread as an institution in the town. The households of successful slave traffickers like Crispina and Jorge were also inhabited by enslaved captives and other domestic dependents. Naturally, they were full of anger and resentment, and the Inquisition trial was a golden opportunity to try and get their own back: some of them made full use of the one real power that they had, the intimate knowledge of household life, of who was coming and going, and of what illicit things might be taking place out of sight of the general maw of life in the town.

There were two types of dependents in households in Cacheu:

those who were legally enslaved (in the eyes of the Portuguese empire, at least), and those who were apprenticed in a contracted form of dependence. The latter were called *grumetes* and often served as ship-hands and on errands around Cacheu and in its hinterland. Captives might do the same, but they had zero legal rights and could frequently be forced into bondage, sent across the Atlantic as slaves or forced to cross the ocean with their masters, where they would continue to serve them in the ports of the Americas; the terror at this outcome underpinned their motivations in much of their lives. Meantime, it was of course the enslaved and the *grumetes* who did all the actual work of the household. The stories of two individuals detailed in this trial may give us a strong idea of what these lives were like, and how they interacted with and shaped the world inhabited by Crispina and Jorge.[27]

The story of Domingos de Aredas, a servant in the house, begins by offering us a view of the texture of the lives it contained. Aredas had lived with Jorge for over ten years as his dependent, until his master had married Crispina; and, after the marriage, he had stayed on for a further two years because Jorge was ill. However, bad blood soon developed between Aredas and Crispina. According to Aredas, things came to a head when he had ordered her slave Sebastião to throw away some sacred liquids from the *chinas* (herbal decoctions made according to Senegambian religious practice) kept under the bed of Bonifacia – one of Crispina's female slaves – into the river. Crispina had then 'turned against him like a serpent', sending Aredas a message through Bonifacia that he was now responsible for her daughter (since these charms were said by the *djabakós* to protect the health of her loved ones): 'and Crispina Peres who had liked and loved the witness like her son, before and until that point in time, thereafter grew to hate him badly, and five or six years since this happened, never spoke to him again'. It may seem implausible that hatred could be caused by this alone – and indeed no doubt for some time tensions between Crispina and Aredas had been rising – but as we will see in this book the *chinas* had great importance for Crispina.[28]

## The Heretic of Cacheu

That there was hatred between Aredas, Crispina and Jorge, they all agreed upon. Inevitably, Jorge's own testimony places things in a different light to that of Aredas. According to him, more than fifteen years earlier, in 1646, he had been trading in the port of Sara, which was reached by sailing some distance upriver and thence through the *bolons* into Casamance. There he had found that the African chief official or *alcaide* of the port had imprisoned the young Domingos, his brother Mateus and a younger brother, as well as their mother, after their father had died. Jorge had negotiated with the king of Sara, petitioned and eventually managed to free the Aredas family. He had brought Domingos to Cacheu, where he had had him baptized and stood as his godfather, bringing him into his household, teaching him Christian doctrine and training him up by taking him on trading missions as far away as the Nunez river and Sierra Leone. Things continued well for some years after his marriage to Crispina in 1655, when Jorge had moved into Crispina's house bringing all his goods and his household. But then the row over the *chinas* had happened, in 1661 – just three years before the Inquisition investigations began. Thereafter, Jorge declared,

> the said Domingos de Aredas, whose blood was boiling at seeing himself bereft of the company of his godfather, the man who had brought him up and done so much for him, spoke great ill of [Crispina Peres] in many parts, wherever he found himself in discussions.[29]

In fact, the differences between the stories are not all that much. Both Domingos de Aredas and Jorge show us a world in which powerful traders would take young men under their wing into their households and seek to train them in the crafts of business, as it was then conducted in Cacheu. The religious dimension was important here, with baptism and relationships to godparents being valued by both sides. Over time, these *grumetes* would develop their own independence and make journeys on their own for the household enterprise: it was on his return from one such journey, to the Bijagós

*Crispina and Jorge*

A *bolon* in northern Guinea-Bissau.

islands in 1661, that Domingos's row with Crispina over the *chinas* had taken place. On the other hand, very little was hidden between patron and *grumete* in the household, for, as Jorge put it, Aredas had lived 'inside his house in its most intimate spaces with no separation whatever'. These were key emotional bonds, valued deeply by both sides: when something interfered with them and broke them – a new marriage, an altered hierarchy of values – it was hard for both sides not to begin a feud grounded in the hatred that so easily follows a love that has been broken.

The tale of Domingos de Aredas also introduces us to the slave of Crispina and Jorge called Sebastião Rodrigues Barraza. It was to Barraza that Aredas had given the liquids from the *chinas* to throw into the river; Barraza clearly did not think much of it, for he later said that Aredas had stolen half of the enslaved captives and other goods with which he had returned from the 1661 journey to the Bijagós, and that this was the root of the feud that followed. This could indicate that Jorge still had warm enough feelings for Aredas

*The Heretic of Cacheu*

that he had tried to conceal this from the Inquisitors. On the other hand, Barraza might have been inventing things through dislike for Aredas. What becomes clear from Barraza's own testimony, written down by him in a letter, is just how complex these ties were in a household like that of Crispina and Jorge in Cacheu – and also how rare a testimony such as this is, since he declares almost at its outset, 'I never at any time knew what it was to testify since I am a slave.'[30]

However, Barraza's testimony quickly makes clear that, while enslaved, his life was quite different from that of the enslaved in the Americas. As he put it, 'I never lived in the home of my mistress and always lived as a free person outside the house.' In other words, even though legally enslaved, he had great leeway as effectively a household servant and was entrusted with errands and important bits of business which he went about the town conducting for Crispina and Jorge. Nevertheless, it's also clear that this trust had ebbed substantially by the time of the trial, since Crispina denounced him as a drunkard, and, as he himself wrote in this letter, he was 'a poor slave interested in the flask of wine and brandy and the shirt and iron bar'.\* Trusted or not, Barraza gave a haunting indication of what daily life was like for the enslaved in a household like this when he said that 'our Vicar did not beat a slave with a stick, which means that he has not spoken'. In other words, beating slaves was as commonplace as talking in this place: remembering that Crispina suspected him of hating her for her violent approach to household management, we can be grimly sure that daily beatings were as workaday as speech for the enslaved in Crispina and Jorge's house in the 1660s.[31]

The place of household slaves such as Barraza emerges in great detail from this evidence. On the one hand, Barraza was literate, saying how astonishing it was that 'as a poor Black slave my master ordered that I should be taught to read and write'. He appears to have had some connections to African nobility, since he later claimed that the king of the nearby kingdom of Cazil was

---

\* Cloth and iron were currencies in Cacheu, as discussed in more detail below in Chapter 6.

the brother of his wife. Yet whether this is in fact true is moot given the many accusations of his habitual lying, from Crispina and others: he had little respect for the world he lived in, for its violence and cheating. Justice in Cacheu consisted of 'getting many people to swear false testimonies by asking some to testify against others'. Trust was in short supply: while colonial residents perjured themselves at the drop of a hat, the evidence of slaves was equally unreliable.[32]

Barraza's evidence, alongside that of Aredas, helps us to gain an insight into what Crispina and Jorge's household was like. Hierarchies in Cacheu were more vertical than most. Beatings of slaves were a daily event, the slaves fearing what might happen should they be sold into the even worse fate of the Atlantic traffic. On the other hand, people like Crispina and Jorge depended on trusted confidants of their household to send on errands, and to be trained up in the business. And yet trust was elusive, and could often be broken: the violence and abuses of power which were at the basis of the imperial project in West Africa made sure of that. This meant that betrayal was never far away. One of the witnesses in the trial, the priest Antonio Vaz de Pontes, described how all these workaday hatreds filtered into Crispina's Inquisition trial:

> And because Cacheu is a land where many and very serious rumours and baseless lies are spread with great perfidy due to publicly known hatreds; and [people] swear falsely, without fearing God, as can be seen every day . . . and because the said Jorge Gonçalves Frances has some known enemies, who regard themselves as rich and [noble], [and] more powerful than him; and these have induced others with lies to take the said [false] paths; they want everything [from him], because the said Jorge Gonçalves is one of the most important persons of this *praça*, a prosperous merchant and [head] of a wealthy house.[33]

The best insurance against such a fraught situation was to rely on kin and kin connections. For why was Sebastião Rodrigues

Barraza in such a privileged position? His name suggests that he had previously been in the household of the Portuguese Barraza family, who had been related to Álvaro Gonçalves Frances in Portugal, and had come to Cacheu at about the same time. Loyalty to kin meant that Jorge had welcomed Sebastião Rodrigues Barraza into his household, as he had welcomed the Aredas. Yet just as his brothers-in-law denounced him to the Inquisitors, so too would the enslaved Barraza, whose word – as he himself said so painfully in his testimony – could always be suborned by Jorge's enemies through his yearning for that painful and elusive dream of freedom.[34]

It was through Aredas and Barraza, in fact, that the concoction of the Inquisitorial scheme to denounce Crispina appears to have taken shape. Enmities which began with the violence and inequality in her home could soon spread around the town, and take a very different form.

After Domingos de Aredas had fallen out with Crispina and Jorge in 1661, he went to live with their rival Captain Ambrosio Gomes, and his wife, Bibiana Vaz. The Inquisitorial trial – the deportation of Crispina, seizure of goods from her and Jorge – would lead to a huge power-shift in this couple's favour. By 1670, Ambrósio would be commander of Cacheu, and after his death in 1679 Bibiana Vaz was to become the most powerful trader there, filling the shoes that Crispina Peres had occupied twenty years before her – and the subject of several discussions by historians. In 1684, she would capture the captain-general of Cacheu, Joseph Gonçalves de Oliveira, and imprison him in her home in Farim for fourteen months; Oliveira had fallen out of favour because of his attempts to prevent ships from France and England from trading in Cacheu. Asking the key question of many political intrigues – who benefits? – it becomes clear that this couple had a key role in fomenting the trial of Crispina Peres.[35]

Aredas moved from the household of Crispina and Jorge to live with Gomes and Vaz around three years before the Inquisitorial investigations began. This was a good career move for him, since by

## Crispina and Jorge

the time of the trial he was an official scribe in Cacheu. The relationship between Aredas and Gomes must soon have prospered through the shared envy and hatred which they had of Jorge. Gomes wanted to take over as the most powerful trader in Cacheu, while Aredas just wanted revenge – something which his new administrative position would facilitate. Soon they became relatives by marriage, as Domingos's younger brother Mateus married the daughter of Gomes's cousin on Santiago island.[36]

Gomes's hatred of Jorge went back a long way. In his declaration to the Inquisitors of his enemies, whose testimony should according to him be discounted, Jorge made this clear:

> The testimony of Captain Ambrósio Gomes against him . . . cannot [be considered] valid, because nine years ago, when [he] was Captain in this *praça* [Cacheu], by an order received from the Governor Pedro Semedo de Cardoso, in the island of Santiago [Cabo Verde], he arrested him . . . and put him in two chains; for this reason the said [Ambrosio Gomes] has always held a grudge against him and they have never spoken [to each other] again, as is public and notorious.[37]

This enmity was born of the rivalry of two men who were very alike, each questing after their share of power in Cacheu. Like Jorge, Gomes had been born there to a New Christian father and an African mother. His mother, Teodósia Gomes, was from the Bijagós islands. She was baptized a Christian and extensively used the healing practices of the *djabakós*. Teodósia lived in Cacheu and seems to have been widely consulted by the people of the town as a healer, since it was to her that Crispina herself had gone when experiencing difficulty in childbirth eleven years before the trial. Clearly she had passed much of this on to her son Ambrósio since he had come to assist with the labour, tying several Mandinga amulets – known as *gris-gris** both then and now – around Crispina's arms and upper waist and stepping on a small mat on the ground.[38]

---

* Pronounced 'greegree'.

Like Jorge, Ambrósio had a New Christian past that linked him irrevocably to the Inquisition. While born in Cacheu, he had been raised in the small town of Montemor-o-Novo in the Portuguese Alentejo. Witnesses in the trial declared that his relatives there had been penanced by the Inquisition, as had the father of his cousin in Santiago Manoel de Matos. Doubtless it was because of this, and the desire to escape the risk that he would be tried, that he had returned from Portugal to Cacheu. Because of these connections to the Inquisition, as one witness put it, people in Cacheu 'called him offensive names, [such as] donkey face'.[39]

For three years, Aredas lived in the Gomes house. The idea that Gomes could foment a trial against someone for consorting with the *djabakós* seems absurd, given that he himself used some of their techniques. Moreover, many witnesses came forward to declare that Ambrosio Gomes was also a friend to these Senegambian healers. One of these witnesses described how he used their *gris-gris* and sacrificed cows on the helms of his ships to obtain prosperous trafficking voyages. Yet this was a power play in which all this was mere detail: none of this stopped him from denouncing Crispina and Jorge for using '*djabakóssarias*' in the trial. This was a trial which Gomes had had a strong hand in fomenting: as Crispina said in her testimony, he had urged her slave Rodrigues Barraza to make his accusation, something which he confirmed in his own letter. In this way, people who knew their household were manipulated by their enemies into denouncing Crispina and Jorge, and unravelling the life that they had built.[40]

Where did the idea of concocting the accusations against Crispina for the Inquisitors come from? Here, the role of another enemy was almost certainly important. As we saw in the Introduction, Crispina's was not the first Inquisitorial trial of the era from this part of West Africa. The priest Luis Rodrigues, formerly vicar of Farim and a frequent visitor to Cacheu, had been tried in Lisbon a few years before. And it was Rodrigues who had come to Cacheu after his acquittal by the Inquisitors, to begin the process of investigation which led to Crispina's trial. His story was well known in

## Crispina and Jorge

Cacheu, and – as an inveterate drunkard and carouser – he was almost certainly a frequent presence in the Gomes/Vaz circle. For if anyone was likely to cook up a scheme like this, it was Luis Rodrigues – a man of whom it can fairly be said that his scruples were weak.

Religious probity was not a mainstay of Rodrigues's work as a priest. In Santiago island, where he worked as a canon in the cathedral, he was famous for drinking and eating all night long before then going to say mass the next day, in spite of the fact that priests were supposed to fast before saying mass. He fired off pistols in the town at night on his drunken sprees, even though this was banned by governors. Famous as a sworn drunkard and womanizer, he had also failed to say mass on Maundy Thursday in Farim because he had been hosting a party with women dancing and singing. His complete lack of respect towards the religious precepts of the Church was made clear by the scandalous sermon he had given in Farim, claiming that he could pardon all forms of incest. Although none of this was unknown in the Portuguese colonial world, as a number of examples from Brazil can attest, it was still shocking to many.[41]

Rodrigues's dissolute character is important in understanding the household of Crispina and Jorge, as it begins to give us an insight into another aspect of the world which they inhabited. As we will see in more detail later, this was a world where alcohol played a key part in social life. Rodrigues was an inveterate drunkard, and one witness in his trial described how 'everything that happened to [him] was caused by wine'. He had swordfights with rivals in love in the streets of Ribeira Grande in Santiago – these were so bad that he ended up with injuries on his head – and was said to be 'incapable of maintaining friendships with anybody'. He solicited women almost daily, and if they refused him he took to humiliating them by standing outside their houses in the night, pretending that he had just left them after having sex. He was also accused of having committed rape several times on the veranda of the church of São Bras.[42]

One witness described Rodrigues's general character as follows:

> it seemed to him that whatever wickedness existed in the world he had a part of, because he kept a lover . . . and even pursued and defamed married women, and since he was a man who got drunk on wine and roamed about by night with weapons hammering on the doors of strangers, and the witness said that he had travelled throughout Spain and the Americas and that there was no man alive who had such a ruinously wicked lifestyle and habits as [Rodrigues].[43]

Of course, Rodrigues claimed that all of this had been cooked up by his enemies. Nevertheless, since his defence against one of the accusations levelled at him was that he had not 'dishonoured the daughter of Beatriz Monteira because she had already lost her virginity a long time before and was by then a woman of the world', we can conclude that much of his character was as portrayed in this trial. In short, he was certainly someone who would have been quite willing to distort the aims of the Inquisition to further his own passions.[44]

These, then, were some of the enemies of Crispina and Jorge. There were their commercial rivals, Ambrosio Gomes and Bibana Vaz, who had taken in the sworn enemies of the couple from their household a few years before. And there was the dissolute priest Luis Rodrigues, who wanted vengeance against Jorge (who he had labelled an enemy in his own trial). Indeed, when we consider Rodrigues's character, it is quite possible that something else entirely also motivated him. Perhaps Crispina had spurned his advances – which he seems to have made to almost every woman he came across – something that he never took lightly. And so he had determined to foment a case to enforce the patriarchal power of the Portuguese empire in Cacheu.

As it turns out, then, it was not a coincidence that this Inquisitorial trial from Cacheu – the only one, as we saw in the Introduction, of the seventeenth century – was taken against a woman. The trial of

## Crispina and Jorge

Crispina Peres exposes in all its details the misogyny of the imperial world, as well as the fury and hatred which was provoked in it when confronted by more complex gendered dynamics in a town like Cacheu.

Those details are precious, almost four centuries later. Crispina's and Jorge's characters are clearly drawn. We get a glimpse of the challenges that they faced in their marriage, as well as the bond which they did have with each other and the common experiences which united them. We learn of their complex backgrounds in both West Africa and Portugal, their fluid approach to religion and their interactions with neighbouring rulers, such as the king of Sara, with whom Jorge had negotiated to free the Aredas family. Beyond this, we also see how the violence involved in their traffic in enslaved Africans – the regular beatings, the constant potential for domestic slaves to be trafficked away to the far worse fate in the Americas – brought hatred and enmity to their household, which would be the seeds of their undoing.

For like most successful people, Crispina and Jorge were the targets of envy and of conspiracies to unseat them from their place in Cacheu. Gomes, Vaz and Rodrigues were just three of the powerful enemies that they had in the town. There was also the religious visitor Gaspar Vogado – an important civil and religious administrator in Cacheu, who worked with Rodrigues to foment the trial – the former captain-general Manoel Rodrigues Salgado and Jorge's brothers-in-law. Working together, these people accused the couple to the Inquisitors of exactly the same 'heretical' practices that they themselves partook in.

As the evidence against Ambrosio Gomes made clear, it was a workaday event for people to go to *djabakós* to seek healing from the many illnesses and fevers that beset people in Cacheu. This was a Senegambian town. The intrusion of Portuguese law was always only piecemeal, even if with Crispina's Inquisition trial there was a concerted attempt to make it more permanent and to bring Cacheu more firmly into the grip of empire, and the ways in which imperial emissaries conceived of the world.

2.

# Women and Power in Cacheu

'Men marrying older women was a laborious matter, implying that he could not do anything with her'

One of the ways in which Cacheu challenged the imperial worldview of the Inquisition was in how women and men related to one another. Cacheu in no way mirrored the world of Counter-Reformation Portugal, where young girls were dressed in nun's wimples in the streets of Lisbon in order to prepare them for a life of seclusion. While in the halls of the Inquisition of Lisbon it was men who commanded – as Inquisitors, notaries, scribes and translators – and women appeared only in the guise of those to be condemned, Cacheu was a very different place. Women were in charge every bit as much as men; and it was precisely the challenge that this setting presented to a chauvinist braggart such as the drunkard canon Luis Rodrigues, who initiated Crispina's trial, that may have contributed to the plot to 'get' her and thereby reassert the presumed morality of empire.[1]

In the previous chapter, we got a sense of Crispina and Jorge's household and of their personalities. We came across the people who they dealt with on a daily basis, and the undercurrents running beneath the dealings they had with them. But to grasp all this well, we also need to see how the standard relationships between men and women in Cacheu differed from those in Iberian cities. For Crispina's was hardly an isolated case: as we have seen, she was succeeded as the most powerful and wealthy trader in Cacheu by Bibiana Vaz. Where in seventeenth-century Europe, women's activities were hampered by (male) administrative power, Cacheu was different. These relations so forcefully offended the sensibilities of Portuguese colonial officials that they tried to constrain them through the Inquisition. So in this chapter we look at the power that women developed here, and the social context of Cacheu in which this happened.[2]

Crispina and Bibiana Vaz are examples of the women known to historians of other parts of Senegambia as *signares*. These were mixed-heritage women who developed significant trading power in many towns of the region from the seventeenth to the early nineteenth centuries. Beyond Cacheu, there are important examples of the power and wealth of these women in towns such as Gorée and St Louis (at the mouth of the Senegal river), as well as further south in Sierra Leone. The ability of dynamic and entrepreneurial women to become the most powerful traders in the port towns of Greater Senegambia is evidence that the gendered dimensions of history

*Signare* from St Louis, Senegal.

## The Heretic of Cacheu

and culture in this area are a good deal more complex than is often supposed by outsiders.[3]

There are several ways in which the power and agency of women emerge through Crispina's trial. The first is the fact that the documents exist at all. This was the only Inquisitorial trial undertaken throughout the seventeenth century in Guinea-Bissau. Given the acknowledged fact that Inquisitorial procedures were often initiated as a means of gaining revenge on one's enemies, this sole extant trial could only have been taken against an exceptionally powerful and influential individual. The number of enemies that Crispina had is clear from the pages of documents, with person after person appearing before the Inquisitors to denounce her. The more powerful the person, the larger the number of their enemies; and so this shows the power she had accrued in the town.[4]

A second factor is that many of the witnesses pointed the finger not only at Crispina's 'heretical' activities but also at those of many women who were friends of hers. These women were said also to make sacrifices in the shrines of the quarter of the town called Vila Quente. For when the original accusation was formulated in the pages of the trial, it was not only against Crispina but also against 'Genebra Lopes and Isabel Lopes, single, Black women resident in [Cacheu]'. This gives a hint of what we will see in this chapter: in Cacheu, women ran their own households, supported one another in commercial business, and were the clear commercial, religious and social rivals of the upstart (male) Atlantic traffickers who were trying to establish themselves in the town.[5]

The evidence of Sebastião Vaz, a boatswain and resident of Cacheu, can stand as representative of all this:

> He knows as a matter of certainty that when there is need, or something is lost, Genebra Lopes, a single Black woman, resident of this settlement of Cacheu, buys palm wine and chicken and sends them and sometimes goes to the shrine . . . And he heard her say many times that it was [done] with that intention because . . . when they buy these things to make sacrifices in order for the stolen or lost

[goods] to appear, they will scream, saying in their loud voices that they want to sacrifice it.[6]

This gives a startling image of what often happened day by day in Cacheu. When thefts took place, successful trading women whose goods had been taken would buy palm wine and chickens from the marketplace and then roam the streets shouting loudly that they were going to make a sacrifice to the *china* – with the known implication that the shrine's spirits might ensure that bad things happened to whoever was the thief, if they didn't give back what they had taken. According to Vaz, all of this happened in Vila Quente, a neighbourhood which was run by women:

> in this place there are many Christian and free women, who inside their houses and outside the settlement, at the above-mentioned shrine, or *china*, sacrifice or libate wine most days . . . so said the witness that most of the time he resides in . . . Vila Quente, and the witness says that he personally knows all these Black women and . . . [that this] is common, and notorious in this settlement.[7]

Women's power and agency in Cacheu was not therefore limited to the likes of Crispina and Bibiana Vaz – to those who could rise to commercial dominance and the autonomy which went with it. There was also a whole neighbourhood of the town in which women ran the households and the religious life. What was it, then, about daily life in Cacheu which meant that ambitious women ran the life of the town, creating the sort of household which we saw in the last chapter? As we will now see, kinship connections, linguistic skills and the commercial set-up all created a world which seemed upside down to the misogynistic Atlantic traffickers from Europe.[8]

Women's capacity to occupy powerful roles in Cacheu naturally mirrored the world around them. In fact, it wasn't just in Cacheu that women could become autonomous dominant figures, like Crispina and Bibiana Vaz. The historian Michael Gomez has noted

## The Heretic of Cacheu

how, in the empire of Mali, Mansa Sulayman was challenged by his chief wife, Qāsā, who rode daily with an entourage to the royal council's doors. In the micro-kingdoms near Cacheu, meanwhile, female rulership was also a factor in political life. In her book on the micro-state of Pachesi, in the Casamance, Gambian historian Ralphina Phillott de Almeida describes how there were at least three female rulers in the earlier phase of Pachesi prior to 1750. Meanwhile, the account books of the slave trafficker João Bautista Pérez, from 1617, recount him providing a bottle of wine to invite the queen of Cassão to share a drink, on the Gambia river.[9]

Male Atlantic traffickers arriving in Senegambia in this period both lampooned and accepted this reality of female political authority. One of the few Inquisitorial trials of the sixteenth century from here was of a man known in the documents as Mestre Dioguo – with the Portuguese 'Mestre' implying that he was a ship's pilot. Dioguo was accused of dressing up at Christmas in a skirt in a farce performed in the town of Bugendo, where he pretended that he was the Virgin giving birth. This mockery of the life of Jesus was enough to see him accused of being a New Christian heretic, but it also may have represented a deeper tradition of the swapping of gender roles (if not their physical attributes) in Senegambia – and of a world in which women held political and at times religious power. Even today, at Carnival in Bissau, men and women may dress up in one another's clothes and adopt their roles for the week.[10]

Crispina's influential position in Cacheu wasn't therefore an anomaly either in the town or in the world around it. In Senegambia, women could be in charge as well as men – just as Isabel of Castille was queen in the early sixteenth century, and Elizabeth of England was so in the later part of the century. However, if this seems as something of an anomaly today, it is because of the intervening charge of the passage of time, and of the prejudices and inequities that it has racked up. It is in fact precisely because of the history of patriarchy since then that it may seem to some readers that Crispina's life defied the world in which she lived, whereas in fact she embodied it – as people in power usually do.

What, then, were the roots of this influence and authority which Crispina held in Cacheu? There were three core elements: language, kinship and healing. Multilingualism of African women such as Crispina, with fluency in a number of West African languages, gave them a huge advantage over male Atlantic traffickers when it came to business dealings. Secondly, the kinship networks which she had with family members in different parts of the region helped her to establish herself. Finally, both language skills and kinship opened the door to her access to healers, the *djabakós*: with illness and physical fragility such a workaday part of life, especially for the Atlantic traffickers, this could only enhance her prestige in the town and the need which people had of her.

The place of language comes first. We know from the evidence of what happened in Crispina's trial in Lisbon that this was one of her advantages in Cacheu. For she did not speak Portuguese, and, as we have seen, her evidence to the court had to be translated by Manoel de Almeida. Since Almeida had an official position in the Cabo Verde islands, where he was sergeant-major, this suggests that she must have spoken to him in the Kriol language which is today the lingua franca of Guinea-Bissau and the national language of Cabo Verde (where no indigenous languages from West Africa are spoken widely). The growing power of the Creoles of Cabo Verde in the seventeenth century went with the establishment of this language, and the ways in which it forged a community and shared identity among them, as language always does.[11]

Beyond Kriol, Crispina spoke Bainunk. This was the language of her mother, Domingas Pessoa, and also of her grandmother Florença, who were so central to her upbringing. Given that it was the stories of her maternal line which she carried with her in life, this was probably her first language. However, Bainunk was then a language in decline, as Bainunk people in Casamance and Guinea-Bissau became challenged by the advancing Floup migrations and the growing power of the kingdom of Kaabu. This meant that, while Bainunk might have been her first language, she needed to be fluent in a number of others in order to gain the successful place that she had in life.

*The Heretic of Cacheu*

A third language of Crispina's was Pepel. Given the strong trading connections which she had with the rulers and powerful traders surrounding Cacheu, she can be assumed to have spoken the Pepel language (for how else would she have been so highly valued by them, so that they had threatened to storm the town on her arrest?). And finally, Crispina's fourth language was Mandinga: given the frequent passage of Jakhanké Mandinga scholars through Cacheu, and in her house, she must also have spoken this language, which at the time was becoming something of a lingua franca and remains so to this day. It is quite possible that she also spoke some Floup, a language of growing importance but also one with many mutually unintelligible variants – and one which a surviving Bainunk–Floup dictionary from the late seventeenth century shows was very different from her native tongue.[12]

Four to five languages may seem a lot, but this kind of versatility remains quite normal in Senegambia today. One Portuguese trader of the sixteenth century called João Ferreira was known locally as Ganagoga, a word that in the Biafada language meant 'someone who speaks all the languages': the fact that such a word existed in Biafada shows that this was a fairly common occurrence. Multilingualism was just a workaday requirement for trading and engaging successfully with the many different peoples who came to work and do business in Cacheu. If you couldn't speak many languages you were likely to be outdone in the market deals that were the basis of daily life – and in fact this was what happened to the Portuguese and their mixed-heritage children on a regular basis, with some accounts stating that they regularly paid more than West African traders for the same assortment of goods.[13]

Without fluency in West African languages, success would not come. These languages were the main vernaculars of daily life in the Peres household. We know this from the evidence of one witness in Crispina's trial who said that the daughter she had had with Jorge had been baptized not with a Christian name such as Maria or Isabel, but – as we saw in the last chapter – Ohanbú. These were the languages spoken in the home, testament to the environment in which Crispina and Jorge had been raised by their mothers and in which their own children would grow up, where they would seek to make a success of their lives – and they would need to speak a number of Senegambian languages to be able to do so.[14]

On the other hand, success in Cacheu also required being able to deal freely with the Atlantic traders. For this, the new Kriol was the chosen language: this was what Manoel de Almeida had learnt in Cabo Verde and in Cacheu, and must have been the main way through which Crispina communicated with Atlantic traders. So Cacheu's Atlantic-facing trade was conducted in an Atlanticized language, Kriol. But West African languages were those spoken in the home, and thus were the languages of most people's emotional lives – even if this emerges only with difficulty in the Portuguese language of the documents which have survived through to us today.

Why did this multilingualism help Crispina to build her commercial success? For one thing, it was certain to be a trading advantage in a political environment where local rulers trading with Cacheu might speak Mandinga (in Farim), Pepel (in Baoula) and Bainunk (in Casamance). For another, it meant that not only could she negotiate with political leaders, but also that she was able to interact freely with traders from all over the place. These language ties connected to her heritage, too, since the kinship ties she had through her Bainunk mother, Domingas, must have been significant in making initial contacts with those rulers who became important to her trading networks.

In sum, those who were born to West African parents, were fluent in a variety of West African languages and had kinship ties in different parts of Senegambia had significant advantages: in Cacheu these people were almost certain to be women, not men. These advantages brought greater security, for the biggest defence against enslavement for anyone inside or outside the town was wealth. It was wealth which brought respect, and freedom from being pawned as a dependent in a slave-trading environment or forced into military service, which could lead to defeat, capture and enslavement.

These linguistic and cultural ties gave women a strong advantage in one other crucial area: health and healing. Good health was a rarity in Cacheu. Crispina's trial pages are filled with mentions of people who witnessed a certain event, one now being investigated by the Inquisitors, but who had since died: virtually on every page, a witness will say that so-and-so would know about an event were it not for the fact that they were now dead, or that they had heard of something from someone else who had since passed on. Crispina's own interactions with the *djabakós* were an attempt to seek better health for her loved ones: her husband, Jorge Gonçalves Frances, who spent most of his time sick in bed, and her young daughter, who had developed a fever and for whom she had turned to the *djabakós* in search of a cure.

Human nature, and the sufferings of ill health, mean that the sick will seek healing. This is why healers have always been able to adopt powerful positions in all societies, from Cacheu in the seventeenth century to the dispensers of biomedicine in our own time. All this meant that integration into African healing networks was vital to daily life for Atlantic communities in West Africa. Their greater proficiency at West African languages, and their kinship ties, meant that Cacheu's women had much better access to networks of healers than did its men. With health and healing such a key part of everyday life, this connectedness to the surrounding cultural world was an important element of women's empowerment in Cacheu.[15]

This power undermined the ideals of patriarchy and empire. This is something that helps us to understand why health and illness lay at the heart of this Inquisition trial. The fact that Crispina's power and her interactions with the *djabakós* centred on their potential healing powers underlines just how vital this was to daily life and to women's position in a settlement like Cacheu. As we saw in the previous chapter, the question of whether using the herbal remedies prescribed by local healers was itself a sign of 'heresy' was raised by the Inquisitors. The realization that healing was a source of power for Cacheu's women explains why this healing was a source of suspicion.

All this makes the roots of female empowerment in Cacheu clearer. The town was characterized by the intermarriage of Atlantic traffickers with West African women. However, unlike in the Americas, the Atlantic heritage of the male traders was not an advantage. In fact, it was the reverse. In Cacheu, their spouses had much greater reach: their linguistic abilities, kinship networks and the greater access which all this gave them to healers and the potential for better health empowered them. Moreover, women too could be *djabakós* in the region around Cacheu – female *djabakós* came to Peres's house alongside male ones – which meant that no aspect of this was a 'man's world'.[16]

This provided much of the context for the rise of a powerful woman such as Crispina Peres. And since trade was at the heart of Cacheu's life, the ways in which it was conducted by the town's men and women were also vital in shaping the roles which each had, and the experiences which they had of life.

Go to any market in Guinea-Bissau today – and anywhere in West Africa – and you will find that most of the traders doing business are women. It is women who dominate what economists call the 'informal economy', covering the ground with their goods laid out on red-and-white-checked sacking or stacked up on wooden stands. They are trading the necessities of life – onions, tomatoes, batteries, mobile phones, Maggi stock cubes, sandals – in a context where, without refrigeration or a steady supply of money, most people must go to the market every day. It is market women who sit in brightly printed dresses awaiting their sales and the small amount of money which is essential for them to supply their household needs.

This is the money without which they cannot do, and so it is the women who keep the market going. Their menfolk may be very far distant: working in Europe and sending remittances back home, or trying to get there if they haven't made it across the Mediterranean already. They may be nearer by, working in Dakar or Banjul or Conakry and still sending what money they can. If this is the pattern today, it is partly because this is what it has been for so many centuries, linked to economic patterns of extraction and debt which are so old. Historical structures die hard once they are institutionalized, and this system of distant, absent men, and of women controlling the local market, is one that stretches right back to the seventeenth century in Guinea-Bissau. At that time, though, the male trading journeys went nearer by, through the maze of creeks and swamps which characterize Senegambia, especially in the rainy season.[17]

Cacheu was always a town of traders, founded to take advantage of pre-existing commercial networks which linked the *lumos* (markets) of the region. Many of the records that survive are testament to the inveterate trading lives of both men and women. As the English trader Richard Jobson put it in his account of a 1623 visit to the Gambia river, describing the children of dead Portuguese traders and their African spouses: 'as they grow up, [they] apply themselves to buy and sell one thing for another as the whole country do[es]'.[18] Of course, European traders such as Jobson, and the Cacheu-based traders whose records are drawn on here, were bound to assume that every aspect of life was bound up with what most interested them – trade, profit, commerce. But all the same it is clear enough that this place was nothing without its business.

If women dominated the marketplace in Cacheu, it is natural that their commercial role there was driven by these patterns of trade. Prominent women such as Peres commissioned ships which then plied on trading voyages from the Gambia river in the north to Sierra Leone in the south. Most of the trading voyages themselves, however, were conducted and crewed by men. The upper reaches of the Gambia river were very far distant, and each journey involved multiple stops en route for trade. Beyond the main stopping points, João Bautista Pérez's trading accounts for a trip of 1617, for instance, involved stops at small ports such as Tandakunda, Tendaba, Tancoaralle, Cabaceira and Nhamena. His brother Manoel's account books involve trade with places as varied as Geba, Bichangor, Bissau, the Bijagós, the Gambia river (including the kingdom of Barra, on the north bank) and the port town of Joal to the south of Dakar. None of this business was quick, as at each of them there was a need for sociability and exchange. These were therefore journeys which all required long absences from Cacheu.[19]

João Bautista Pérez's ship captain, João de Andrade, gives a good example of the range of destinations that such a journey might involve. In one 1617 voyage, he owed Bautista Pérez goods based on trade in Cassão on the Gambia river, Bintang and Sanguedogu in Casamance. In the Introduction, we saw how these journeys from Cacheu operated through the creeks of Casamance. This was a route which was easiest in the rainy season, when the creeks flooded and linked up the waterways of the São Domingos river near Cacheu with the Casamance river near today's Ziguinchor, and thence to the wide, mangrove-lined thoroughfare of the Bintang *bolon*. Once this tributary hit The Gambia itself, it was another fifty leagues upstream to the port of Cassão, and further still beyond that to the highest reaches of the river navigable by ocean-going vessels, which were known as Barreiras Vermelhas ('Red Limits/Barriers').[20]

With trading men frequently absent, the commercial life of Cacheu was in the hands of the women. This helps us to understand how and why it was that the whole neighbourhood of Vila Quente was said to be run by them. For not only were the men absent for much of the time, but the other side of the coin was the women's command of the commercial networks – driven also by the cultural and linguistic advantages they had – of the town. Of course, women's power and authority had many roots to it beyond the absence of men. As we have just seen, this was a pattern which had a long history in the Greater Senegambia region. All the same, the frequent absence of men was certainly a factor.

Moreover, it wasn't just the fact that the men were absent which mattered, but also what it was that they did when they were away. The records show us that these were debauched expeditions, which meant that many men returned from them with little ability or appetite to run anything. There were constant halts for bits of trade: a bit of cloth and wine here, some kola nut there, some ship repairs as well, all working with a range of different African traders

## The Heretic of Cacheu

and craftsmen (caulkers, carpenters and so on) on a contract basis. Cassão on the Gambia river was one of the liveliest trading stops. Here, Mandinga market women hosted markets when trading ships arrived, selling rice, millet, eggs, milk, butter and hens. Ships were often repaired on the beach-side by Mandinga carpenters and shipwrights, because of the large amount of wood that was available at this place.[21]

At Cassão people had to take care, because of the elephants that frequently came to bathe in the water and the many crocodiles found nearby. A frequent trader was João Bautista Pérez, whose accounts provide a good example of the range of goods paid out, one day in 1617. One Mandinga trader, Maroalle, bought kola nuts, *aguardente* (rum), wine and raisins; another bought a gold sword; and a third, Tomane Mancara, bought kola nuts, wine and some handkerchiefs. All of these goods were bought on credit against the value of captives: the male Atlantic traders provided the goods desired by West African elites, in return for the commodity which had highest value for them, which was enslaved African labour.[22]

Booze both made and broke these exchanges. In the Bautista Pérez account books, alcohol was everywhere: where wine is mentioned this must have been imported, and not palm wine, which tends to become rank (and smell of rotten eggs) quite quickly. Luis Gonçalvez owed to João Bautista Pérez the cost of half a flagon of wine which he drank with one Duarte, and a flask of wine which he had shared with the *grumetes* of Sangedogu – as well as another when he had fought in the same place with someone from there (presumably after the drinking and gossip had got out of hand). In each port, permission for trade had first to be got from the local rulers, which involved further negotiation and the giving of gifts/taxes – and often, as the sources tells us, the liberal spreading of invitations to come and drink wine and *aguardente* with the traders by the river, in sessions which presumably carried on, and on. It wasn't just the queen of Cassão that took advantage, as we saw in the opening to this chapter. One entry in the account book describes the payment of a flask of wine during a stay in Jagara when 'the king came on board'. João Bautista Pérez traded horses with the king of Casamance and cloth with the king of Rufisque. Other account book entries talk of flagons of wine being given to kings as part of the trading encounters and goods exchanged.[23]

The place of alcohol is curious. As we have already seen, Islam was growing in importance in the seventeenth century, and many of the towns on the Gambia river were governed by Islamic rulers. So how come wine and *aguardente* were so important? According to Jobson, visiting the Jakhanké scholarly centre of Sutucó on the Gambia river in the 1620s, what distinguished the Islamic clerics from the rest of the population was precisely their refusal to drink alcohol. This suggests, therefore, that the rest of the population did not share these scruples, not even the kings and queens (something that remained true into the nineteenth century). As we have already seen, West African religious traditions often used alcohol in the form of palm wine in the making of offerings at *chinas*, and thus this was clearly a religious as well as a social pattern which Jakhanké preachers were still finding hard to shift in the seventeenth century.[24]

This drunkenness is important in trying to understand the gender relations of men and women in Cacheu. As we will see later, the papers of Crispina's trial make it pretty clear that people in the town itself often fell into binge drinking. The constant pauses for drink here and there on these long trading voyages made the men increasingly dissolute by the time they returned to the town – as many of the statements from the Inquisition trials of both Crispina Peres and Luis Rodrigues made clear. This drunkenness made them more likely to either revert into drunken sprees or to fall ill, as the Inquisition documents demonstrate. This was another nail in the coffin of male dominance and misogyny in the town, something that, as we have seen, many of the Atlantic traffickers did not take lightly.

Meantime, while the men lived it up and aged fast, things were different for the women of Cacheu. These same account books also provide precious information which show how they had their own independent trades. Unlike the itinerant men, purveying imported goods in exchange for enslaved Africans, the African women of Cacheu did not tend to work in slave trafficking. These records show that they tended to work in a range of small-scale trades, as well as running small businesses. They made their living selling goods on credit to these itinerant male traders, while at the same time developing their own independence.

Women of Cacheu often made small purchases from traders such as João Bautista Pérez, either for themselves or to sell on in some small business deal. One woman, Guiomar, brought some wax and wine from him in 1619. Domingas Lopes bought two measures of kola nuts, chickpeas, Rouen cloth and some handkerchiefs, while Esperança Vaz bought the same items in addition to wine. The account books are littered with the names of other women living in Cacheu – almost certainly in Vila Quente – and making small purchases either for their households (wax, cloth) or for their own consumption (wine, kola nuts, chickpeas). These women ran their households, sorted out the provisioning and also it seems often sold small bits of stuff here and there to their friends and neighbours who came passing by. This was in keeping with the culture that many people in Cacheu knew from Ribeira Grande, where – as we have already seen in the Introduction to this book – women controlled the Caboverdean trading environment and ran most of the small-scale stores.[25]

This detail adds another layer to the sense of what this town was like. The busiest area was down by the port, where much of the haggling for provisions, wax and cloth was done. These women traders in Cacheu thronged the place. They were known in Kriol as *regateiras* (hawkers, or peddlers). Then they would go back to Vila Quente, where little bits of business here and there also went on as people came in and out of one another's houses for what they needed. Meanwhile, other women who were not yet living in their own independent households, but still worked as servants or household slaves of Atlantic traffickers, also did business on their own account: one, Maria Rodrigues, the servant (*criada*) of António Vaz, bought raw cotton, a variety of different types of cloth and wine from Manoel Bautista Pérez in 1614. Thus, while the men were away on trading missions, the women were in control of the marketplace.[26]

This last piece of evidence on raw cotton also indicates a core element of the economic life of women in Cacheu and the surrounding area. This was in spinning and supplying cotton for the looms that were so important to weavers of the cloths that dominated town fashions. We know that many household slaves and dependents in Bintang span cotton, and also that women in Ribeira Grande earned their living spinning raw cotton; and that one of those mentioned, Leonor Ferreira, had also traded between Cabo Verde and Farim, where she had spent some time. Maria Rodrigues's purchase of raw cotton suggests that the same patterns were in play in Cacheu, and that spinning cotton was important to the economic life of the town's women. This pattern was in keeping with general Senegambian practices, where women tended to spin cotton while men did the weaving. In Cacheu, not only did women run the marketplace, therefore, but there were other trades open to them through which they could achieve economic independence – and through which a skilful negotiator like Crispina might eventually rise to prominence.[27]

All this helps us to develop a clearer picture of the social and economic life which underpinned Crispina and Jorge's household. Men like Jorge travelled widely and were often absent, while women like Crispina dominated the everyday commercial life of the town as they do today. Many other women who did not live in the colonial town but in Vila Quente earnt money through small-time trading (the *regateiras*), and also from their micro-industries of spinning cotton. Cloth was one of the most prized goods across the Greater Senegambian region and was a unit of account in Cacheu, and so women's role in its production also safeguarded their economic position.[28]

When the men like Jorge did return from their trading journeys, they had spent months drinking with their trading partners, workmen and local rulers. Often, they fell ill. On the one hand, this meant that they were in no position to constrain the activities of their servants, women such as Maria Rodrigues who were trading on their own account (as was in any case commonplace in other parts of the Portuguese empire). On the other hand, they were dependent on the ties to healers which women in the community had built up.

The fact that women owned the marketplace was key in the power they had in Cacheu. They were economically independent, which meant that they were not about to be pushed around by men. This was why Crispina's daughter was not likely to obey Jorge by kowtowing to his choice of marriage partner for her, as we saw in the previous chapter. On the other hand, Cacheu's prosperity also depended on its close political and cultural ties to its surroundings – and this was also based on the connections built by its women. All this shows that, in the tales of male debauchery and illness which run through Crispina's trial and that of Luis Rodrigues, we can also read the wounded pride and impotence that many of these male Atlantic traffickers felt in the lives which they led in this West African port town.

Economic and social independence usually go together. Crispina was the most successful trader of her era in Cacheu, but she was also just the tip of the iceberg. Most successful women traders in the town also acted as household heads, as she did. Far from being an anomaly, Crispina's life and household embodied the world she came from, something which tells us how far different this world was from that of the Inquisitors who arraigned her before them. It was small wonder that they felt threatened by it. Looking at women's histories in Cacheu, and the transformations that took place in the household, is an important way of grasping the social and political changes of this time and place.[29]

The way in which gender relations mirrored the economic power structure of the town is clear. Just as in patriarchal societies, older men often marry younger women, so in Cacheu the reverse was the case. In fact, women appear often to have married younger men, as was the case with Crispina and her bedbound husband Jorge: as he put it to the cotton-spinner Maria Mendes, 'men marrying older women was a laborious matter', which according to Mendes 'impl[ied] that he could not do anything with her' – and also implied that it was not something that was all that rare in Cacheu.[30]

Another way of interpreting this is that an older woman in such a partnership, such as Crispina, was in power when it came to daily affairs, trade and many aspects of household life. Older women might well marry younger men in a setting like Cacheu, where ambitious men from Portugal and Cabo Verde might arrive, and where economic networks were usually the province of women who were older. This was upside down to the usual way of things in the Portuguese empire, and was another indication of the perceived reversal of gender norms that Crispina's trial then sought to undermine. The fact that in this region parents of brides received dowries from the groom rather than paying them – as was the case in Portugal – rammed home this reality, and was often the cause of dispute with Atlantic traders who did not want to accept this custom but had no alternative. Jorge described this when he made a list of his enemies in his wife's trial, and said that: 'Domingos Duarte . . . married a girl of their house without asking any dowry; and afterwards he wanted to receive it, but they did not give it, for which [reason] he started hating them a lot.'[31]

Beyond the inverted relationship of age and marriage, Cacheu upended the gender norms of the Portuguese empire in countless ways. Many economically independent women not only ran households, as Crispina did, but also lived in all-female households in Vila Quente as the evidence we saw at the start of this chapter showed. Here, they ran their small-time trading businesses that we saw in the previous section. Their homes were often also the destinations of the itinerant men who roamed about the town when they returned from their trading voyages, rich and dissolute from the trade in enslaved Africans, looking for a relationship of some sort.

All this underscores the reality that, in Cacheu, women were generally in charge. That women were seen as household heads in the manner of men in Portugal is shown by the way in which one of the enslaved members of the household of Peres and Frances referred to Crispina as 'his master'. That women ran their own households is further made clear by a piece of testimony from Crispina's trial, in which the Friar Sebastião de São Vicente said that he had heard that the priest and vicar of Cacheu, Antonio Vaz de Pontes, was 'having an affair with another *parda* [mixed-heritage] girl whose name he cannot recall, who lives in the house of Isabel Lopes, a Black woman, and single, resident in [Cacheu]'. In other words, Lopes ran the house, in which other women also lived; from the evidence we have already seen, this must have been in Vila Quente, and was in keeping with many other contexts in precolonial West and West-Central Africa in which women managed households and were in political authority.[32]

Vaz de Pontes had clearly assimilated well into the ways in which the town worked. Other witnesses confirmed that he was a frequent visitor to Lopes's house, some saying that there his partner Catalina was expecting a child with him, and others that he had visited her straight after mass on Ash Wednesday (when he should have been more spiritually engaged). Meanwhile, when Vaz de Pontes gave his own evidence, he mentioned 'the white and *parda* women, who headed their households'. All this shows that female-run households were the norm, not the exception, and that there was nothing remarkable for people in Cacheu in the type of household that Crispina and Jorge had created. Indeed, the fact that it was Jorge who went to live in Crispina's house when they got married shows how far Western gender norms were reversed in the town: with women in economic power, it was the men who moved in with them when they formed a union.[33]

If the freedom and autonomy of women in Cacheu was grounded in their economic independence, other elements of their daily lives of course connected to deeper aspects of the life cycle: mortality, parenthood and the desire to preserve health. While on one hand the desire for social freedom brought women to live with one another in Vila Quente, and to lead their own households, on the other women often formed their own households because of the deaths of their male partners. An entry from Manoel Bautista Pérez's accounts, of

1617, shows one of his clients to be Ana Lopes, the widow of one Antonio Pinto – meanwhile, another client on the same page of the account book was Izabel Miranda, 'who lives in the house of the widow of Antonio Pinto [i.e. Ana Lopes]'.[34]

In other words, the trading journeys of the itinerant male traders discussed earlier often came at a cost of their premature mortality. As they embarked on prolonged binge-drinking sessions, both while travelling and then on their return, their health suffered. In Cacheu, the women's linguistic and kinship networks meant that they had better access to healers, and so they could try to help them to get better. But often, the men died. Women then looked after each other: they lived in one another's houses, and, where one had inherited a house following widowhood, others would come to join them and trade on their own account, as Izabel Miranda had done with Manoel Bautista Pérez from the house of Ana Lopes. Women were generally the heads of households, and determined from here the course of their commercial, social and emotional lives.

The centrality of the emotional aspect of the life-cycle is writ large in Crispina's trial. As she said herself, in the confession which she gave to the Inquisitors in Lisbon, she had begun to wear the amulets or *gris-gris* provided by the *djabakós* in the hope that they would cure her daughter of an infant illness, and as many people in the town had recommended them. However, 'when she saw that her daughter who had had them put on her, and for whose benefit she herself had worn them, had died, her heart grew small'. The emotional freedom of these commercial women – to love, grieve, heal, and die in the manner of their choosing – was enabled by their economic freedom: but it of course did not mean that their lives were easy or at all without suffering and sadness.[35]

With such strong economic, social and emotional autonomy, women in Cacheu had sexual independence. Even a priest like Antonio Vaz de Pontes thought nothing of having a relationship with his girlfriend Catalina in Isabel Lopes's house. The trial of the priest Luis Rodrigues also makes it clear that in these communities women were free to choose their sexual partners. It was, after all, Rodrigues who was placed in the Inquisitorial dock as a priest, for soliciting women in the confessional. The women of Farim, on the other hand, clearly felt they had the social freedom to participate in drunken and raunchy parties at his house. As one witness put it,

> the said priest always went around with a shirt half-undone, and full of wine, ordering dances to take place at his house where he brought together both pagan and Christian women, and all this with a great fanfare and producing a huge scandal in everyone since he committed sins with them.

Meanwhile, one woman of Farim, Domingas Afonso, stayed for three days in his house 'receiving confession', apparently of the opinion that, whatever the Inquisitors thought of it, the social censure she would receive for this would be a small matter.[36]

In Cacheu itself, fights between Atlantic traffickers over the love

Postcard of the river at Farim, 1910.

of African women were common enough. It wasn't just the envy that was caused by the public affairs of people like Vaz de Pontes that brought things to a peak. Sometimes people came to blows as rivals, which alone confirms the power that women had sexually, economically and socially in the town. In his defence during his own trial, Luis Rodrigues accused the Caboverdean archdeacon Diogo Furtado de Mendonça of fighting another captain, Salvador Rodrigues Mermellada, in Cacheu, in rivalry for the love of the Black woman Florença de Andrada.[37]

Women's sexual freedom was complementary to the many roles that they had in Cacheu. It was they who kept the town's economy and social life going, while their men were absent, ill, raging drunkenly at their social impotence, or dying. Their economic dominance and cultural capital gave them the freedom to run their own households, welcoming in other women who needed a place to live. There they sought to care for the health of those they loved as best they could, whether children, lovers, girlfriends or spouses in decline.

This context of gender relations shaped the household of Crispina and Jorge, which we looked at in the previous chapter. It was here that the enmities that led to Crispina's trial were born. As we have seen in this chapter, a key factor shaping these enmities was the fact that men and women related to one another in Cacheu in a way that was utterly different from what Atlantic traffickers had known before. Many did not like it: when Domingos Duarte 'grew hatred in his heart' for Crispina and Jorge at their refusal to pay him a dowry, he was manifesting not only his hatred of the couple but also his hatred of the world which had produced them.

Women had many roles in Cacheu. They were traders, heads of household and had an independence in their daily lives which was shocking to arrivals from Portugal. This matched the surrounding environment, in which female rulers in Cassão and Pachesi were common enough. Women's independence in Cacheu became the source of many rivalries and tensions in the town, pitting a patriarchal Portuguese empire into a differently gendered sphere on which that empire sought to intrude. These tensions then spilled over into these Inquisitorial trials – as the constant references to quarrels, drunkenness and disputes make clear.

The women of Cacheu were able to move about with freedom from one place to another, as the cotton-spinner Leonor Ferreira did from Cabo Verde to Farim, and as Crispina herself had done in her life. This was again just normal. One person accused of practising witchcraft in the trial was Júlia de Aguiar, who had been born in the trading settlement of Geba and had then left there, taking her son with her, to move to Cacheu and thence to Farim on the borders of the powerful kingdom of Kaabu. This kind of freedom of movement and autonomy was just a workaday aspect of daily life for many of the women who lived here.[38]

All this can begin to bring together a sense of what these women's lives were like. They moved around, traded and often shouted loudly in the streets of the town if they needed to go and make a sacrifice to the *china* in Vila Quente. Their voices and inclinations shaped the town. As the work of Ferreira and of the other

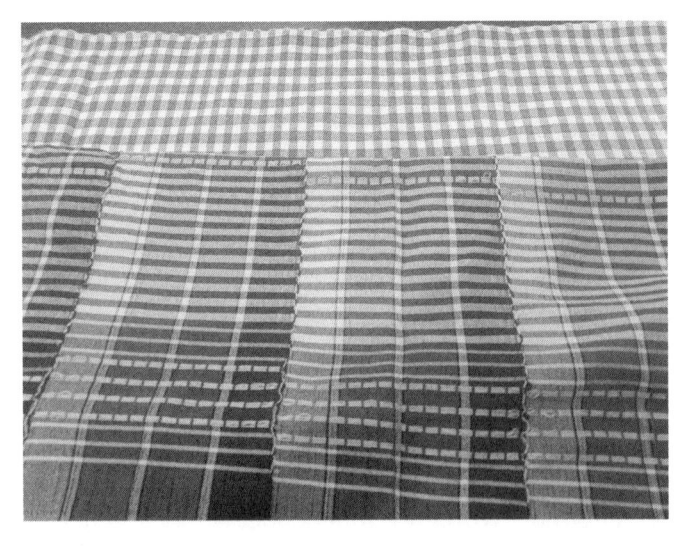

Pepel cloth from the early twentieth century.

women we have discussed here shows, cotton and textiles were important to them. Fashion counted, and women had an important place in supplying cotton to weavers and in selecting fabrics. While they prepared all the food, both for themselves and for the men of their household, pounding the grain in pestles and mortars, they also were important consumers of textiles, both locally made and imported, and were decisive in shaping styles in the town. They often wore blue-and-white cotton shifts, made of the same cotton the men wore, with another hanging loose from their shoulders.[39]

On the other hand, it would be a mistake to think that these relations were somehow static. Some historians have argued that there is strong evidence that the increasing violence associated with the transatlantic traffic in enslaved Africans had a strong impact on gender relations. Times were changing fast. With men lost in warfare and captured for enslavement (with the strong preference by traffickers for male captives), women in rural settings and away from the urban spaces of the ports and other commercial towns had to take on a much greater labour burden. While there may have been freedom and autonomy for the women in Cacheu and Vila Quente, they were the lucky ones. For in some ways, their autonomy had been purchased at the price of their sisters in the *tabankas* (or villages) round and about.[40]

The trader Lemos Coelho described the life of women in the Bijagó islands in the 1660s:

> The women are the ones who work in the fields, and plant the crops, and the houses in which they live, even though small, are clean and bright, and despite all this work they still go down to the sea each day to catch shellfish.[41]

In other words, in the two centuries since the Portuguese had arrived in Senegambia and the slave traffic had begun, a divide had grown up between the urban spaces of Cacheu and others like it (Farim, Geba, Bintang) on the one hand, and many of the rural

*The Heretic of Cacheu*

Rice bushels hanging from a roof, Guinea-Bissau.

communities under pressure through the Atlantic traffic on the other. While, as the historian Walter Hawthorne has shown, among the Balanta the heavy work of rice-growing pushed much of the fieldwork into the domain of men, in many other places farming was becoming more and more the work of women – alongside the countless other things that they had to do. If women ran the marketplace, it may have been because they had to come to market the produce that they had reaped from their work in the fields. In Cacheu, by contrast, the dynamic of male travel and female commerce gave women the scope to run things as they wanted to. Free women were socially and economically empowered, and in many ways in charge. But there were also, of course, many enslaved women in the town, lying in chains and imprisoned in the houses of traders like Crispina, women who had little such autonomy over their lives in what was then the most important Atlantic slaving port on this part of the West African coast.[42]

## 3.
## *Cacheu: The Setting*

'there can be no doubt that if the Africans wanted to destroy [Cacheu] they would have done so already'

Cacheu the town was a place which defined the lives we are getting to know. It was a town shaped by the history of enslavement. Over the course of the more than 350 years of that devastating history, the largest numbers of what historian Ana Lucia Araujo calls 'humans in shackles' departed from today's Democratic Republic of Congo and Angola for the Americas. However, it was here, in the borderlands between Guinea-Bissau and Senegal, that the transatlantic trade in captives first took shape during the early sixteenth century. After the 1550s, the volumes of captives from West Africa – destined at first for Mexico and Peru – increased in number, reaching approximately 5,000 per year by 1600.[1]

During the sixteenth century, Cacheu was a small riverine settlement without much business. The Portuguese traders lived some miles away among the Bainunk communities on the north bank of the São Domingos river. They resided in the settlement of Bugendo, a short distance up a creek from the north bank of the river, near to the modern border town of São Domingos. From Cacheu it was one league (about three miles) further upstream to the creek which cut in to Bugendo's port; beyond Bugendo, this waterway met the Nhonho creek, which led to Ziguinchor, on the Casamance river and its adjacent mudflats.[2]

At this time the Portuguese appear to have been quite well integrated into West African societies. Some of them performed masquerades, as we saw in the previous chapter, while others followed African religious practice. The main commerce from Bugendo seems to have been in food provisions and not in captive Africans, according to one report from the 1560s, noting how a ship had sought provisions there before moving south. This suggests that in these early decades, the violence of the imperial demand for labour was not as yet the only factor shaping these African–European relationships in the Cacheu region.[3]

However, two pressures changed the dynamics in the 1580s. The Kassanké people began to rebel against the Bainunk, attacking Bugendo and the Portuguese there, perhaps owing to their anger at the growing traffic in the enslaved and the social and economic crisis that this was creating. Meanwhile, a severe drought in the Cabo Verde islands in the 1580s drove many islanders to settle on this part of the coast. The arrival of these colonists in large numbers, amid the political conflict of the Kassanké attacks on Bugendo, upset further the balance of power. Under the direction of the colonial governor on Santiago island, in 1589 the Caboverdeans established a fortified settlement in Caticheu – meaning 'Where we rest' in Bainunk – which they abbreviated in short order to the name the town has had ever since. However, this attempt to create a barrier between the colonial community and the Senegambian world in which it dwelt was to prove more successful on paper than in practice.[4]

All this means that both Crispina and Jorge were born in a period when Cacheu was still establishing itself (both being born between c.1615 and 1620). Only thirty years old then, the town was going through a period of expansion, driven by the rapid growth of the traffic in enslaved Africans in the early seventeenth century. Having got a sense of the human relationships and tensions which underpinned their household in the previous two chapters, in this one we gain a detailed understanding of the environment which they inhabited: the houses, streets and neighbourhoods which made up Cacheu, and the objects which made up the fabric of material life.[5]

## Cacheu: The Setting

This provides a sense of the town itself – the sights and smells, the sounds, the texture of social life – but also of its broader physical environment and how that was changing. Cacheu was not somehow isolated from global affairs. It was deeply connected to broader social and environmental transformations worldwide. Changes catalysed by the mini Ice Age* were contributing to profound environmental transformations which shaped the physical experience of daily life in Cacheu in the middle part of the seventeenth century. At the same time, this was a West African environment, which did not take intrusions from the outside world lightly.[6]

Over the coming centuries, the creative and at times destructive tension produced by this dynamic of African agency and power on the one hand and external force and influence on the other came to shape many aspects of the continent's histories.

Cacheu lay about twenty miles from the Atlantic Ocean, in the land known as Mata. The town was sited on the wide brown waters of the São Domingos river. On the far northern side of the river the land was covered in mangroves, as it is today. From this bank, canoes were brought by villagers every day in the dry season laden with provisions – millet, rice – and with dried fish to trade. There were several very populous villages here, Bosól, Usól and Safunco, from which occasional attacks were made on Cacheu. Soon enough, however, the attacks might be interrupted, especially during the rainy season, when according to one document from 1656, 'nothing is done because of the torrential rain'. Then, once the rains had gone by the end of October, the old pattern of trade resumed.[7]

---

* A cooling period in the North Atlantic region that occurred in three stages: scholars argue that it began in the fourteenth century and reached its coolest extent in the 1660s. Disputes about the causes of this environmental crisis (and its 'economic' consequences) remain fierce to this day. Some historians attribute it to sun-spot changes, and others to climate change driven by human greed, violence and destructiveness.

## The Heretic of Cacheu

Markets are often located in border areas, and Cacheu too lay in a border area between the Pepel and Floup peoples. The Pepel lived in the area further inland from Cacheu, upriver, while Cacheu and Mata itself was also Pepel. However, the area between Cacheu and the coast, the so-called Mata de Putame, was Floup territory. The Floup were a diverse group of peoples, some of whom spoke different languages, but who seemed to be united by shared religious practice – and also by their hostility to Portuguese traders and to the Atlantic traffic in general. Over time, the Floup would migrate further north into Casamance and eventually as far as to the Bintang *bolon* in The Gambia.[8]

For all the attempts made by the colonists to recreate a space that was familiar to them, this was a Senegambian town. One letter from Santiago island in 1656 said that there were just five or six white people living in Cacheu, and that most of them were absent on trading trips for much of the year. Of these whites many were in fact, like Crispina and Jorge, of mixed heritage, more African than European. This didn't stop some of them from trying to import some Portuguese ideas of honour and respect. Swordfights sometimes descended onto the town's streets, probably over trifles, to pass the time. It was deemed a sign of hatred if people passed one another in the street without raising their hats, as they might have done on the waterfront of Lisbon. But in reality, this was all a colonial performance, as the hopeless state of the town's defences against the Pepel made clear: self-evidently, five or six people cannot defend anything very well, and the records we have make it abundantly clear that the Portuguese were barely tolerated guests, and that the Pepel were certainly the ones in charge, attacking the Portuguese redoubt in Cacheu many times.[9]

Indeed, the Pepel had begun to launch attacks against Cacheu as soon as the town had been founded in 1589. They had attacked the fortified settlement the following year, but had been repelled. By the 1620s, one author described how the town was 'often at war with the Africans who live around it, who are brave, hostile and eager to fight'. So adept at warfare were they, that 'there have been ships which have entered [the river] in times of war to defend the people and all the people and officers [of the ship] have been killed'. The Pepel eventually allowed the Portuguese to remain on sufferance: as the military captain Luis de Magalhães wrote in 1640, such was their military dominance, that 'there can be no doubt that if the Africans wanted to destroy [Cacheu] they would have done so already'. This may, of course, also indicate that there were different factions among the Pepel, formed most likely on the basis of class: those who suffered most through the inroads of the Portuguese colonial presence were most likely to fight against it.[10]

In the years running up to Crispina's trial, things had steadily deteriorated in Cacheu as far as the Portuguese empire was concerned. Writing one of the most detailed accounts we have of the region in 1669, the trader Francisco de Lemos Coelho – whom, as it happened, Jorge accused in his wife's trial of being his sworn enemy – described how the captain-generals of Cacheu had had many battles with the king of Mata, and that 'in the last one our people were defeated with many dead, which led to the peace treaty which has lasted until today'. This had probably been in the mid-1650s, but in 1662, when the new captain and factor arrived, he found the town surrounded by troops, 'without any defence whatsoever . . . neither a fortress nor any defence which could prevent the Africans from setting the town on fire'. There were not even any rifles or bullets, and there was hardly any gunpowder: every time that the Pepel leaders wanted to force the captain and residents to do something, they just sent their people to occupy the water fountains, forcing the Portuguese to comply or to die of thirst.[11]

This political dimension is vital to understanding the Inquisition records that we are drawing on to enter into this time and place. On the one hand, Crispina's trial was an attempt to assert Portuguese imperial control when it was under attack from all sides: locally from the Pepel, whose military superiority was manifest, from the growing influence of other European imperial powers along the whole Senegambian Atlantic coast, and from Islamic Jakhanké preacher-traders in the region. On the other, as

## The Heretic of Cacheu

the dominance of the Pepel showed, anyone with strong connections to the political leaders that surrounded the town was bound to be in a good commercial position, as the accusations against Crispina made clear.[12]

These commercial connections defined Cacheu. The streets were filled with household servants and captives carrying huge loads: rounded bundles of wax sold in 'loaves' (which was highly prized in the Atlantic trade, and often destined for making the candles of the many churches of the Americas), alongside millet and rice for the town and for the captives imprisoned in the trafficking ships. Provisions came from across the river, but they also came from further afield, with some millet being brought from the Bijagós islands. Beyond the coerced and unfree labour, some of this work of carrying loads in the streets of the town may have been paid, as the account books of Manoel Bautista Pérez suggest: in one entry from 1613, he describes the costs involved in sending goods to the trader Dioguo Teles, in exchange for him sending wax back to Bautista Pérez's home.[13]

These details offer a window onto a town busy – in the dry season – with the loading and unloading of goods, bundled up and taken here and there. One of the most important things to grasp about Cacheu is that this incessant activity meant that it was also a very mobile town. The stereotype of a static, unchanging Africa could not be further from the truth. No one stayed put for long. Just as the canoes came laden with goods from surrounding villages, most people moved around frequently – for reasons of trade, or of healing, or of religion. The night was no barrier to movement, and in fact the *djabakós* who came to see Crispina to heal her children often came at night.[14]

It was because of this constant movement of people that news travelled quickly. Just as history in this part of West Africa remains largely an oral genre, so news spread by word of mouth far more quickly than it did by written word or fiat. News was vital both to being able to know who could corroborate a story, but also to keeping hold of some precious piece of gossip which might become useful – who knew how many years later? As Jorge's envious brother-in-law João Nunes Castanho put it about the infamous 'pots' in which Crispina was alleged to keep her heretical 'witchcraft' remedies, she had hung these pots 'at the same time as he was living in her house, which was seven years ago, more or less, and that the said pot remained for two years hanging in the same place': someone in the household – probably Sebastião Rodrigues Barraza – had told him what was happening, years after the event, so that he could get his story straight.[15]

All this can begin to give us a sense of the atmosphere of the settlement of Cacheu. This was an African town, under African political control, even if Portugal's imperial presence could not be completely ignored. The streets were busy with activity. Enslaved household servants and apprentices such as Domingos de Aredas were busy, bringing goods from the port to the houses of the Atlantic traders; though the enslaved feared being sold into the worse fate of the Atlantic traffic, this was in practice unlikely because the major traffickers depended on them for their work bringing goods to and from the house, and for the connections they had in a town in which the Portuguese were not in political control. Meanwhile, and because of the fear and envy which they had of them, these same messengers from the household gossiped and connived to undermine the power of the leading merchants of Cacheu.

At the same time, many daily concerns were much like those anywhere else in the world, as we learn when Manoel Bautista Pérez describes returning a cat to Simão Machado in 1617 because he had discovered that it was female. Bautista Pérez might not have wanted a litter of kittens on his hands, but hunting mice which might destroy the grain stores was a concern in Cacheu, as it was anywhere else in the world.[16]

The town of Cacheu today is divided into two main parts. First, there is the old administrative centre which grew up during the era of formal Portuguese colonialism in the twentieth century. There is the main avenue which runs down from the entrance into the town on the Canchungo road to the jetty on the riverside, passing the old municipal buildings – the council, the main church, the *sobrado* (two-storey) houses of the old merchants. But perhaps it's no surprise that the people of Cacheu have little love lost for these remains. Most of them exude an air of peeling abandonment, the sort of half-life in which defunct empires so often live on. The main part of the town is in fact some distance away from this more visible 'centre', in the palm groves which greet the waterfront and the avenue and stretch off some distance from them. This is where the compounds of the townspeople are found, where the real life of Cacheu today is located: it's here that the people live, almost as if ignoring the shell of the colonial town and its painful histories which in some ways shaped the lives they live today.

The curious thing is that this footprint of Cacheu mirrors the town as it was in the seventeenth century. At that time, the town was also divided into two parts. There was the colonial part, connected to the transatlantic traffic: this was the focal point for the daily lives of Portuguese colonial administrators and the traders who visited to do business for some weeks or months, and for those who worked with them. And then there was what was in fact – though you would never know this from the colonial documents – the main part of the town, where most people lived. As we saw in the previous chapter, this was called by the Portuguese 'Vila Quente' – the hot town. And while the colonial town was connected to Atlantic cultures – the site of honour-bound swordfights and social slights given by those who would not raise their hats to one another – Vila Quente was an African town, with African religious, social and cultural ways of life, a place run by its women.

What was the material world of these spaces like? In order to understand Cacheu as a space, we need to get a sense of how people lived. This doesn't just mean a sense of their social or political lives, but also of its material fabric: the houses people inhabited, the ways they were built, the texture of what they saw and felt as they went about their daily lives. To do this, we're

## Cacheu: The Setting

fortunate to have several descriptions from the seventeenth century which can give us an impression of what the urban space of Cacheu was like then.

Writing in the 1610s, the missionary Manoel Álvares gave a good sense of the townhouses of the Portuguese merchants. These were set in a square shape, and some were built with a *sobrado*. The walls of these larger houses were constructed of dried earth, covered with palm leaves. These had been built in response to some of the conflicts with the Pepels mentioned above. For, while originally the houses had been made of wood, as one anonymous account puts it, many of these buildings were then burnt down in the conflicts with their African hosts, as was the church (which was set ablaze in a great tragedy in which many people died, including enslaved Africans). The Portuguese colonists were thus increasingly forced by the Pepel to adopt their own architectural styles to stave off the threat of having their wooden houses burnt down. By the 1630s, the main street of the colonial town offered a mix of styles: some wooden houses, the larger earth-built storied houses, and smaller thatched houses for the free African residents of Cacheu.[17]

Another characteristic building that the Portuguese copied from their African hosts was the storehouse, which were known as *combetes*. These stores were towers built in a square shape, like the houses. They were constructed of sun-baked earth, probably modelled on the rice granaries found in many villages of the Senegambia region. According to one account, and as with the adobe construction of the houses, the Portuguese used the *combetes* to store their property so as to protect themselves from the risk of losing everything to arson. Manoel Bautista Pérez described holding a large amount of wax in his *combete*, for instance, in 1614. In the early days of the town, the roofs appear to have been made of wood and then covered with dried clay, but it seems that then the wood was dispensed with because of the risk of Pepel hostilities.[18]

There were two main streets in this part of Cacheu. There was the main street along the waterfront, which was called Rua Direita ('Straight Street'). And then behind Rua Direita, there was Rua de Santo Antonio, which was set back one block from the port. The dock of the riverside was marked out by a platform, which was made of stone and lime. Rua Direita not only gave on to the river, and was the main site for trafficking activities; it was also the street that linked up the two worlds of Cacheu, running from the town's main church to the Pepel neighbourhood of Vila Quente, as a legal document from 1612 described it. Though the church had originally been built in wood, by the 1660s it was made of stone and lime.[19]

Vila Quente was therefore, on this 1612 account, at the opposite end of Rua Direita from the church. The best description that we have of the neighbourhood was given by Francisco Lemos Coelho in his 1669 account. Coelho said that by this date there was a hermitage dedicated to St Anthony at the entrance, named after the street that led to the neighbourhood from the portside and built of adobe and thatched with palm leaves. But while a Euro-African trader might have tried to emphasize it for his readers in Portugal, in reality the footprint of Christianity was nominal, as the Inquisition records make clear. Here, Vila Quente was singled out as the place where the people of Cacheu went to make offerings at the *chinas* which dominated: these were separate shrines covered often by a roof made of palm fronds, and set aside from the populated areas of the settlement, in which offerings could be made.[20]

As the summary of the prosecution case put it:

> Vila Quente, which lies a gunshot away from the settlement of Cacheu where the heathens* have their idol, to which they sacrifice and offer palm wine, and the blood of chickens, cows, goats and other animals, and libate the idol for the purpose of sacrifice.[21]

---

* As noted before, this refers to non-Christian Africans (i.e. the vast majority of the population).

*Cacheu: The Setting*

It was in Vila Quente that the funerals following the Pepel religious traditions were practised. As another witness in Crispina's trial put it, in Vila Quente 'heathens live with Christians, and in this place there are many Christian and free women, who . . . sacrifice or libate wine most days always in the company of heathens'. This was the palm wine tapped from the trees around the town, and not the Portuguese wine imported expensively from Madeira.[22]

So, though Christianity was present in Vila Quente, its significance was overshadowed by the African character of the settlement. According to Lemos Coelho, the neighbourhood itself was 'inhabited by free Black *grumetes*, and African fishermen who have not been baptized'. They worshipped at Pepel shrines, and drank palm wine. They also lived in houses built in the Pepel style, many of which were, as we have seen, women-only households. The town was protected from attack from peoples of the surrounding country by a stockade or *tabanka*, built of sharpened stakes from mangrove trees, beyond which was a moat. The *tabanka* was named after a form of protection for settlements derived from invaders known as Manes, who seem to have come from the Mali empire (centred on the Niger river in the south of today's Mali) to Sierra Leone in the 1540s, around a century before Lemos Coelho was writing. By the seventeenth century, fortifications of this type were the norm for settlements throughout this region of West Africa; and in fact several accounts indicate fortified villages among the Floup and in the Casamance region even in the early sixteenth century.*[23]

The English sailor Richard Jobson described what these fortifications were like in the Gambia river region in the 1620s:

> their habitations [are] round together, and for the most part have a wall, though it be but of Reeds, platted and made up together, some six foot in height, circling and going round their Town, with doors of the same, in the night time to be orderly shut.[24]

---

* To this day, villages in Guinea-Bissau are called *tabankas*.

These towns and villages were defended, and there were city gates, much as there were in the towns of Europe at the time. But what were the houses that made up the settlement of Vila Quente like? A number of sources can give us a real sense of the materiality of these African homes. Most people lived in these fortified villages – the *tabankas*. Meanwhile, in the late sixteenth century, the Caboverdean André Alvares d'Almada described the homes of the Pepels, where 'people were forced to live in dwellings that were more labyrinths than houses'. This protected them from attacks, making it hard for raiders to find their way back out of the maze of interconnected courtyards.[25]

Vila Quente's fortifications were typical of the region, therefore. Many of the houses in the settlement itself were probably also built with protection in mind, given the frequency of attacks on Cacheu from the surrounding villages. These kinds of fortified houses with palisades became quite normal in this period of the history of Cacheu and the surrounding region. At the same time, this style of architecture also served a different purpose when adapted by the Portuguese in Cacheu: these buildings could also serve as a type of prison for those captives awaiting transport in irons to the Americas.[26]

How different, then, was Vila Quente from the towns and villages of the surrounding area, where people like Crispina and Jorge also spent so much of their time? As in Vila Quente, most buildings in the Greater Senegambia region were constructed with sun-dried clay (called adobe by the Portuguese in their descriptions) and had roofs thatched with palm fronds. The well-to-do houses had vestibules in which visitors were received, while there were also often fences made of wood and palm fronds. Most houses had benches here, on which visitors could sit. Their doors had locks which had wooden keys, the outer walls were whitewashed with lime, and the houses were generally round with the thatched roofs tied to the rafters: according to Richard Jobson, this was because the round shape made it harder for the gusting winds of the rainy season to blow off the thatch from the roofs. Houses with more than one storey were also not limited to the colonial town of Cacheu. Building a

*Cacheu: The Setting*

A fence bordering a vegetable garden, Bijagós islands.

*sobrado* was a sign of status across the Senegambian region. In the port of Cassão on the Gambia river – a Mandinga settlement regularly visited by traffickers from Cacheu, as we will see in the next chapter – there were several *sobrados*.[27]

As a whole, these descriptions help us to understand how the material fabric of Cacheu embodied its complex West African and imperial Portuguese context. The theory of empire, designed in Lisbon, was one thing, but the practice was different. While the ideals of Portuguese imperial hierarchy were embodied in the financial and human costs that were exacted by the stone construction of the new church, these were a painful façade which concealed a different material reality. Most of the town's houses were for African workers and their families, built by them using African construction styles (though the 'European' houses were square-shaped and not round). The *combete* storehouses had been adapted from local granaries and using local materials to protect the property of the Atlantic traffickers. The two-storey dwellings were not an innovation, as they were found elsewhere in the region.

Meanwhile, the building materials of the colonists' houses had been adapted from the Pepel in order to protect them from attack. Cacheu's architecture was in fact a material recognition of the fragile grip which the Portuguese empire had on this part of the world – a grip which it would seek to tighten through Crispina's Inquisition trial.

In the same way that the construction of the houses in Cacheu reflected their setting – and the materials that were available, and most useful – so, too, did the social and material worlds of the households. Just as the houses drew on Senegambian techniques of construction, so these households embodied their political and social context. This was, of course, West African. In fact, the local architectural techniques underpinning the construction of houses also helps us to understand Crispina and Jorge's household: as modern architects have so often claimed, the philosophy that shaped their built environment also signified how they lived their lives.

This is clearest through the way in which Crispina and Jorge's home embodied the extended kinship network (*gan*) more characteristic of a Senegambian family compound than of a European household. As we saw in the previous chapter, members of Crispina and Jorge's extended family frequently came to stay with them for long periods of time while they waited on business deals or just hoped to get rich through association. As with most extended families, they did not always get on well, but this did not matter to the set-up. Brothers-in-law, stepchildren, nieces and nephews all had walk-on parts in the Inquisition trial, as witnesses who could be trusted to know what had been going on in the household because of the fact that they had spent periods of time living there. This was an extended West African *gan* homestead: just as the material context of the built environment shaped the architecture of

## Cacheu: The Setting

Cacheu, so too did the social and kinship context in which the town was located.

Though reflecting these local relationships, Cacheu's urban environment was also distinctively part of the Atlantic world. People constantly passed through in pursuit of business, their needs catered for through Senegambian structures. There was a ready market for renting rooms and houses in towns like Cacheu and Farim, just as there was in other parts of the Iberian empires. The scribe Pedro Pais rented rooms in houses owned by Jorge. This was a longstanding business, since fifty years earlier Manoel Bautista Pérez noted down a debt for the rent he owed for living in a creditor's house. Some historians have seen the ease with which outsiders could arrive in places like Cacheu, and settle in for a time before moving on, as an inheritance of the tradition from this part of West Africa where landlords were often ready to accommodate strangers.[28]

On the one hand, therefore, the framework of renting rooms and houses seems familiar. And yet, on the other, these and other snippets of information give us a sense of complex social settings that were far removed from the traditional family household of the European imaginary. Many of the witnesses in the two Inquisition trials of these years make it clear that they lived in shared housing with other residents of Cacheu and Farim. In these households, the gender dynamics were very different from those of Portugal and its empire. Just as there were all-women households in the town, so there was no taboo to stop women traders from renting rooms from houses owned by men and living with them. Jorge's nephew Rodrigo Gonçalves Frances said that, when he was living in Farim, in 1655, one of the residents of his house was a single woman called Bonifacia, a baptized resident of the town.[29]

Thus, the social worlds of these households reflected a wide range of influences, far beyond that familiar to people who knew only Portugal and its empire. The households were extended. They were never static, incorporating not only family members but also apprentices such as Domingos de Aredas. Conversely, there was an active, often successful and mobile population of men and women who rented rooms or shared houses with one another. One witness against the priest Luis Rodrigues testified that she had spent two weeks living together with him in the same house in Cacheu, alongside others – which can give a sense of lives lived in this urban setting that were both shared and collective, and where men and women occupied spaces in a way that Portuguese visitors found unusual.[30]

This blend of West African and Atlantic ways of being also typified the material trappings of the houses themselves. The possessions which people surrounded themselves with characterized the mixed environment. On the one hand, the large households of Rua Direita were filled with the sorts of goods that would be expected in an Atlantic trading settlement. The bedrooms had wooden-framed beds made locally, and mattresses that were traded on the ocean-going ships. Blankets were one of the most frequent items in the account books of Manoel Bautista Pérez, both for use by free visitors to the houses of the townspeople and by the Africans who also occupied them, either imprisoned in chains behind the stockades or in irons on the ships soon due to cross the Atlantic.[31]

The sheer number of references to blankets suggests they were in high demand, whereas mattresses – mentioned only rarely in the account books – were a luxury item. It is quite easy to imagine Jorge laid out on his bed – as witnesses in Crispina's trial said he so frequently was – shivering away malarial fevers beneath the blankets which had arrived in Cacheu through this business. But the blankets were also described specifically in one document as being 'for Africans'. This suggests that they were also in use in Vila Quente and in the round dried-earth houses along Rua Direita and perhaps also were traded to some of the towns in the surrounding area. The volume of wax traded suggests that candles were also widely used by night, in bedrooms and elsewhere, which gives a sense of what these rooms were like both by day and by the flickering candlelight at night.[32]

If sleeping is one of the most important functions of a house, high on the list beside it are cooking and eating. There were fixed

## Cacheu: The Setting

benches in the kitchens of the houses known as *cantareiras*, on which people might sit and talk to those cooking or cleaning. The richer households like Crispina and Jorge's, with an interest in maintaining a European lifestyle, ate off imported kitchenware which was a sign of status as they saw it. This included Chinese porcelain, and also silver plates melted down no doubt from Potosí's silver (the silver mines in Bolivia being then at their zenith of production) – there were both larger and smaller silver plates in some of the households of Cacheu and silver spoons, while some people drank out of silver cups. Cooking was done with large cauldrons bubbling away on braziers, heated with charcoal, which offers another glimpse of the streets of Cacheu with bundles of charcoal and firewood carried to and from the large *sobrado* houses on the waterfront. There were also ovens made of copper in the richer houses.[33]

Food itself, like most other aspects of life in the town, offered a globalized mix of African products and imported luxuries. After two centuries of intensive interactions between the peoples of Senegambia and the Portuguese, the culture which had emerged was mixed. Senegambian cuscus and palm oil were staples of cuisine, and the sheer amount of the grain accounted for by Bautista Pérez suggests that it was a firm favourite for the African population. On the other hand, there were large amounts of foodstuffs imported through the Atlantic trade which provided European status to those in the town who craved it. This included the basics of Portuguese cuisine such as wine, oil, olives and sugar, and also clear luxuries: figs, almonds, oranges, cured sausage, jam, cheese from the Alentejo (a firm favourite of Bautista Pérez, who was often in debt for the purchase of it), chickpeas and dried figs. There was even the extravagance of imported pepper through the spice trade to Asia, and some Dutch cheese was available as well.[34]

This mix of foods was one which suited the identities and cultural worlds of a household like Crispina and Jorge's, where life sat in between the African and the Atlantic worlds. All of these details give us a richer picture of the houses of Cacheu. The bedrooms of the wealthier trafficking houses seem to have been sparsely furnished.

By night, they were lit by candles illuminating the beds with their imported mattresses and blankets. The kitchens were hives of activity. There were fixed benches where people sat and gossiped, and charcoal and sacks of provisions were constantly being brought in and out by household slaves. The serving of food reflected the poisonous hierarchies that were growing up alongside the transatlantic traffic: silver and Chinese porcelain service for the traffickers, and not for those enslaved and kept captive behind the stockades that guarded the house and its 'property'. In these homes, the trappings of wealth and success were imported: status signals that indicated who was in power in the colonial world at least, and where the roots of that power and wealth were being set down.

This parading of foreign luxuries as status symbols was reproduced in perhaps the clearest material manifestation of the place of imports in Cacheu: fashion. This was shown off flamboyantly through the streets of the town: the wealthiest colonists in the town preferred to wear silks and damask from India and China and wouldn't dream of being seen going about in 'English cloths'.

The account books of Bautista Pérez are very clear on the visual impacts of foreign clothing styles in Cacheu. As in so many other times and places in the history of the world, what people wore – and their ability to change according to new fashions, as they came in – was one of the most important facets of their lives. Access to the latest trends in textiles meant that it was always vital for your life to be on display. There was a huge variety of cloth for sale in the warehouses of the Atlantic traders. From Europe, there was cloth from England (known as perpetuan), from Rouen (where the textile houses were famous for it), as well as from the well-known looms of the Dutch weavers. There was a fashion for *picote*, a sort of purl-stitched clothing then in vogue in Spain and Portugal, which also found its way to the streets of the town. Black hats were worn, and traded, as were insults when people failed to doff them to one another in the street.[35]

The range of textiles on offer was certainly not confined to

Europe. By the later eighteenth and nineteenth centuries, indigo-dyed dark-blue Indian cloths were among the biggest imports to northern Senegambia, but the records of Bautista Pérez show that the import of cloth from India had begun much earlier. One of the most common items in these accounts are 'cannekins', cloths woven in Gujarat in India. Shirts were on sale woven with Indian cloth, alongside taffeta from both China and Mexico. With Chinese manufactures available, the many silk socks that also can be found changing hands in these records may well have been woven on the silk looms in that part of Asia.[36]

The range of textiles available in the 1610s – from virtually every corner of the world, from Mexico to China and India via most of Europe – shows starkly just how globalized Cacheu and West Africa were by this time. Clothing from literally every corner of the world was available for sale in huge bundles in the warehouses of the Atlantic traffickers. The value ascribed to textiles is shown by the fact that it was the major unit of account in most of the records that we have from Bautista Pérez, woven into plain white strips or bolts of cloth for the cloth-currency trade. This also helps us to gain a sense of the flux of life in the town, where each new ship arriving bringing these goods was impatiently awaited, to see what the new styles and trends were that it brought, and which would soon be found paraded up and down the Rua Direita and in Vila Quente.[37]

Amid these imported material goods, there was also a thriving business in locally produced cloth. Textiles woven in many different parts of Senegambia constitute one of the major items found in the account books. In 1617, João Bautista Pérez bought literally hundreds of bolts of both black and white cloth woven in the Gambia river area, alongside many of the well-known blue-and-white *barafulas* woven in Cabo Verde, and also it seems being reproduced by Fulani weavers in The Gambia area. Some of this weaving may also have been done by enslaved captives trained in this task. Cloth was traded in Cacheu that had been woven as far north as among the Jolof, as one itemized list in the account books makes clear. Meanwhile, textiles woven in closer ports like Degola often changed hands, alongside the more valuable and prized Senegambian cloth known in the books as *Pano de Rei* ('king's cloth'). It becomes clear not only how important and prized cloth was but also how enormously varied the styles and weaves were, and how much this mattered to the people of the town.[38]

What emerges is that, in spite of the place of imports among the Atlantic traffickers and in their homes, the material context of Cacheu was solidly West African. Though textiles from Europe and Asia had a place in the colonial town, and in the houses of people like Crispina and Jorge, most people wore clothing produced locally. Major textile-producing regions included Bundu (the east of present-day Senegal) and Fuuta Tòoro on the Senegal river in the north. Textiles were woven on a horizontal treadle loom, and the threads were dyed indigo, black and yellow. So important was the textile production and trade in Senegambia that, by the 1670s, European traders on the upper Gambia river had to buy large volumes of textiles there to compete in trade. Moreover, Senegambian textiles were also an Atlantic product, since they were traded across the ocean to Cartagena in today's Colombia.[39]

Oral histories make it clear that the trading of dyed cloths was a key part of the business of the region. On the south bank of the Gambia river, one of these woven cloths was known as Kantong, and was also made by women into a wrap which they wore. The significance of textiles made in Senegambia – and the potential competition which they posed to the wider Atlantic textiles trade – was such that a denunciation was made to the Inquisitors in 1619 of one trader originally from the Malay Peninsula port of Malacca. Manoel da Silva was accused of being a heretic for using the amulets widely in circulation, and for wearing 'a shirt [made by] the heathens'.* Fashion mattered, as it always has, and revealed the cultural identities which people held and the ways in which they were – or were not – influenced by globalizing trends. The fact that a denunciation to the Inquisition was seen as one of the best ways of addressing the weak hold of Portuguese clothing styles in

---

* 'Camisa de gentio'.

the town shows how far the fashions most in use here were locally designed and produced.[40]

Beyond the fashions on view, the furnishing of Cacheu's houses themselves also emphasized the African setting and barely even paid lip-service to the imperial context. In the first place, as we have seen, the doors to the houses were made of wood and had wooden keys – something that seems to have been a regional style, since there were plenty of blacksmiths who could have made metal locks had they been preferred. Additionally, elephant-hunting brought ivory into the trading towns, both for export and for carving. While ivory was an important item of export into the Atlantic trade, carvers also transformed it into beautiful and important objects which became prized in southern Europe. Of course, many of these goods also stayed in towns like Cacheu for everyday use – salt cellars, candlesticks and the like – and formed an important part of the material culture of the houses.

The most famous carvers hailed from further south of the Nunes river region, towards Sierra Leone. Known to the Portuguese as Sapis, these people shared a culture based on their religious shrines and on their linguistic and cultural commons. Already in the early sixteenth century, the Sapis had become famous in Portugal for their ivory carvings, which carried motifs both of indigenous and of Catholic iconography and activities, as well as making use of the ropes and rigging of the Portuguese caravels as part of the design. There was a great carving tradition in this part of the West African coast, with remarkable stone carvings also having been produced here at this time. As the historians Luís Afonso and José da Silva Horta have shown, the Sapi carvers also made beautiful oliphants (or hunting horns), some of which carried European hunting scenes as their sculpted embellishments. These horns were used in warfare in Casamance and around Cacheu; they were divided into seven to eight cylindrical sections, from the mouthpiece to the bell. However, while representing European fauna in these scenes – stags, wild boars, horseback riders – some of these scenes also represented the animals of the region such as elephants, lions and rhinoceros.[41] We can be certain that these ivories featured prominently in Cacheu from their afterlives. Once Manoel Bautista Pérez moved to Lima, in Peru, he did not forget the tradition of ivory carving which he had seen as a young man in West Africa. Ivories were widely available in Peru, and the Inquisition inventory of his possession after his arrest for heresy shows that Bautista Pérez was a great appreciator of them. He owned an elephant tusk and had a range of ivory furnishings including cabinets on stands, chests, bureaux and escritoires. It is almost certain that this was a taste that he acquired in Cacheu, since many Sapis had moved to the town from the Sierra Leone region after the invasion of the Manes mentioned above, in the second half of the sixteenth century. They brought these skills and knowledge with them, and their manufactures circulated widely in the houses of Cacheu by the seventeenth century.[42]

Another important aspect of material culture in these homes was shaped by the presence and growing importance of Islam across Senegambia at this time. Crispina's Inquisition trial is full of references to the 'Mandinga strings', or *gris-gris*, which were made by Jakhanké Mandingas and were themselves the outcome of cultural encounters between African religions and Islam. These amulets carried verses of the Qur'an sewn inside pouches woven of animal skin

Olifant. Ivory, carved. Sierra Leone, c.1500–1550.

*Cacheu: The Setting*

and were designed to protect the bearer from harm. They circulated very widely in Cacheu, as did the *alúas*, or wooden writing tablets, on which young children learnt Arabic and specific verses of the Qur'an, and which are still frequently seen in the villages of Guinea-Bissau. These *alúas* were mentioned by the trader Lemos Coelho in his 1669 description of the Jakhanké preacher-traders who often came through Cacheu.[43]

All of this shows us that Cacheu's material worlds were many. There were Senegambian carvings and clothes, Islamic religious materials and imports from Europe, alongside Chinese porcelain and taffeta and Potosí silver. This was a cosmopolitan material world, representative of the many different peoples who lived in the town. In this way, Cacheu's material culture reflected how the seventeenth century was an era in which peoples all around the world were incorporating the styles and tastes of other cultures. Just as West African towns like Cacheu incorporated the influences of the wider world, so too did people in Portugal. Some folk tales from the Cacheu region ended up being transported and reproduced in the Alentejo. The Sapi ivories themselves circulated widely in Portugal, especially in the sixteenth century, and the motif of the rope

Ivory pyx with scenes from the Passion of Christ, from Sierra Leone, with clear illustration of the rope motif.

from the rigging of the caravels was so striking that it may have influenced the emergence of this motif in the architecture of Portugal's 'golden age' of Manuelline architecture (first two decades of the sixteenth century).[44]

In sum, Cacheu's was a mixed material setting. The houses were Senegambian, built with local materials and in local styles. The defences of towns such as Vila Quente were widely used across the region. The items of daily use came from all around the world: from China and Bolivia, as well as, of course, from local sources. Cacheu's was a material world that reflected a globalized cosmopolitan West African town of the seventeenth century.

The globalization of Cacheu's material world ranged beyond the objects of daily life. For in the two decades before Crispina's Inquisition trial began, the town was hit by serious climatic instability. Droughts affected even the mangrove swamps around Cacheu and the Casamance region. This was an era which brought swift climatic changes. Of course, it wasn't just Cacheu that was affected by this in the 1640s. This decade saw mass global climatic fragility, which went with a huge increase in conflict. One of Manoel Bautista Pérez's debtors in Peru in the 1630s included a resident of Ica, south of Lima, who had not been able to pay 'because of the bad harvests which this town has suffered in the last few years . . . as is notorious . . . so that [the only crops] that ha[ve] been sewn are those necessary to sustain the African slaves who work there'.[45]

A harrowing testament of the climatic instability of the age was provided by the Capuchin missionary Antonio Cavazzi, who spent many years in Angola in the middle third of the seventeenth century. According to Cavazzi, devastating plagues of locusts (which often accompany droughts) had stripped fields bare and eaten everything in their wake in 1642, 1643, 1654, 1658, 1662 and 1664. These locust swarms left the land seeming 'arid and sterile', and so devastating were they that the missionaries went out to perform exorcisms against them. Cavazzi's account of plagues and famines

## Cacheu: The Setting

is connected to the general ecological disturbances then having profound political effects all over the world.[46]

Cacheu's experiences were thus a microcosm of a global pattern of extreme weather conditions that heralded change. The written record is clear on the hunger provoked by these changing conditions. When in 1641 the residents of Cacheu wrote to the new Portuguese monarch, John IV – following the breakaway from the joint monarchy with Spain – they told him of the difficulties that they faced. These had 'originated principally in a large famine that this settlement and the districts of Guinea [i.e. the broader Senegambian region] have been enduring for three years now'. There had been a 'general famine', and a large wave of mortality had struck.[47]

Evidence from the rest of the seventeenth century confirms that climatic instability persisted throughout it. Visiting the Gambia river region in 1690, the English slave-trafficking agent of the Royal African Company Cornelius Hodges noted that there was much famine there. Hodges also indicated the disruption to seasons that had continued since around 1640. On 20 April he wrote that they experienced a great rain storm, even though the rains did not usually begin for another month. It was this unreliable rainfall pattern which doubtless had brought about the problems with the harvest and the ensuing drought – much as the residents of Cacheu said had taken place in the 1640s.[48]

When the rains did come, of course, material life around Cacheu changed completely. One missionary sailing off the coast of Conakry – north of Sierra Leone – in 1663 described a different world completely from the busy life and activity which was the norm for the dry season: 'For five days solid we had big thunderclaps at night, and terrible storms: with such infernal and dreadful flashes of lightning, that the night seemed to be always on fire, making the waves swell with great force.'[49]

There are different theories as to the causes of this climatic instability. The traditional view was that it was caused by sunspot variations, which appear to have intensified in the first half of the seventeenth century. More recently, a team of Colombian archaeologists have argued that the cause of the colder temperatures was the depopulation of the Americas following the Spanish conquest: on this account, with the disappearance of an estimated 95 per cent of the population in the sixteenth century, carbon sinks were effectively created through reforestation, which then decreased carbon content in the atmosphere and so allowed temperatures to cool.[50]

In either case, the climatic changes that took place in Cacheu and the surrounding area occurred because the region was part of a globalizing world. Either it was the sun's physical changes that were affecting everyone, or alternatively the demographic impacts of the genocide of the Native Americans were affecting all world regions. The impacts in the town made it clear that it was part of a global world, connected to it in many different material ways which only now can be pieced together.

As we have seen in this chapter, this global framework intersected with a setting which was distinctively Senegambian. Politically, Cacheu was under the control of the Pepel and their rulers. The houses and urban architecture were essentially local, even if the square-shaped large trafficking houses seemed 'European' to some visitors – distinguished from the round shape of the West African homes. But the dried earth of the walls, their whitewashing with lime – a Mandinga practice – and the thatch of the roofs suggested otherwise. Many of the imported luxury objects were European, Asian or from the Americas, but these mixed with the basics of daily life, the clothes people wore, the *combete* stores in which the bolts of cloth were kept, the ivory salt cellars and the wooden *alúa* tablets on which the town's Islamic communities practised their learnings from the Qur'an.

Cacheu was a town in a delicate balance. But its social and cultural equilibrium was now under threat. The increasingly erratic climate was producing hunger, driving conflict and warfare around the region. Competition for resources stoked division and enmities. This may also explain in part why Cacheu so often seemed to be under attack from neighbouring peoples, as many at the time suggested. On the other hand, growing European competition was leading to a free-for-all among imperial powers seeking to assert control over the Atlantic trade of the town. In this situation, for the Portuguese – who were struggling to assert their independence from Spain – a powerful organ like the Inquisition offered a chance to entrench their position in Cacheu. Thus did a European institution come to play a role in the daily life of what was in most other respects a very West African town.

## 4.
# Cacheu in Regional and Global Context

'he had gone [binge drinking] with the said canon more than forty times, both by day and by night, in his house and in the house of the said canon'

On my first visit to Guinea-Bissau, in 1995, I went to a remote island in the Bijagós archipelago. Before I went, the fishermen who took me advised that I should buy some gifts for the king of the island where they planned to leave me for a few days. The usual offerings were a bottle of rum and some leaves of tobacco, which I bought at the market of the main commercial centre of the Bijagós islands, Bubaque. At the time, I did not compute that these items were representative of the global relationships in which Guinea-Bissau had been intertwined for centuries. Tobacco was, of course, a plant from the Americas, while rum also was a major part of the trade from Brazil to Africa in the eighteenth and nineteenth centuries.[1]

By the middle of the seventeenth century – when the people whose lives we are trying to understand lived and died – these networks were flourishing. Through them, textiles and crockery from Asia arrived in Cacheu, and also silver from the Americas (along with, it turns out, tobacco and booze). Historians can sometimes talk of these networks as if they are real things, like neural or computer systems. But of course, these networks were made by people in all their fraught complexity: individual human lives and their stories, like Manoel da Silva, who somehow or other had by 1619 come from Malacca to live in Bugendo, where, as we saw in the last chapter, he was accused of heresy for wearing a shirt woven in Senegambia. The ways in which these life-stories became enmeshed in so many others are bewilderingly complex, and this is what causes us to try and simplify them through a seemingly objective description as a 'network'. In this book, however, my approach is to try to understand that enmeshing of lives through their individual strands themselves, and the emotions which they produced.

In this chapter, the strands begin slowly to unravel from the tight ball in which they have so far been kept, in the small urban space of Cacheu, because, as is already clear, we can't understand this town in West Africa without getting a sense of the ways in which it was connected both to its region and to the world. By understanding Cacheu's nuances and contours in detail, we can also gain a broader grasp of what the nature of daily life in other port towns of western Africa might have been, places such as Calabar and Ouidah. As we'll see, beyond its many Atlantic connections, Cacheu was closely linked to ports up and down the Senegambian coast, from today's Dakar in the north to Sierra Leone in the south, as well as to many places hundreds of miles inland to the east. These links shaped the culture of the town: they brought together peoples from all across the region, with their different languages, textiles, religions and foods, and they also shaped the human geographies, and the long periods of absence on voyages of trade.

The global links – to India and Malacca, to the Americas, to Constantinople across the Sahara and to Europe – mattered just as much. They contributed to the cosmopolitan material culture of the town but they also manifested the ways in which, just as global contexts of the environment shaped the droughts and famines of the seventeenth century in Cacheu, so the global context of shifting traffic was having a profound impact on the town's daily life. Here, the granular detail matters in grasping the challenge which the materials in this book offer to conventional narratives of history. The opportunity of recovering these unique strands of political, cultural and social history from Cacheu shows just how much is

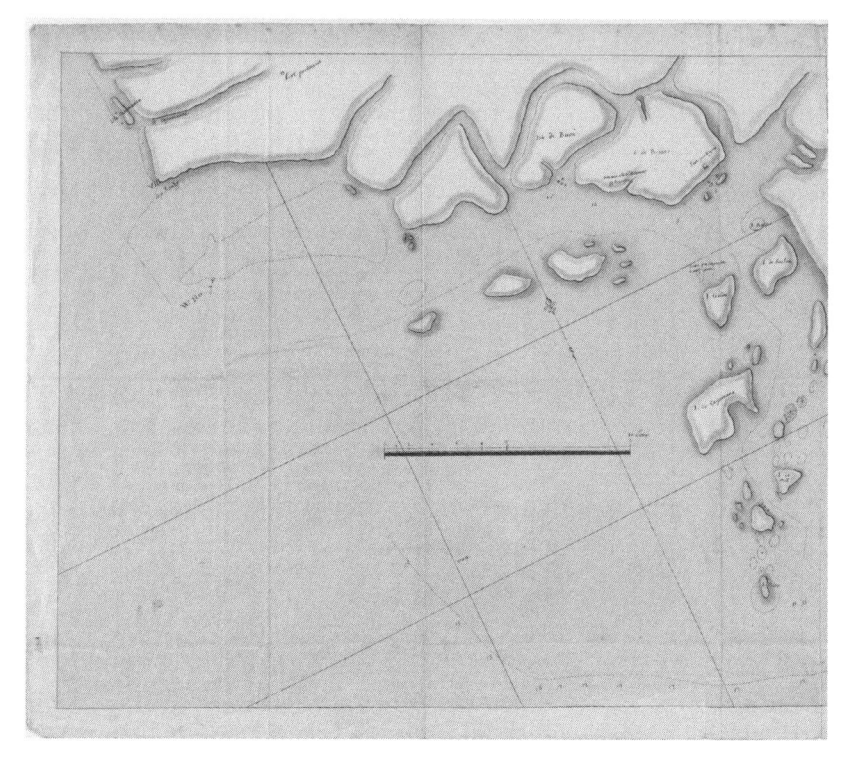

French map of the Casamance river and Bijagós islands, 1767.

lost in the understanding of world history when places like this are written out of it.

Cacheu was located amid Pepel communities, with Floup villages nearby. At this time the Floup were in a process of northward, migration in Guinea-Bissau, moving through the Casamance to the south bank of the Gambia river, where – now known as the Jola – they remain among the most important groups today. Meanwhile, those Pepel who live near this coastline, and on the adjacent islands of Jeta and Pecixe, are now known as Manjako. A different Pepel-origin community near today's town of Bula (Baoula in seventeenth century sources) is that of the Mancaigne. The linguistic, cultural and religious frameworks of these three peoples are shared, and when they arrived in the region they founded their centre at Cobiana, in the creeks and forest to the south of Cacheu.²

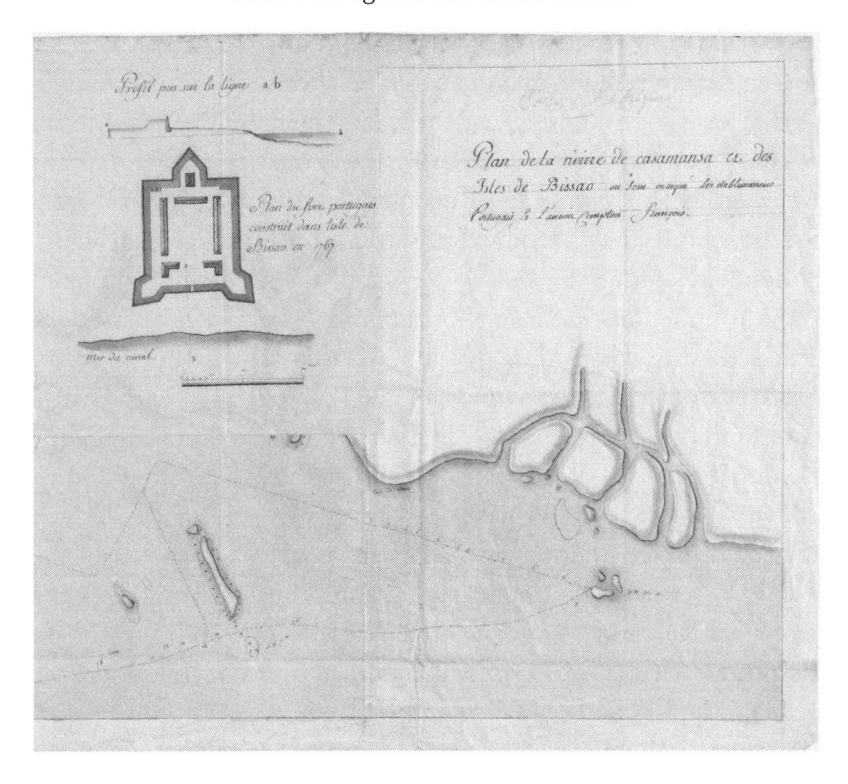

The Pepel had themselves been migrants to this part of Guinea-Bissau, probably arriving since the early fourteenth century in the Cobiana region. In the 1300s, this Pepel movement came in response to the expansion westwards of warrior armies from the empire of Mali, as this most powerful polity in West Africa founded an outpost in Kaabu under the military leader Tiramaghan Traoré. Some 150 years later, in the late fifteenth century, further migrations were led by a Fulani army marshalled by Koli Tenguela: Tenguela led his troops from the Futa Tòòro region on the banks of the Senegal river, south across the Gambia river, before eventually settling in the highlands of the Fouta Djalon (in Guinea-Conakry). The modern cultures of the Greater Senegambia region were established through these

## The Heretic of Cacheu

processes of migration, which displaced many communities from the Gambia river region and the upper reaches of the São Domingos rivers. These communities made towards the mangrove swamps of the coastline, which were harder for the armies to navigate: many of the oral histories of these peoples describe their arrival from the east, before they founded the settled communities near which Cacheu was later established at the end of the sixteenth century.[3]

The foundation of these communities by refugees shaped the social structure which they developed. Perhaps in response to the pressures they had faced from Mali and then from the early Portuguese empire, they formed egalitarian societies. Whereas societies linked to the empire of Mali were strictly hierarchical, with working-caste guilds – blacksmiths, weavers, leather-workers – and a division between enslaved and free people, these peoples of Guinea-Bissau tended to be both isolationist and more communitarian. Living together in *tabankas* as a form of protection from military attacks was another characteristic which embodied this collective approach to the world: it took shape during the sixteenth century.[4]

This meant that the century or so prior to the founding of Cacheu in 1589 was one of consolidation. Mali's influence was waning, after the usurpation of its power by Songhay in the second half of the fifteenth century. In Senegambia, the communities displaced by the Mande and then the Fulani migrations were seeking to establish themselves. In the meantime, the Portuguese traders had also begun to arrive. It was a time of rapid change, in which at first the Portuguese must have seemed like just another band of wanderers in a difficult world. No doubt this explains why they were initially welcomed through the old Senegambian model of landlords and strangers. But once the fortress at Cacheu went up, it became clear that the dynamic was changing.

The Pepel and the Floup had not escaped from one marauding army only to fall into the power of another. Thus, the attacks on Cacheu which we saw in the previous chapter didn't take long to unfold. From the outset, struggle and conflict characterized the response to the attempt to impose European imperial traffic here. By

1600, a clear political framework was emerging. Hegemony belonged to the Mandinga, in the kingdoms of Kaabu and elsewhere, while the Portuguese were struggling to establish something similar near the coast. These Mandinga were descended from the original migrants from Mali and then developed their own autonomy in the 1500s with Mali's decline. The more egalitarian states of the Pepel, the Floup and other peoples lived at the margins of Mandinga and Portuguese power. They resisted it.[5]

The seventeenth century, which we are concerned with in this book, was a time of expansion of these Mandinga kingdoms that were legacies of the empire of Mali. Writing of the time around 1600, the Caboverdean trader André Donelha described four rulers, or *farims*, of the region, all of whom spoke Mandinga: the first in Kaabu, who ruled between the south bank of the Gambia and the north of Guinea-Bissau; the second in Bidassou (the Casamance), ruling over the Balanta, Biafada, Bainunk, Kassanké and Pepel peoples; the third at Cocalí, in the Nunes river area; and the fourth of the Susu people, near to Sierra Leone. Boundaries between the different polities were quite clear: by the 1660s, Lemos Coelho said that the port of Geba (south of Cacheu) was ruled by the Farim Bidassou, but that it was a border town since on the other side of the river the land belonged to Kaabu. Each kingdom was ruled by Mandinga *farims*, and yet the boundaries between them offered opportunities for trade. It was at these boundaries – at Farim and Geba, bordering Bidassou and Kaabu – that goods could be exchanged by the middlemen. These middlemen were increasingly the mixed-heritage Africans of Portuguese descent and their *grumetes*, who moved goods from one part of the region to another on their sailing ships and began to join up the dots of regional commerce.[6]

A good example of these dynamics was the town of Farim, about 100 miles upriver from Cacheu. According to Lemos Coelho, the Atlantic trading post of Farim was founded in the late 1640s by residents of Geba (though in fact its role in the region's trade was much older, since João Bautista Pérez had visited to trade in the 1610s). It was known to the Mandinga of Bidassou as Tubabodaga – 'the white man's village'. By the end of the seventeenth century, the captain-general of Cacheu, Vidigal Castanho, wrote that 'the preservation of the settlement of Cacheu depends in large part on the trade of this town [Farim]': there had been trade with the English Royal African Company fort on James island in The Gambia, but this was intermittent, and it was Farim and the kola-nut trade with Kaabu that counted most.[7]

What was the mainstay of that trade? Thirty years earlier, Lemos Coelho gave a good description of what that trade was like:

> Every year, at least twelve ships visit annually, and I once saw eighteen go, all laden with cargoes of [kola nuts] . . . and at times five thousand barrels of these came, and they are sold in lots of 100 with it being ordinary for 100 to be given for one measure of cloth.[8]

The Portuguese had thus come to act as middlemen for a Senegambian production cycle. Kola nuts were grown in Sierra Leone. They were sifted at the site of production and could be sold with or without their shell. They were then transported thence on the Portuguese ships to Cacheu and Farim. Here they were exchanged for textiles, woven by the famous weavers of the region; Fulani in particular, who also especially valued the kola. Once having sold the kola for textiles, the Portuguese would take them a further two tides upriver to the town of Bafeta (the modern town of Bafatá, in Guinea-Bissau), where they would buy a lot of wax, some ivory and many enslaved Africans. They would then return to Cacheu for trade with the Atlantic traffickers, bringing of course some of the textiles that were so fashionable in the town. If Vidigal Castanho is anything to go by, this system was the mainstay of Cacheu's economy by 1700.[9]

In fact, the Bautista Pérez account books suggest that by then this system dated back at least a century. Kola were by far the most valuable goods traded at Geba by Manoel Bautista Pérez in the 1610s, as many different account book entries can show. Meanwhile, when João Bautista Pérez's ship captain Antonio da Nunes Costa itemized a trading voyage to the Gambia river in 1617, the forty measures – or *godenhos* – of kola were far and away the most valuable good on his list of merchandise. These nuts were sold in large and small measures, both wholesale and in small quantities for use as gifts or offerings by individuals. They were so valuable that in one shipment laded by Manoel the kola on board were nearly four times as valuable as the ship itself. Meanwhile, one measure – or *godenho* – of kola cost the equivalent of five enslaved captives in a business transaction conducted in Geba in 1617.[10] The political world that empowered this trade saw the cooperation and working together of different peoples. The Mandinga of Bidassou and Kaabu were influenced by Islam and prized the kola nuts as a stimulant in part because alcohol was increasingly frowned upon. As Lemos Coelho put it, 'They believe that nothing can be well done, neither a marriage nor a legal judgement, if kola is not taken first, and that illnesses cannot be cured without it either. And they say above all that it keeps them from sin.' The trade that kept this Mandinga hegemony going, and that linked it up, was carried out by the Catholic and/or New Christian Portuguese and their *grumetes*. And meanwhile, in the rivers and *bolons* in between lay a host of smaller kingdoms that professed allegiance to one or another of the *farims*, such as the three small Balanta kingdoms of Bahár, Soár and Ginció, which lay between Cacheu and Farim.[11]

Cacheu thus lay at a cultural and political crossroads. It was in a Senegambian land of Mandinga political hegemony, and yet the

Kola nuts as a wedding gift.

peoples who lived around it had been driven there by the Mandinga expansion from Mali and often sought to struggle against it in one way or another. On the other hand, Cacheu itself was a settlement representative of the Atlantic empires of Europe, in which attempts were often made to cement European traffic and priorities. Cacheu therefore depended on the political framework of the Mandinga and of their *farims*, and yet it was also a colonial town. This tension was bound to provoke the conflicts that lay at the root of the lives that we follow in this book.

There were three main trading axes linking Cacheu and the surrounding kingdoms. To the east, thirty leagues (about ninety miles) up the São Domingos river, lay Farim on the borders of Kaabu and Bidassou. South, reached by tracking the Atlantic coast past the Bijagós islands and then along the coast of Guinea-Conakry and the land of the Farim Susu, was Sierra Leone and the lucrative kola-nut trade. And to the north, through the maze of *bolons* and along the Casamance river, was the network of waterways that linked up to the Gambia river. Beyond this, there was the more immediate trade around Cacheu itself, which linked to markets at Bugendo, Baoula and Guinguim.

Each of these axes had its own character and attractions. The trade linking Cacheu and the most immediate surrounding villages and towns was structured through the *lumos*, or regular weekly markets. These still take place in Guinea-Bissau, where they attract many people into the towns on a regular basis to buy cloth, household and electrical goods and food. This is a system of rotational markets which is as old as documentary history itself. *Lumos* are places where friends meet and knowledge is exchanged. And it is clear that *lumos* have always been like this: when people spoke in Crispina's trial of other acquaintances or witnesses to events who were now in one place or another, we can be fairly sure that this information came to them by word of mouth, probably because someone was seen or met at a *lumo*. The fact that these markets have existed for many centuries gives a strong sense of the continuity of

*Lumo*, Bula, Guinea-Bissau.

social and historical processes over time, in spite of the enormous ruptures which have also taken place.

One aspect of the business of the *lumos* at that time connects clearly to the nature of markets in other parts of western Africa and its diaspora. In markets in today's Benin and Nigeria, and also in the Yòrubá diaspora in Salvador da Bahia in north-eastern Brazil, markets are places where healers and ordinary people go on a regular basis to purchase a variety of items to perform religious and curative rituals: these include animals, dead or alive, feathers, snake skins and pottery in which to place the offerings. Similarly, in the *lumos* of Senegambia, one of the goods that appears to have been traded in the seventeenth century was the power to heal, alongside the material objects that today make them tick. In Crispina's trial, we learn that there was clearly some kind of regular trade in health and healing of this kind, since we are told of Crispina and Jorge sending goods across the river to Bugendo so that sacrifices and offerings could be made to the *chinas* before their marriage. We also learn of the time that Jorge sent his nephew to the *lumo* at Bujé, four or five days' distant in Casamance, to fetch a particular *djabakós* to cure him.[12]

Bujé was the centre of the kingdom of the Farim-Bidassou, according to Lemos Coelho, and also a major market for wax and some ivory. Thus, this market in healing went with the material and spiritual exchanges which still characterize the *lumos*. In the account books we have from the 1610s, we can easily see this. At one time, Manoel Bautista Pérez sent one of his business partners with 427 pieces of cloth and three slaves to trade at the market at Baoula (a distance of some thirty-five miles). On another, one young trader, Gaspar Carneiro, is stated as taking goods to trade 'in the bush [i.e. in the West African trading system] on my own account'. Doubtless, Carneiro was aiming for some of the *lumos* where it would be easiest to make the most from these trades.[13]

These two snatches of information offer a more detailed picture of how Cacheu's connections to the *lumos* – and so to its surrounding towns and villages – worked in daily practice. There were, of course, the large trading ships from the town which the governors and richer traders such as Lemos Coelho took notice of: the eighteen ships going annually to Farim carrying kola nuts from Sierra Leone. But much more workaday were the many canoes plying up and down the *bolons*, propelled by Pepel and Floup canoemen, taking traders of all kinds with their own assortments of goods to the next stop in the schedule of *lumos*. These canoes were filled with bundles of cloth woven locally, hessian sacks bursting with beads and jewellery, and many other goods besides, weighing down the vessel while the navigators perched at the prow and steered their way up and down the rivers which made up the transport system.[14]

These were the trading voyages which almost everyone who lived in Cacheu knew. They defined a core part of their experience of life. It quickly becomes clear from the sources we have just how dependent the people in Cacheu were on this existing system of *lumos* and the networks which they provided. These were thriving markets in well-known villages and towns which grew big because of the business that came their way. People would often come to trade somewhere,

Canoe on Orangozinho island, Bijagós.

and then settle when the going seemed good: a new marriage partner in life, a welcoming family or a leading trader in the settlement, perhaps some other emotional pull or tie which quickly made one place and its *lumo* more attractive and profitable than another.

A good example is Pedro Nunes, a witness in Crispina's trial. By the early 1660s, Nunes was a resident in Farim, where he was married, but he had not visited Cacheu for fifteen years 'to spend any time, but [had] only passed through in transit'. Cacheu might have been the most important Atlantic town in Guinea-Bissau, but people could easily find better places to put down roots, as Nunes's evidence suggests. Nunes was giving evidence here about Luis Rodrigues and noted that, of the women involved in that case, 'today many of them would be dispersed across different parts of the country'. And, of the men who knew about it, one was resident in Bissau and another in Sierra Leone. We do not know what brought them there, but we can begin to imagine: trading voyages of several days – upstream from Cacheu to Farim, or along the *bolons* south to

Bissau and Baoula – spending time at the *lumos*, and then some swift connection that made the trader want to settle down.[15]

Of all the places which Cacheu had ties with in Senegambia by the middle of the seventeenth century, the eastward route to Farim was certainly one of the most important. Farim lay on the borders of Kaabu, the most important of the Mandinga kingdoms by this time. Kaabu was a hierarchical society, with a warrior aristocracy – the *nyantios* – and guilds of artisan craftsmen, including the *griots* or praise-singers whose role in Senegambian societies has endured to this day in singing the praises and histories of families at important events such as marriages and naming-ceremonies. Islam was present but had no political power, with the Muslim clergy living in separate neighbourhoods just as the Christian traders did in Tubabodaga. The major religious shrine was to the sacred serpent, Tamba Dibi – something that was not irrelevant to life in

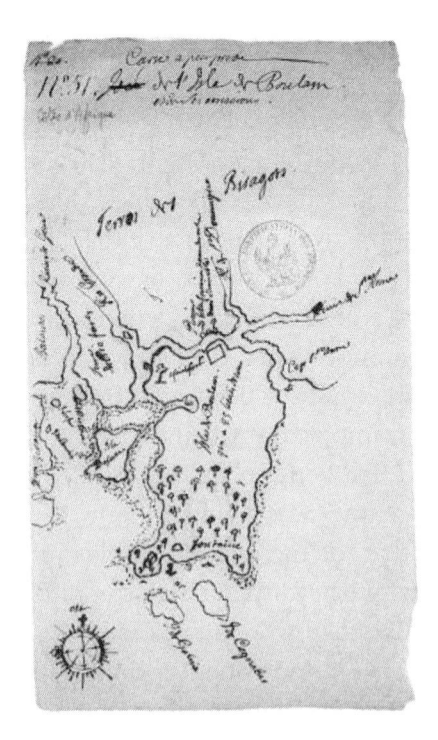

French map of Bolama island offshore from Bissau, 1718.

Cacheu, as we will see in the next chapter. Kaabu's importance to Cacheu lay in its being a key destination for the kola nuts from Sierra Leone and a warrior state whose wars contributed to the supply of enslaved Africans who would depart in chains on Atlantic ships.[16]

The importance of Farim – and of Kaabu as a trading partner – meant that the links between Cacheu and the town were strong. People originally from Cacheu lived not only here but also in the surrounding villages. One witness in the trial of Luis Rodrigues for his scandalous behaviour with 'single and married women' in Farim lived about two leagues (six miles) away from the town with his daughter, Domingas Afonso. Many people were mentioned who lived in one or another of the Senegambian settlements – the Nunes river, the Cabo-verdean island of Fogo, Cacheu – and had been present in Farim when Rodrigues had lived there and caused such a scandal. These included Manoel de Almeida of Cabo Verde, who ten years later would serve as Crispina's jailer and then translator in her trial before the Inquisitors in Lisbon. The sheer range of people constantly passing through Farim is marked in this trial and confirms the view that by the later seventeenth century Cacheu was dependent on Farim for its trade, and therefore in fact was interdependent with Kaabu.[17]

The second axis from Cacheu – southwards to Sierra Leone – was the one which had the biggest connection to Farim, through the trade in kola nuts. Given the importance of the kola trade to Cacheu, this was one of the most common voyages made. Jorge testified in his wife's trial that this had been his habitual trading itinerary, and that he had frequently gone south to the Bijagós islands, the Nunes river and Sierra Leone. Crispina, too, knew all of these places well. Pilots were paid to take traffickers as far as Sierra Leone and back on these voyages. A frequent stopping point on these journeys was Bissau – capital city of the country today – and people often sent gifts of wine and cloth from Cacheu with others who were going there to repay a debt or as a present to a trading partner.[18]

This begins to give a sense of how Cacheu was a small part of a much larger regional community. Everyone in the town knew these

## The Heretic of Cacheu

other places and had friends, family and connections in some of them. One of the major trading towns en route south to Sierra Leone was Geba, some distance inland from today's city of Bissau. Geba's main business was in wax from Casamance and kola nuts from Sierra Leone, traded in exchange for iron. In the first decades of the seventeenth century, the town had been the settlement with the biggest volume of trade in all of the region. As one account put it, '[Geba] is a settlement two times bigger than Cacheu, where many men had married and lived and did not want to obey the Captain [of Cacheu]'. In the 1660s, there were 200 residents, all of them of mixed African and Portuguese heritage. In other words, it was as suggested above: traders had arrived from Cacheu and soon found business ties and love and had settled in a place where theoretical Portuguese control could not touch them.[19]

Finally, there was the third axis mentioned above, north to the Gambia river. The Gambia was connected to Cacheu by sea and by the inland networks of *bolons*. The sea route appears to have been used especially by Atlantic traffickers, as one account from 1635 of two of their ships meeting a day's sail out from Cacheu – one bringing captives from The Gambia – suggests. But, for those who lived in Cacheu and the surrounding area, the inland route was the more usual: it was more familiar, and travellers could call in and greet old friends, family and acquaintances on their way.[20]

The priest Lucas Mendes e Franca makes this clear in a letter written in Cacheu in May 1665 which was included in Crispina's trial documents:

> within three days I will go by land to the Casamance with João de Torres and Tomás de Villa Lobos; the ship that Francisco Vaz sent immediately after she went to sea let so much water in that she had to return to Bintang and send the money by land.[21]

These inland links connecting Cacheu and the Gambia river followed the routes described in the Introduction: north along the creek past Guinguim to Bichangor, then along the Casamance river and up past Sanguedogu along the Bintang *bolon* to The Gambia. Some of these trading routes reached the north bank of the Gambia river, with mention of Tendaba in one of João Bautista Pérez's trading expeditions of 1619. This was a well-defined route, especially in the rainy season, through the kingdom of the Farim-Bidassou in Casamance and thence up the Bintang *bolon*. Casamance was a region famed for its wax, with it said that 'the bees which are tended to in this land are incredible'. The honey was used by some of the people in Casamance to make alcoholic drinks, but there was so much of it that it could still have filled shiploads. Some of the honey also made its way to Cacheu, where it was bought by traders like Manoel Bautista Pérez.[22]

What were these voyages like that went through Casamance to the Gambia river? Lemos Coelho gives us some idea of what it was like in the 1660s, at the time of Crispina's trial. The canoes from Cacheu brought kola nuts, iron, cloth, jewellery, rum, gunpowder and rifles and returned with wax and some ivory. And then, there was a trade in captive Africans from Casamance, who also filled the canoes in their chains as they made their way slowly back to Cacheu and their wretched fates. The misery of what must have been almost a daily scene has a saddening impact when you are standing on the banks of these *bolons* today, generally quiet since the advent of metalled roads and apparently abandoned by the world and its cruel economies of supply and demand.[23]

These, then, were the three axes which connected Cacheu to its surroundings. By the middle of the seventeenth century, however, the political equilibrium which had been reached sixty or seventy years earlier was collapsing. These routes and their importance were changing. From the Portuguese side, by 1640, a concerted move had been made to squash Geba's independence to the south of Cacheu. It was for this reason that the captain-general of Cacheu, Gonçalo Gamboa de Ayala, had forced some residents to move to Farim, where to his mind they could be more useful. Through Kaabu, Farim could provide enslaved Africans for the Atlantic traffic, while in Geba they could not be found. Instead of chained captives, on this kola-nut route to Sierra Leone, the residents 'sold much ivory, wax, silver, gold and amber'.[24]

The later seventeenth century also saw the consolidation of Kaabu itself as the most important state in the Senegambian region. Kaabu's provinces on the south bank of the Gambia river were growing in power. This came with the rise of the *nyantio* warrior classes and through the demand from the Atlantic side for the captives which all this produced. In other words, what emerges in these details of Cacheu's regional ties is the growing importance by this time of its Atlantic traffic. The wars fought by Kaabu produced captives who entered the transatlantic traffic through Farim and Cacheu, and through the creeks of Casamance. Those whose memories were older could recall when the trade in kola and wax, through Geba and Sierra Leone, had been the more important – when the constant warfare and discord linked to the Atlantic traffic had been much less. This shows that these decades in the middle of the seventeenth century were key in disrupting the balance of power between West Africa and the Atlantic empires.[25]

This earlier produce trade was not as profitable as capturing human beings in the ways already described – through warfare, raids and indebtedness – and transporting them so that their labour turned into silver and gold, thus to capitalize the world economy. This realization was also an important element of the emotional lives and struggles of people in Cacheu and its surrounding region in these years, as daily life in the kingdoms and creeks around them changed in accordance with the new and relentless patterns of demand arising from the Atlantic world.

As well as belonging to a regional community, Cacheu was connected umbilically with the islands of Cabo Verde. The first few chapters of this book have presented many occasions where characters who lived in the islands were passing through the town, as well as visiting other places such as Farim. Cacheu itself had been founded by Caboverdeans: this Atlantic port town was part of an extended ocean community with the islanders, where people shared in-laws, cousins and trading relationships with one another. What happened in the one could only affect what was happening in the other. News tended to spread like wildfire, and all kinds of social, cultural and political affinities (and conflicts) were growing in the sixteenth and seventeenth centuries – a relationship which endured for hundreds of years.

Understanding daily life in Cacheu therefore also means getting a good sense of its ties to Cabo Verde, and what these meant for the town. Virtually everyone who lived there was connected to the islands by kinship ties: enslaved, *grumete* and trafficker. Crispina's trial offers countless examples. There was Jorge's nephew Francisco Tavares and his brother-in-law João Nunes Castanho, both originally from Santiago, as was Maria Mendes, aunt of the scribe of Cacheu. There were also those born on the island of Fogo, famous for its fertile wine-producing soil and its eponymous volcano spewing hot lava into the Atlantic throughout the seventeenth century: the trader Francisco Correia and the official scribe Antonio Gomes de Sousa had both been born there. And beyond those living in the town, there were the many islanders passing through, women such as Leonor Ferreira, who was a cotton-spinner living in Ribeira Grande and who visited Cacheu and Farim to do business at some point in the late 1650s.[26]

An important element of the bond between the islands and Cacheu was in the similarity of gender relations in both places. In this aspect, Ribeira Grande was in many ways a twin to what we saw of Cacheu in Chapter 2. Prosperous traders in the town were often women, such as Ferreira and Maria Mendes, who was also a cotton-spinner and trader. As in Cacheu, these women often ran their own households, and carousing male parties like those which the priest Luis Rodrigues was famous for often tried to gain access to them: as his former friend Domingos Rodrigues Viegas said in his trial, he often went to 'the houses of women'. Many of the examples in that trial show that, as in Cacheu, women lived together, ran households and small-scale trading operations and worked in cotton-spinning. This was an important commonality which appears to have grown up in the two places together.[27]

These ties were deep. On the Cabo Verde islands themselves, almost everyone had kinship ties to Cacheu and its region. The importance of the slave traffic from Senegambia meant that the enslaved population of the islands came from this area. There was, for instance, the evidence of Esperança in the trial of the priest Luis Rodrigues, a slave of Maria Gonsalves in Ribeira Grande, who had been born in West Africa but had lived on the islands for many years. Some members of this diaspora had managed to return to the land of their birth, since according to one report of the 1640s many of the *grumetes* of Cacheu, though now free, had at one time been household slaves of islanders of Santiago. News travelled quickly between islands and coast, and people in Cabo Verde did not lose touch completely with the worlds they had known before enslavement. A good example of this is that, in Luis Rodrigues's trial, one witness described how he had heard in Cacheu of the fights which Rodrigues had had with rival factions on the island of Santiago: gossip spread rapidly from islands to coast and vice versa, and this meant that all those in Cacheu and the islands might hear of one another, and of their loved ones, even if separated by distance and enslavement.[28]

The connections between Cacheu and Cabo Verde thus happened on different levels. There were those framed by the Portuguese empire and its requirements: the priests despatched from the cathedral chapter to work in places like Cacheu and Farim, the administrative officers of Cacheu, almost all of whom had previously served in some capacity in the islands, and the military links, with Cabo Verde sometimes sending troops to protect the settlement from attacks by other European empires, such as the Dutch and the Spanish, who were at war with the Portuguese at various points during the period covered in this book. For the African populations of the islands – both those born on the continent and those whose kin had been there for one or two generations – the connections were embodied in their persistent attempts to return to Africa, either in autonomous trading missions such as that of Leonor Ferreira, or in establishing themselves in Cacheu and then buying their freedom through their own work and trade.[29]

And then there were the commercial ties of the island merchant traffickers, most of whom visited Cacheu and had relatives and friends there. One of the reasons why the traffickers were so drawn to Cacheu was that by the middle of the seventeenth century the islands remained the administrative capital of the Portuguese empire in West Africa, but their 'heyday' had gone. A series of droughts beginning in the 1580s had created a fragile ecological and human ecosystem and contributed to the way in which Portuguese imperial trade had moved on elsewhere. In the famine of 1609, the people of the islands had relied on shipments of grain from the Mandinga of the Gambia river to stave off collapse. The environmental changes, and the newly dry conditions that we saw at the end of the previous chapter, meant that ships on the Portuguese imperial route to Brazil or India (the *carreira da Índia*) could no longer guarantee picking up a good load of provisions here. They often called elsewhere instead, particularly the island of São Tomé in the Gulf of Guinea, while the main focus of the Portuguese empire was now in Angola and Brazil – especially once the Dutch had usurped them as the main European power in Asia. This new economic fragility meant that many islanders went to Cacheu to seek their fortune; Jorge's scheming brothers-in-law offer a good example of the envy and greed which followed. Meanwhile, a new class of Creole landowners and merchants took control of the island of Santiago. By the 1650s and 1660s they had come to dominate its political scene.[30]

As far as the struggles for imperial dominance went, therefore, by this time the power of Santiago island was definitively on the wane. The decline of the Portuguese empire in general – with its prolonged civil war with Spain throughout this time, from 1640 to 1668 – meant that there were few resources, and fewer ships still that called in at the port. Meanwhile, trading vessels from Portugal's growing imperial rivals such as the Dutch and the English called in on some of the smaller islands such as Fogo and Maio to lade salt or provisions, and there was nothing that the Portuguese captain-general in Ribeira Grande could do about it. In the conception of the Portuguese empire, the Cabo Verde islands were ruled

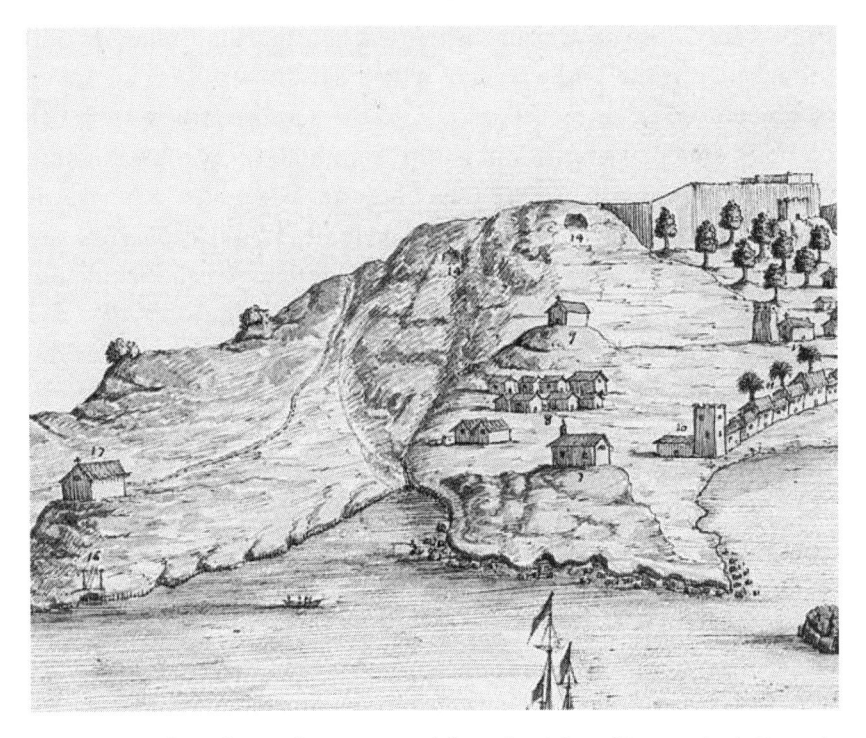

Ribeira Grande, Cabo Verde, 1655. Detail from the Atlas of Leonardo de Ferrari.

from Santiago, as was Cacheu. However, in practice, the power of the military and religious officers of Ribeira Grande was toothless by the 1650s – both in the archipelago and on the West African coast.

What, then, was the urban and physical space of this Portuguese colony in the Atlantic Ocean like? Having been apparently uninhabited in the fifteenth century, by the 1650s the islands had been settled for two centuries. There was still quite a large population. However, the community felt small: when asked in Luis Rodrigues's trial how they knew him, people would often reply that it was because 'the place was small and everyone saw each other every day'. By these years, there were 20,000 people who could fight for the militia, and a population of around 12,000 in the capital of Ribeira Grande. The fortress of São Filipe loomed on a cliff above the town, where several whitewashed churches stood in the valley. The city was divided into three neighbourhoods: São

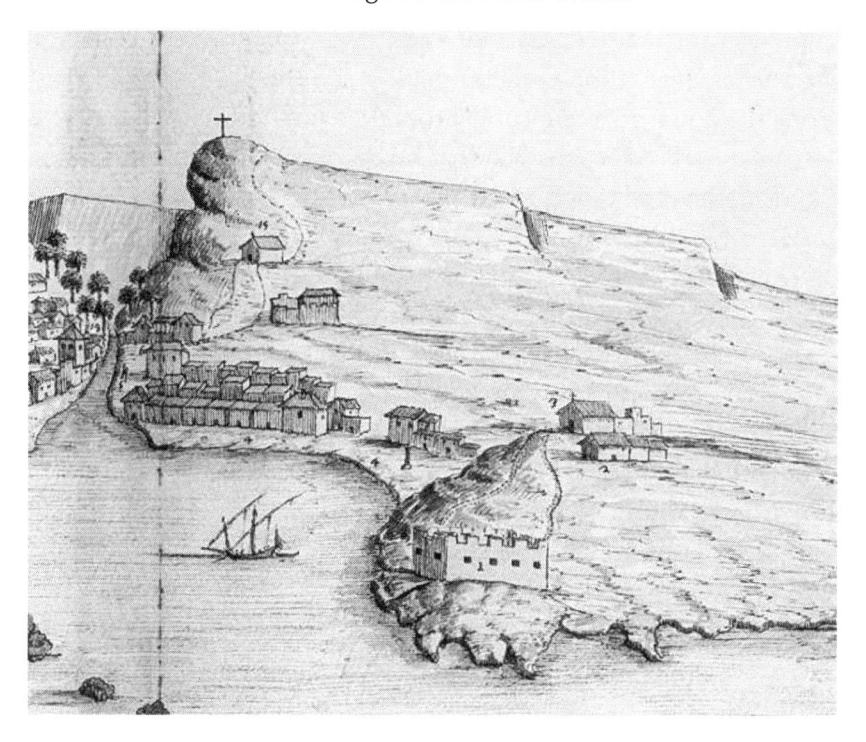

Sebastião, São Bras and São Pedro. From São Pedro, a road ran down to the port where the ships arrived, which lay in a narrow bay. Ribeira Grande's two other main streets were Rua da Carreira and Rua da Banana, which still bears its name to this day in the now somnolent remains of this first town built by European empires in the tropics.[31]

Just as Cacheu was deeply connected to its hinterland in the seventeenth century, so too was Ribeira Grande. People would come into the town from the countryside to do business, selling their produce and buying necessaries unavailable in the mountainous interior. This was the case of the Black trader Agostinho Rodrigues, who then claimed that Luis Rodrigues had spiked his drink and stolen his money in a card game, sending his health into a general decline; it ended in his death shortly afterwards. Meanwhile, the richer residents of the town often owned *fazendas* in the countryside worked by enslaved labour, those Africans and their descendants who had come as captives from Cacheu and its surrounding region. These *fazendeiros* (plantation owners) made frequent and extended visits from the town to their rural properties: in Rodrigues's trial, for instance, Barbosa Barros said that he had been absent from Ribeira Grande when the canon had been arrested and so knew little about the arrest.[32]

These details allow us to begin to build up a sense of the emotional and social worlds of Santiago island. The passing of the imperial shipping traffic on to other places meant that external economic demand had collapsed. Those places – like the port of Ribeira Grande – that depended on that traffic saw an upsurge in theft and general lawless behaviour, as the framework of political order based on the power of empire crumbled. This decline went with a generalized increase in corruption among those in charge. During the 1650s, money was robbed from the Misericordia alms house by its own officials, and even the tiles were filched from the roof. Other officials stole silver from the church of Our Lady of the Rosary (the temple of the Black religious confraternity) and buried it in their back gardens. Meanwhile, corruption was so endemic that one witness in Luis Rodrigues's trial said that all of those who hated him could easily be bribed to swear falsely against him.[33]

This corruption oozed out of the imperial miasma. It was embodied in the drunk, thieving and corrupt officials who remained. The sort of drunkenness of which Rodrigues was accused was daily fare. Many were known as 'men of the taverns'. The wild drunken sprees which Rodrigues participated in were so frequent that in his testimony his friend Domingues Rodrigues Viegas said that he knew about them 'because he had gone on them with the said canon more than forty times, both by day and by night, in his house and in the house of the said canon'. However, as a month before his arrest the canon had fought Rodrigues Viegas and his friends with swords in the street, it is pretty clear that friendship was a fragile commodity in a town propped up by the violence of slavery, empire and alcohol. The endemic cruelty of 'legalized' enslavement and its consequences produced a society that was violent in many different ways.[34]

Yet while the imperial economy and society of Ribeira Grande was in decay, things were different for those who did not depend so much on it. The loss of munitions and firepower meant that it was much harder to stave off the growing power of the Creole class from the highlands, who were regularly said to be about to attack Ribeira Grande. The descendants of those trafficked from the mainland wanted revenge, or at the very least a seat at the table. For many people, the decline of Portuguese imperial interest was positive: 'decline' did not seem so bad from the perspective of those who had less to lose. The workaday lives of most people on the islands was summarized by one witness in Rodrigues's trial, who described the world of the accused canon's parents as one in which 'they lived by the general business of this land, buying and selling from their house'.[35]

How important, then, were the institutions of empire, Church and state in the lives of those who came from Cabo Verde to Cacheu? In Santiago island, some effort was still put in to maintaining the façade of power. But the growing dominance of those outside the usual power structures, of the Creoles from outside the city, showed that this empire was really an empty shell. In the other islands, its influence was even less. When in 1660 the Inquisitorial emissary Friar Paulo de Lordello was charged with investigating the life and habits of Maria da Luz from the island of Maio – just across the sound from Santiago – he found that her husband had died eight years before and that since then she had had an open relationship with the factor of the island, having two children with him. None of the Maio islanders thought anything bad of this, and in fact Maria da Luz had a good reputation among them.[36]

In the face of such indifference, the Portuguese imperial structure would seek to reassert itself through these Inquisitorial investigations. But at the same time, its power to shape the links between Cabo Verde and Cacheu was far weaker than the other factors driving them: the kinship, memory and yearning to return of the Africans of the islands of Cabo Verde on the one hand, and the craven greed, desperation and desires of the Atlantic trafficker-remnants of a lost imperial heyday on the other.

By the 1650s and 1660s, Cacheu was a place where many of the residents had global connections of one sort or another. Commodities from around the world found their way to the town and were part of many people's daily lives – alongside the Senegambian textiles, foods, furniture and utensils which also characterized the place. Naturally, the goods did not arrive alone: they came with the people from the town whose journeys defined the cosmopolitan atmosphere that made Cacheu what it was. By the 1660s, it presented a meeting of different worlds. On the one hand, there were the Jakhanké traders who connected the town to the Dar-al-Islam, and with places far across the Sahara in cities such as Tripoli, Cairo, Madinah and Makkah. On the other, the Atlantic trading diaspora to which Jorge and Crispina belonged pointed north and west, to Portugal, Spain and the Americas, most especially to Brazil, Peru and Colombia, while also at times connecting to Portugal's empire in the Indian Ocean and places like Malacca.

Though many of these journeys were out into the Atlantic, Cacheu also had links reaching east. By the seventeenth century, itinerant Jakhanké marabouts, or preacher-scholars, were regular visitors to Cacheu, tending to travel with an entourage of Qur'anic pupils. They were connected to centres such as Sutucó on the Gambia river, at the heart of the Jakhanké diaspora. The Jakhanké were historic culture-bearers from West Africa, being said to have come originally from the settlement of Dia in the Middle Niger valley, one of the oldest centres of urbanism in West Africa (dating from around 500 BCE). Along with other trading diasporas, the Jakhanké linked up the trade from Senegambia as far afield as Constantinople. One visitor to Sutucó in the 1620s described a discussion with one marabout, who said that he had travelled far inland to the east. And according to one anonymous account from the 1640s, discussing the importance of the kola-nut trade near to Geba, '[the Muslims] hold it like a precious relic ... and they take this fruit inland as far as Constantinople in order to sell it.' The regular pilgrimages to Makkah also linked to Senegambia, as one account from 1599 suggested – and were connected, through the Jakhanké, to Cacheu.[37]

Meanwhile, the Atlantic trade offered links across the Atlantic to the Americas, and also to Spain and Portugal. This connection produced both emotional and commercial ties. Men from the Spanish Americas lived in the town, married to townspeople of mixed heritage such as Chica Mbena, whose mother was Sapi and whose father was Portuguese. On the other hand, the priest Antonio Vaz de Pontes turned out to be more of a merchant than a man of the cloth: one witness claimed that he had amassed enough capital to then go and live in Spain for two-and-a-half years, while nominally the priest at Cacheu, before returning to the town via Cabo Verde. Indeed, as Vaz de Pontes's story shows, the place of religion was always contradictory in these commercial connections. While many of the priests were drunkards or slave-traffickers, this did not mean that religious practice did not matter: wax for use in the churches of Portugal and the Americas, where it would be sculpted into candles of penitence or for the souls of the departed, was also a major export of New Christian traffickers such as Manoel Bautista Pérez, and some of the wax was also traded to be melted down for candles used to remember the dead in the church of Our Lady of Victory in Cacheu.[38]

The city in the Americas with which Cacheu had the closest ties was Cartagena in today's Colombia. Cartagena was then the main city for the arrival of enslaved Africans in Spanish South America. Many were destined for the mines of Zaragoza, in Antioquia, while others were trafficked through Panamá across the isthmus, and then south to Lima and Peru. This constant influx of large numbers of enslaved Africans from both Senegambia and Angola made Cartagena into a cosmopolitan city which was substantially shaped by its large African population: healers, day labourers, market traders and the large community of maroons (Africans who had escaped slavery) who had established themselves in the Palenque de Limón, all expressed the significance which Africans had in the culture of the city and its surroundings.[39]

Cartagena was the principal destination for Atlantic traffickers from Cacheu in the seventeenth century, and most of them could be found there at one time or another. A 1651 legal declaration made in Cartagena noted two people born in Cacheu and now in their mid-twenties who 'were now present in this city'. All these traffickers from Cacheu who came to Cartagena, of course, did so on the slave ships, in which they usually had a share. The royal official Antonio Rodrigues de San Isidro Manrique declared in 1630 that the Portuguese came to the city 'on the ships which come with Africans from the Kingdoms of Guinea': as an example, Diogo Barraza declared in 1635 that he had travelled as a passenger in one of these ships.[40]

In Cartagena, the workaday cruelty of these ships met that of the Spanish empire in the Americas. Just as in Cabo Verde, the violence of empire shaped the corruption and cruelty of this imperial 'jewel'. One Native American cacique (leader) described the impact of colonial policies on his people near to Cartagena, in a declaration to friars of 1624:

> Don Francisco a Native American born in the province of Cartagena, as the cacique that I am of the towns of Perina, Tomina, Montar and Monil ... declare that with our people having lived since antiquity by the shore of the Senu river, Doctor Juan de Villabona a judge of the Royal Court arrived to visit us and founded a town that he called San Juan de las Palmas ... in which he brought together ten Native American towns. And that we have lived there for eleven years, during which time many of us have died and others have fled to distant provinces, since we had been taken by force away from our natural land where we had much better land which was better suited to our cultivation, better water and fisheries and woodland.[41]

Seven years later, in 1631, the curate of this town of San Juan de las Palmas confirmed this. In a letter mainly lamenting the way in which the brutal labour regime made it impossible to work for the saving of souls, he described how the Spanish *encomenderos* (landowners and thieves) had forced the Native Americans into all kinds of shattering labour, day and night and seven days a week. Many died. The workaday expropriation of land, and the massive ideological violence that went with conversion, was central to the entire ideological project of Spanish empire.[42]

Of course, this was replicated wholesale with the traffic in enslaved Africans. Much of the traffic to Cartagena from Cacheu involved massive contraband and the callous overcrowding of captives in the foetid ship holds. The consequence of this violence was, naturally, repeated revolts by the Africans on the traffickers' ships and also once they arrived in Cartagena – for Spanish power in the continent was often weaker in remote and inaccessible areas. As early as the 1580s, a community of escaped Jolof people lived along the Gulf of Urabá to the north of Cartagena. They had developed settled communities with fields of crops that they cultivated. The Spanish sought to establish fortified towns to harry them and prevent them planting crops, but all the same there were uprisings on traffickers' ships when they neared this point: on one ship in 1581, the Africans on board caught sight of palm trees, which were often the source of provisions in West African societies (of oil, palm wine and thatch for houses), and fought the Spanish crew with guns to try to overpower them.[43]

Thus the city of Cartagena was interconnected with Cacheu in a number of ways: humanly, commercially, materially and ideologically. The cruelty of the sixteenth-century Spanish conquest and the colonization of the Americas created the demand for enslaved African labour. But it also created the ideological and imperial connections between the two towns and the immense violence of enslaved labour regimes which characterized these places. Of course, Cacheu was a colonial island in a West African setting, and the impact of these regimes on the town itself remained relatively confined in this period. The settlers of Cacheu could not control the hinterland and its peoples, and the cultural and political influences from Senegambia were dominant, along with the commercial routes which brought these influences into the town from places like Farim, Geba and Sutucó.

Nevertheless, as the demand from Cartagena for enslaved Africans grew, so too did the ways in which the violence of the Atlantic empires seeped into this globalizing town, slowly influencing how the community took shape in the seventeenth century.

## 5.
# Religion, Politics and Power

'he said that sometimes he heard *djabakós*, and Mandingas who follow
the law of Mohammed, in Crispina's house, which she consulted
for cures of infirmities of persons in her household,
paying them a salary for doing so'

In 1663, the missionary André De Faro travelled from Cacheu to Guinguim. It was just over a year before the order to arrest Crispina was received in Cacheu. Faro would have a walk-on role in her trial as an Inquisitorial scribe, and one of his companions on this trip to Guinguim was the Franciscan friar Paulo de Lordello, who would be deputed as Inquisitor in the trial (and select Faro as scribe). Both were keen to expand the place of the Church in West Africa, for unlike in the Americas or in African kingdoms such as Kongo it had not settled in to resounding success here. In Senegambia, Christianity jostled for position with African religions and with Islam, alongside the place which Judaism had also had for some of the settlers who had come from Portugal. Indeed, the political power expressed by religion was a mirror to the changing balance of African and European power which was playing out in Cacheu and its surrounding region: grasping where this balance lay, and what it meant to people, is crucial in understanding the lives of those who lived here.

Religion and trade were not in truth very far apart. Faro, Lordello and their companion friar Francisco de Braga reached Guinguim easily enough, where they met two Portuguese traders installed there and doing their business. The friars settled in to stay with them. All seemed well, until one night,

> a great crowd of Africans rose up with weapons against one of the said merchants, over debts from his business . . . their fury was so great, and such the arrows and spears raining down on the Portuguese [traders] and on us, that we were all at risk of death.

However, the next day, whether it was the merchants who were the targets of this assault or Faro and his two friar companions was a question that hung in the air.[1]

The friars and the two merchants all walked a few miles inland to visit the king of Guinguim, a baptized Christian called Dom Diogo by Faro. We can get a sense of what this meeting might have been like from the description of Richard Jobson's audience with a king on the Gambia river forty years earlier:

> The king is commonly sitting on his mat, laid on the ground, which in our entrance he observes, not offering to rise . . . we do not use to move our hats, or uncover our heads when we come to him, but drawing near, somewhat bending our bodies, we lay our hands upon our breasts, which he also performs to us.[2]

According to Jobson, the king would never speak directly to foreign visitors, but only through an intermediary. In this way, then, the friars explained in so many words to Dom Diogo that they were following the by-then historic practice of Catholic religious warriors, honed in the conquest of the Americas at shrines such as that to the Virgin of Guadalupe just outside Mexico City, where churches were built on a pre-existing site of indigenous religious worship. In short, the friars proposed building a church in Guinguim that was next to the *china* of the settlement. They wanted the shrine of African worship to be removed, because they did not want it near the church, where they would have to see the Africans 'worshipping the devil'. It becomes clear that the assault the previous night may have been linked to the missionaries' aim to remove the sacred shrine as much as to the activities of the Portuguese traders – although, of course, this was not how Faro and Lordello chose to report it.[3]

The king of Guinguim said that he would ask his people to remove the *china*. However, the chief of the settlement – known to Faro as Xacôbraga – refused and gathered a crowd of people there to defend it. Even the king's nobles, who had come armed, could not make them leave. So the next day the friars returned to the king, Dom Diogo, and said that if the shrine was not moved they would leave, and along with them the Portuguese, who would never return to trade with him. Dom Diogo did not want this to happen, not at all: the way in which political power and access to trade and its profits were connected was plain to all in the Atlantic world. He sent a large force the next day to impose his decision to move the *china* from its sacred land, something which was the cause of great grief in Guinguim. As the shrine was removed, 'there was no shortage of cries, and sobs, and especially among the women who all gathered together in one body'.[4] Understanding well the compelling power of theatre as spectacle and entertainment, the missionaries then made good their ritual of possession of the sacred site:

> Friar Paulo then put on his stole and surplice, the Portuguese lit their candles, and then Friar Francisco walked holding a great cross in front of him, while the others followed behind with holy water, one of them ringing a bell, and all the Christians gathered together and then on this same day [when the African shrine was banished] we performed this procession.[5]

What Faro recounted was more than just the local conflict of African religions and Catholicism at Guinguim. Here is a clear description of how commercial and religious power were interconnected, and how this increased the influence that Christianity had in some parts of Senegambia through the fear that local rulers had of being cut out of the new Atlantic commercial networks. Power in Cacheu and its surroundings was constructed in economic, political and religious

*The Heretic of Cacheu*

Manjako religious shrine on the edge of a village, Jeta island, Bijagós.

dimensions. Whatever the particular emphases that historians may make, these cannot be disentangled. The three factors worked in tandem. Crispina's trial is the clearest proof of all of this fact: it was because of widespread envy of her economic power that a religious charge was brought against her, and the trial itself was an embodiment of the way in which Atlantic empires sought to challenge and weaken the power of political leaders on the African continent.

There was of course nothing unique about this interrelationship of economic, political and religious power in Cacheu. Historians of the Atlantic world have shown in recent years just how deeply intertwined these aspects were for African peoples, as for all peoples. Indeed, in the diaspora, the main way of challenging European imperial power developed by Africans was through religious unity. This was shown recently by the historian José Lingna Nafafé in his history of the Angolan abolitionist prince Lourenço de Mendonça Silva, who took his case for abolition of slavery to the Vatican in 1684, and can also be seen in a number of other movements of Black resistance. The Palmares maroon community of the seventeenth century in north-eastern Brazil was led by a figure known as Nzumbi, which was the name for a religious leader for the Umbundu peoples of Angola. And when, in the nineteenth century, there was an uprising of enslaved Africans against slavery in Salvador da Bahía, in Brazil, it was known as the Malê rebellion for being organized by African Muslims in the city.[6]

Thus, the attempts in Crispina's trial to challenge the *djabakós*, and their power in Cacheu, was a political as well as a religious act. This related to the fundamental role which Catholicism itself had in the politics of the Portuguese empire. The importance of the *djabakós* in Cacheu spoke to the fact that African political power remained dominant. Moreover, many of the *djabakós* summoned by Crispina practised Islam, while the itinerant Jakhanké traders manifested the growing influence of this religion in Senegambia at this time – something which the Portuguese saw as a threat to their power. The capture and deportation of the richest trader in the town was a statement by the Portuguese empire that it remained a force to be reckoned with – and wanted to see off the challenges of its commercial and imperial competitors.

There was one further piece to add in to the religious stew. Jorge's father's family were New Christians, as were Ambrosio Gomes's, and the Inquisition was always alive to the dangers of a 'Jewish plot' against Catholicism. However, in truth, by the time Crispina was arrested in 1665, the influence of Judaism as a religion had all but disappeared around Cacheu. 'Heretic families' such as Jorge's were so fully integrated into the Catholic Church that he had asked to become a member of the *Ordem de Cristo*. There had been a new rush of heretic crypto-Jews from the Americas after the Inquisition trials of the 1630s in Cartagena and Lima, with penanced fugitives arriving in Cacheu, such as João and Vicente Rodrigues Duarte – nephews of Manoel Bautista Pérez – and Manoel de Matos. However, their Jewish practice lapsed and was soon virtually non-existent, and, as Lemos Coelho wrote in 1669, the missionary work among the Portuguese Jews south of Gorée had been so successful that they had all fully converted to Catholicism by then.[7]

In other words, we will see in this chapter how Christianity, Islam and Judaism all interconnected in Cacheu alongside African religions at this time, just as the three monotheistic religions had done in Spain and Portugal before the rise of the Inquisition in the late fifteenth century. Today these faiths are often seen in conflict, but it has not always been thus. The Convivencia of late medieval Spain is one well-known counter-example, and seventeenth-century Cacheu offers another instance. Of course, there was a good deal of conflict as well as cooperation, both in medieval Spain and in the setting of this book, and yet nevertheless both do offer striking examples of coexistence. For at that time someone like Jorge – whose father had been penanced by the Inquisition for Jewish heresy – was quite happy to turn to Islamic healers when they were sick. Further north of the Gambia river, in the port of Joal, the Jewish trader Manoel Pelegrino had a relationship with the Islamic Jolof king's daughter in 1619. Meanwhile, according to Jorge, virtually every Catholic in Cacheu drew on both Islamic and African religious and healing knowledge through their dealings with the *djabakós*. These religions may have represented empires that were in competition with one another – and there may at times have been violent disagreements, as the case from Joal suggests, since the Jolof king stripped Pelegrino of all his goods – but all this took place within a context in which people shared in one another's lives.[8]

Conflict and competition were the geopolitical backdrop to all this. The broader context was one where the power of the Portuguese empire was in long-term decline. In Asia, the Dutch had taken their place among European maritime middlemen. The Portuguese had managed to defeat the Dutch and regain Angola (in 1648) and Brazil (in 1654), but only at the price of a negotiated treaty with the English, which meant that they were now a rival growing in strength. In Senegambia, the English fort at James island in the Gambia river had by now been established, where emissaries of the Royal African Company were buying enslaved captives for the Barbados plantations, alongside leather, wax and ivory. If Portugal was to bed in its 'interests' in the region for the long term, they needed some show of imperial strength.[9] This context is vital in understanding the stand-off

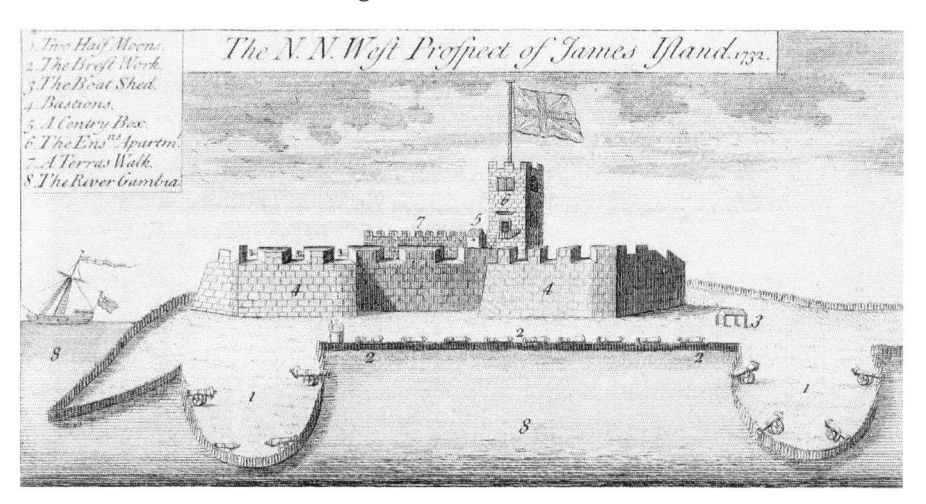

James Island Fort, The Gambia. From Francis Moore's book *Travels into the inlands of Africa*, published in 1738.

of the Franciscan missionaries with the people of Guinguim of 1663. The religious usurpation of the *china* of the settlement was testament to the growing competition for religious power here. This in turn symbolized the increasing power of Atlantic empires and of the cycle of extractive economic demand in Senegambia. Crispina's trial came to a head soon afterwards, making it clear that this was the thin end of a very thick wedge. Her deportation to Lisbon symbolized an attempt to erode African political power, under which the colonial enclave of Cacheu had lived hitherto on sufferance. Although the attempt was fairly unsuccessful in the medium term, the expansion of missionary activities and the further inroads of Atlantic empires on Cacheu and its hinterland would soon follow.

In the pages of Crispina's trial, the *djabakós* are among the principal actors. We never get to know their names from these pages, but their significance in the daily – and night-time – life of the town is clear. As we have seen, it was because of her interactions with them that Crispina was arraigned before the Inquisitors. One of the ironies of her trial is that it was clear that she was just doing the same as everyone else in the town: these healers helped with fevers, difficult childbirth, worked with the bodies of the dead and provided

## The Heretic of Cacheu

succour to all those still hanging on to the worlds of the living. They were part of most people's lives, and so to arrest Crispina for this showed that this was a political trial dressed up as a religious one.

The *djabakós* embodied the plural religious world of Cacheu. Some were Islamic, even though much of what they did hardly fell within the purview of conventional Islam. Just as Jorge was a Catholic who was open to African and Islamic religious practice, and whose father had been accused of being a Jewish heretic, so many *djabakós* were Muslims who brought aspects of African religious belief to their practice. Not everyone appreciated this plural approach to religious practice, and it is also clear that many (though not all) Catholics in the town saw all non-Christian practice as being performed by '*djabakós*', lumping Islamic and African religious practitioners in together. This inability to see any difference in the lives and beliefs of others was to become a hallmark of later European imperial worldviews.[10]

In his evidence, Vicente Rodrigues Duarte – a trader and captain of the town – provided a pithy summary of this approach:

> Asked whether he knew about those *djabakós* which he said were Heathens [non-Christians], he said yes and that they were Mandingas, who follow the Law of Mohammed; and that all the Blacks of this settlement travel to foreign kingdoms, and this settlement, performing witchcraft, in order to receive their payments.[11]

In other words, Duarte believed that all the *djabakós* were Jakhanké Mandinga, travelling from one settlement to another, where they performed acts of healing and augury alongside their teaching of Arabic to children, for which they were well paid by the people who lived there. However, a subsequent witness made it clear that the reality was more complicated. Francisco Tavares was also asked about the presence of *djabakós* in Crispina's house:

> asked about the seventh question, he said that sometimes he heard *djabakós*, and Mandingas who follow the law of Mohammed in Crispina's house, which she consulted for cures of infirmities of persons in her household, paying them a salary for doing so.[12]

Tavares saw a distinction between Islamic healers and those following African religions, who on this account were competitors for preeminence in the healing regimes of the town. Many other witnesses recognized this distinction as well, implying that Crispina clearly did too, describing how she 'usually had *djabakós* in her house, *feiticeiros* [i.e. *djabakós*], and Mandingas'. This is more in keeping with evidence we have, which shows a growing influence of Islam and its competition with African religions – but not at this stage a complete supplanting of these faiths. This competition led to a form of syncretism, which became crystallized in the use of the *gris-gris*, amulets which had become near universal in their use by the middle of the seventeenth century. When Crispina's brother, Antonio Peres Balcasar, gave evidence, he recounted how Crispina and Jorge's rival and enemy Ambrosio Gomes 'wore a conch around his waist, as the Mandingas who follow the Law of Mohammed are accustomed to, and [practice witchcraft], in order to stop any damage from entering him [his body] by diabolical arts'. What is described here is a mixture of historic African beliefs about the power of the spiritual world, blended with the use of Islamic prayers written out on the amulets which then were wrapped around the body in the *gris-gris* – as Francisco Tavares put it, 'the said Blacks would bring along their little books, and letters written by them, which are their diabolical arts.' Indeed, as the art historian Cécile Fromont has shown, such hybridity continued further in the Atlantic empires, as Mandinga charms or pouches were made in the Americas using ostensibly European designs and materials.[13]

These sources may show how African and Muslim practices were mixing in the 1660s, but they also show that African religious practice remained dominant in Cacheu. The *djabakós* were more prominent and sought-after than the Jakhanké as healers by people in the town. When Jorge and Crispina had sent to Bugendo and Bujé for healers, they had been dealing with settlements of Bainunk and Kassa peoples that were definitely not Islamic by this time. Meanwhile, the denunciations of Crispina's 'fetishist' heresies all focused on religious practices that were distinctively Senegambian, and not those brought by itinerant Jakhanké clerics from the wider Dar-al-Islam: in

## The Heretic of Cacheu

fact, since it was women who ran the commercial life of Cacheu, so it appears that their commercial power in the town was the partner to the significance which African religious practice had in their lives.

We have already seen many facets of this practice discussed in previous chapters. Crispina kept pots on her wall that were said to be *chinas* to bring health to her daughter. She encouraged sacrifices of animals on the helm of Jorge's ships in order to bring good fortune in a trading voyage, and her ability to command this almost as a proxy-*djabakós* may also have been symbolic of the power which she had accrued. When people were ill, she was accused of making sacrifices of goats and mixing their blood with certain herbs and with palm wine, and then placing the mixture in the pans or *chinas* under their beds as an offering; so when Jorge's brother-in-law João Nunes Castanho commanded that these liquids be thrown into the São Domingos river, she flew into a fury and never spoke to him again. Moreover, participation in African religious practice was clearly the dominant form of religiosity of many of the women of Cacheu, since their houses in Vila Quente were said by witnesses to be the site of these offerings, and since all those accused in the trial of worshipping at *chinas* were women.[14]

Jorge himself gave a good summary of what this meant for daily activity in the town when he discussed the beliefs of many of the women who were also accused of witchcraft in the trial:

> Genebra Lopes, a Christian, when her son was in bad state, took him two or three [times] . . . to Bugendo, land of heathens, to cure him with the heathens; she said she would cure him with the magic arts; and also that one Isabel Lopes used to attend the funerals of the heathens, believing in their wrongdoings, against our Holy Catholic Faith, and in their *Chinas* . . . And also, one Nicolaça Dias, when Brásia Dias died, she took the clothes of the deceased to the *China*, saying that the *China* killed her.[15]

All of these acts of worship and ritual depended on the counsel of the *djabakós*. One witness described how, after Crispina's daughter had died, Crispina had tied the wrists of both of her arms with *gris-gris* given to her by the *djabakós* and had put some on herself as well, 'so as to ensure that the [witches] would not eat her, which they call killing in these parts'. These figures were spiritual counsellors, healers and intermediaries between the living and the dead through the offerings they recommended and the worldviews which they disseminated. This made them certainly among the most important people in the town for most of Cacheu's inhabitants – and far more important, in practical terms, than the captain-general or his pasty-faced acolytes, yellow with fever, writing interminable screeds lamenting their impotence in this environment.

This realization is abundantly clear from the pages of the trial and also emphasizes that it was the dominance of African religion which was the partner to the other ways in which the town upended the norms of the Portuguese empire. This dominance of the *djabakós* empowered the women of the town who were the key participants at the *chinas* and thus went hand in hand with their commercial and social dominance. If the dominance of African religions could be challenged, then so too in time could perhaps these 'unChristian' gender norms and the associated economic empowerment of the women of Cacheu. This was precisely the trajectory of religious, gendered and economic power over the centuries that followed.

Many other aspects of Crispina's trial give a sense of the daily significance of *djabakós* in shaping life in Cacheu. Witnesses described how Crispina employed them to give her auguries 'in order to know some things which one expected to happen'. One, Pedro Pais, gave a specific example of this, saying that he had asked a *djabakós* to give him an augury to test the accuracy of their skills, and that the *djabakós* had replied with details of the arrival of a big trading ship from Santiago in Cabo Verde bringing news from the new captain of the town, who himself would arrive later in a smaller ship – 'and the witness [Pais] stated that it all happened *in terminis*, just like the [*djabakós*] had said.' And there was one further aspect which confirmed just how significant African religiosity remained in the household of Crispina and Jorge, and thus in Cacheu as a whole.

This was the fact that they were both accused of keeping a giant snake in their house as part of their religious practice.[16]

Snakes were important religious symbols in Senegambia, as they are in other parts of West Africa such as Ouidah in today's Benin. As we saw in the previous chapter, the most important shrine in Kaabu was dedicated to the snake known as Tamba Dibi. Snakes were abundant. There were the huge pythons, and the green and black mambas who sometimes lived with them in the large *kapok* silk cotton trees. In this part of Africa, they were associated with shapeshifting and believed to be spirits able to assume human form (beliefs that were also widespread in Europe at the time, regarding shapeshifting and spirits assuming the forms of animals). They were a connection between the visible and invisible worlds and remained so for centuries. In his memoir *The Africa Child*, published in 1954, the writer from Guinea-Conakry Camara Laye described the important role that snakes had

A *kapok* or silk-cotton tree, Bijagós islands.

in the spiritual life of his family. He recounted how, as a child growing up in the 1930s, he had once seen a black snake heading towards his father's workshop. He had run to warn his mother, who usually beat snakes to death with sticks. However, she admonished Laye and told him that this snake was his father's guiding spirit; his father then added that it provided him auguries and told him everything that would happen. This was how he was able to tell the apprentices in his workshop the details of all the people who had come to the workshop in his absence, where the snake lay unassumingly, curled up in a corner.[17]

These considerations are important. They show that the many accusations that Crispina and Jorge consorted with spirit-snakes are testament to the Africanity of their beliefs and social structures. One such accusation is worth repeating in full detail:

> Jorge Gonçalves, and Crispina Peres ... [kept] in their *combete* (which is a house buried in the ground where they keep all their goods) ... a big snake; for having strong feeling and being the sin of the heathens ... they keep a snake like that in their house, which they bring from the woods by the devil's art ... for the house to be very successful, and make a lot of money; and they say that it is customary for those who keep snakes like that in their house, to sacrifice an animal from time to time.[18]

This snake was known by many witnesses to be important. Crispina's own relative Baltasar Lopes 'said that she kept a [snake called an] *iran* in her house where she was used to receive heathens for whom the snake took on a human appearance, and said that she kept it so that nobody would arrest her'. Here is a clear sense of these *iran* snakes providing auguries, able to protect Crispina from harm, just as Camara Laye's father told him as a child nearly three centuries later.[19]

In her own testimony given to the Inquisitors in Lisbon, Crispina herself showed just how important these snakes were to the beliefs and daily lives of many in Cacheu and beyond. She described how as a child, when she had been living with her father, Rodrigo, on the Geba river, rumours had spread there that he and his business associate the barber Antonio Gomes had become rich because of some snakes which Gomes kept in his hut, 'even though it is certain that the said Antonio Gomes died poor; and even though she, the confessant, never saw such a snake, nor does she know if what these people said was true.' Gomes had been born in Portugal, like Crispina's father, which also shows just how much European arrivals adopted Senegambian worldviews.[20]

Crispina tried to present herself to the Inquisitors as someone who could see beyond these beliefs – and had no truck with this African 'sorcery'. Not only had such use of these spirit-snakes failed for Gomes, but she herself had always tried to steer clear of becoming involved in this kind of thing:

> approximately eight years ago in the settlement of Cacheu, when she was in her house with Maria Mendes . . . Mendes said to the confessant that in order for her to have goods, and riches, she wanted to bring an *iran* snake to her house, that she would ask the Black *djabakós* to bring her one, as these people were accustomed to carrying them; the said snake asked for goods and riches for the person who had them in their house, or sent for them through the Black *djabakós* to the bush; to which she the confessant replied, to the said Maria Mendes, that she did not want to have the said snake in her house, which could do her harm, since she was scared of the creepy-crawlies (*bichos*) that hatched on their skin.[21]

The testimony about the snakes is inconclusive. A number of witnesses, including Crispina's relatives, claimed that she and Jorge made use of them. On the other hand, Crispina herself tried to present herself as with no illusions as to their efficacy when it came to the arts of commerce, wealth and protection from harm. It may be that she had at one time believed in these spirit-snakes, before the death of her daughter 'made her heart grow small'. What this evidence confirms beyond doubt, however, is the significance of African religious idioms in Cacheu at this date – and the way in which they coincided with the empowerment and dominance of African women in the town, who were the main adepts at the *chinas*. It is in fact this evidence on the importance of African religion in Cacheu's daily life which helps us to see that the Inquisition's religious war was also an economic, political and gendered war rolled into one.

Crispina's trial makes clear that there was an effective market for religious practice in Cacheu. There were the institutions of Catholicism – the Church, the brotherhoods – alongside the *chinas* in Vila Quente. There were the *djabakós* who came from villages and towns by canoe, from Guinguim and Bujé in Casamance. And then there were the itinerant Jakhanké Islamic preachers, who were also a significant presence. All this gives a powerful impression of a different facet of daily life in the town: of wandering preachers, covered in *gris-gris*, the sounds of laments from funerals, the loud cries of women off to make sacrifices at the *chinas*. Cacheu is nothing without understanding the religious context in which it existed.

Religion was not completely rigid here. Catholics drew on *djabakós*, while the Jakhanké syncretized Islamic verses from the Qur'an with African beliefs in the power of the amulet. The importance of these *gris-gris* is clear from these documents at the time, as is the way in which they heralded the growing power of Islam in Senegambia. In her own evidence, Crispina described these 'Mandinga strings' as being 'of white and black cotton, of the thickness of string of a whipping-top'. She herself had used them at times, having them tied to her upper arms and her waist next to the skin; and Ambrosio Gomes, who had given them to her at a time before they became rivals and enemies, said that he had used them to protect himself from being wounded in war. The ubiquity and use of these amulets across the region is shown by the story in Luis Rodrigues's trial, where he was accused of fabricating relics and selling them to credulous people in Ribeira Grande to protect them from all harm from gunfire – just as the *gris-gris* in Cacheu were said to do.[22]

The importance of the *gris-gris* in Cacheu was due to the increasing presence of the Jakhanké traders and the growing influence of Islam in Senegambia in the seventeenth century. While historians usually saw Islam as a religion of Senegambian elites at this time, it is clear that it had become a popular religion by 1700. This was thus a turning point in the religious history of the region, as the social base of Islam expanded significantly. The heartland of the Jakhanké itinerant clerics who were vital to this change was on the Gambia river, but by the seventeenth century there are many other pieces of evidence which show that Islam had also become widespread in Guinea-Bissau. While Kaabu itself was not a Muslim state, there were Islamic communities across the region which made Islam a viable competitor to the African religions which still retained primacy.[23]

This can be seen in the many descriptions of Muslim preachers passing through Cacheu in Crispina's trial, but also in other details which make clear that Islam was a religion with many adepts by this time. When the Jesuit missionary Baltasar Barreira tried to found a Catholic school in Geba, in 1605, he complained about the number of Islamic preachers then passing through the town. And, writing in 1685, the French traveller Jajolet de la Courbe wrote that there were many Muslims in and around Geba too. That Islam was widely spread across the region was shown around 1600 by the Caboverdean André Donelha, who described how the prayer mats so widely used across the region were woven in the territory of the Farim Cocalí, on the borders of Guinea-Bissau and Guinea-Conakry.[24]

The growing significance of the kola-nut trade – the nuts valued across the Islamic world as a stimulant which was not alcoholic – through the seventeenth century is alone testament to the growing role of Islam in the region. Probably, it had the status of an attractive outside religion with a connection to a powerful world – something that promised a different potential to the usual exhortations of the *djabakós*. Literacy was also an attraction for some, and the role of spreading education was an important one for the Jakhanké clerics. The Gambia river was their base, with many madrassas established by the seventeenth century in which children learnt to read and write Arabic on the *alúa* wooden tablets, in the light of day and by fire at night.

Sutucó, the centre of these Jakhanké clerics, was described by

## Religion, Politics and Power

Richard Jobson in the 1620s as the largest town he had seen in The Gambia, and as a place where many clerics lived, and where they also provided lodgings for other itinerant preachers passing through the town. By the 1660s, Lemos Coelho was describing the entire settlement of the Gambia river as Islamic, except for the Kombo kingdom of Floups by the coast.[25]

All this helps us better understand the religious life of Cacheu itself. While the Gambia river region was ruled by Islamic communities, communities in Guinea-Bissau were more mixed. Jakhanké preachers and traders passed through often from The Gambia, along the axes of trade then growing hand over fist, with their pupils in tow. They offered *gris-gris*, which provided a counterpoint to African religious practice. But African religions themselves remained dominant, in keeping with African political power in the town in general. As the *Ta'rikh* (History) composed in the nineteenth century in Bijini in Guinea-Bissau put it, in Kaabu itself there were 'no Muslims'. Or perhaps, to be more accurate, Islamic preachers often passed through, but their practices mixed with African religions, and they held little political power. Meanwhile, Cacheu's global influences were coming from all sides – both from the Dar-al-Islam and from the Atlantic empires to the West.[26]

For the Atlantic trading community in Cacheu, the Church offered a further site of religious practice, and one that could not be ignored. While the *djabakós* embodied local religious and political power, and the Jakhanké connected Cacheu to the Gambia river and the rich worlds of the Dar-al-Islam beyond, the Catholic Church looked west to the Atlantic. The wealthier traders of the town had to embrace Catholicism, even though in practice they turned to it as one religion among many.

The reputation of the Church as an institution was mixed and depended most of all on the position which people had in the town. Catholicism was of course a core part of the Iberian empires, and so was important for anyone who had dealings with Lisbon or Cartagena. The most powerful colonial figures in the town held offices in the church too. Gaspar Vogado, the religious visitor of Guinea and one of the major instigators of Crispina's trial, had been captain-general of Cacheu in 1649–50. Jorge had been both captain-general of Cacheu and the major-domo of the church of St Anthony. Those who were ambitious needed to find a role for themselves in the church in order to symbolize their authority both to other people coming from the colonial world and to the rest of the town's inhabitants.[27]

This connection of the Church to the colonial world was symbolized further by the fact that all of the officers and priests came from Santiago island in Cabo Verde. As we have seen, both Vaz de Pontes and Rodrigues had been sent as priests from there, while Inquisitor Lordello was president of the Franciscan monastery in Ribeira Grande, the institution where the initial interrogations in the trial of Rodrigues took place. There were also established doctrinal religious institutions attached to the cathedral there: a religious school with a teacher run from the chapel, for instance, and alms

The restored Franciscan monastery in Cidade Velha (Ribeira Grande).

houses through the institution of the Misericordia, which was well known across the Iberian worlds. Daily mass was also said in Ribeira Grande's cathedral, and Rodrigues himself caused a scandal there one day when he consecrated the host carelessly in a piece of animal hide. Cabo Verde was much more closely connected to empire than Cacheu, through its links both with Lisbon and with other parts of the Atlantic world, and because Portuguese political power was unquestioned there: where imperial power was stronger, the Church was also, and since that power was weaker in Cacheu, so was the power of the Church.[28]

Moreover, this close connection to empire was the other side of the coin of the bad reputation which the Church had for some. For a number of its most senior officers were closely connected to the trade in enslaved captives, something which we will explore in much more detail in the next chapter. The vicar Antonio Vaz de Pontes was described in Crispina's trial as 'a man of trade', a 'big businessman and merchant and hard bargainer', and 'one of the biggest traders in this settlement of Cacheu'. In the trial of Luis Rodrigues, Rodrigues claimed that Vaz de Pontes had been appointed by the governor of Cabo Verde, Pero Ferraz Barreto, and had been sent to Cacheu with a large amount of goods to sell in the trade, which he had done before sending the 'proceedings' back to the islands, almost certainly meaning enslaved people.[29]

Not only were key officials of the Church in Cacheu involved in slave trafficking, but the vicars also were closely connected to it through the process of baptism. Africans received the most cursory of baptisms from the vicars in Cacheu before being despatched in the 'floating tombs' of slave ships to the Americas. For this, the vicars were paid, as the account books of the New Christian Manoel Bautista Pérez from 1614 make clear: the vicar of Cacheu was paid for 'baptizing the Blacks in Guinea', as was the scribe who annotated and made 'legal' this supposedly religious procedure. The account books made clear the tension between the religious justification of enslavement and its commercial purposes: 'from Guinea there is owing [an amount] to the vicar and to the scribe for the baptism of all of these

## The Heretic of Cacheu

[enslaved Africans*] and of those who died'. With the core officers of the Church so closely connected to the traffic, clearly not everyone in Cacheu had a good opinion of their religion – this may indeed be one of the reasons why the church of Our Lady of Victory was burnt down by one attack from the Pepel, as we saw in Chapter 3.[30]

Moreover, not only was the Church closely connected to the business of enslavement through the ritual of baptism and the financial interests of the clergy, but even those priests who weren't traffickers were poor emissaries of the faith. Vaz de Pontes was shacked up with his mistress in Vila Quente. Meanwhile, Luis Rodrigues, the first vicar of Farim, was a thoroughgoing reprobate. The sermon he gave in which he said that he could pardon all acts of incest scandalized not only his Catholic congregation but also many of the Africans in the town. This was hardly a good advert for the probity of Christianity. According to one witness, João de Valdeveso, the Africans in Farim started 'mocking the Catholic faith, since they observed among themselves continency between parents and children, brothers and sisters, and even between first cousins'.[31]

Nevertheless, although there were a number of reasons why Africans in Cacheu might have had little love for the Catholic Church, it was not a religion they ignored. As described at the start of this chapter, the religious officers and friars in West Africa were keen to mount religious processions: at investitures of new churches (as in André Faro's mission to Guinguim), but also on other holy days. Baptisms were significant events among the trafficking elite: Jorge, for example, was godfather to at least two of the witnesses in his wife's trial. And while African funerals were important in Vila Quente, accompanied by loud laments known dismissively in Crispina's trials as 'wails' (*choros*), Catholic funerals were mounted with solemnity and processions in the town. Wax was bought for candles to accompany the procession, which was led by the vicar, who bore a large cross in front of him before saying mass for the deceased. After

---

* The word used in the document is *peças*, or 'pieces', a usage which came originally from the terms used for cattle in Spain.

this, a grave was dug and the body interred – and all of this came at a cost which helped sustain the finances of the church in the town.[32]

Alongside the processions at funerals and religious festivals, religious confraternities also had a significant role in Cacheu. The confraternity of the Rosary was an important institution, as it was in Ribeira Grande in Cabo Verde (where the restored whitewashed walls of its church remain). One of those mentioned in Crispina's trial was Susana Lopes, who had been 'Queen of Our Lady of the Rosary' in Cacheu, showing that she had been elected as one of the carnival queens during the feasts before Lent. Carnival in Bissau remains famous and popular to this day, with hundreds of thousands of people thronging the streets of this small city: from the evidence here, this is a Catholic tradition incorporating African religious traditions that is very old.[33]

This is a significant detail, showing that Cacheu belonged to a broader African Catholic culture developing in the seventeenth century across the Atlantic world. As a number of historians have shown, the confraternities of the Rosary were important institutions for Africans in colonial Iberian societies: they spearheaded political movements campaigning against abolition as early as the 1680s, and they also allowed for the recreation of African political and spiritual cultures. The fact that the carnival processions of these confraternities took place in Cacheu helps us to grasp the town's place in a broader Catholic world, but it also shows that the Catholicism practised was an African version – for Susana Lopes, the carnival queen, was also accused of going 'to the land of the heathens, to a caste which they call [Pepels], and to another called [Bainunk], to a funeral that the heathens hold for their deceased . . . to pour palm wine and blood . . . on their *Chinas*'.[34]

All in all, it becomes clear that, just as the people of Cacheu adapted Islam to their own religious practices and belief, so they did the same with Christianity. For the vast majority of the people of the town, this was one shrine among many – and valued as such. The Church existed through its core institutions – the buildings, offices, brotherhoods and ritual roles in funerals and at baptisms – but in terms of faith what was practised was certainly in Inquisitorial terms 'heretical'. People blended their beliefs and attendance at shrines (whether *chinas* or churches). There was nothing to stop someone from being the carnival queen one week, and then going to a funeral in Vila Quente the next. As Jorge himself said in his wife's trial, there were only four Catholics in the town who observed the faith without any admixture of African beliefs.[35]

Crispina's trial therefore represented in part a concerted attempt by the Church to challenge the status quo. The Jesuits had established a mission in Cabo Verde in 1604, from which missionaries had worked in West Africa; but they had struggled with ill health and poor finances, and the mission had been disbanded in 1642. The second half of the seventeenth century saw an attempt at renewal in which the trial played a key part. It followed the installation of the Franciscans in Guinguim and the stand-off with Xacôbraga, displacing the *china* to build a church. Then, in 1664, the Pepel king of Mata de Puxame was converted to Christianity by the same missionaries. All this made clear that the importance of religion as a proxy for economic and political influence was a priority for the Portuguese empire, in which Crispina's trial could stand as an exemplary demonstration of the dangers of heresy and the powers of the Church to punish it.[36]

This renewed proselytizing mission continued with the Capuchins in the second half of the seventeenth century. In 1678, two Spanish Capuchins installed themselves in Bissau, to the south of Cacheu, where they stayed for at least a decade. Their stay bore fruit with the baptism of the king of Bissau and members of his nobility in 1694. Thus, in the twenty-five years following Crispina's trial, the work of the religious missions to combat the hold of Islam and to 'root out heresy' continued strongly. As the power of European empires in the Atlantic grew, so, it seems, did the power of their religion. Nevertheless, the conversion of these rulers was probably in the main a political choice, structured by the growing power of the Atlantic empires and the need to have access to its trading networks (as the king of Guinguim had made clear to André de Faro in 1663). This conversion was seen by them to be to one shrine, among many.[37]

## Religion, Politics and Power

All the same, it would be wrong to dismiss this Christian belief as hollow. By the time of Crispina's trial, and in the years that followed, the place of Christian belief had grown in Cacheu and its surroundings. It is clear from the trial that very many people held devoted beliefs in an invisible spirit-world, and for some this was manifested through Christianity: in Crispina's trial one witness, Maria Mendes, returned to amend her statement before Inquisitor Lordello because 'she was in danger of dying . . . and she relieved her conscience, for fear of God to whom she was going to give her account'.[38]

The priest Antonio Vaz de Pontes may have been a profiteering trafficker, but as far as he was concerned life was still tough for people like him in Cacheu. For all its fortifications, for all its connections to other ports of the Iberian empires, Cacheu was an African town, where African religious practice dominated – and this reflected the African political control in place. So, once the Pepel and Bainunk ally Crispina had been arrested by the Inquisitorial commissary Friar Luis de Chaves, from the Franciscan monastery in Ribeira Grande, things got tough. As Vaz de Pontes put it:

> We have all asked and advised the said [Chaves] that he should leave [here] immediately because our lives and belongings [are] in great danger, which was very inconvenient for all of us, and that it was common for the said heathens to steal from us and do us harm, as they do every day without any grounds or reason.[39]

Inquisitor Lordello also railed at the lack of 'obedience' of the Africans in Cacheu in a letter which he sent to his religious superiors from the Franciscan monastery of Cabo Verde in August 1658. He was trying to make inquiries of the faith as he had been commanded to, through the sergeant-major of Cacheu, and yet according to him this was a very difficult task, 'because the people are rebellious and do not know what this is [for]'. In other words, so weak was imperial power in the town that the people did not even recognize it, or pay heed to its summons.

## The Heretic of Cacheu

Through the trial of Crispina which he prosecuted in the years that followed, Lordello was determined to do something about this.[40]

As seen in Chapter 1, once she was arrested by Chaves, a stand-off arose between the Bainunk and Pepel near Cacheu and the Portuguese. Chaves himself put it that the arrest warrant 'was executed . . . putting not only my own life at risk, but that of an entire village'. After the arrest, the 'priests [in Cacheu] stayed in their houses with guns in their hands and all day and night they stood watch, because we feared that the Black heathens would invade the settlement'. André de Faro, scribe in the trial (whom we have come across in a different guise already in this chapter), wrote that, after the Pepel and Bainunk 'gathered to free the prisoner Crispina Peres', Jorge moved with her brother and one of her daughters to live with the Bainunk in one of their nearby settlements. Crispina and Jorge's household slave Sebastião Rodrigues Barraza had also fled from Cacheu to the kingdom of Cazil near Casamance, where he had relatives, but he was seized in a village outside the town on the orders of Crispina's brother, 'saying that they would kill him, because he caused his sister to be arrested'.[41]

It is here that the threads of politics, kinship and religion become clearer. For, according to the vicar Vaz de Ponte's declaration, Peres's arrest was made all the harder since she was 'a close relative of the Bainunk Black heathens, who live [at a distance] of half a tide from this port'. She was also well known 'among the other Black heathens who are our neighbours and among the main kingdoms . . . and she controls all of them because they use her house as a canteen, where they eat and drink'. Crispina herself gave a list of all the peoples she welcomed to her home in her defence: 'Papel Blacks; Black women of Caboi;* Felupe Blacks; Ca[ss]anga† Blacks, Blacks from the [Bijagó] islets; and Black men from Capei; Blacks from Baxere and Blacks from [Pabuto]; Blacks of Baoula and all the *grumetes* from Farim'. According to her, they 'all came to her house with everything they made; and everything was bought there, without

---

\* Today a Manjako village in north-western Guinea-Bissau.
† Kassanké.

selling to another party . . . because she gave them more [things] than all the others, she spent a lot on food and drink'. In other words, Crispina's kinship ties gave her political connections, and this drove her economic nous, along with the linguistic and social skills that were part of her cultural DNA. This made her house a more popular trading site than any other in Cacheu: a centre of sociability.[42]

This context makes the fears of the Portuguese priests as to the outcome of Crispina's arrest more understandable. For all the sedimentation of one account of reality in the piles of paper accumulating in archives around the empire, Catholicism had only a tenuous hold here. Without the political power to enforce it, Christianity would only ever have a weak grip in Cacheu. Real religious power still lay with the *djabakós*, representative of the Bainunk, Pepel and Floup kingdoms that lay around this West African port town. Arrivals from Portugal quickly became swept up in African religiosity, perhaps partly because they saw it as a route to more worldly success such as that manifested by Crispina. One accusation to the Inquisition in 1630 claimed that someone in Cacheu had said that as a child he had always wanted to be a 'fetishist', and that he still wanted to be one; while in 1694 there was a trial in Cacheu of a Portuguese man who was using *gris-gris*.[43]

Nevertheless, and as Crispina herself also showed, there was a religious (and therefore political) coexistence between African religions and the Portuguese Church. In her own life account, Christianity had had a significant role. She had been baptized and learnt the major credos of the faith. And yet she was fully integrated into Senegambian belief systems and rituals, consorting almost daily with the *djabakós* and Jakhanké preachers who passed through the town. This was just normal religious life in Cacheu, where many Christianized Africans lived in Vila Quente – which was also the centre for the worship of *chinas* and for African funerals in the town. This was something that came from the mixed heritage of many people there, as the tale of Crispina and Jorge's enemy Ambrosio Gomes makes clear:

> [Barnabé Siqueira] overheard many people say that Ambrosio's mother has a house in Guinguim . . . in a *baga-baga* [termite mound],

Termite mound, Bijagós islands, Guinea-Bissau

which in our language is an ant hill which forms a big mound of earth, a place she visits every time her son has some work to get done, attributing to it the power of God.[44]

There was such a close cultural relationship between Cacheu and nearby towns such as Guinguim, often grounded in kinship ties like these and those of Crispina's. People in Floup villages quite far from Cacheu would ask after people in the town and say that they had heard news about mutual acquaintances there from others. Even priests like Lordello wrote letters about their establishments in Cacheu, saying that it was in the Mata de Putame 'on whose land we are staying', suggesting that there was knowledge of customary land rights in Pepel culture that precluded an outright sale of *tchon* (land), which could only be leased as it belonged to the people and ancestors of the *tchon*. The cultural norms of Senegambia thus influenced even how the emissaries of the Catholic Church and the Inquisition saw their own role in the country.[45]

What this shows us, in fact, is just how interlinked all religions in Cacheu had become by the 1660s. The *djabakós* had adopted facets of Islam, while the Jakhanké had also melded some Islamic beliefs with the African religious use of amulets. Christians practised African religions and gratefully turned to Jakhanké preachers too – as did people like Jorge, whose slave-trafficking father had been penanced by the Inquisition for being a Jewish heretic. Even the priests of the town understood and acknowledged aspects of African customary law. And all of this intermixing was symbolic of the balance of political power that characterized life in Cacheu by this time. Nevertheless, the 1660s was also a decade of change, heralding a decisive shift in the intensification of the demand for captive African labour in the Americas – and with it a sweeping imbalance loomed in the scales of political power.

On a visit to Bula in 2011, I saw an old friend who had lived in the town on and off for years and was married to a Fulani woman from there. He told me that there was a new marabout (Islamic cleric) in the town who could give very powerful blessings. So we went to the room which he had rented in a compound a short distance from my friend's. The man had been trained in Mauritania – whither many of the great clerics from Timbuktu had dispersed with their libraries following the Moroccan invasion of 1591 – and had then spent many years with different marabouts across Mali and Senegal. Now he made a living moving from one town to another, arriving and becoming known for the depth of his esoteric knowledge and the wisdom that he could impart.[46]

During that same visit, we met my friend's brother, who lived just across the Senegalese border in Casamance. He rode down on his motorbike, and we spent several days talking in the oppressive heat at the end of the dry season. In much of what he said, he lamented the corruption of governing elites in West Africa. They drove past in smart four-by-fours, with hardly a clue of the nature of daily life for the people in the countries they ruled. 'All they do is eat,' he said in Wolof: *'Lekal, rek.'*

All this is relevant to the seventeenth century too, for it shows how systems established then have endured over the last 400 years. The concept of 'eating' has moved from the consumption through malicious sorcery of the healthy bodies of the people of Cacheu to a political concept whereby the governing class consumes the bodies of the people of West Africa through their eating of the political commons. Meanwhile, it was in that phase of history that itinerant Muslim clerics began to pass through the towns of Guinea-Bissau with increasing frequency, offering counsel and spiritual succour to people in their daily struggles with the travails of life brought on by these new class dynamics. It turned out that the patterns detailed in the inquisitorial trials of the seventeenth century were the starting points in the establishment of a system of belief and governance that has endured.

Just as demand-driven greed encapsulates the concept of 'eating' today, so too the structure was being established in the seventeenth century. This relationship between economic greed and political power was one of the cornerstones of the emergence of this pattern of belief, politics and consumption in the seventeenth century. In 1682, French traders on the Senegal river reported making the almost incredible profit of 800 per cent on their trading missions. That similar fantastic profits were made around Cacheu was made clear by Lemos Coelho at about the same time. He recounted that he had once lost one of his trading ships south of Cacheu, with the death of almost 100 enslaved Africans on board. However, as he put it, in the trademark matter-of-fact style which conceals untold misery in historical documents, 'such is Guinea that I had recovered the loss [of money] within a year'.[47]

This is the context of the repeated attacks which Cacheu experienced from those who lived around it. African rulers wanted to resist the encroachments of the colonial enclave of Cacheu, and so did many villagers in the surrounding area. They sensed that, with the entrenchment of Atlantic commerce and its religious allies, political and economic autonomy would be eaten away from them. As we will see in the next chapter in more detail, some Senegambian peoples attacked the Cacheu ships involved in the regional trade to Sierra Leone or The Gambia, killing the captains and holding the crew hostage. That this was not infrequent is shown by the fact that the Cacheu traders developed a category to describe these 'Africans at war' (*negros de guerra*). However, the growing importance of Atlantic markets in order to maintain status and prestige meant that many rulers, such as Dom Diogo of Guinguim, whom we encountered at the start of this chapter, felt that they had no option but to retain access through granting space to missionaries like Faro and Lordello.[48]

Thus, Christian and African religious practices were blended as African political autonomy was weakened, just as the *djabakós* had also incorporated elements of Islam. This religious hybridity was symbolized politically through the increase in the traffic of enslaved Africans, which was an aspect of daily life in Cacheu that involved everyone who lived there.

# 6.
# *Slavery and Human Trafficking*

'The slave traffickers buy some captives who have been stolen, and in fact many of them are . . . bringing them to the ships by night, thieving them from the Biafada and Bainunk peoples'

Trafficking in enslaved Africans was the economic lynchpin of the town of Cacheu. It is impossible to get a full sense of daily life in the town without understanding this history. It was this business that brought in external finance from the Atlantic empires, and which thereby also brought to Cacheu many of the traders from the Americas, Cabo Verde and beyond. Of course, the manufacturing and trade of textiles and ivory carvings remained important within Senegambia, alongside agricultural production, financing the trade in kola nuts between Sierra Leone and Farim. However, it was with the traffic in people that the changing political and religious dynamics of the seventeenth century became institutionalized.

Senegambia had been the first African region to be drawn systematically into the transatlantic traffic. Until around 1617, this westernmost part of Africa supplied about half of the captives who were taken by force to Cartagena. After this time the Angola region predominated, but this signified more the overall increase of the traffic than a diminishing impact around Cacheu. The consequences were vast, although the numbers of human beings involved were concealed from the eye of the imperial taxman. Ships from Senegambia were said by a Jesuit in the 1620s to cram in 700 people where the captains claimed to be carrying 200. One ship arriving in Cartagena in 1635 had 510 captive Africans who had not been officially registered. With between six and ten ships departing Cacheu annually, this would suggest a total of 4,000–7,000 captive Africans taken each year through the streets of Cacheu, loaded onto the lighters and taken out to the departing ships in this wide stretch of the river.*[1]

Most of the major actors in this book were involved in the traffic. The earlier historical documents that we have been looking at – the account books of Manoel Bautista Pérez and his brother João – were produced to account for the profit and credit produced by this cruel business. Manoel later went on to be the richest man in Lima, the main reason why he became a target of the Inquisition there. The depth of his personal involvement was recently unearthed by the historian Chloe Ireton, through a legal case taken in Cartagena in 1614 by Francisco Martín. Martín claimed that he had been illegally enslaved in Cacheu by Manoel Bautista Pérez. Martín had been born to Sapi parents, who were free Christians in the town, and had worked as a *grumete* on the ships plying to Sierra Leone and Gambia: he claimed that his freedom in Cacheu was widely known, and that he had been sold illegally to Bautista Pérez, who had then taken him to Cartagena.[2]

Crispina and Jorge were themselves deeply involved in this traffic in the 1650s and 1660s. Jorge's father Álvaro had frequently done business in Cartagena in the 1620s and 1630s, and there were many accusations against him for carrying far larger numbers of Africans in his ships than he declared in order to avoid paying the requisite taxes to the Spanish crown. Meanwhile, although Jorge was ill and

---

* It is important to remember that numbers do not give a full sense of impacts, given that the world's population in c.1600 is estimated to have been around 500 million people, or approximately 6 per cent of the population today. Therefore the numbers involved had an impact on their home communities much larger than similar numbers would produce today, and have to be multiplied by fifteen or twenty times to give a comparable figure in today's population terms.

## The Heretic of Cacheu

travelling little by the time of the trial, his frequent trading trips to Farim and Sierra Leone in better years were all part of the complex jigsaw in which the traffic was central. The row he had with his godson Domingos de Aredas developed in part because Aredas had 'stolen' some of the captives with whom he had returned to Cacheu from a trafficking mission in the Bijagós islands. As for Crispina, she claimed to the Inquisitors that the word of enslaved members of her household should not be taken at face value because of the cruelty with which she treated them all.[3]

The significance of the traffic to the daily life of Cacheu and of the towns and villages nearby was evoked by the priest Manoel Álvares in the early 1610s:

> Here between six and ten large ships come each year to buy slaves for the Indies . . . and for this reason all the merchandise from the world, and from Guinea, congregates here, being redistributed from here to the other trading ports; and all forms of currency are converted into that of slavery.[4]

This last point is central: for the enslaved human being was the ultimate unit of economic value for the trafficking economy. As documents from the 1630s show, the entire economic ecosystem of the imperial world of this region depended on this system of value. In 1636, for instance, the senior vicar of Ribeira Grande in Santiago, Cabo Verde, wrote to Cacheu to underwrite the purchase of fifteen captives, whom he received so that they could be 'bought according to the orders of the most Illustrious Bishop of [Cabo Verde]'. The vicar then ordered that the accountant of the town should bring the captives to Santiago island for the bishop's use, in exchange for 712 bundles of Caboverdean *barafula* cloths.[5]

Everyone, at all levels of administration, was involved. But beyond the economic significance of the traffic, Manoel Álvares also provided a haunting glimpse of how people were captured and enslaved in the first place.

> The slave traffickers buy some captives who have been stolen, and in fact many of them are . . . bringing them to the ships by night, thieving them from the Biafada and Bainunk peoples . . . many are captured being said to practise witchcraft, accused by caprice, only for the whole house and family to be finished off.[6]

The stolen captives were taken aboard the Atlantic ships on lighters. On one 1635 ship, the *St Vincent* captained by Juan Diaz Copete, the captives were then taken off the ship in these small boats while the customs inspection was being made – all to 'make the numbers add up'. Huge distortion and abuse of human life, and the imperial coffers, was being carried out. Of the 130 people accounted for by Diaz Copete, twenty were young boys and girls. 'Ten per cent' of the cargo was written off in the account books for deaths en route. When the ship was eventually inspected on its arrival in Cartagena, the crew said that a far higher number than this had lost their lives during the Middle Passage. And yet the numbers never added up: the inspector found 153 captive survivors on board the ship, who had been crammed onto this vessel in the port of Cacheu, along with those many human beings who had died at sea.[7]

This immense cruelty was made possible by a process of dehumanization which was implicit in the ways in which the enslaved were treated in the town. Captors made systematic attempts to strip the humanity of enslaved people in Cacheu and other colonial towns of the region such as Farim, beginning with the refusal to ascribe to them a name. This was even the case among many household captives not necessarily destined for the Atlantic traffic: by denying them a name, their captors were making clear that their legal status did not protect them from anything, and that they too could be destined for the holds of the trafficking ships, in spite of all the work they did for the household.

The evidence on the lack of names is exemplified by the testimony of Pedro Nunes from Farim, who, when asked the names of the women whom the priest Luis Rodrigues was said to have slept with there, replied 'that he did not know their names or dare to know them, since some were slaves, and others free, people of low standing'. A similar attitude was shown by the boatswain Sebastião Vaz, who lived in Vila Quente, and who claimed that 'he knows personally all these Black women but that he does not know their names'. This workaday belittling of humanity was common in Ribeira Grande as well as in Cacheu: in Luis Rodrigues's trial one witness claimed to know all the female slaves of Maria Gonsalves, who was his neighbour, even though he had not learnt their names.[8]

Nevertheless, it is worth noting that things were a little more complicated in Crispina and Jorge's household. Here, some household slaves did have African names. One of Crispina's slaves was called Eiria, and, as we have seen, the couple's daughter was called Ohanbú. Crispina also had a daughter called Cassilha. Many names of Christianized women in Vila Quente revealed their ethnic origins, such as Isabel Bahelampa, where the surname means 'moon' in the Biafada language. Just as their house was a meeting point for peoples from all backgrounds, so Crispina and Jorge's attitude to names and the humanity of the enslaved was perhaps more nuanced than that of others in their peer group – no doubt largely because of the close ties which they had forged with surrounding communities.[9]

Stripping the enslaved of their names was a key step in the process of objectification and commodification which, in the corrupted eyes of the tormentors, legitimized captivity. This workaday horror of the trafficking business sat alongside daily life, which continued almost without a pause for thought. The people of the town bought clothes and prepared food, carpenters and carvers produced benches and salt cellars, everybody said their prayers, and many consulted oracles. Life continued, even as the cruelty which also made all of this possible continued beneath people's noses.

One of the enormous problems in writing about the history of slavery in Africa is in the generalizations that surround the debates.

Since 'Africans' participated in the capture and sale of captives for the traffic, there are those who say that they are equally responsible for the crimes committed. Such generic judgements may salve consciences, but they do not aid in understanding what went on. For the people who lived in Cacheu in the seventeenth century did not see themselves as 'African'. They were Floup, Kristón (Catholic Africans who often were or had been *grumetes*, often of mixed African-Portuguese heritage), Biafada, Pepel or Bainunk, they worshipped at this or that *china*, consulted Tamba Dibi and other snake-spirits and might also consult the Jakhanké Islamic clerics or go to the Catholic Church. If they were attacked, this was not an attack by other 'Africans' but by enemies who wanted their land or to make a profit, or who worshipped at a different shrine.

Among these peoples there were those who participated in the traffic, and there were others who fought it fiercely. Often this came down to a question of class. The Bainunk king of Guinguim was prepared to compromise with the Portuguese on religious matters for fear of losing access to trade. Despite this, the Portuguese trading settlements in both Bugendo and then Cacheu were under constant threat of assault, presumably from those with nothing to lose and everything to gain by this. Meanwhile, there were other groups who frequently attacked the Portuguese traffickers and would kill them if they could.

One account written by two Capuchin missionaries in Bissau in 1686 described quite clearly a gulf growing up between the different peoples of the region in their views on slavery. The Capuchins – Francisco Mota and Angel Fuente de la Peña – wrote how two major purveyors of captives to the traders in Cacheu were the Bijagó islanders ('where the big ocean-going ships and most of our vessels in these parts go just to buy slaves') and the Fulani from the Fouta Djalon mountains ('whose profession and office is that of bandits, and they have no other except to rob Blacks in these rivers . . . and these form a large part of those who are sold'). The major buyers were the Kristón, 'Creole Christians of this land, who are those who most go in to buy them', something which the Englishman Richard

## The Heretic of Cacheu

Jobson had noted in The Gambia sixty years earlier, when he had written that it was the mixed heritage Afro-Portuguese who dominated the traffic in the enslaved.[10]

Meanwhile, the profits and loss associated with the trade in humans meant that there was increasing political disorder. The Floup, Pepel and Bainunk who lived near Cacheu also conducted raids on one another, which led to some being captured and sold as slaves. The people of Cacheu such as Crispina and Jorge had many household slaves and were themselves deeply connected to the traffic. However, it was the Bijagó, the Fulani and the Kristón who were the main groups involved in Guinea-Bissau. The Bijagó continued to worship at *chinas*, the Fulani were Muslim, and the Kristón were Catholics who traded with the Atlantic traffickers, themselves often converted Jews escaping the Inquisition: people belonging to all these groups were involved in this nasty business.

However, this 1686 Capuchin account also made it clear that many of the people who lived in Senegambia resisted the traffic. Cacheu was frequently attacked by Pepel warriors for much of the seventeenth century. Meanwhile, near Cacheu, groups of Floup warriors often raided passing ships, gathering when the sound of their *bonbolón* drum was made. They aimed to kill the whites and capture the Africans on the ship. The killing of a European was something 'which they are very ostentatious about, holding themselves to be a great knight, and brave, he who has killed a European, and to show this off they put their head at the tip of their lance, and show it off as with triumph'. Manoel Bautista Pérez's captive, the Sapi Francisco Martín, had himself experienced this in around 1612 when working as a crew-member on one of the ships plying the coast: his ship had been captured by a group of Africans at war, who had killed the captain and the pilot and tied up everyone else on the vessel, whether free or enslaved.[11]

In fact, according to the Capuchins Mota and de la Peña, it was impossible to find anyone along the São Domingos river who would defend the trade in enslaved Africans. It is worth bearing in mind that all the peoples whom they identified as the traffic's strongest adherents were outsiders to Cacheu. The Fulani came from the highlands of the Fouta Djalon and had themselves migrated almost within living memory from the north of Senegal. The Bijagó were descended from people who had fled the mainland and the advance of the armies of the Mali empire in earlier centuries and perhaps nursed grievances of their own against the peoples who now lived there. And the Kristón purchasers were outsiders by definition, Catholics of mixed African-Atlantic world heritage. Those Africans who came from Cacheu itself and its hinterland were often fiercely opposed to the traffic, and the everyday realities of slavery in the town were accompanied by many acts of struggle and resistance against it.[12]

While the different peoples of Senegambia had different approaches to slavery, this was also a time of changing views for some from Europe. The new mood followed a *cause célèbre*: two years before the Capuchin memorandum from Bissau, in 1684, the Angolan prince Lourenço de Silva Mendonça had taken a legal challenge to the Vatican for the abolition of Atlantic slavery. Mendonça was a prince of the kingdom of Ndongo and the representative of the Black religious brotherhoods of the Rosary from across the Atlantic world – both in Lisbon and Seville, and from the Americas and Angola. He had argued that slavery was against divine, civil, natural and human law. The result of the Vatican case was concern in the colonial councils of Portugal and Spain that the divine court on earth might rule for the abolition of Atlantic slavery: this had led officials in Lisbon to make the tiniest change in their approach, instituting new laws against the overcrowding of captive Africans on trafficking ships, in a cursory attempt to smooth things over with the Papacy.[13]

As we saw in the previous chapter, the Black brotherhood of the Rosary organized processions at Carnival before Lent in Cacheu. The Mendonça case must therefore have been known to people in the town. Doubtless, the two Capuchin missionaries felt that this was a good moment to make the case for the injustice and illegality, in divine and human law, of the traffic. Mota and de la Peña conducted interviews and concluded that 'the said contract for slaves is

## The Heretic of Cacheu

illicit, sinful, and unjust . . . since most and indeed almost all of the enslaved are tyrannically and unjustly brought into captivity.' This was considered by their superiors in Rome for some time, until a decree was issued that in every trading town a priest should be stationed to inquire whether those enslaved had been captured in 'just war', and to catechize them before they were despatched in chains to the Americas; as far as they were concerned, this concluded the matter.[14]

In the end, moral scruples would not get in the way of the traffic. The forces of empire and of the nascent capitalism which made this world tick had decreed that nothing should stop it. As the seventeenth century unwound, and with the economic and political pressures in Senegambia from the Atlantic empires growing stronger year by year, a world without this institution functioning as a core aspect of daily life had become almost unthinkable.

The daily presence of slavery in Cacheu leaps from the historical documents considered in this book – from the earliest ones in the 1610s to Crispina's trial coming to a head in 1665. Manoel Bautista's account register from 1613 is as apt a place as any to start trawling through this tale of sorrow.

One folio begins, 'Blacks that I have in my house', and then itemizes a detailed list which begins to give a sense of what these realities meant in Cacheu. Bautista Pérez accounts for the costs of branding a Bainunk young man for Domingos Fernandes. He sold a young woman to a Kassanké nobleman, while Roque Pereira 'paid me nine Blacks' on account for the ten he had given 'in merchandise' the last time (with an enslaved person the unit of account). The religious visitor of the town bought a Pepel young woman in chains from him. On 1 November he bought two young women from Pero Moreno for forty-five bundles of blue-and-white *barafula* cloth from Cabo Verde. Three days later, Pero Vaz paid him two young men – one Biafada and one Mandinga – in exchange for others whom Bautista Pérez had 'lent' him. He branded one captive to give to the *griots* of Cacheu, and on 25

## Slavery and Human Trafficking

November bought from Pero Nunes a young Floup man and woman for forty-five bars of iron. The captives that he had in his home were all thus accounted for in terms of profit and loss, the purchases and sales annotated punctilliously in his account-book entries.[15]

Captives were kept in irons in the store-buildings of the fortified houses we came across in Chapter 3, awaiting transport to the Americas. This was so normal that, in one of his account book entries, Manoel Bautista Pérez noted that someone owed him '6 chains which I lent him'. In these circumstances, it was vital that everyone knew the status of everyone else in the settlement. This is clear from all these documents, which routinely show witnesses describing others according to whether they were enslaved or free. Naturally, the condition of enslavement therefore also went with a desperation to regain freedom. In Crispina's trial, her own household slave Sebastião Rodrigues Barraza claimed that he had only denounced Crispina because he had been promised freedom. He was, he said, 'a piece of cattle with no pasture': as he put it, 'there are slaves in Guinea who would throw away their lives for a fishbone or a flask of wine or brandy, and even more so for the manumission they promised me.' According to him, both the captain-general of Cacheu, Antonio de Fonseca de Ornelas, and Ambrosio Gomes had got him drunk on wine and brandy and promised him his freedom, bribing him 'with ribbons and shoes and buttons and all that which I most needed': believing that the elusive freedom was within his grasp, according to Barraza, he had therefore sworn falsely in Crispina's trial.[16]

It becomes clear from looking at these details just how routine the buying and selling of human beings was in Cacheu. The Atlantic merchants were constantly exchanging captives for merchandise, and vice versa. When traffickers like Bautista Pérez were preparing their 'shipments', they produced detailed lists of their transactions. On 8 August he might buy a Bainunk young woman called Violante; on the 10th he might buy a number of captives from different people, perhaps in some social event at his house in exchange for four barrels of wine; and on the 12th he might buy a Floup young man from the *griots*. Six people were bought over five days, while wine was exchanged, and drunk, and merchandise put away by those who had come to trade. None of this was viewed as remarkable in the account books, or unusual: this was normality, as much a part of normality as the drinking of wine or listening to the *griots* sing their histories of the derring-do of the ancestors from the distant past.[17]

The involvement of the *griots* – praise-singers playing instruments such as the *ngoni* and *balafon* – gives a wider sense of how the practice of slavery took shape within a broader framework of daily life in Cacheu. Many accounts of the time describe the role of the *griots* in Senegambian society, especially among the Jolof and the Mandinga. The *griots* of the kingdom of Kaabu became especially famed, and the kora harp known widely today originated in this part of West Africa, probably in the eighteenth century. The presence of the *griots* in Cacheu is an indication of the importance of the Jakhanké preachers and traders that we saw in the previous chapter, since *griots* were also a core part of Mandinga society.[18]

However, *griots* had a mixed role in Senegambian society. Lemos Coelho wrote in the 1660s that 'their profession is to play their instruments . . . dance and sing, and to be like buffoons who accompany their warriors into battle to encourage the troops with their songs.' They only married among themselves and no one else would touch them, since they were held to be shameless, forming themselves as something of a pariah caste.[19]

In his account books, Bautista Pérez used the word in the Kriol language for *griot*, which is *djidiu* – derived from *judeu* ('Jew') in Portuguese. This label emerged as early as 1506, as one account puts it:

> In this land [of the Wolofs] and among the Mandinga there are Jews called *Gaul* [gawol] and they are black like the people of the land although they do not have synagogues nor practice the rites of the other Jews. And they do not live with the other Blacks but apart in their own villages.[20]

In other words, the label occurred because of the fact that the *griots* were ostracized in Senegambian society, as the Jews were in Portugal, and lived in their own ghetto neighbourhoods just like the Jews lived in their *juderías*. These were people who lived apart, married one another and were buried not in a communal cemetery but in the hollowed-out trunks of baobab trees. Nevertheless, from the accounts of Bautista Pérez it appears that *griots* did live close to Cacheu. When he was preparing his shipment of captives to Cartagena in 1613, Bautista Pérez bought captives on four separate occasions from 'the *griots*', three Pepels and one Floup. And in 1614 he accounted for buying a pregnant slave 'from a *griot* in his [the griot's] house'. Why, then, were the *griots* involved in this business? As we have already seen in this chapter, many who lived locally to Cacheu could not defend the traffic. This was something which outsiders profited from the most: Atlantic traffickers, the Fulani, and the Bijagó. Since the *griots* were also deemed as outsiders in Senegambian society, their participation in this business formed part of their general isolation and marginalization from the core community.[21]

So harrowing were the conditions of enslavement that illness and death were, of course, commonplace. The Atlantic slaving ships were known in Brazil as *tumbeiros*, floating tombs: in Bautista Pérez's account books they are given a related name, *tumbaquos*. Captives awaiting transport were sometimes taken off the ships in the harbour because they were ill. On one shipment in 1618, Bautista Pérez removed eighty captives from a ship in Cacheu's dock because they were suffering from a range of illnesses in the stomach, the arm, the teeth, or from fever. This was not some kind of humane generosity: he could not risk the economic loss which would follow if their illness infected the rest of the ship. By March, Bautista Pérez was accounting for the deaths of many of these people who had not survived the trauma and despair of their capture, enchainment, transport to the ship and the anticipation of what seemed a certain, cruel and dishonourable death: one beautiful young Nalú man died from smallpox, a woman who was 'very good' died on 3 March, and another 'very beautiful' young man on 11 March.[22]

The relationship between slavery and death was a central one. The struggles over life and the power of death were essential to enslavement. The will of some of the enslaved to live was naturally weakened by the appalling conditions of capture and transport. On the other hand, the captors needed to eke out the lives of those they tormented in order to reap their own account-book profits. The power to heal, to make life endure, was something that related not only to the sanctity of life in Cacheu, but also to the rise of modern capitalism. Only by winning the struggle over life and death would traffickers be able to realize their profits in the plantations and mines of the Americas.[23]

If the captors lost, they needed all the same to account for their 'losses'. Bautista Pérez's accounts for 1614 contained a 'Memorandum of the Blacks who died on me in the ship belonging to Antonio Rodrigues da Costa, and of the people who they belonged to'. The list accounted for twenty-six human beings and noted also on which parts of the body they had been branded: whether on the right or left arm, or on the right pectoral. It was followed by an accounting of the thirteen human beings of his property who had then died on or before their arrival in Cartagena, including one whom he had 'given as alms to the friars of San Diego'.[24]

Thus do the accountings of profit and loss reveal the workaday cruelty of the traffickers who lived in Cacheu in the seventeenth century. A different facet of the town's life emerges. Alongside the market-vendors and the busy trading canoes drawing to portside with their wares, a sadder picture comes into focus, in which cruelty and the death that followed were also central to the town, alongside the laments from the funerals so often heard coming from the direction of Vila Quente, where people were desperate – for reasons both noble and greedy – to find the salve of healing and eager to turn to those who offered it.

The details of this accounting begin to give a deeper picture of the role of slavery in daily life in Cacheu and the many ways it was manifested. This institution kept a house like Crispina and Jorge's afloat – economically, socially and in terms of the work that was done there. The imprints of enslavement could not be erased. They were there in the storerooms in which captives were kept awaiting shipment, in the agony of the brandings that took place there to mark ownership and in the passage of captives in chains to and from the house, bought and sold as part of complex ledgers which made sense at least to the couple and to those who were their debtors.

However, perhaps the most salient aspect of the economic role of slavery in a household like Crispina and Jorge's was in the capital that it enabled them to acquire. It was this capital, after all, that allowed them to acquire the extravagant taffetas from China and Mexico, and the luxury foods like almonds, dried figs and Alentejo cheeses. But how did they go about it? Capital had to be exportable: that is, it had to come in a form of money that could be converted into goods that could be carried overseas and exchanged there in other commercial transactions. What forms of money existed in Cacheu which could be taken out of Senegambia? As we have already seen in this chapter, the enslaved captive was becoming the ultimate arbiter of economic value. This means that understanding the relationship between enslavement and money is essential in understanding how the traffic was linked to capital accumulation in the seventeenth century: a pithy summary would be that enslavement produced the financial credit which lubricated the entire trading system and helped it to expand in this period of history.

The Bautista Pérez account books are the best place to start to try to figure this out. For here, in countless places, it is the human being that is the measure of account against which other goods are measured. In one 1617 list, for instance, flagons of wine are accounted for at '28 per Black', while iron bars are listed as having the same price. Valued cloth such as the Indian cannequins also held their own price in human beings, as did handkerchiefs – with one bundle worth 'a Black and a half'. There was also a differentiation between enslaved humans as an accounting measure ('A Black of payment'/*um negro de pagamento*) and enslaved human beings as persons in captivity moved from seller to buyer (*um negro por si*). The reality that people were currency emphasizes how significant the trade in enslaved Africans was to generating economic capital in world history.[25]

The other core account-book currency was the bolt of cloth. Sometimes this was the *barafula* from Cabo Verde, often listed as an accounting currency (with, in one transaction of 1613, a *barafula* accounting for the purchase of some millet). And it was very common for lists of merchandise to be valued in their cloth valuations, as one list from 1613 of the goods owed by one Antonio Pinto make clear: flagons of wine, bottles of rum, cases of jam, blankets and the value of an apprentice (*mancebo*) were all measured in their cloth currency equivalents. This does not mean that actual bolts of cloth were measured out for each transaction, but it does show the importance and ubiquity of Senegambian textiles in the town: this was a universally valued item of trade, whose worth every merchant could understand as it was transferred to other items.[26]

Yet, while cloth was a transferrable form of currency within Senegambia, it coexisted with global forms of money in Cacheu and the surrounding areas. Gold was mined in the upper reaches of the Senegal and Gambia rivers: this was why Richard Jobson had visited in the 1620s, and was also of interest to the Royal Africa Company trader Cornelius Hodges in 1690. The Bautista Pérez account books show meanwhile that silver circulated quite widely. There were silver bars in the town, alongside minted coin (the *reales*). On 20 June 1614, Manoel Bautista Pérez accounted for going to one Mateus da Costa's home and giving him 100 *reales*, or silver pieces of eight (*reales de a ocho*). Over the next two months, Bautista Pérez gave him a total of 976 *reales*, which were spent on a very wide range of goods, and also loaned out to other people in the town. Gold also changed hands, with Manoel also accounting for giving 1,064 *reales* in gold to Jeronimo de Torres in 1614.[27]

In other words, capital in Cacheu was made through the intersection of Atlantic and African currency zones. Traffickers made money by maxing out their payments to African traders with African-centred currencies, while exporting 'goods' that were convertible elsewhere: gold and human beings. This system meant that there were multiple currencies in operation, as has often been normal in world history.

Silver '*daalder*' (forerunner of the dollar) coin minted by the United Amsterdam Company in 1601, equivalent in weight to the Spanish 8 *reales* coin.

Payments in the town and in the surrounding region were made in Senegambian currencies: iron bars, cloth, kola nuts and hides. Very low-grade purchases – such as confession from the priest in Cacheu – could be satisfied by paying a chicken. Crispina sent money to the *djabakós* in Sara and Bugendo before she got married so that they would perform the relevant offerings at the *chinas*. This meant that, for small purchases and payments, money had to be quite easy to move around.[28]

For bigger trades, merchants kept bolts of cloth in rolls of forty in their warehouses. When Manoel Bautista Pérez's brother João died in 1617, he noted that the executor of his goods had 'a roll which has 40 cloths to pay out to people'. This cloth was then used to pay traders and workmen for merchandise and other services, with the merchants peeling off the measures of cloth for flagons of wine, pieces of copper and chickpeas as the fancy took them. Some African traders would come to Cacheu to receive cloth on credit to then take to sell in the bush. Meanwhile, the role of the iron bar as a form of currency – important for blacksmiths in making weapons and agricultural tools – was shown by Rodrigues Barraza in Crispina's trial, when he described himself as 'interested in . . . the shirt and the iron bar'.[29]

On the other hand, the Atlantic economy prized different sources of value. Gold and silver circulated and could be 'cashed out' and exported by the winners in this cruel game. Fines in the Inquisitorial trial of Crispina were measured in *cruzados*, not cloth and iron bars. The silver in the town came, indirectly, from the mines of Potosí and was a source of exchange and capital. Much of the gold was mined locally, and both gold and silver could be convertible globally – as could the enslaved human beings whose work underwrote the whole brutal and brutalizing system, a system so integral to daily life in Cacheu that many visitors hardly mentioned it.[30]

One of the questions that has preoccupied many historians of slavery is how far this terrible history built on existing African institutions. Some have tended to emphasize this relationship as somehow organic, imputing thereby at least mutual responsibility for the growing trade to Africa and Africans. However, in an essay written almost sixty years ago, the Guyanese historian Walter Rodney pointed out that the earliest accounts of Europeans in this part of Africa made very little commentary on forms of slavery. The only exception was in areas to the north of the Gambia river, where the political elites had already converted to Islam by the 1400s. Yet within a couple of centuries the social context had changed radically, and forms of slavery were routinely described by visitors in Senegambia. Rodney's argument was that this was strong evidence that the Atlantic institution of slavery had corrupted forms of dependence known in West Africa prior to the Portuguese arrival there. In other words, the forms of violence we have just encountered were produced by the growing influence of Atlantic imperial forces on the societies of Senegambia, and by economic demand.[31]

Various additional pieces of evidence support Rodney's contention. Certainly, there were many in Guinea-Bissau who attributed the trade in captives to the demand coming from the Atlantic. The legal status of people in Cacheu depended absolutely on the Roman concepts of slavery from which Iberian empires derived their practices. In their 1686 memorandum arguing for the injustice and illegality of the Atlantic traffic, the two Capuchin missionaries recounted the response given to them by a nobleman from Bissau when discussing the issue:

> Father, we know very well that this is wrong, but we see that the whites employ all their money in seeking out slaves, so that it seems they don't want anything else. And so we go to look for them too ... because they give us money for this; if they bought something else, we would trade in that instead.[32]

According to these perspectives, the Atlantic institution of slavery had a guiding influence in Cacheu. Relationships of dependency and compelled labour had, of course, existed beforehand in Africa, like anywhere else in the world at this time, but the concept of the ownership of another person – and the consequent stripping of rights and agency that were implied – came from the Roman legal system. It was this institution which shaped the way in which slavery existed both in Cacheu and in the wider region. Crispina's trial provides strong evidence that as the seventeenth century unwound imperial European concepts of enslavement were in the ascendancy, even if African traditions of dependency and associated labour remained in place.

As we saw in the first chapter, Crispina herself was quite happy to acknowledge the cruelty with which she used her own slaves; presumably she thought this would not surprise the Inquisitors, since after all there were many enslaved people in Lisbon, where she was then imprisoned. This meant that all their evidence about her 'heresy' should be discarded, according to her. Other witnesses gave testimony which supports her account. According to Vicente Rodrigues Duarte, at one point she had imprisoned one of her household slaves called Eiria and refused to let her go to confession, 'saying that she would die without confessing, as indeed she did'. Another witness, Gaspar Pegado, noted that she had spent all this time 'keeping her in shackles, which were only taken off her after she had died': according to Pegado, Jorge had been angry about this act of cruelty, and argued with Crispina because of it.[33]

On the other hand, household slaves could often move with

considerable freedom in the streets of Cacheu and beyond. Sebastião Rodrigues Barraza put it like this: 'I never lived in the home of my mistress and always lived as a free person outside the house.' Rodrigues Barraza was often sent on errands to the towns and creeks outside Cacheu. Crispina also sent 'her women' to perform errands for her, and one witness recounted that she had sent one 'to the land of the heathens to . . . make sacrifices to the idols'. This was the enslaved woman Bonifacia, whom we met in Chapter 1, who according to Rodrigues Barraza was Crispina's accomplice in the matter of the *chinas* and kept pans and pots with blood from the sacrifices of goats under her bed, which were then mixed with herbs and palm wine and taken for offering to the shrines.[34]

However, as with much of Rodrigues Barraza's evidence, there may have been more to this denunciation than met the eye. The trial papers show complex emotional worlds behind much of what was said here. Rodrigues Barraza was married – according to him, to the sister of the king of Cazil – and yet, at the same time, others said that he was in love with this slave of Crispina, Bonifacia, who went to make offerings to the *chinas*. This denunciation may therefore have come because of a sense of ill-feeling at some emotional loss, since Bonifacia had since died – something that might also explain his apparent turn to being an inveterate drinker.[35]

The priest Friar Sebastião de Sao Vicente, the scribe of the trial, put it like this:

> Crispina Peres . . . had two female slaves, one of the Bainunk caste and the other from the island of Santiago, who performed *chinas* for her in the land of the heathens; and because the said slave Sebastião had fallen in love with the said Black slave woman, from the island of Santiago, as he had raised her, he reprehended her once, saying that she should not engage in the arts of the Devil, as she was a Christian, and knew what was Christian.[36]

This detail makes it quite clear that the life of the household slave was quite different from that of the enslaved person in chains awaiting transport to the Americas. Household slaves were taught to communicate in Portuguese so that they could be useful in Atlantic trade. They developed their own emotional ties in Cacheu and could be married in the town, as Rodrigues Barraza was. He had his own social life and had been able to spend two weeks away from Crispina and Jorge's house in the run-up to the trial – getting drunk in the houses of their enemies, according to Crispina. That this kind of social life and exchange was normal is clear from the trial of Luis Rodrigues, where a witness called Sebastião Vaz describes a conversation he had had with 'the Black slave of Luis Gomes called Pascoala' about the priest's drunken parties and sexual behaviour: these kinds of casual conversations hint at the broader social life and exchange for household captives in these small Atlantic trading settlements of West Africa.[37]

This ambiguous social position derived from the fact that Cacheu was between two worlds and legal systems, the African and the imperial Atlantic. African institutions of dependency and belonging allowed for this kind of movement. Household slaves in the colonial worlds of the Americas also could often move within urban spaces, conducting errands for the house and sometimes setting up their own businesses as healers, through which they might eventually be able to raise enough money to buy their liberty. On the other hand, the fact was that under imperial Portugal's inherited Roman law these individuals were the property of the house in a way which was quite different in places like Cacheu and Farim to the situation in other parts of Senegambia.[38]

This created a fraught and fearful emotional world, which was never far beneath the surface and might help to explain the desperate drunkenness and casting around of someone like Rodrigues Barraza in search of his freedom. Fear of being deported to the Americas, and a deep knowledge of the cruelty and inhumanity that this would mean, lay at the bottom of all this. Although most captives destined for the Atlantic ships came from further afield as war captives or criminals, anyone could suffer this fate – even a trusted household member. The reality of this is brought home in an account of one of Crispina's slaves, almost certainly the Bainunk companion to Bonifacia who had been her ally in the sacrifices to the *chinas* with the liquids kept beneath beds in the house. The witness Maria Mendes described how 'the blood . . . was poured into the sea by a Black female slave of Crispina Peres who later would go to the Spanish Indies.'[39]

In other words, status as a household slave was not enough to protect people from being clapped in chains, branded, canoed out to one of the waiting floating tomb-ships and transported to the Americas. In this way, the institution of chattel slavery from the Iberian colonies was never far from the minds of those who lived their lives as household slaves in Cacheu. It was a fate which could await any one of them, if the accounting books of credit and debt so demanded: given the way in which the demand for forced labour from the Americas had transformed the political dynamic of the region, by the middle of the seventeenth century this became almost inevitable.

Sitting just a short distance offshore from the African mainland, the Bijagós islands have for many centuries been a place of escape from coercive state power. In the thirteenth and fourteenth centuries, people from the continent fled here from the advance of armies from the empire of Mali. During the twentieth century, the islands were the last holdout against Portuguese colonial power, only finally being 'pacified' in 1936 – just thirty-five years before the start of Guinea-Bissau's war of independence. In the early years of the twenty-first century, airstrips built in the colonial era were said to have been rehabilitated by drug-runners from Colombia as a means of flying in cocaine from the Americas en route to Europe – with little anyone could do to stop them.

During the seventeenth century, the Bijagó islanders became well known in Cacheu for their role in the trade in enslaved Africans. The Bijagós' history of escape from persecution meant that they had no scruples about repaying their history with interest, launching off in war canoes in order to raid their neighbours on the mainland. One account from the 1640s described their impact on their Pepel, Floup and Bainunk neighbours in stark terms:

> the people of these islands live from the robbing and kidnapping raids which they make against others, especially in kingdoms which border them, where they have destroyed seventeen or eighteen kings . . . the cause of a great loss for the [Spanish] royal treasury since when these kingdoms were in good shape many more Africans left from here.[40]

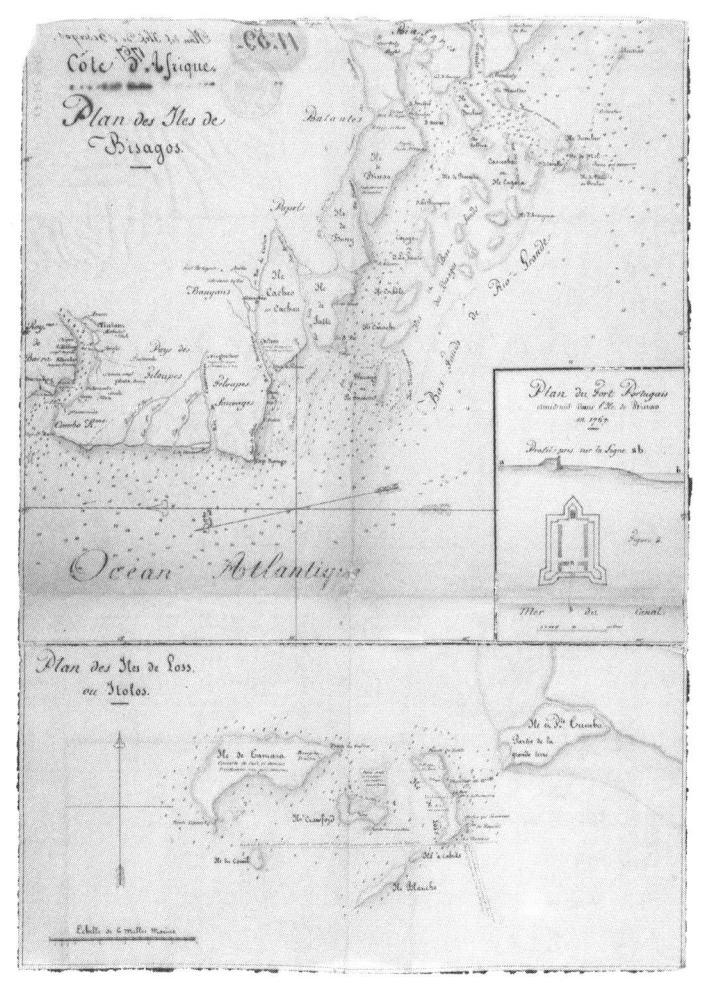

Map of the Bijagó islands, 1767.

## The Heretic of Cacheu

While the legal framework of chattel slavery thus came from the Iberian colonies, the demand for captives drove strong political impacts in Africa. On the one hand, it catalysed political change, as this quote suggests, and on the other, as we will now see, it also produced a strong tradition of struggle against this economic framework and a commitment to try to renew the strength of existing institutions in Senegambia. Both responses coexisted and were in conflict, as the various struggles for power – imperial, religious and economic – took shape.

Increasing competition was a central part of the changes. It was this that led to the willingness of rulers like the Bainunk king of Guinguim to host Catholic missionaries, in order to safeguard access to the trade which had become necessary for political survival. Without access to the Atlantic trade in weaponry, and to the iron bars which the smiths melted down to make the tools that could shape stockade defences and agricultural tools to increase food security, collapse seemed a certain fate: whether in the face of attacks from the Bijagó or from the rulers of Kaabu, who were now equally involved in procuring captives for the Atlantic traffic. The irony was to be that the Bainunk rulers who did engage with the trade, in Guinguim and further north in Casamance, near Sanguedogu, were also the people who experienced the greatest political decline in the centuries ahead – very few people in Casamance and Guinea-Bissau identify as Bainunk today.[41]

By the mid-seventeenth century, therefore, the growth of chattel slavery in the Atlantic empires had begun to have some impact both in Cacheu and in the surrounding region. This was an impact not just on political elites dependent on trade but also on the institutions of Senegambia. In the 1640s Jorge had been able to negotiate to buy the freedom of the Aredas family from the king of Sara, meaning that the concepts of hostages and of enslavement had apparently begun to influence some rulers by then. On the other hand, these rulers clearly also felt that there was corruption of existing institutions involved. Some of them, according to Sebastião Rodríguez Barraza, 'did not trust those [enslaved Africans] who came from the Whites but returned them to the Whites'.

Others, like the Floup who raided European ships and killed their captains and pilots, kept the enslaved whom they freed from these vessels until they felt that the debt had been repaid, whereupon they were released – incorporating them within a more Senegambian framework of debt, dependence and eventual freedom.[42]

There were therefore different responses to the impact of Atlantic concepts of slavery in this part of West Africa, something which generalizations will usually miss out. Some rulers accommodated the new dynamic to some degree but tried to maintain distance – other peoples, such as the Floup who attacked European ships and the Pepel who attacked Cacheu, challenged it with force. This crystallizes the patterns traced in this chapter and the one before. The rising economic demand for captive labour prompted the Bijagó raids and the changing views of enslavement, since, as the Bissau nobleman told the Franciscan missionaries in 1686, if other goods had been demanded they would have gone looking for them instead. Bijagó raids led to the political collapse of the Bainunk kingdoms around Cacheu, and their inability to continue the attacks on the fortified town which had greeted its foundation in the late sixteenth century. The political weakness that followed created an opening for Christian missionaries, leading to the conversions of the kings of Mata de Putame, Guinguim and Bissau. This then led the way to closer relationships with Atlantic empires and their Catholic religion in general: the ground was prepared for the intensification of these relationships in the centuries that followed.

Crispina's trial is a marker for this shifting balance of power in the seventeenth century, and the attempt by Portuguese institutions to stake a political claim in West Africa. Though the scales were tipping, however, traces of the pre-existing frameworks can also be found in the documents of the time. What these show us is that frameworks of law existed in West Africa different from those brought from the Atlantic: there were distinct concepts of slavery and freedom, and some leaders sought to retain these as one type of response to the changes driven by the demand for captive African labour for the Americas.

## The Heretic of Cacheu

Lemos Coelho describes this clearly when giving an account of the kingdom of Bujé in Casamance (whither Jorge had sent his nephew Francisco Tavares to seek a *djabakós*, as we saw in Chapter 4). Bujé, he said, was:

> very prejudicial to the residents who live in Cacheu, and in all of Guinea, because they refuse to return to the whites the Blacks who flee there for any money whatsoever. And today they have made a very large settlement of runaway Blacks, who would be worth a lot of money. And I felt this very keenly, because one time when my boat ran aground 15 captives fled, all of them carpenters, shipwrights, and blacksmiths, who were worth the same as 40 slaves to me, and in spite of the most careful efforts I could get none of them back.[43]

Clearly, in Bujé, the doctrine of chattel slavery meant nothing. Humans were not for sale at any price, and there was a different conception of money and value and the relationship these had to the human being. This differing legal system regarding enslavement is also clear in Crispina's trial. Rodrigues Barraza said of the captain-general of Cacheu de Ornelas that 'he did things in Guinea that heathens would not do, selling free people.' This suggests a clear concept of freedom in Senegambia, and also that the arguments of the Capuchin missionaries from 1686 on the illicitness of the trade in captives had strong grounds: those enchained and enslaved, transported to the Americas, had not been caught in 'just war'.[44]

Since this alternative political ideal was still alive and well in the region in the seventeenth century, it is not surprising that many enslaved captives in Cacheu sought to escape. Manoel Bautista Pérez's accounts are full of instances of this. In 1614, he accounted for the 'cargo which came to me in Guinea with the late Pedro Alberto', including two Africans who 'escaped from me', one Nalú man and a Black woman. The costs were annotated for those who 'brought them back to me', here and elsewhere in the accounts.

## Slavery and Human Trafficking

At other times Bautista Pérez himself organized the search and would charge this to his debtors, as with Diogo Rodrigues in 1615 who owed him 'for looking for eight of his slaves who fled to the bush'. These cursory financial details conceal worlds, of course: the worlds of those captives so desperate to escape their incarceration, plotting with others in their storehouses, trying to bribe guards, sneaking away, and the worlds of their captors, paying others to track them down, to return them in chains, so that the 'loss' could be avoided. Sometimes, the person could not be recovered and they fled for good – and were marked down as an irrevocable economic loss in the system of accounts.[45]

This again shows how different the concepts of dependence and slavery were in Senegambia from those in the Atlantic. There would have been no reason to flee had the institution of slavery in Africa been the same as the condition faced by captives in chains in Cacheu. The constant possibility of escape is clear not only from the accounts, but also from Crispina's trial. When she was arrested by the Inquisitors and the uprising from her allies in the surrounding region took hold, Jorge tried to quell the rebellion. Some of his slaves saw this not as a crisis but as an opportunity (as crises so often can be seen by some). As Jorge told the Inquisitors, 'some of his own Black slaves went out of this settlement, freeing themselves, [along with] some of the others [who] had fled into the bush since they were in their own lands.'[46]

In other words, proximity to lands of origin, to sacred land, shrines and kin, alongside knowledge that a different system of slavery and dependence was at work in Senegambia from that in Cacheu, made escape a constant desire for captives in the town. Resistance was everywhere. Enslaved people sought alliances with those who might help to restore their freedom; and others also sought advantage in such alliances, hoping to curry favour with the traffickers and make clear how indispensable they were (and why they should never be auctioned off to a different trafficker). Fear of the Atlantic slave system and a deeply painful knowledge of what it meant were thus at the heart of the conflict over power, life and the spirit which took shape in Cacheu over the course of the seventeenth century.

When the English Merchant Richard Jobson visited the Gambia river in 1623, he travelled far upriver from the Atlantic Ocean. At the town of Barrakunda, which was nearly as far east as the Atlantic vessels could sail, he met a merchant from a well-known Mandinga trading clan, whom he called 'Buckor Sano' in his text. Sano came aboard his ship one day 'about noon . . . with his music playing before him, with great solemnity, and his best clothes on, and about some 40 [people] more, armed with their bows and arrows'.[47]

This was a meeting which has become famous to historians of The Gambia and of the traffic in humans. Sano assumed that Jobson was interested in the trade in captives. However, when he put this to the Englishman, Jobson refused, saying proudly that the English did not traffic in people. This was true at the time, but Jobson's pride of course came before the fall:

> He showed unto me certain young Black women, who were standing by themselves, and had white strips across their bodies, which he told me were slaves, brought for me to buy . . . [and at my refusal] he seemed to marvel much at it, and told us, it was the only merchandise they carried down into the country . . . and that they sold there to white men, who earnestly desired them, especially young women as he had brought for us.[48]

Jobson described here the disturbing relationship between the Atlantic trade in human beings and the sexual objectification of the body by the people traffickers. The Atlantic men 'earnestly desired' these young enslaved women, as objectified beings for their own gratification. And this corrupted view of humanity is apparent not only in Jobson's narrative but also in the account books and Inquisition trial records, through their discussion of people as objects of trade.[49]

For it was through the objectification and measurement of their physical qualities that the enslaved mostly were described in these documents. In the trial of Luis Rodrigues, the doctor João de Palma who lived in Ribeira Grande described how 'one of his slaves, a beautiful girl called Lazara who is now dead' had refused to go and confess with Rodrigues since he had solicited her before in the confessional. Meanwhile, the Bautista Pérez account books were full of the description of captives who had died or escaped as 'beautiful'; otherwise, the books generally described the enslaved according to their heights, with captives being so-many palms tall. This sexual and physical objectification of human beings was just the other side of the coin of the account-book capitalism which could, to the eyes of commerce, justify their capture, purchase and sale.[50]

The inevitable conclusion of this objectification is evident in the way in which human beings themselves became accounted for as a form of transferrable currency, how the slave was a unit of account in which the transfer of other goods could be measured. This emerges from virtually every page of the Bautista Pérez accounts, which talks of 'a Black of payment', or of Bautista Pérez being 'paid' one Black woman by the king of Busis. Meanwhile, according to one witness, when the philandering priest Luis Rodrigues was in Cacheu in around 1656, he had told the New Christian João Rodrigues Duarte, who had been penanced by the Inquisition in Lima, that he needed to pay him 'eighty bars of iron which amounted to four Blacks' or else Rodrigues would force him to wear the penitential Sanbenito worn by those condemned by the Inquisition in the streets of Cacheu.[51]

This dehumanization of others became a core part of the outlook of the Atlantic traffickers in Cacheu. This was why Manoel Bautista Pérez could write blithely of having sent ships with '40 Blacks-worth of merchandise to [Cacheu] and another to the Bijagós with 75 Blacks-worth'. The reduction of human subjects, of personhood, to objective materiality was complete in this way. Once this had been done, any act of cruelty could be explained away. And then if the traffickers themselves died in Cacheu, their debts could be paid, as happened to Damião de Franca in 1618, when his executor paid 'seven slaves to João de Escovar . . . and I paid one Black to Fernão Duarte, and two slaves to Baltazar Gonçalves Querido . . . and to Ines Mendes a Black woman I paid one slave'.[52]

All this provides a crucial perspective on the way in which the violence of the institution of slavery was experienced in Cacheu. The enormous cruelty of the treatment of the enslaved meant that their 'owners' like Crispina did not trust them an inch, for they knew that they would do anything to escape – as many did. The objectification of the enslaved went with their sexual exploitation and the dehumanization of the enslaved as bodies to be accounted for according to their size, or their beauty in the eyes of their tormentors. All of this was then 'cashed out' in the reduction of people to units of account, which provided the clearest summary of all of the violent conversion of human capital to an 'objective' economic basis.

This meant that the health of the human was valued in purely economic terms – an outlook which some might say has continued more or less unchecked ever since. One document summarized this, a list of 'the injuries of the Blacks who belong to Mr Manoel Andrade': these included a Floup called Juan with a burn on his face, another Floup called Manoel with a cataract in his right eye, while a Bijagó called Bartolomeo had a cataract in his left eye, and a number of the captives had festering sores in their legs. All this mattered because of the economic value which could be apportioned to these people, and for no other reason at all. Thus did health, and economic prosperity, come to seem connected from the very beginning of the Atlantic trade in human beings.[53]

This outlook provoked a new way of defining relationships of human dependence in Senegambia. Local institutional ideas survived in the freedoms which some household slaves like Rodrigues Barraza retained. But the power of demand from the Atlantic meant that the more violent institution was in the ascendancy. There were many who forcefully resisted it: the Floup of the nearby creeks and forests, the Pepel who continually attacked Cacheu and the enslaved who found ways to escape and made their way to Bujé, where they formed a maroon settlement under the protection of the king in Casamance. For outsiders, however, this traffic was a way of strengthening their power and position in a region in flux.

For the Atlantic traffickers, this human suffering and trauma was transferred into economic capital which could be exported away from Cacheu. As the Bautista Pérez account books show, silver mined by Native American enforced labour in the mines of Potosí was the currency usually paid for enslaved Africans in Cacheu. This direct capitalization of human bodies was the clear outcome of the process of objectification and violence at the heart of this institution, and the workaday experience of it in the streets of Cacheu.[54]

# 7.

# *Work*

*'They live only from their labour, and their day-rate which is paid every day, some of them are caulkers and others are sailors, and then there are also many other men of the sea'*

Towns and cities are built by the people who work in them, and seventeenth-century Cacheu was no different. It was a town which existed because of the work people did to maintain it. Much of it was done by household slaves. It was they who often did the heavy-duty lifting and carrying of loads from the portside to the merchant houses, without which the commercial fabric of the town would have collapsed. Once they had stowed this merchandise away in the *combetes*, the bolts of cloth, provisions, luxury items of jewellery and tableware formed the backbone of the town's mercantile economy.

While this enslaved labour was key to those households, however, there was a whole other world of work in Cacheu without which the town would have collapsed. This was the work done by its carpenters, builders, cobblers, caulkers, cotton-spinners, bakers and blacksmiths. The work of these craftsmen and -women was commissioned and paid for. Wage labour was an important facet of most people's experience of the place. These workers lived in Cacheu and enjoyed themselves because of the money they earnt through their labour. That is one of the reasons why it's necessary to understand the currencies and financial transactions which underpinned the economy, as it helps to show how wage labour was integral to most people's experience of life in the town.

## Work

The missionary Manoel Álvares described in the 1610s just how important this labour was to the fabric of Cacheu, when he described 'the neighbourhood houses' (*cazas do bairro*) of the town (i.e., the neighbourhood where almost everyone lived):

> The neighbourhood belongs to the common and working people, all of whom are independent. They live only from their labour and their day-rate which is paid every day, some of them are caulkers and others are sailors, and then there are also many other men of the sea.[1]

This shows how much of the work of the town was done by people paid on day-labour rates. According to this account by Álvares, the majority of those who resided in the biggest neighbourhood of Cacheu made their living in this way. There was, too, a market in hiring out day labour from those who had household servants or dependents. In this case, dependents were hired out for work by their masters (who, of course, kept the proceeds), just as Manoel Bautista Pérez 'lent' seven young men to Pero Vaz de Morais on 3 September 1613 for a day's work, making a charge against it in his account book.[2]

Given how important work is to people's identities, it is impossible to understand the experience of daily life in this time and place without getting a meaningful sense of how it functioned there. In the urban spaces, women dominated the markets, traded widely and spun cotton for the weavers. They also worked as healers and bakers. Men tended to work in the shipping industry as caulkers and carpenters and were also cobblers and blacksmiths. Everyone worked, and through the money they earnt they were able to enjoy the entertainments that the town offered, as we will also see in the next chapter.

One of the most common-or-garden forms of work in Cacheu was trade. Senegambia offered nothing if not a market economy: not the kind that a little over a century later Adam Smith would dismiss as solely based in barter, but one which was financed through the currencies we came across in the last chapter. Richard Jobson said that trade was the main form of business of the whole of the Gambia river region, something that 'the whole country doth'. Certainly, the evidence of the records we have left supports his observation. Most free people in Cacheu earnt at least some of their money doing business: entrepreneurship based in social connections was at the heart of the way most people got along in life.

This is one of the reasons why the *combetes* of the big Atlantic traders were the centre of working life in Cacheu. Here, exhaustive lists were made of the goods received from traders in Lisbon. Then, merchants like Manoel Bautista Pérez would give some of these on credit to other merchants who were plying their trade in the rivers and creeks nearby – people whom he trusted because of the social networks that he shared with them. In 1617, he produced a long list of goods which he was giving to the pilot Francisco Rodrigues, half for him to trade on his account and half on credit for him to trade on behalf of Bautista Pérez. His brother João, meanwhile, gave out small bits of merchandise here and there to whoever came to see him: flagons of wine, bits of crystal, measures of kola nuts, all offered on credit to small-time merchants in the town, who would then have to repay through the universal value equivalents, captives or cloth. That this business life involved most people in the town is shown by a list of João Bautista Pérez's transactions from 1616: this included giving a shirt to a carpenter, a flagon of wine to a *grumete*, another to a ship-pilot who called in and several cloaks which were handed out to some more *grumetes*.[3]

This gives us a better sense of what the texture of this merchant working life was like. The *combetes* of people like the Bautista Pérez brothers were always busy, at the heart of Cacheu's sociability and networks of gossip. Some of the people who worked for these merchants would call in and demand cast-offs of some of the latest imports: overcoats or flagons of wine. Pilots whom they knew, or carpenters whom they needed to work carefully with, would ask for bits of clothing or some drink. This could be given out on credit, to be repaid through profits from trade in an upcoming voyage north to The Gambia or south to Sierra Leone. There was also, of course, a flux to this business: when ships had just arrived from Lisbon or Cartagena, these *combetes* must have been jam-packed with people seeking out new bargains or just curious as to how styles and demands were changing. Once the big players had satisfied their curiosity, then the day labourers and *grumetes* called in to have their picking for smaller-scale business and personal needs. Either way, what comes across most vividly is the range of people coming in and out of the storehouse, and then making off with some of the newly arrived goods: the clothes to show off in the streets of the town, the wine to drink with their friends to assuage some of the difficulties of this world.

It is important also to bear in mind that this was a working environment where there were specialist merchants who had particular goods to offer and also particular requirements. A good example comes with the merchants of wax. As we have seen, the Casamance region, upstream from Bichangor, was famed for its wax: it is hardly surprising, therefore, that many of the traders who came from Bichangor were bringing the loaves of wax which are described in the records, and were paid in turn with cloth. But what is also interesting is that Manoel Bautista Pérez had a dedicated *combete* for wax, which he gave out to a whole range of different small traders who came to the store. Wax was sold in both big and small loaves, suggesting a range of different markets for buyers. Moreover, the weights of the loaves of wax were accounted for in the books, which gives us a strong sense of the atmosphere here: of scales operating with iron weights made by the blacksmiths of the town, weighing out the wax, which was then taken by small-time businessmen for use in the *lumos* of Senegambia further afield, because candlelight was clearly something that many people used in the towns and villages of the region.[4]

Just as some people specialized in wax, others focused on kola nuts. The trade to Geba was one where kola predominated, just as it did in the business with Farim by the end of the seventeenth century. When Bautista Pérez laded a ship to Geba in 1617, the value of the kola nuts on board – at '27 Blacks and 30 pieces of cloth' – was almost nine times that of the next most valuable commodity traded, 3 barrels and 40 flagons of wine (coming to '3 Blacks and 121 pieces of cloth'). Again, this gives us a different picture of the working life of the *combete*: measurement, weight and evaluation were a core part of the life of the merchant here, and of those who came to take small bits and pieces here on credit. Everyone had to have a strong sense of how the stocks were in the *combetes*, what was in demand and where the best destination for business was with what was at hand. If you were plying the southward run to Sierra Leone and Geba you were into kola nuts; if you were headed north into Casamance, you were in the market for wax.[5]

Fundamentally, the merchant's working life in Cacheu was one of evaluation. Everyone involved needed to know what was in stock, how the account-book prices in bolts of cloth and enslaved human beings measured up and where they might best turn a profit. The evaluation went with specialization, as people developed expertise in one or another location and its preferences. And this expertise so often came with human and emotional ties, as people formed relationships and had families in one or another place and so grew to know and love them.

The lists of goods on account seem simply to confirm the perspective of those who made them: that trade and business was the only thing that mattered in the Atlantic world's outposts in West Africa. It has also been far too normal for historians to look at these records so many centuries later and reproduce exactly this outlook, a materialist view of the world and the ways in which it has changed, precisely measured, evaluated and accounted for – and with so many of the human and spiritual meanings stripped away. But a closer look tells us much about labour in Senegambia at the time, not only in Cacheu but in the villages and towns nearby.

Probably the most common item mentioned in the account books is the bolts of cloth that were so ubiquitous in the town. A number of historians have shown how central cloth production was in many parts of Africa, from here in Senegambia to the Angola region of West-Central Africa. This is why the best match to an industrial setting at the time was in textile production. The labour associated with textiles affected most areas near to Cacheu. There were some areas that were more famous for weaving than others, but it is also clear that cloths were woven generally in many of the *tabankas*. Weaving micro-industries can be found in the Bautista Pérez account books from the coast of Guinea-Conakry, towards Sierra Leone, as well as from Geba, The Gambia, the Casamance and fine-quality woven cloth produced by the Jolof north of the Gambia river. This is pretty strong evidence that weaving – and also the manufacture of the horizontal treadle looms on which the weaving was done, alongside the vertical looms which were widespread in West Africa – was a typical form of labour for many of the men of the region. This went with the associated labour of cotton harvesting and picking, generally done by women and also increasingly by captive labour in the cotton fields of the Gambia river region.[6]

There were many labour tasks associated with weaving, including winding thread onto shuttles of the loom and dressing the loom itself. Good descriptions of the centrality of weaving as a form of work are given by Lemos Coelho. In his book he describes the weaving workshops which were developed among both the Fulani and Serèer communities living north of the Gambia river. Both peoples wove the white cloths, which they sold widely as cloth currencies, as we saw in Chapter 3 – and which no doubt were the source of the 'white cloths / *panos brancos*' often found in the Bautista Pérez account books. Lemos Coelho also wrote that the main goods bought with kola nuts in Farim were bolts of cloth, presumably woven in the villages of the kingdom of Kaabu and then brought by ship to be exchanged there for the kola. In other words, the manufacturing conditions were clearly strong enough to produce a surplus of cloth beyond the needs of each community, which was sold into the growing market in Senegambia and the Atlantic world.[7]

The cloth was woven with the picked cotton spun by women. There also seem to have been female entrepreneurs who bought

### The Heretic of Cacheu

*Vertical loom, from today's Nigeria. 1910.*

picked cotton in bulk from merchants like Manoel Bautista Pérez. In one account book entry for 1613, he describes selling 1 *arroba* of clean-picked cotton to Maria Nunez, to the value of 24 bolts of cloth. Nunez presumably then took the cotton to sell at the *lumos* near Cacheu to teams of weavers, who then could weave the cloth. Probably on reaching the *lumos*, Nunez would also buy some of these same textiles to take back and sell in Cacheu, thereby making a profit at both ends of her enterprise. As we have seen throughout this book, therefore, women were lynchpins in the network of labour which kept the system of Senegambian trade afloat.[8]

All this helps us to begin to put together the working environment of the *tabankas* around Cacheu. The clacking noise of the wooden batons in the loom, as they moved back and forth, must have been ever-present. The industry was structured in many ways like the textile industry of the Netherlands in the same period, where cloth was 'put out' by big traders to various households who had micro-industries

## Work

and could help meet the orders. Many households had sacks of raw cotton being spun and prepared for weaving. Others were making indigo dyes to bring out the blue-and-white colour of the *barafulas* woven in Gambia and also in Cabo Verde. This happened alongside chatter and gossip, which was a central part of the entertainment of daily life, as we will see in the next chapter.[9]

Beyond the centrality of the textile industry and associated labour, which is clear from the account books, there are many other aspects which help us to grasp the character of work in the region around Cacheu. We can begin with the loaves of wax, which were such an important part of trade in Cacheu and had their own dedicated *combetes*. Honey was also sold and in widespread demand in Cacheu, as several accounting entries show us. Yet where did this honey and wax come from? Beekeeping was an old practice in Senegambia, and some of the first Portuguese visitors found that the peoples of the area were making hives of straw covered with clay, and hanging them in the trees. A century later, around 1580, the Caboverdean Almada wrote that in Casamance 'they keep bees in basket-shaped hives made of straw, plastered with cow-dung'. The making of hives was clearly an important economic activity, something that beekeepers could do in their compounds having gathered the straw and bound it carefully together. Once they were hung in trees in the bush, the beekeepers would go and check them periodically until the honey was ready: then they became merchants, since the honey could be traded or converted into mead (a honey liquor), while the wax was sold in loaf-shapes. Thus does one 'product' in a book of accounts conceal a whole economy of work.[10]

The gathering of straw at the end of the dry season was a major agricultural task, connected to a number of micro-industries. Beyond the hives made with it, there were the Islamic prayer-mats woven in the Nunez river area and found widely across Senegambia, including at the Jakhanké centre at Sutucó on the Gambia river. But the most important use made of straw was in the basketry industry. There was a strong market for baskets, in which other products such as kola, cloth and grain could be stored. Manoel Bautista Pérez bought two bundles of baskets in one trade in 1613, and ten other baskets on 8 June in another purchase. The baskets gathered in the *combetes* had been woven by women in the villages and towns near Cacheu, doubtless as an afternoon activity once grain had been pounded or fields tended to: this was another way for villagers to access cloth, iron bars and other forms of money which they needed to gain heft in the local economy.[11]

Another major part of work in village life was the gathering of wood. This was important for cooking fires, and the longer tree-trunks could be sharpened and turned into the stockades of the *tabankas*, such as those used in Vila Quente. However, timber of one kind or another was also, of course, an important part of the construction business. When, in 1619, a merchant in Cacheu contracted one Falabane to supply 900 bundles of sticks, this was probably linked to the thatching of houses in Cacheu. Falabane in turn worked with nine people, including Mansa Bare and Faroutamba, to supply 100 bundles each. The work must have been done in villages surrounding Cacheu, since otherwise it would have been uneconomic to bring such an inexpensive product a long way. The work of gathering the brushwood from the bush, measuring it and tying it up was something that occupied nine separate households. This is an example that shows how very many people in the area immediately around Cacheu were involved in labour activities connected to the town.[12]

What emerges is the close connection of labour in the forests and glades around the villages in Senegambia with the micro-industries of Cacheu's economy. Men and women went out, probably in the early morning and late afternoons, to gather straw and to hang their hives in trees in the forests, not too far from the villages they lived in, for fear of both threatening humans and other creatures. Brushwood and straw had to be gathered, for that labour soon to be converted into revenue-generating work: the production of hives, the gathering of honey and making of mead and the weaving of baskets and prayer-mats which could then be sold far and wide. As the example of Falabane and the procurement of thatch for Cacheu shows, most households – if not all of them – were involved in labour which contributed to the town's well-being and defences in one way or another.

Alongside these market-oriented crafts, agricultural work was naturally one of the main forms of labour. This was also in fact part of the market economy, since the account-book records show that the idea of an African subsistence economy is a myth. Large amounts of millet and maize were sold to the merchants in Cacheu from the villages surrounding the town. Much of this came from Bugendo, as one account book entry from 1613 shows, when Nicolão Rodrigues took merchadise for Manoel Bautista Pérez there to 'get provisions'. But there was also a trade in millet from as far afield as the Bijagó islands. The archipelago was known for its millet production, and several people owed money in the account books because of their purchase of it from Bautista Pérez. As we saw at the end of Chapter 2, this work in the islands was done by women, who planted and harvested all the fields there. Maize was another widely grown crop, and had been since its introduction from the Americas in the sixteenth century: stocks of it were taken to Cacheu for trade, adding to the amounts of surplus that needed to be produced in the Mata de Putame, the Bijagós islands and Casamance for consumption in the town.[13]

The trade in millet from the Bijagó islands illuminates the way in which labour and the Atlantic economy were connected. The surplus production was needed not only to meet the requirements of those who lived in Cacheu but also to feed the enslaved captives who were taken on the very same trading ships from the islands to the port, and thence across the Atlantic. This surplus work in the fields was done by women and reflected the demand for men coming from the Atlantic trafficking economy and from the wars which the increasing political conflicts of the time were generating. In fact, just as in Britain women staffed the factories during the First World War as the men were slaughtered, so during the political conflicts in Africa generated by the transatlantic traffic women's labour burden increased – as also did the opportunities to capitalize on this for some women, like Crispina. For, as history shows, times of crisis are also seen as opportunities by some.

In other words the work of trade – whether trade in textiles, picked cotton or provisions – which so many people from Cacheu were involved in was the other side of the coin of much of the labour done in the region around the town. The products in the account books of Atlantic merchants were there because of the labour and entrepreneurship of men and women who lived nearby and who saw an opportunity to create a more secure economic basis for their households. They did this through marketing baskets and honey and by producing more grain and textiles than their own households required. This surplus work created a market economy, financed with currencies used both locally and across the world. In this way, Cacheu's working environment was part of the globalized marketplace of production.

Global influences on daily work can be glimpsed in many of the traces that we have left from Cacheu, the faint impressions of history on paper. Many of the skilled craftspeople who worked there, and lived in 'the neighbourhood', had jobs which related in one way or another to the Atlantic shipping trade. The traffic required people who could work on the ships, steer them and repair them as required. For the ships that arrived in Cacheu from Lisbon and Cartagena generally came after months at sea, and often after some dangerous moments.

Repairing ships was a skilled job, generally divided between the work of carpenters and caulkers. Carpenters appear at several points in the Bautista Pérez account books. We know that they must have worked on ships and not in building construction, since, as we have seen, the use of wood in housebuilding in Cacheu was rapidly phased out because of the risk of arson. On one day in 1617, one João Cardozo incurred a debt of two bolts of cloth which he had paid to 'Manoel the carpenter of Bastião Fernandes'. This is an interesting piece of evidence, as it suggests that carpenters in Cacheu could be contracted to work for particular merchants, but that this did not stop them from hiring themselves out to work for different clients. Probably their merchant contractors wanted them on hand to work on repairs for their boats when they came in to port, in sawing new boards and filing them to size where they had been broken or needed replacing. Most likely, they also worked in building the barricades and platforms on lower decks for the transport of enslaved Africans. But at the same time this did not stop them from hiring themselves out to work for others in similar need – which suggests that their labour skills were in demand and could not be controlled by their contractors.[14]

We also know from Crispina's trial that carpenters worked in most of the major trading towns of Senegambia. One of the witnesses in the trial, Pedro Nunes, discussed the drunken parties held by Luis Rodrigues in his house in Farim in around 1656, and the news he had heard from the servant of a carpenter in the town, Antonio Pires. With the river trade to Farim vital for the commerce of Senegambia as a whole, clearly carpenters were in as much demand here as elsewhere, working with the ships of the trade.[15]

Carpenters like Pires worked alongside caulkers in the work in the port. Caulkers were those who repaired leaks in ships, something which virtually every vessel to arrive in Cacheu suffered from. The work of the caulker was to seal the seams and joints in the boards of the boat. This was done by soaking cotton fibres in pitch, and then hammering them into the gaps in the boards with a caulking mallet or chisel. We know that this was one of the most common jobs in the port from the number of references to caulkers in the account books and in Crispina's trial, and also because of the number of entries for the sale of pitch. Entries in the account books were almost always associated with wine – 'caulkers who are preparing the ship owe a bolt of cloth's worth of wine', reads one entry from 1617 – which suggests that the work of caulking, though painstaking, was leavened by drunken chat.[16]

Alongside the work of making the ships seaworthy, there was the business of actually sailing them. Many of those who lived in

*The Heretic of Cacheu*

Cacheu worked as pilots and boatswains, and one witness in Crispina's trial even said that he was the 'second helmsman' on one of Jorge's ships when it had left Cacheu for a trafficking voyage to the south. Some of these sailors had quite long-term contracts with the ship-owners: one of them in Crispina's trial, Sebastião Vaz – a boatswain – said that he had worked for Vicente Rodrigues Duarte in this job for three years and so had got to know him by sight very well. A number of witnesses, meanwhile, were pilots. Some were quite old and experienced in the traffic. While often of Portuguese heritage, they were generally married to African women, and their children were rapidly entering the class of Kristón traders.[17]

Finally, there were a number of professions found in Cacheu linked to provisioning ships for the Middle Passage. Coopers were important cogs in the wheel of trade, making the barrels that would store drinking water and other provisions on the long Atlantic crossing. Alongside them, there were *tortugeiros*, people who supplied turtles, which were laded onto the ships to provide food and oil. One account book entry for 1614 speaks more powerfully than any modern historian: '20 June, for the cost of last week's meat for the Blacks and turtles, and other expenses for the Blacks, 42 *pesos* and 7 *reales*': the turtles must have been important, since they were fed with meat on shore before being stowed on the ships alongside the rest of the passengers on board.[18]

Taken all together, this evidence gives us a strong impression of work at the portside in Cacheu. This was not a quiet place. There was the noise of hammering and sawing from caulkers and carpenters as they drank wine and chatted to one another, repairing the ships and readying them for the next leg of their voyage. On dry land, coopers were at work hammering and shaping their barrels and making sure they were conditioned for taking provisions on board. Meanwhile, those involved in the art of sailing were negotiating their next voyages, discussing routes and provisions with the merchants whose credit financed the operation and preparing their own side-hustles as they did so which would allow them to put a bit of money by for their families.

*Work*

What is also interesting is that it was not just in Cacheu that this kind of atmosphere characterized people's working lives. As we have seen, there were carpenters in Farim. And we also know from some of the travel accounts that we have left that the crafts associated with shipbuilding were found in many of the ports of Senegambia. Writing of the late sixteenth century, André Donelha described how the port at Cassão on the Gambia river (not far from the modern town of Janjangbureh) was a place where ships were repaired. Here there were caulkers, and rigging and ropes were repaired using materials brought from nearby. In this way, the shipping industry and the work associated with it was found in many parts of Senegambia and not just in the Atlantic-facing port of Cacheu.[19]

On my first visit to Guinea-Bissau, in 1995, I visited the town of Gabú, which is today in the easternmost part of the country. Not too far to the north of Gabú, just off the road to Vélingara in Senegal, is Kansala, which was the capital of the old kingdom of Kaabu until it fell to invading Fulani forces from Fouta Djalon in the late nineteenth century. I had come here to catch a lorry to Senegal, and it was my last day in the country.

After I had arrived, I went to the market. I bought some bolts of cloth by the metre and then went to a tailor, who took my measurements and told me to come back the next day for natty and colourful shirts and trousers made with the printed cloth. Then, moving a little way from the tailor's, I came across a silversmith selling exquisite necklaces with leaf-shaped designs that he had made in the workshop behind the market-front, the metal melted down from some of the silver that had been circulating in the country since the seventeenth century. And beyond these stores there were leather-workers (some of whom made amulets, or *gris-gris*) and blacksmiths.

When, decades later, I began to read through the sources that I have drawn on to write this book, one of the most remarkable things I discovered was the longevity of many of the crafts and professions that I had come upon in that visit in 1995. Much of the working activity of Gabú in 1995 was grounded in skills and crafts that were longstanding, and spoke of historical techniques of craft and work. There had been tailors and leather-workers at work in Cacheu 350 years before, and the records suggest that the working lives of those people – with apprentices doing much of the menial tasks in the workshop while learning their craft – were not that far removed from what I found in Gabú in that 1995 visit.* Blacksmiths also have a very long history associated with politics and power across Senegambia, and especially in Mandinga communities: in the sixteenth and seventeenth centuries, their work melting the iron bar imports into weapons and agricultural tools was vital to produce surpluses and defend communities from the increasing insecurity.[20]

While the Atlantic-facing professions seem in the sources to keep the economic life of the town afloat, Cacheu itself depended all the more on the labour of those who rarely ventured beyond Vila Quente. There were many who made their livings in the town doing the sorts of job that could have been found in many other ports of the Atlantic world. A good example is the baker Francisca Fernandes. There were copper ovens in Cacheu, and perhaps she owned and managed one of them. Her business dealings occupy a whole page of Manoel Bautista Pérez's accounts from 1617, but she can also be found as early as 1614, which suggests that she had a well-established business in Cacheu. Francisca Fernandes was often found coming to his *combete*, where she would buy flour, sweet biscuits, *barafula* cloths and iron bars. She had a thriving business, judging from the number of times she came in to the store in 1617: she bought quarts of flour from him on 27 May, 3 June, 12 June and 20 June, which suggests that she had a strong clientele and kept on having to top up her supplies to keep the loaves coming. That her bakery had an important place in the town's life is shown by the various times that Manoel Bautista Pérez sent over six iron bars with her employee Natalia (*a sua Natalia*). Bread was, of course,

---

* Or indeed which can be found today in tailor's workshops in Senegambia, where young apprentices also sit by and learn from the trained craftsperson.

essential to Holy Communion, a part of Catholic life and identity, so the role of this woman baker in the town was important enough for her to have dependents whom she sent on errands.[21]

Many working people could earn their living in Cacheu. There were shoemakers, as the account books show when Manoel Bautista Pérez gave three bolts of cloth for his debtor Antonio Nunes de Andrada 'to the cobbler'. People paid money to have their laundry done – 4 *reales* was paid out by Miguel Antonio 'to have his clothes washed' in 1615, while Lemos Coelho said that he employed a washerwoman while living in Cacheu. There were fairly frequent mentions of tailors, who turned the measures of cloth into clothing for people to wear around the town. And then there were the institutions connected in some way or other to the colonial world, with a jailer employed in the town in the 1610s (paid two bolts of cloth in 1614).[22]

Again, these details are precious because they allow us so many centuries later to zoom out and get a broader sense of what working life in the town was actually like. Beyond the noise of the carpenters and caulkers doing the ship repairs, the hammering and sawing of wood on shore for the coopers to make barrels, beyond the noise of enslaved household members and other workers carrying large bundles of cloth, raw cotton, millet and other provisions to and from the merchant houses and the port, there was another world of work: the practical, daily tasks which made sure that the town as a whole could function.

Most of this work was done by the people who lived in Vila Quente and 'the neighbourhood'. While Cacheu's port was the centre for the market-based activities and shipyards, the streets around it were the centre for much of the work that kept the town together. On the stretch downriver from the port towards Vila Quente, the laundrywomen came to do their work, having brought in bulk orders from some of the merchant houses in the town with whom they worked. In the streets behind the harbour were the workshops of the blacksmiths, cobblers and tailors, the last two buying animal hides and bolts of cotton wholesale and then working them into the clothing and footwear worn in the town. Walking the streets were the traders, seamen and household members who were coming to and fro on errands: buying bread at the baker's, where they could exchange news and gossip and wonder what new fashions and products the next ships to call in to port might bring.

All this detail shows is how the working lives and ambitions of so many peoples across the world were becoming intertwined through these first centuries of globalization. The people of an urban settlement in Senegambia did not have a working life that was any different in nature or activity from that of many people in Europe or in other parts of the world. In fact, the demands of production and the market meant that the nature of work is very recognizable even today, centuries later. The experience and practice of labour was widely shared across the world, even in the seventeenth century, offering a common ground to experience and social class at a much earlier time than is often recognized. On the other hand, overlaying this common experience in Cacheu was the violence of the objectification of people and objects, something which also went with the rise of the modern world economic system.

There was one group of workers in Cacheu whose job was to leaven (or, some might say, to prolong) the violence of this system: the people whose work it was to heal those who had fallen sick in large part because of it.

Healing was at the root of Crispina's trial. The fact that people like Crispina and Jorge routinely turned to the *djabakós* was something that the Inquisition and the Portuguese imperial state could not tolerate. But it was something that everyone did. However, this could only be seen as heretical because there were also other people in the town who worked in what was to Portuguese eyes a more conventional approach to medicine. As we have seen, daily life in Cacheu challenged imperial views of gender and hierarchy, and so it wasn't surprising that the struggle between West African and European visions of life and human society might crystallize in a struggle over who had the power to heal those many human bodies which the Atlantic trading system was making ill.

*Work*

An interesting set of entries in the Bautista Pérez account books is over payment to the *boticário* – or pharmacist/apothecary. On 24 August 1614, Manoel Bautista Pérez noted that Mateo da Costa had borrowed 30 silver pesos to pay to 'Gonçalo the *boticário*'. This apothecary Gonçalo was almost certainly a Kristón, since imperial residents were always privileged with family names in the imperial archive. The following year, the role of these apothecaries was made clearer in an accounting entry for July and August: Diogo Rodrigues de Lisboa owed money for the 'cures offered by the apothecary and doctor and surgeon until these slaves had been sold'.[23]

In other words, there was a range of healing professionals in Cacheu who hired themselves out to the traffickers in order to try to maintain the health of their captives until they could be rowed out to sea and despatched on the Middle Passage. As we saw in the previous chapter, sickness and disease were rife among the enslaved awaiting transport to the Americas. Sometimes sick captives had to be taken off ships waiting offshore, for fear that their illnesses would infect the rest of the enslaved on board. In these conditions, those who worked in the arts of healing, and claimed to be able to bring the sick back to health, had a powerful position in the town: one that was linked both to their claims to have powers over life and death and to the economic role that they performed for the traffickers.

These records suggest that this healing work was practised by both Africans and Europeans living in Cacheu. While the apothecary may have been a Kristón, some of the doctors were European. In 1613, Manoel Bautista Pérez paid a bolt and a half of cloth to 'Domingues Pires, for bleedings which he gave to Luis Afonso, who has now died'. The cures that were prescribed often involved bleeding the patient, as was also the case, of course, in Western medicine of the time. At one point in 1617, Manoel Bautista Pérez paid a doctor for 'bleeding my people and giving them the necessary medicines in my house'.[24]

Those who worked in the Western conventional arts of healing clearly faced challenges in Cacheu. In the era of leeches, Western medical practitioners were less equipped to deal with the fevers and disease of West Africa than the *djabakós* and herbalists. Intermediaries were often barber-surgeons, who in the seventeenth and eighteenth centuries were known for bleeding the sick, something that remained the case in many parts of both Africa and Europe into the twentieth century. In the Atlantic world setting these medical practitioners drew on West African healing practices of bleeding and cupping in their work with the sick. Barber-surgeons were sometimes called on to bleed people in Cacheu, as some of the records show, with one Miguel Antonio paying the barber who had bled him in the town in 1617. They were often employed in a medical role on the Middle Passage, and some historians have seen them as key figures in the cross-cultural medical influences, as African knowledge of healing herbs and skills was exchanged with techniques of European medical practitioners, where barber-surgeons had their own guilds. Activities performed by barber-surgeons in other parts of Africa, but for which there is no specific evidence in Crispina's trial, included tattooing, circumcision and administering smoke-cures, as well as some forms of specialism which included contraception and the treatment of mental illness.[25]

This relationship between barber-surgeons and other West African healers was set out clearly in Crispina's trial. In her testimony in Lisbon, Crispina described how she had asked 'a Christian woman who had been born in the same settlement of Cacheu and was married to a barber whose nickname was Frique Fraque to look for someone who could cure her said daughter'.[26]

It has been all too easy for historians and the historical record to pass over the way in which across the world humans used a vast pharmacopeia: countless exchanges and experiments were going on across the entire Atlantic world throughout this period. Barber-surgeons and healers, too, were workers in Cacheu, and in many ways among the most emblematic of them all. In Senegambia, the healers travelled from towns like Bujé, Guinguim and Farim to Cacheu to try to cure Jorge at Crispina's behest. They worked in their house, often at night, and, as we will see in the final chapter of this book, had extensive botanical knowledge of plants with healing properties. For their skills, these healers were paid salaries by Crispina according to some witnesses, with one saying that 'she consulted [them] for cures of infirmities of persons in her household, paying them a salary for doing so'. Another witness described how they travelled to foreign kingdoms to receive payments, suggesting too that they were involved in trade, as almost everyone in the town was.[27]

All this provides a different perspective on working life in Cacheu. In some ways this was a town like many other in the Atlantic world, with many of the same crafts and professions to be found. But this was also a town where so many people could fall sick, perhaps through the conflicts generated by the competition between worldviews which were brought into contact by the new cycles of economic demand. As we will see in the final chapter of this book, the struggle for life, and the love and anguish that went with trying to heal those who were sick, characterized the emotional worlds of the town. Those workers who claimed to be able to provide some kind of salve, and who – like the barber-surgeons and the *djabakós* – bridged the African and European worlds becoming in so many ways intertwined, had the biggest claim on people's trust.[28]

# 8.

# *Entertainment and Gossip*

'Agostinho Rodrigues [had been] there, drinking wine and rum with Canon Luis Rodrigues, and [the witness] saw that the said Black man was drunk, playing cards without any care with the said Canon, without a clue what he was doing in the game.'

There was plenty of work to do in Cacheu, but there was also plenty of time which people devoted to having fun. Work could be put aside for days at a stretch, depending on the cause – something which suggests that the concept and awareness of time was quite different from that which we have today. Sometimes the cause was one of the raucous drinking sprees, where people consumed flagons of wine imported from Madeira, palm wine tapped locally and bottles of rum imported from Brazil and the Americas. The palm-wine tappers could be seen scaling the trees in the districts around Cacheu, with harnesses tied around their waists made of leather. They would bring the white, viscous drink straight into town in calabashes, since the older the palm wine, the more rancid and putrid it becomes. Sometimes, the parties finished in the kind of 'decadent' dances that the priest Luis Rodrigues was accused of hosting when vicar in Farim.

Alcohol was one of the things most frequently bought and sold in the warehouses of Cacheu. People went partying, or just used the wine as a companion to their work, sitting on the decks of the vessels in the shipyards and drinking as they repaired the leaks or the cracked boards of the decking. The frequency of the drinking bouts, and the tight-knit nature of the community in Cacheu, meant that gossip and quarrels were never far away, something that also seems to have been a form of entertainment for the people who lived here. Quarrels often arose out of rivalries in love and sex, driven into the open by too much wine or rum. The Inquisition trials are filled with scandalous details which make it clear that the hold of the Church over daily life and morality in this distant time and place was very weak: there were street fights in the town over new lovers, while young women and men caroused on the streets alongside reprobates like the priest Luis Rodrigues, who then went on to say mass fresh from a night on the tiles.

The way in which quarrels and gossip circulated so quickly in Cacheu also tells us something perhaps more profound about the way that people lived and enjoyed their lives. While in the twenty-first century the printed text has a defining influence on human experience and identities, in seventeenth-century Senegambia these were shaped by the spoken word. Word of mouth shaped daily life, through the news that people received, the stories and scandals that they heard of one another and the gossip that was stowed away in the memory-bank to be made use of when the time was ripe. Speech, and the sociability which produced it, was therefore one of the most central forms of entertainment and enjoyment to be found at the time: a testament to the oral culture and the oral histories which have endured in West Africa both before and since.

This tells us that life and the joy that went with it were public performances. Many acts were performed for public show, so that entertainment and social fun were part of the public sphere. The concept of privacy was something that did not exist much in Cacheu. Dependents in Crispina and Jorge's household knew exactly what was going on there. Nothing was a secret. Entertainment was meant to be public: whether it was the enjoyment of drinking sociably with friends and rivals, the social delight in sharing a ribald piece of gossip, the loud shouting that went with an announcement that someone was going to make an offering at the *china* to recover some object that had been stolen or the collective enjoyment that came from playing games and producing performances for one of the festivals of the town.

Some of the most public acts of celebratory performance in the town came through religious life. The way in which these were intended as public demonstrations is quite clear from Crispina's trial. A good example is from the story of when the liquids contained in the *chinas* which the *djabakós* had told Crispina to keep under her bed were thrown into the river by her slave Sebastião Rodrigues Barraza:

> the witness said, that [João Nunes Castanho] shouted at the said slave Sebastião [Rodrigues Barraza] to fetch and bring those objects, and the slave did so; and he showed them the pots and pans, which were full of the [liquids] mentioned above, and after being seen and admired, they sent the said slave to throw them in the sea, or the River of São Domingos. The witness also stated that as Crispina Peres could not find the said *Chinas*, or idols, [she heard] gossip from his companion, João Nunes Castanho, about her, telling her that he, the said witness, had thrown her *Chinas* or idols into the sea.[1]

In other words, João Nunes Castanho had made sure that the materials from the *chinas* were thrown into the river. This was a public act, given how busy the riverfront and shipyard of Cacheu were with all kinds of work. To cement the public demonstration of Catholic purity on the one hand and repudiation of African religious practice on the other, Castanho had then spread gossip about his behaviour around the town – something that no doubt he enjoyed doing very much.

Another example to help shape our understanding of the enjoyment of the public practice of religious life is the story we heard earlier, of how people often went to make sacrifices at shrines to recover stolen goods. One witness described how 'when they buy these things to make sacrifices in order for the stolen or lost [goods] to appear, they will scream, saying in their loud voices that they want to sacrifice it, and to libate the *china*'. In this way, everyone

## Entertainment and Gossip

in the town knew that the sacrifice was being made, and moreover when this was done 'the stolen object immediately reappears'. We can well imagine that the victim of theft was angry but also enjoyed the loud announcement of their departure to the *china*, and the fear that this provoked in the guilty party.[2]

There were so many facets to life in Cacheu. However, few of them were private. This is what made Crispina's Inquisition trial such an anomaly, for most such trials in Portugal and Spain were of people tried for secret heretical practices. There was nothing secret about religious life in Cacheu, or about most other aspects of the sociability and enjoyment which made life – for all its harshness and struggles – so valued and worth living.

Religion and the celebration of life were among the most public demonstrations of enjoyment in the town. Religious theatre was compelling, and a central part of the struggle for influence and the power over life. Even so, much of this had to do not with life, but with death. It is pretty clear from the sources that we have that funerals were among the biggest forms of celebration that took place in Cacheu – something that still rings true to anyone who has spent much time in Guinea-Bissau.

On one visit to the country about a decade ago, I was walking along a path through some cashew plantations, a few miles from a small town. A party was taking place near the path, in a compound with mango trees and a picket fence which separated the household from the field. There were bottles of palm wine on the ground, and dancing. I was told that this was the funeral celebration of someone who had died some years before: because they had had leprosy, the family had needed to wait until the body had decomposed to celebrate the life of the departed person. But now they were doing so with gusto – something that reminded me of a conversation I had some years before with a young woman, who told me that her biggest difficulty in life was how to pay for the funeral of her father (who was then still alive). Indeed, recent research confirms that funerals (*toka-churs*) in Guinea-Bissau remain events which brings

## The Heretic of Cacheu

people from all different communities and religions together, in which everyone is keen to share, to acknowledge their collective belonging.[3]

As the Brazilian historian João Reis has put it of life in the African diaspora in north-eastern Brazil, 'death is a festival'. Death was an opportunity to celebrate the importance, and supremacy, of life. It was also a way of reinforcing values and worldviews which celebrated the importance of life and of living rather than those which hastened death and disease. In Cacheu, each person had a vital life force which did not leave this world lightly. Its passing had to be celebrated and commemorated, so they could know that they would be missed by those who they had left. Otherwise, they might return and cause mischief.[4]

The Bautista Pérez accounts make clear how important funerals were to enjoyment and to public religiosity in the town. In one entry, Bautista Pérez describes how he had given someone twenty bolts of white cloth – probably woven by the Fulani and Serèer north of the Gambia river – 'which he took at the time of his departure to the burial'. The cloth was a gift, and perhaps also a contribution to the consumption of food and drink that was also part and parcel of these commemorations. This amount of cloth had a value equivalent to four swords, which shows the considerable expense poured into these funerals both by the families and by people who happened just to be going along to participate in the mourning rituals and festivities.[5]

The account books also reveal that there were costs involved in the burial of enslaved Africans in the town. On 19 July 1614, Diogo Rodrigues de Lisboa spent 20 *reales* for the cost 'of burying a male Black who had died', and the same again on 13 August for a female captive. This could be an expensive undertaking, since death was so common in Cacheu, especially among the enslaved. In fact, twenty-nine enslaved persons belonging to Rodrigues de Lisboa died that year while awaiting transport, all annotated in the account book at a cost of 20 *reales* per person for burial. This can be compared with the cost of renting a house in Cartagena at the same time, which was

12 *reales* per month. The burial costs per enslaved captive in Cacheu were equivalent to one and a half month's rent of a townhouse in Cartagena, which was not an inconsiderable sum – perhaps £5,000/US$6,500 in today's money. Much of the costs would have gone to paying the officers of the Catholic church in Cacheu for performing the necessary religious functions (we know that women took chickens with them to pay priests for receiving their confessions, which is indicative of this).[6]

However, it is in Crispina's trial that the celebratory aspects of many of these funerals become clear. One witness, Manoel Lopes Godins, gave the following evidence:

> 'he knew that Teodósia Braga, Susana Lopes – Queen of Our Lady [of the Rosary] – and Domingas Braga, often go to Pagan funerals to attend their ceremonies, which is public knowledge and well known, and that all in the neighbourhood of Vila Quente know this.[7]

Many other witnesses confirmed this. Some said that, when these women went to the funerals in Vila Quente, they 'went to the funerals of the Heathens to make a sacrifice to the *china*, which we call idols, with cow's blood, or that of chickens or goats'. According to Vicente Fogaça, 'most of the people of this land . . . attended the *choros*, and wails, and other Pagan ceremonies, being baptized Christians'. In other words, the witnesses confirmed that the West African funeral ceremonies were very public events, attended by most of the people in Cacheu. They brought animals to make sacrificial offerings at the shrines of Vila Quente, which were accompanied by public expressions of grief and distress.[8]

Funerals were important religious events and celebrations of the life of the deceased, therefore, in Vila Quente. Given the ubiquity of death, which we will see in more detail in Chapter 10, they were very common. However, they also mattered in the Christian community of Cacheu, where the costs associated with the funerals of the enslaved tells us as much. The narrative of the religious ceremony conducted by the missionaries at Guinguim in 1663, which we came across in Chapter 5, is suggestive of the manner in which they were conducted by the Church officers. Formal ceremonial processions, with the priests of the town dressed in their sacred garments, proceeded with the corpse of the deceased through the streets of the town. The formality of the ceremony, and its ritual solemnity, was no doubt intended as a deliberate counterpoint to the noise coming so frequently from the African funerals in Vila Quente.

Alongside the formality of the interments, however, there were other Christian festivals which were more joyous. We know that baptisms were significant in the town because of the number of times in Crispina's trial that the role of godparent is mentioned. In her defence, Crispina denounced several people for their hatreds of her and Jorge, hatreds made worse as they were co-godparents (*compadres*) of a child. This was the case of Vicente Rodrigues Duarte, a *compadre* of Ambrosio Gomes. Of another man, Luis de Moura, Crispina put it that he was 'a great enemy of her and her husband because he was *compadre* of Ambrosio Gomes and Vicente Rodrigues Duarte and Captain de Ornelas'. In other words, the celebration of baptism was not only an important ritual of the church in Cacheu, but also provided the cement for social bonds which were vital to the life of the town.[9]

Foremost among the church's religious festivals, meanwhile, were the carnival processions which retain such importance in Bissau to this day. Here, the church could attempt to show how it was not such a fusty old house of religion as all that. Carnival kings and queens were elected, and the evidence from both sides of the Atlantic suggests that the celebrations went with dancing in homage to the chosen monarchs for the week. Carnival costumes, made by the tailors of the town, drink and food were part of the festival that preceded Lent (though whether the prescribed penances and fasts of those forty days were ever closely observed in Cacheu is cast doubt on by the evidence in Crispina's trial).

Perhaps, for that week before Lent, the focus of celebration in Cacheu moved from Vila Quente to the street by the port with the colonial installations. All this brings home the atmosphere of religious competition which characterized life, as we saw earlier, not only among Christians and African religionists but also among the Jakhanké Muslims. In this noisy and very public entertainment/struggle over the rituals of life and death, the struggles over life played out.

Having fun in Cacheu was a noisy and expensive undertaking for both men and women. But while women seem to have specially favoured the celebrations at funerals, for men it was often a drunken undertaking. Sometimes there were good excuses for a blowout like carnival. But there were also many times when people just went on heavy drinking sprees, often the itinerant traffickers who only wanted to pass the time before one ship sailed or another one arrived.

The frequent exchanges between Cacheu and the Cabo Verde islands means that there was a shared culture of partying, as people from one place were often also found in the other at a different time. We can get a good example of the atmosphere which resulted from the accusations and evidence that accumulated in the trial of that infamous drunkard the priest Luis Rodrigues, who brought his lifestyle with him to Farim when he went there as priest. Many observers of his parties in Farim described the dances that he put on in his house: music of some kind was clearly involved, alongside the palm wine, the wine from Madeira and the rum.[10]

Who were the musicians involved here? It seems unlikely that *griots* would have participated, even though we know that *griots* were a part of the experience of daily life. Drums were found widely, and perhaps they were involved, although their use often had some kind of military aspect, something that remained true as late as the 1960s, when the *gumbé* drums were used to pass information during Guinea-Bissau's war of independence against the Portuguese. Stringed instruments were almost certainly played at these parties: either guitars brought on one of the Atlantic ships or the stringed lutes played by the Floup known as *akontings*. We know that there was also a lot of dancing, since Rodrigues's accusers called them 'dances' (*bailes*) in the testimony rather than parties;

## The Heretic of Cacheu

both men and women certainly enjoyed themselves through dancing therefore, and this was common throughout Senegambia.[11]

As for the atmosphere of these parties themselves, it is better to turn to Luis Rodrigues's behaviour on Santiago island for a fuller sense of what went on. Rodrigues was, after all, according to witnesses, famous for this. One witness, Bras Rodrigues, described a conversation with Luis Rodrigues in the small hours of one of these carousing nights out:

> When [Bras Rodrigues] had wanted to leave and go back to his house Canon Luis Rodrigues had pressed him to stay, saying Let's eat and drink some more, to which the witness replied, How can your grace want to eat any more when you have to say mass in the morning?, to which the said Canon answered, Let's eat and drink and then in the morning I won't say mass; but that then the next morning he had found out from many people that on the contrary this Canon had gone to say mass.[12]

Luis Rodrigues's character is pretty clear from this. He was someone quite happy to exert peer pressure on others, to try to get them to stay out with him as long as possible to enjoy the freedom of drinking and creating a noise that might annoy the rest of the town (who annoyed him). But drink alone was not enough to make these nights out really memorable: there was also the risk and reward that came with leading others on and taking advantage of their naivety. One witness described a sad tale from Santiago island which involved the drunken canon:

> That in this island [Luis Rodrigues] brought one Agostinho Rodrigues to his house, a simple country man who he then got drunk with rum and spicy wine which he gave him, and then stole a lot of money and other important things from him, which [Agostinho Rodrigues] kept in a bag; and then he ordered some Black [slaves] to take him away by night, and leave him in the river course which runs from the square to the Rua da Carreira of this city; and there the said Black

[slaves] left him for dead, not knowing who or where he was, such that the Captain-General Thome Fidalgo da Costa ordered him to be taken to his house where some medicines were given to him, and the said Agostinho Rodrigues returned somewhat to himself; but that the said wine and rum were so strong that this Agostinho Rodrigues never again came back to full health, just roaming around staggering and with poisoned blood, suffering terrible pains over a period of five months, more or less, at the end of which time he died.[13]

The theft of the money was one of the major accusations against Rodrigues, but it was put in a different light by one of the witnesses who gave more details as to what had gone on. Rodrigues had acquired the money through being a card-sharp:

Agostinho Rodrigues [had been] there, drinking wine and rum with Canon Luis Rodrigues, and [the witness] saw that the said Black man was drunk, playing cards without any care with the said Canon, without a clue what he was doing in the game; and he then said that the Canon had said to him [the witness], Let's both play with this Black man and take the three thousand *reis* that he's got from him, to which the witness replied to the said Canon that it was not a Christian act to take his money.[14]

Card games seem to have been part and parcel of these binge drinking nights, in Cacheu as in Ribeira Grande. Gambling was common, and all kinds of things were bet in these games. Manoel Bautista Pérez won twelve crates of jam from Pero Vaz de Morais in one night out in 1613, and another crate of jam from Dioguo Soares later that year. He often sold packs of cards to people in the town – buying in twelve packs on one occasion in 1613 – some of which he had bought from Jorge's own father, Álvaro Gonçalves Frances. Credit was often given to people who came wanting to bet it away, as Manoel accounted on one day in 1615, for the debt owed to him by Paulo Rodrigues d'Aguiar for 'having given him 30 *pesos* to play with at sea'.[15] All this gives a different sense of the desperate atmosphere that often went with these

## The Heretic of Cacheu

Playing cards from c.1650. The values of the numeral cards were indicated by a single suit-mark and numeral, and the rest of the card was illustrated with the relevant number of birds, animals, flowers or vegetables according to the suit.

nights of drinking, of partying and of gambling. People clearly often went to the trading houses to buy packs of cards alongside the wine and the rum. Then they took them to one of the houses they were living in, or down to the riverside, where they spent long periods of time playing cards, drinking, listening to music – and waiting. Perhaps this waiting was one of the main things that trading men in particular were doing in Cacheu: they were waiting for ships to sail, or to arrive, they were waiting for provisions to come in from the Bijagós islands, for kola nuts to come from Sierra Leone, for bolts of cloth to come from Casamance and Kaabu. And while they waited, they drank and gambled their time away.

This social atmosphere created enmities. Luis Rodrigues's trial shows that there was a group of hardcore drinking men in Ribeira Grande who often met up for nights out like this. There was a division in the town between them and the rest of the population – probably the majority – who resented the disturbances they created:

coming and hammering at the doors of the houses of women to try and get them to sleep with them, staggering through the streets to the city gates and back again and frequently getting into brawls and worse. Doubtless something similar went on in Cacheu: we know from Sebastião Rodrigues Barraza's testimony that he had spent virtually weeks getting drunk on wine plied to him by Crispina and Jorge's enemies, who presumably constituted the drinking section of the town, while none of the witnesses against Crispina said anything about their household being a place for drinkers. This division in lifestyles, too, was probably one of the sources of enmity in Cacheu, revealing as it did a different approach to life itself.

This division in lifestyles also corresponded to a split between those parts of the town connected either to African or to European ways of living. There certainly were alcoholic drinks indigenous to Senegambia: mead was widely drunk among Floup communities in Casamance, alongside palm wine, of course. Most Muslims in Cacheu followed a plural approach to their faith, since, as we saw in Chapter 5, it was only the itinerant Jakhanké clerics from Sutucó who did not drink; this approach would change over the course of the next centuries, and especially in the nineteenth century.

African forms of celebration were ubiquitous, especially in the regular funerals in Vila Quente. Leisure activities were varied. There was the game of *warri*, played with a wooden tablet carved with a number of hollows, around which players move beads, seeds or other objects. This is a well-known game found from East to West Africa and was known in Senegambia in the seventeenth century, as Richard Jobson described in 1623: 'In the heat of the day, the men will come forth, and sit themselves in companies, under the shady trees, to receive the fresh aire, and there to passe the time in communication.'[16] While they were doing this, Jobson described them playing *warri*:

> [They have] one kind of game to recreate themselves with, and that is in a piece of wood, certain great holes [are] cut, which they set upon the ground between two of them, and with a number of some

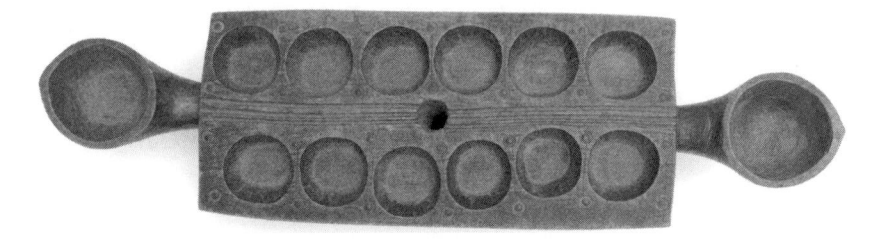

*Warri* board.

> thirty pebble-stones, after a manner of counting, they take one from the other, until one [of them] is possessed of all.[17]

There was another aspect of West African culture which provided enjoyment for many people in the town, and that was the pleasure of speech. Just as performance – of religion, of acts of sacrifice or penance – was central to pleasure in the town, so was the art of the public pronouncement. Gossip ruled in Cacheu and the towns round and about. Crispina's trial is virtually a litany of tittle-tattle: the number of times people say that they have heard so-and-so say something, or have been told about some scandalous and heretical behaviour on the part of another person (usually someone they do not like), is just about countless.

A good example of how gossip circulated occurs in the following story from the trial, given by Crispina and Jorge's enemy and rival Ambrosio Gomes:

> about five years ago, more or less, when Jorge Gonçalves Frances travelled to trade with foreigners in his own vessel, in order to know the end and success of his voyage, a goat or cow was slaughtered under the covered deck by their slaves; and its blood was spilled on the foot of the big mast or the helm, which the heathens take for a *china*, and a divine and mysterious object. The witness stated that he knows about this by hearsay, having heard Sebastião Fernandes Mascarenhas, born on the island of Santiago, and now residing in The Gambia . . . who at the time was master of the ship, and saw it with his own eyes.[18]

There is no personal evidence here, simply gossip passed on because it was known that it might provide power to those who had knowledge of it, secrecy having often been connected to power in many cultures. This wasn't necessarily the purpose of the gossip. It might have provided part of the entertainment of a drunken night out, or have been a way of passing the time in the interminable waiting for ships to arrive or depart. Talking about the heresies or sexual peccadilloes of others was as good a way as any to make others laugh and to gain a reputation and social standing. There was always something to be gained from upping the ante, and Crispina and Jorge's enemy and rival Ambrosio Gomes offers the shining example of this in the trial.

In another part of his testimony, he discussed the sexual behaviour of the priest and trafficker Antonio Vaz de Pontes, who was 'known for, and rumoured as a sodomite':

> The witness also stated . . . that when the said Canon Luis Rodrigues, towards the end of November of the previous year, 1662, travelled to the coast, and arrived there, he heard a story from a young man called Domingos de Andrade . . . he heard the said Canon say that when the said Domingos de Andrade stayed in the house of Priest Antonio Vaz de Pontes, where he had been living for some time, that the said Priest Antonio Vaz de Pontes quarrelled with a *parda* harlot, whom he publicly keeps in his house, called Madalena Dias, with whom they say he lives in concubinage, and not contenting himself with her alone, let other women into the said priest's house, as many as he wants, and he likes: and being reprehended for that (*sic*), the said Priest Antonio Vaz de Pontes answered him very wearily that he did not have any reason to complain about her, because he did not give it to others by the same way as he gave it to her.[19]

It is hard to make sense of the numbers of layers of gossip and hearsay which are revealed here. Gomes had heard from Andrade, who had heard from Luis Rodrigues, that Pontes, who lived with a woman called Madalena Dias – 'with whom they say he lives in concubinage' – had anal sex with her, while he slept with other women as he chose. This was clearly a story with substantial mileage on a drunken night in Cacheu.

Of course, people do talk about one another, and, as the thirteenth-century Icelandic *Njal's Saga* puts it, 'few are spoken of as they would wish'. That this was a source of pleasure and collective entertainment in Cacheu is clear from the trials that we have. This is, of course, natural in human societies, but the ubiquity of public speech about others was not just a product of this aspect of human nature, it also came about because of the culture of orality in West Africa. In Cacheu, power and history were created by speech, and this meant that it was not only enjoyable to talk, but a claim on power and prestige to do so. Indeed, in many ways, Crispina's trial was an attempt to challenge the primacy of the oral culture of West Africa and to assert the primacy of written text, through constant and interminable repetition of the accusations in what was effectively a form of bullying.

The way in which Senegambian culture influenced the oral world of the town – even when spoken in Portuguese – is clear from the idioms of the trial. These often employ metaphors from African languages even in Portuguese, which show how the style of these languages influenced the cultural worlds of Cacheu. Twice in letters reproduced in the trial, Jorge described how 'in this land from a fly people can make an elephant': what he meant was to describe this world of exaggerated gossip, where someone like Ambrosio Gomes would take a tiny detail that had travelled through several transformations from one person to another, and then blow it out of all proportion. On another occasion, when Crispina flew into a fury with Domingos de Aredas for ordering the *china* liquids to be thrown into the river, her household slave Bonifacia said that Crispina had 'said that she had given her daughter's nose, which amongst the heathens means that she had left her daughter's life in their hands'. Clearly, Crispina was more used to speaking in imagery and idioms from the languages she had grown up with and translated this into the Kriol that she spoke. Thus did West African oral culture influence the way that speech was used in the town.[20]

## Entertainment and Gossip

The pleasure of speech and gossip was an important aspect of how friendships were cemented. However, it also produced enmity. Some gossips were said to be 'caustic ... with a sharp tongue'. Speech could wound, as well as create bonds of friendship and laughter. When the wounds cut deep, the speech would break out into fights and quarrels, which in a perverse way provided another form of entertainment in the town.

Once Crispina had arrived in Lisbon in 1665, she was repeatedly arraigned before the Inquisitors. In one of her earlier hearings, she was asked to disqualify any witnesses who she claimed might swear falsely against her, because of the hatred that they had for her. An extraordinary list of denunciations followed from her, which shows the extent of gossip and hatred that ran through the town like water, and how often it degenerated into fights. Almost everyone in the Atlantic side of the town was immersed in this, which appears to have brought them a vicious sort of pleasure.

Crispina's most significant enemy was, she said, the new captain-major, António da Fonseca de Ornelas. Jorge had refused to give him gifts and bribes on his arrival, 'and for this reason he hated him so deeply that he openly chased him'. As the most powerful commercial couple in the town, with far better connections that de Ornelas, Jorge was not about to pay fealty: his African networks were far more important than anything de Ornelas could bring. In response the new captain-general destroyed any petitions made by Jorge, refusing to hear them, and 'forced his enemies to denounce and swear false statements before the Reverend Friar Paulo [Lordello]'. This meant that the witnesses would confirm the rumours spread by de Ornelas's own nephew from the island of Madeira, 'who was now living in his house, under his protection and dependent on his charity because he came here poor, and did everything he told him'. In other words, rumours and gossip had been spread by the nephew because of the open hatreds which de Ornelas enjoyed parading around the town.[21]

Ambrosio Gomes was a great friend of de Ornelas, according

## The Heretic of Cacheu

to Crispina. His hatred for Jorge went back to the time when Jorge himself had been captain-general of Cacheu. At that time, Jorge had thrown Gomes into prison, on the order of the governor of Cabo Verde. Gomes had resisted imprisonment and been abusive, and so Jorge had clapped him in irons. However, when a new governor had arrived, he had been bribed to release Gomes; then he had ripped open the prison warrants and burnt them. And then afterwards, as Crispina put it, 'when her husband no longer served as captain-general they had many conflicts and used their swords publicly . . . they were many times seen without talking to each other, not even greeting with their hats publicly'.[22]

Swords were one of the more common items traded in the Bautista Pérez account books, and we can be sure that this kind of collapse of drink, rumour and gossip into quarrel and bloody street-fight was all too common in Cacheu. Another street-fighter and enemy of Crispina and Jorge was the trader whose written descriptions we have often come across in this book, Francisco de Lemos Coelho. According to Crispina, he was an enemy because 'he had a public fight with the nephew of her husband [Jorge], called Manoel Luis Frances, during which the latter was humiliated, fell on the ground, and was wounded.' But Jorge hadn't just fought Gomes and been involved in a fracas with Lemos Coelho, he had also almost had a sword-fight with the merchant-priest Vaz de Pontes: Jorge had called him 'an avaricious person and a *puto* [male prostitute], and that he was known to be a drunk', and Vaz de Pontes had come to his house to provoke a fight, and the two had had to be separated.[23]

In Vaz de Pontes's case, the relationship between drink, gossip and swordfights was made clear by another witness, João Nunes Castanho, Jorge's brother-in-law, who was also declared by Crispina to be an enemy of the couple. Castanho said that one day Vicente Fogaça had been drunk and had claimed that Vaz de Pontes 'had committed sodomy with a Black person but that nobody believed him [when he said this] as he had been very drunk'. Castanho said that others had told him this, including Ambrosio Gomes, 'with whom [Pontes] quarrelled, resulting in the use of arms'. And

## Entertainment and Gossip

eventually, when the religious visitor Gaspar Vogado took a case out against Pontes about this, he did so with 'great glee'.[24]

All these stories make clear both the ubiquity of gossip and its contribution to quarrels, enmities and street-fights. This dynamic leaps off virtually every folio of Crispina's trial. Gossip was always at the root of this, usually founded in enmities and rivalries in wealth, history or sex. Vicente Rodrigues Duarte was an enemy of Jorge, who had testified against him that his brother João had been penanced by the Inquisition in Lima and escaped the galleys in Spain when he had been sent there to see out his sentence. All this knowledge was the result of hearsay, as was Jorge's oath that Vicente had also come secretly to Cacheu and that 'he publicly says, as it is known in Cacheu, that he secretly boarded the ship hiding in a barrel'. Gaspar Vogado was an enemy of Jorge, who had prevented him from fleeing Cacheu after inquiries were made into his appropriation of royal funds: Vogado had responded by 'spreading many rumours and collecting false testimonies' against Jorge.[25]

This 'spread of rumours' – the oral culture which as we have seen was the bedrock of community life – was also the beginning of many of the fights that we have encountered here. It didn't take much for it to degenerate into swordfights which could leave the loser bloodied in the streets. And while this was a form of entertainment, of sorts, many preferred to avoid it if they could. One witness in Crispina's trial was Pedro Correia Tavares, who had been born on the Caboverdean island of Fogo. He described himself as 'a reserved person who is always at home, and does not observe or notice other people's lives'. Some people might try to recuse themselves therefore from the general culture of entertainment that characterized the Atlantic face of the town, of gossip and drinking while waiting for ships to come and go, of rumour, losses from gambling, and the ill-humour, quarrels and fights that followed.[26]

But however resolutely these people tried to stick to this approach, there would always be loudmouthed social butterflies who would arrive from somewhere – Farim, Cabo Verde, Geba – and make sure that little changed. One, of course, was the priest Luis Rodrigues, who had often passed through Cacheu. In his trial before the Inquisitors in Lisbon, he mentioned that one of his own enemies, whose testimony should be ruled out of court, was Manoel Dias de Moura, not only because he had criticized his poor religious observance as priest in Farim, but because they had had a row over a loan. In Cacheu, in Gaspar Vogado's house, the two had had 'a serious and furious quarrel, which was witnessed by [Vogado], his secretary Sebastião Carvalho, Captain Bernardo Rodrigues Pereira, Captain João Rodrigues Duarte, Captain Francisco Correa and Captain Manoel Rodrigues Salgado'.[27]

Here, another echo of Cacheu's long-ago noisescape comes to us. There was the sound of hammering and saws on the ships by day, and of the work of blacksmiths and tailors and coopers on shore. By night, a louder and more distended noise echoed by the riverside. There was the music of some parties, and laughter around gossip and games of cards: and then there were the drunken arguments which so often took hold, leading to furious shouting at the middle of the night, the drawing of swords and the attempts to hold people back from murder.

For death was never far away from daily life in Cacheu.

The king of this partying culture of drink, gossip, enmity and fighting was none other than our old friend, the priest Luis Rodrigues. Having been hauled before the Inquisitors largely because of the enmities he had sown through his own behaviour, he returned to dredge it all up again – fomenting the trial in which Crispina was arrested and deported to Lisbon.

We have seen already that Rodrigues was an inveterate drunkard and womanizer, someone who was happy to slander and denounce others when the mood took him. As one witness put it, 'the canon Luis Rodrigues has many enemies as he is trenchant in his speech.' One of the common insults which he threw about was that people were Jews; as Rodrigues himself put it, 'the majority of the residents of Rua do Calhão were his enemies as he generally called them all Jews'. Another witness said that Rodrigues insulted all his enemies as Jews, whether or not they had any Jewish ancestry, and that 'they heard the insults as coming from ill will and so everyone bore him ill will.'[28]

Sometimes, of course, the fights and enmities were based in material struggles. Factionalism grounded in a zero-sum struggle for control of the material wealth of empire was at the root of many of the fights which then emerged – as we have also seen in the turf war between Ambrosio Gomes and Bibiana Vaz on the one hand, and Crispina and Jorge on the other. It was this factionalism which stoked Crispina's trial, as Jorge and his network had refused to pay tithes to Rodrigues when he had been vicar in Farim, which brought about some of the hatreds for which he sought revenge with the trial of Jorge's wife.[29]

Just as Crispina's trial was grounded in existing commercial rivalries, so, however, was Rodrigues's own imprisonment by the Inquisition. His trial was fomented by the provisor and archdeacon of Santiago island, Diogo Furtado de Mendonça. Rodrigues claimed that he had been preparing a case against Mendonça for trading fifty horses in return for contraband trade with a Dutch ship – when the Dutch had by this time been at war with the Portuguese in Brazil, Angola and across West Africa for almost a quarter of a century. However, there was more to the case than this, as one witness, Manoel Viçoso (who had been born in Cacheu), testified. Viçoso's testimony places the cruelty and viciousness of those in colonial command in clearer relief – illuminating how desperate the quest for worldly wealth made their lives.[30]

Viçoso put it like this:

> [He] declared that the canon Luis Rodrigues had been a great friend of the Archdeacon Diogo Furtado de Mendonça. Then he had brought a petition against Mendonça to the council, so that they would reconsider their consent to the Archdeacon's order that his own brother-in-law should be banished, a man called Miguel Lobo

who was married to the Archdeacon's sister Marina Peres. Because they had agreed that his said brother-in-law should be banished from his wife on [the Archdeacon's] own orders six or seven years before, and now he was dying of hunger, having been rich and married with his sister, before being banished to Guinea and prevented by the said Archdeacon from returning from Guinea and living with his wife. And as the said canon Luis Rodrigues had come back from Guinea, where the said man was living in banishment, he had made this petition in the council. And the Archdeacon had been angered by this, and they had stopped being friendly as before, and this petition made by the canon Luis Rodrigues had been about a year or so [before this trial].[31]

This was a world where close family ties counted for so little, when it was more important to bring low a wealthy commercial rival such as Miguel Lobo than to help out your own sister in her life. In such a world, people inevitably swore routine false testimonies to protect themselves. There was so little trust. It is hardly surprising, therefore, that rumour led to gossip and fights to the death, and even a priest like Rodrigues himself was quite happy to admit to the Inquisitors that he turned to his sword whenever the mood took him – like so many of those did in Cacheu.

Rodrigues was probably a fairly clumsy swordsman, given the amount of drink that he tended to consume. But that he was a regular brawler is pretty clear from his description of an event in Ribeira Grande shortly before his arrest by the Inquisition in Cabo Verde:

Manoel Rodrigues Jorge and his brother João Fernandes Tavares and his brother-in-law Rodrigo Anes Senteio, who all denounced [me in my trial], were at the time of the said accusation my enemies. [And this was] because of a big fight which they had with [me] in the Rua da Misericordia of [Ribeira Grande], next to my front door, with all three of them drawing their swords and wanting to kill me; which without doubt they would have done if the Reverend Cantor

Rodrigo de Figueiredo and the Canon Antonio Mascarenhas had not come running, separating the fight.[32]

Moreover, this was not the only swordfight that Rodrigues had got into shortly before his arrest by the Inquisition in Ribeira Grande. One of the witnesses, the priest Thome Vaz Mascarenhas, described how, shortly before his arrest, Rodrigues had got into hot water with some of his regular drinking friends: Domingos Rodrigues Viegas ('a hasty person who often fell into fights') and Manoel Rodriguez Zurze. Everything stemmed from an argument in the cathedral council, which Rodrigues Zurze had come to lobby Thome Vaz about: Vaz had told him to go away, that everything was over, and when he had told Luis Rodrigues about the argument in Rodrigues's house, he had replied that 'if he had been there, he would not have been as polite with this Manoel Rodrigues Zurze as [Thome Vaz] had been, but would have grabbed him by the head and thrown him down the stairs.' In a small town like Ribeira Grande, it didn't take long for Rodrigues Zurze to find out about this. He soon turned up in broad daylight with Domingos Rodrigues Viegas as his second, challenging Luis Rodrigues to a fight with their swords and pistols drawn. Rodrigues Zurze's brother, João Fernandes Tavares, hammered at the door of Luis Rodrigues's house with his sword.[33]

Other witnesses to this swordfight in the middle of the day, in Rua da Misericordia where Luis Rodrigues lived, added important details. One agreed that it had all gone back to an argument between Luis Rodrigues and the treasurer of the cathedral council, Rodrigues Senteio, who was the brother-in-law of Manoel Rodrigues Zurze. However, another witness said it was because Luis Rodrigues had refused to lend them all a small amount of money and had gone about calling them all Jews. Others said that both the fight in the cathedral council and the refusal of the loan were at the root of it. All witnesses agreed that the fight was the talk of the town, which shows just how far gossip and quarrels were connected and shaped the experiences of the people who lived there. Once the sparring parties were separated, Rodrigues's enemies went off and began to plot his arrest by the Inquisition, which followed fifteen days later.[34]

One witness, the canon Manoel Gonçalves Tinoco, described what happened next, on the account of someone else who was there, João Rodrigues Freire:

> Being in Manoel Rodrigues Zurze's house, all of them badmouthing the canon Luis Rodrigues, Belchior Monteiro (who was there) said to João Fernandes Tavares, 'Aren't your graces getting tired of the canon Luis Rodrigues, who is the wickedest man there is: do you want us to get him arrested? I can look for witnesses who will swear how the Canon Luis Rodrigues has sold relics.' And the witness said that he heard it from Captain Acenso de Abreu, that when he had been in the town of São Domingos, three and a half leagues from this city, the said Belchior Monteiro had called some witnesses, and that he had made it public in front of the said Captain (Abreu) and the vicar of São Domingos, Agostinho Lopes, that he was going to denounce the canon Luis Rodrigues and find witnesses to support his denunciation.[35]

This being the sort of place that it was, it did not take long for Luis Rodrigues to get wind of the put-up job. He soon went to João Fernandes Tavares and Manoel Rodrigues Zurze and 'flung himself at [their] feet', begging them not to proceed with the accusations and the details of them. But by then it was too late. Luis Rodrigues had run out of friends and had a full account book of enemies: the culture of both Ribeira Grande and Cacheu meant that there were very many people who could testify to his culture of drink, gossip and fighting, and soliciting in the confessional.[36]

What was true of Crispina Peres was also true of Luis Rodrigues: taking away the soliciting in the confessional, there was nothing particularly unusual about his behaviour. He was a victim of the large number of enemies that he had accumulated over the years, and not of anything particularly out of the ordinary in his behaviour.

## Entertainment and Gossip

One thing is clear from both cases. There were few secrets in Cacheu and its surrounding region. People moved in and out of one another's homes, renting rooms while they waited for something to happen: a ship to arrive, merchandise to come in to be bought and sold, people to appear and to disappear, in life and in death. In this movement of people, they knew all the intimate details of one another's lives and enjoyed the speech and the power that came with this knowledge. Exaggeration was normal in all of this: for this was, as we have seen, a place where 'from a fly people make an elephant'.

Life was at the centre of this speech, because death was never far away. Death was a festival, one of the main forms of celebration in the town at the funerals in Vila Quente and the more sombre Christian interments in Cacheu. And death was also present in the illnesses that beset everyone, the weak health of the captives being marched around the town in irons, down to the port, out on lighters to the ships – and then back again on shore if their health gave out, where they would be treated by healers, as life went on.

One of the main forms of entertainment was to talk about other people. This conversation usually was widely lubricated with alcohol, either imported (grape-wine from Madeira, rum from the Americas) or African (palm wine and mead). There was music from drums and lutes at some of the parties, there were card games – and then there were quarrels, and there was violence.

All of this helped to pass the time. This was an era in which the experience of time and space was quite different from that which is known in the twenty-first century – something which spoke of the different approaches to life and to living in and around Cacheu, so long ago.

# 9.

# *Time and Space*

*'this had been in the small hours, because the cock had already crowed, although he was not sure if once or twice'*

Anyone from the West who spends long enough in the places at the heart of this book knows that they encounter a different concept of space and time in Senegambia. It is impossible not to become aware of this. Over the centuries, both African and European cultures have formed a strong idea about this difference. In European cultures, this was summarized through the idea that African peoples were not as 'quick', that Africa was somehow 'timeless', that speed was a form of intelligence and that this considered relationship to time was a justification for every racist stereotype constructed about Africans. But, of course, the reality is not that Africa is without time, but that time is differently experienced and thought about on the continent. In Africa, the idea of 'African time' is well worn in countries where some English is spoken; and in Gambia, when you make an arrangement with someone and try to fix a time, they will emphasize 'Gambian time'. Sometimes this is defined further, as 'English time' / *Ora Inglesa* in Guinea-Bissau.

What does 'Gambian time' mean? On a recent visit to participate in teaching workshops in the country, someone asked my host what time the next workshop – held at the megalithic Wassu stone circles, close to the old port of Cassão – would begin. The answer was that it would begin whenever we arrived, after the journey along the bumpy track through the rice-paddies from the small town of

Kuntaur. In other words, some theoretically objective moment or time does not determine the 'when' of something at eight o'clock, nine o'clock or ten o'clock. On this way of thinking, it is the events themselves that determine that 'when' – a view not so far removed from that of the contemporary French philosopher Alain Badiou, and his idea that our essence as human subjects is brought into focus through events.[1]

Each of these two approaches to time is grounded in a fundamentally different worldview and philosophy of the relationship between people, space and events. This is the opposition between what the writer on time Jay Griffiths calls 'clock time' and 'mythic time'. The rhythms of mythic time have structured all societies and continue to do so, however much we might seek to push them into the background. And yet for Griffiths the demands of clock time have unwound their pressure upon societies from the seventeenth century onwards, as a key part of the process by which human beings and their societies were rendered as objects; moreover, this was part of the rise of a patriarchal approach, since, as she notes, women's experience of time is far more cyclical than linear because of the interaction of their menstrual cycles with the lunar waning and waxing.[2]

All this tells us that time and imperialism are closely connected, and that the same goes for time and patriarchal societies. This is a fundamental finding. And yet, curiously, historians are usually pretty bad at writing about time. Time – perhaps like patriarchy – is just 'there', the real canvas against which the rise and fall of empires, the flux of commerce and the changes in ideas and human relationships are all measured. It is the unquestioned assumption from which a historical narrative – unfolding against the passage of time – must follow. In fact, the battle over perceptions of time – and the experience of this conflict in daily life in seventeenth-century Senegambia – was important in the relationship between Atlantic empires and West African societies at that moment in history: indeed, while some recent historians of time have seen the nineteenth century as central to the concept of universal time and its role in socioeconomic change, the changes which allowed this to happen can be traced further back, to the period we are looking at in this book.[3]

How can we best understand the basis of this conflict over time, as a proxy for the conflict over empire? In her pathfinding book, Griffiths describes the commonalities in most approaches to time in world cultures, where so many different human traditions have perceived temporality as a flow, a river, which is unceasing and without division. The capacity to subdivide time into moments, to break it up, is part of the way in which matter can become an object rather than part of a whole: 'If, as by worldwide imagery, time is a river then the clock is merely a mechanical pretender.' But what does it mean to experience time more as a flow than as a series of moments with their specific referents in time – specific moments when we can make appointments, catch planes or attend meetings?[4]

As a way into imagining what this experience was like for the people who lived in Cacheu and roundabout, we can return to the end of the previous chapter. As we saw there, many of the entertainments took place as a way to 'pass the time'. People who lived in the town were generally waiting for something to happen, often related to trade and merchandise. But this experience of waiting was not necessarily something that we would today understand by that term. Anyone who has travelled much in Africa will have had the experience of waiting for a share-taxi or bus to leave: this is not a question of waiting for some specific time, but of waiting for an event to happen, the event when the vehicle is full of passengers. This waiting for an event helps us to understand that it is the event itself – the arrival or departure of a ship, for instance, in the case of seventeenth-century Cacheu – that structured time, and even the experience of waiting. It did not matter whether that event happened on this or that day, or at this or that time.

Of course, this also meant that the character of the event itself might change and be connected more to what Griffiths calls 'mythic time'. One of the main denunciations of Crispina, and pieces of

## Time and Space

evidence of her participation in occult heresies, was that she had performed animal sacrifices on the helm of one of Jorge's ships – something which in the eyes of many in Cacheu was symbolic of her economic and religious status in the town. As one witness put it:

> as he was second helmsman of the ship of Captain Jorge Gonçalves Frances, one day or two before leaving this port, for the Guinea coast, a free Black called Domingos Mendes, now deceased, by order of Crispina Peres, slaughtered a goat and libated the ship's helm with palm wine, and corn flour of the land, so that her husband would have a fortuitous voyage.[5]

Other witnesses added some details to this. One noted that the sacrifice had happened at dawn, and another linked it to the religious practices of the Bijagós peoples in particular, pointing out that

> when ships leave from this Cacheu to buy slaves on the Bijagós islands, the said Bijagós bring along a goat, or a rooster, to slaughter it on the helm of the ship, so that it will be successful, offering the said sacrifice to the same helm, which they regard as God.

And who could say whether the sacrifice had not then created the need to wait for its libations to take effect? In other words, the event of Jorge's ship's coming and going had been (in Western terms) delayed by Crispina so as to perform a religious practice, something which she had the power both to command and to execute in a way that was symbolic of her power in the town – and this sacrifice had been connected to time as well, through its taking place at dawn.[6]

This account reminds us that in a world where very few people had clocks, people's experience of time was not determined by them. Their approach to events was determined by other structuring features, linked to weather – the rainy and dry seasons, the flooding of rice paddies and accompanying onslaught of orchestras of frogs – as well as to the cosmic time constructed by the passage of the sun and the moon across the heavens. And in our world, where it is impossible to look at a digital device such as the laptop on which I am writing this book without being confronted by 'the time', this helps us to understand just how different the experience of the world was in this remote time and place – even as so much of it has yet seemed familiar as well in this book.

An important aspect of modern theories of time is its relationship with space. The theory of relativity famously holds that there is no time in separation from space, and that what properly exists is spacetime, where both space and time exist in relation to each other. Interestingly enough, this was also the way in which time and space were understood by most people in seventeenth-century Cacheu: time and space were seen as a unified continuum, and each was described by people in relation to the other.

Space and distance were often measured through natural cycles of time (not clock-time). When describing how Jorge had sent people from his household to the market at Bujé to seek out a *djabakós*, for instance, the witness Pedro Pais described how this was 'four or five days' distance from this settlement'. This tallies with the description we've seen by Richard Jobson of his interaction with the Mandinga merchant whom he called Buckor Sano. Jobson recounted a discussion they had had about a distant town, which Sano told him had houses 'covered only with gold'. Jobson tells how they asked Sano 'how long he was going, and coming thither: he answered four Moons'. In other words, the distance to the town with houses topped by golden roofs was measured by Sano through the passage of time and the cycles of the lunar calendar. This was probably a tall tale spun after he had consumed the copious amounts of wine that Jobson describes, which again shows how alcohol, gossip and the passing of time were all connected in the lives and experiences of the people who lived here. Sano was a Muslim, but he was no cleric who would shun alcohol like the Jakhanké from Sutucó: clearly, he was quite capable of spinning tall tales if he felt like it in order to impress, and hoped that the idea of a four-month journey would be

*Time and Space*

more than enough to deter Jobson and his crew from actually trying to reach this West African El Dorado.[7]

As these examples of space and distance show, space was often described by people in relation to natural rhythms that were as much measures of time as they were of space. In her trial, Crispina was said to be 'a close relative of the Bainunk Black heathens, who live [at a distance of] circa half a tide from this port'. Here the description of distance was related to the tidal estuary of the São Domingos river and the distance between high and low tides – which of course themselves were ultimately determined by the temporal cycles of the moon and its magnetic pull on the waters of the oceans. That this use of tides as a measure of distance was widespread is clear from the account of Lemos Coelho, who often used tides as units of distance: when discussing the location of Bujé in the Casamance, for instance, he described it as being four tides upstream from Bichangor and Guinguim.[8]

These measures of space coexisted with a more standard measure from Europe, the league. One witness in Crispina's trial described how the Nunez River was seventy leagues distant from Cacheu. Another said that Guinguim was six leagues from Cacheu. In fact, Senegambian measures of tides had an equivalent in leagues, since, according to one witness, Jorge 'had money sent outside this settlement [of Cacheu] to a place at a distance of one tide, i.e. two leagues, called Bugendo'. This European measure of space was also, however, linked to activity rather than distance itself: a league was generally regarded as the distance that could be travelled in one hour on a horse moving at walking pace.[9]

On the other hand, there was one important distinction in the measurement of space. While what we might call the spaces in the natural world were linked to natural cycles of time, in urban settings space was often described through objects that had been made by humans (as the town itself had been). The boatswain Sebastião Vaz described how the *china* at Vila Quente 'lies a gunshot away from this settlement [Cacheu]'. And in her evidence against Luis Rodrigues in his trial, one witness described how her uncle lived 'a wall and a half' away from the priest. This also helps us to understand how people viewed distances and the spaces between objects. These were not fixed in a definitive point of spacetime but were always relational: the distance that a gun might shoot would link one point and another, as would the width of a wall built by people to construct their separate dwellings in what was actually the same town.[10]

How, then, did ideas of space relate concretely to the passage of time? This seems to have been most marked when it came to the question of journeys. The distance of a journey to places was described through the length of time it took to get there. However, this time was not fixed, like the length of time that a train journey or air flight should take. In one letter written to his superiors from the Franciscan monastery in Cabo Verde on 4 August 1658, soon-to-be-Inquisitor Friar Paulo de Lordello described how Sierra Leone was a 'distant journey of 40 days, and sometimes 2 months'. It was understood by everybody that events might get in the way of the passage of time, that life was not entirely predictable – and nor were journeys when there might be flash storms in the rainy season, or when stops en route might be prolonged for all manner of reasons.[11]

In this book, we have seen a number of ways in which this extending of a journey might happen. The crew of the ship might get drunk around a game of cards in Cacheu and be unable to sail. Or there might be a delay because of a funeral of someone everyone knew, or the need to attend to a religious ritual to provide good fortune for the voyage. Alternatively, on arriving in a port, there might be a need to wait for a different ship and its merchandise to come in, if word has spread that it was in the offing: this could bring better products and a higher profit margin, if the rumours about it were true.

As we have seen, all these might have offered good reasons for journeys to take a few days more or a few days less. And this tells us that people had a much less rigid approach to time and events than is the case in our own era. They might have some plans, but these could be interrupted by unforeseen events. If that happened, they

## Time and Space

were happy to wait, because a journey could not be finished until it came to its end – and there might be all kinds of reasons for a delay. Space was therefore often measured through the passage of time, and this tells us also that ideas of space were themselves fluid and could change according to how time 'went'. Nevertheless, European ideas of space (the league) coexisted with Senegambian ideas, and this was part of the geopolitical coexistence and competition that was taking shape.

While space was often measured through time, time itself often was accounted for according to events during the day. This was the customary mode of relating the time at which some event happened, far and away more common than the use of clock-time.

First, it is worth being aware of how rare the knowledge of clock-time was. Even in Ribeira Grande on Santiago island – which was a much bigger outpost of empire than was Cacheu – there was no clock in the city. It would seem also that few people had access to clocks. As one witness in Luis Rodrigues's trial put it, the scribe João Mascarenhas, after returning from a night out drinking and eating until the small hours with Rodrigues, 'did not know what time this was since there was no Clock in this City'. It is probable that some of the traders did have timepieces as status symbols – a canon giving evidence against Luis Rodrigues did mention 'ten o'clock at night' (presumably just meaning that it was late) – but with no public working clock in the town there was certainly no reliable way of setting the time accurately. That timepieces were traded is shown by the fact that the king of Kaabu was reported in the 1680s to have European curiosities that included clocks – although, again, these were not set at all accurately and were most likely there as testament to the curiosity of such a different approach to time.[12]

Instead of publicly acknowledged clock-time, therefore, time was told according to the things that people did. Evening time was discussed in relation to mealtimes. A witness in Luis Rodrigues's trial described how she had gone to collect her written confession from the canon at the cathedral 'at dinner-time'. Mornings in Ribeira

Grande were measured in part by the ritual of mass in the cathedral, which was said by canons such as Rodrigues and his peers – and was a source of much gossip, for he so often stood up drunk in the pulpit for the ritual, which was also a sacred marking of the passing of time.[13]

As for the night-time itself, this was measured according to the morning callouts of the cockerels. Before they began, this was the deepest night; and after the cocks had begun their morning calls, it became the early morning. A late night out was measured according to this noise, as the witness Bras Rodrigues put it, describing how one time 'he had been eating and drinking with this Canon until after the cocks had crowed' – and that when the canon had wanted to continue he, Bras Rodrigues, had reprimanded him since it was 'after the cocks' (*passante dos gallos*) – a time when inveterate drunkards like the canon might give respectable drunkards like Bras Rodrigues a bad name.[14]

Another witness, João d'Alvarenga, gave a different piece of evidence which also helps to understand the relation between events and time. Alvarenga described another of Luis Rodrigues's nights out, saying that 'this had been in the small hours, because the cock had already crowed, although he was not sure if once or twice; and that this had all happened in the month of January, five or six years ago'.[15] If the cock crowed once, this was a sign that it was still night-time. But a second call was definitely a sign that the night was moving into early morning. It was the event of the call of the cockerels, and the understanding that they had of the relationship of this to the natural cycles of day and night, which structured how most people understood time. After the cocks crowed was, as some witnesses put it, a time that was so late that it was 'beyond hours [time]', or 'outside of hours [time]': a moment that could not be measured and was not really to be understood in relation to any other event or activity.[16]

The idea of something happening 'beyond hours/time' also shows us that there was a broader sense of the passage of events outside of measurement. Much of this was related by people to

## Time and Space

what they called 'midnight'. Luis Rodrigues's parties were seen as becoming scandalous when they went 'beyond midnight into the next day'. Another witness, the bailiff Manoel da Serra, admitted that he had often gone out drinking and eating with Rodrigues, '[until] it had got very late, but that he had always retired to his house because he was a married man, and so he does not know what used to go on after midnight'. There was a general sense that it was the time after midnight which was 'beyond time', in the deepest part of the night. But from what we have seen here, this idea of midnight was more likely structured by the turn of events as things became ever more drunk, quarrelsome and lustful – as when Rodrigues went to hammer on the door of his co-godparent Maria Gonsalves to demand to sleep with her – rather than an idea that it was now past twelve o'clock at night.[17]

This more general awareness of the passage of time, something not linked to hours or necessarily to points in the calendar, marked the deeper sense of how people experienced the passing of their lives. This can be seen most clearly when people describe their ages, for there was a real sense of vagueness about how people in Senegambia saw their ages in calendar-time. Inquisitors always asked people about their age at the start of their testimony, and this was always noted down as 'more or less'. With some witnesses, this seems to have been quite precise: Pedro Furtado de Mendonça said that he was 'forty-eight years old, more or less', for instance, while Maria Rodrigues Duarte said that she was 'twenty-six years old, more or less'. But while these people seem to have had quite a firm idea of their age in calendar years, with other witnesses matters were different.[18]

Some of the best examples of this come from Crispina's trial. One witness was Maria Mendes. Mendes had been born on Santiago island but had lived in Cacheu for many years. When asked her age, 'she said it was 70 or 80 years, more or less'. Meanwhile, in Farim, Domingos Afonso (who had also been born in Cabo Verde) said that he was 'sixty years old, rather more than less'. In both cases, the passage of years seems to have been something that increasingly Mendes and Afonso did not bother with marking precisely. This was something they knew to be important to officials from the empire, but it was not something that mattered to them very much any longer, even though they tried their best to make an educated guess. The same feeling can be read in the reply of the household slave Esperança, living in Ribeira Grande at the time of Luis Rodrigues's trial, who had been born 'in Guinea': when asked by the Inquisitors, Esperança said that she did not know her age, but then clarified that she was 'twenty-four years old, more or less'.[19]

Clearly, this was an estimate that Esperança had, more or less, made up to try to satisfy the requirements of imperial time. And these requirements increasingly sought to corral people into the rigours of clock-time, where the passing of life was measurable and could be split up into definite moments, as part of the broader process of the objectification of the world and humans which went with the rise of the Atlantic empires.

When I was first getting to know the region of Senegambia in the 1990s, I made a number of friends. Some of them I still know today. I remember when one of them showed me his Senegalese national identity card. This told me that he was five years older than I was. Except, he then pointed out, he had probably been about five years old when his mother had taken him to register his 'birth' in the nearest town. In fact, this meant that my friend was nine or ten years older than me – more or less – although for bureaucratic purposes we were not so far apart. Years later, as I comb through these old records which speak of how people thought about time and the passage of their lives so many centuries ago, I realize how long-lasting this disjunction between clock-time and the Senegambian meanings of time has been.

My friend's story also helps to understand one of the main drivers of the imposition of clock-time. This was the rise of imperial bureaucracy, the forerunner of the French imperial bureaucracy that my friend's family had also experienced under French rule in Senegal in the twentieth century – and whose requirements they too had taken with as much of a pinch of salt as possible, just as their ancestors had in seventeenth-century Senegambia. It was in the distant seventeenth century that the first harbingers of the modern imperial state were consolidated, along with all its angry and violent screeds of text which attempted to form one prescribed and factual view of reality rather than the multiple experiences of it. A detailed parsing of these angular, erect lines of script tells us that one of the main ways that this state was imposed was in fact through the construction of a linear form of time. Whereas it may be that, as Jay Griffiths eloquently puts it, 'we are linear, and we are cyclic', the erasure of the cyclical form of time and its experience was part of the ethnocentric imperial approach to time, objectivity and science itself – ever the handmaiden to imperial dreams.[20]

The violence in the construction of linear time through bureaucracy emerges most clearly if we return to the governor of Cabo Verde, Jorge Mesquita de Castelbranco, whom we met in the Introduction to this book. Castelbranco produced vast reams of documentation during his short tenure as governor, all of them precisely dated and annotated according to their place in the imperial line of time. Castelbranco's main concern was to justify his actions and what was claimed by his detractors to be the theft of 50,000 *cruzados* from the imperial state. In order to do this he produced trials and attestations on every subject imaginable, all running to several pages (at a time when paper was a valuable commodity). Writing and the power to determine the validity of an account through its appearance at a specific moment in time were central strategies in his approach – which reveals the power of the linear construction of time and how closely related it was to the objectification of time, space, merchandise and people.[21]

As soon as we read the original documents of that moment, we are confronted with the epistemic force and violence of this approach. A sample of entries from Luis Rodrigues's trial brings out the centrality of time in the power of empire:

> On the twentieth of October of 1657 in this city of Ribeira Grande on the island of Santiago of Cabo Verde in the Franciscan Monastery . . .

*The Heretic of Cacheu*

On the twenty-fifth of October 1657, in this city of Ribeira Grande on the island of Santiago of Cabo Verde in the Franciscan Monastery, being there present the provisor and governor, the following witnesses were asked about the contents of the above testimony . . .

Year of the Birth of Our Lord Jesus Christ 1657, on the thirtieth day of October of the said year, the provisor Diogo Furtado de Mendonça went with me the scribe to the residences of Canon Luis Rodrigues, whom the said provisor seized and took as a prisoner with the help of Governor Pero Ferraz Barreto, to whom he was handed over in custody.[22]

What is striking is that the most important detail is seen as the date in calendar-time. The date always has precedence. In the final part of the text, it is the date that comes first, followed by the actual event: the seizure and imprisonment of the drunkard canon Luis Rodrigues, following the case cooked up by his enemies, who had had enough of his insults and escapades in the town. In other words, imperial time as written down by the scribes of the Inquisition was also conceived as the polar opposite of most people's workaday experience of time. In the linear time of patriarchy, the date came first and then the event; whereas, as we have seen, for most people it was events themselves which structured the experience of time.

The growing sway of the imperial bureaucracy could be imposed on people's own experience of time through the actual power that it had over their lives. In a situation where people could be arrested, their assets seized and their lives ruined, all according to the demands and evidence accumulated in paper-trails – as happened with Crispina – it was vital to be able to keep track of the imperial measures of time which would make sense within this enforced linearity. Inquisitors themselves would refer to calendar-time in their enforcement of their protocols and powers, and so defence against them was best achieved through being aware of this dimension of time as well.

We see this in the first pages of Crispina's trial, where Inquisitor

## Time and Space

Lordello begins by making reference to the original trial taken against Luis Rodrigues 'Canon of the see of the town of Ribeira Grande in Guinea on the seventeenth and other days of January 1658', and noting that this was now to be reinvestigated. Lordello was well able to refer to these documents, since he had been involved in this trial too and had access to the records – a privilege not accorded to those he interrogated. The first witness, Pedro Nunes, was called on 1 January 1661 in Cacheu and asked again to recall what he might have said in the original trial: attention to memory, the awareness of dates and how they might be used to support evidence and testimony, all this was vital in ensuring the security someone had against the arbitrary power and cruelty of the institutions of empire.[23]

One witness in the trial, Vicente Fogaça, gave a specific example of how people made sure to be aware of calendar-time (or clock-time), even if this was not mostly how they experienced the cycles of life. In giving evidence in 1663 about Crispina's sacrifice of animals on the helm of Jorge's ship, Fogaça said that this had happened, 'at daybreak, approximately, on 19 February, in the year 1648'. In the margin, the scribe (none other than the friar André de Faro, whom we came across in Chapter 5), wrote 'I say 50'; which probably meant that Fogaça had revised his view of the date to 1650 rather than that Faro had a different opinion (scribes were not really permitted to have opinions, at least not on paper). This is significant, as it shows that Fogaça had constructed a general memory about the date in February, although the number of years that had passed since – whether thirteen or fifteen – was less clear to him. This shows that in Cacheu dates were known to be important as potential pieces of evidence against an enemy, that it was key to note down the details – but also the slippage of this so easily into the more general river of time which was in fact how most people experienced their lives.[24]

The centrality of empire in enforcing calendar- and clock-time is made clearest by looking at the perspectives of those most involved in it. Manoel Bautista Pérez, for instance, was someone who certainly ran his view of the world according to clock-time. In 1612, he noted down that his daughter Maria had been born in Cacheu on Monday 2 July. Many years later, now a man grown rich through the traffic in African captives, he would still be sending goods over to her from Lima in order to support her daily needs. This was a world in which fear, violence and the passage of time separated people from their emotional bonds. Travel could become a cause of separation, loss and the need to remove oneself from emotions and from the world through a pseudo-objective distance and clock-time specificity of approach, a distance that went with the objectification of so much else.[25]

People who lived in Cacheu in the seventeenth century thus shaped their view of time through two competing and diametrically opposed influences. On the one hand, there was the growing power of imperial demand. While the importance of Cabo Verde itself as an outpost of empire was in decline, the forces of multi-empire economic demands – from the Dutch, the English, the French – were growing year on year. This also meant that it was important to be aware of clock-time and calendar-time, both as a means of self-protection and in order to be able to manoeuvre within this growing power.

On the other hand, most people's experience of time did not fit with this approach. The fact was that things took a long time to happen. A ship might arrive next week, next month or in six months' time. It might easily be attacked by enemies, or founder in a storm and sink en route, which meant that letters and imperial instructions might just get lost. As an insurance policy, administrators made copies to send on multiple ships, in the hope that one would get there. Someone sending a letter from Cabo Verde to Lisbon in the 1660s might well send it via Brazil – hardly a speedy enterprise in the age of sail. All this meant that it was events which structured the experience of time, and not the humanly conceived unfolding line of time itself, or even the workaday strategy of waiting for a reply to a letter – a reply that was as likely to arrive as not.[26]

A good example of what this might mean in practice to people

*Time and Space*

living in this world was given by the Capuchin missionary Antonio Cavazzi, who spent many years evangelizing in the kingdoms of Matamba and Ndongo in West-Central Africa (the northern part of today's Angola). Writing in March 1662 – just a couple of years before Crispina's arrest 3,000 miles north-west in Cacheu – Cavazzi noted that he had that day received a reply from the Papal Curia to a letter which he had sent to Pope Alexander VII in late 1657. In other words, it had taken a little over four years for him to receive a response to this letter. In a world where this sort of experience was the norm, even imperial emissaries could hardly depend on the calendar for their main experience of time, howsoever they structured their texts and petitions through it.[27]

Nevertheless, there are signs throughout the documents that have survived that clock-time was gaining a significant hold on popular consciousness. This was symptomatic of the growing power of the Atlantic empires. Where mythic time has a cyclical view of the passage of events and experience, something that is then communicated in speech, it was in the seventeenth century increasingly interrupted by the linearity of time as marked by writing. This explains too a different approach to reality and to history itself: where myth is oral and time is cyclical – and much history in West Africa remains oral to this day – history is seen by its Western traditionalists as something that is written down, requiring therefore chronology and a linear view of time. Cacheu was a place where these visions clashed: mythic time lived powerfully in Vila Quente and in most places round and about, but in the imperial centre by the portside clock-time dominated and was used to order the evidence through which Crispina would be arrested. Through this constant insistence on dates and times in the texts that were produced, history would eventually be written and set down as fixed in time, just as orality was dismissed as the fabric of myth.[28]

The corollary of a linear view of time was the sense of its universality. Working in the later seventeenth century, and beginning to develop his ideas of gravity precisely in the same era as Crispina's trial, Isaac Newton's view of time was of one that was not only mechanical but also absolute. So did an absolute, universal view of time arise alongside the view of universalism which came to characterize Atlantic empires. This imperial universality was linked also to the objectification of value in capital, so that the use of time was vital in making money (or, as the saying has it, 'time is money'). Indeed, some have argued that the rise of market capitalism in late medieval Europe was closely connected to the growing desire to measure time. Those who had political or economic power were, in this approach to reality, in the position to make claims and enchain the time of others: the power to measure time was increasingly important in the structure of human relations.[29]

So it shouldn't be surprising that the experience of time was vital in seventeenth-century Cacheu, and emblematic of the struggle taking place between West African political and economic frameworks and Atlantic empires. The Senegambian experience of time and its links to key points in the life-cycle, the cyclical view of time and experience, was far and away the dominant one. Space and time were always interconnected, and this was not a link that needed to wait for twentieth-century science to confirm it. Space was conceptualized through natural features or through the passage of time, and time itself was linked to events – was created by the things that people did with one another, collectively, and which many could remember.

On the other hand, as the power of the Atlantic empires grew, and with it the cycles of their economic demand, the things that people did were increasingly being rendered as objects within an imaginary continuum. It was through this objectification and claimed universalism that money and power were becoming concentrated in the West – and that, year by year, accumulated economic value was declining in Africa.

# 10.
## *Living, Healing and Dying in Cacheu*

'I am unable to get out of bed because of my knees and feet; all the joints of the arms are stiff; I am therefore always in infinite pain.'

The cornerstone of Crispina Peres's inquisition trial was not in fact Crispina's alleged deployment of witchcraft, or even the hatred, rancour and rivalry which the witnesses so evidently felt for one another: the pages of the trial make clear that what really mattered to everyone in Cacheu beyond all else was health and the ability to heal. And the claim itself to be able to heal was closely bound up in the processes of objectification that we saw unfolding in the last chapter – objectification towards people, objects and even space and time from the imperial centre. In this chapter, we will see how the imperial assault on West African ways of healing both inaugurated a form of medical colonialism and was a key factor in the shifting balance of power between European empires and West Africans at this time.

Cacheu was an unhealthy place. People spent months and even many years bedridden, suffering from fevers, swellings and distempers of one kind or another. This was especially true of the immigrant Portuguese white men from all corners of the empire, but it was also true of African children who were born and raised here – children such as Crispina's daughter, whom she tried so hard to save from illness and death, resorting to the visits of the *djabakós*, all in an effort to save her, and all to no avail, as she herself tells us in her deposition in Lisbon. Illness was part and parcel of daily life and something that almost everyone was concerned with from one day to the next: their own health, the health of their partners and children, and – for the traffickers – the health of their captives.

Illness regularly produced massive personal and economic, losses. In such a situation, those who claimed the ability to heal were powerful. Medicine and power were – as in all societies through history – connected. As we saw in Chapter 7, there were both European and African healers at work in Cacheu. Those whose powers as healers went unchallenged represented dominant political power, and, inevitably in an African setting, African medical knowledge was preferred. It was the Senegambian healers who knew the uses of local plants to reduce swellings and fevers and who could apply them with success, while European apothecaries tended to rely on imported salves from Europe which were of questionable use in such a different setting. This meant that in many parts of Western Africa in these decades, as a number of historians have shown, Europeans routinely consulted African doctors and also learnt from some of their techniques to deploy them in other parts of the world.[1]

However, this pragmatic approach was also a threat to the supremacy of the Atlantic empires and the objectification of knowledge that went with it. If the consultations of *djabakós* could be made to appear politically risky, and liable to lead to personal destruction, then this would confirm that European imperial power was on the rise. In this way, Crispina's consultation of *djabakós* came to be symbolic of all her 'heresies' in the Inquisitorial trial. Her use of African medical practices, and consultation of their practitioners, was also a confirmation and an acknowledgement that African political power and knowledge remained primary. If this could be weakened, then the political and ideological independence of Africa itself could be contested.

Thus, European deployment of medicine in Africa began in a colonial framing. This started with the almost open recognition that medicine and colonial power were connected. This was a relationship that would only intensify in the centuries that followed.

★

## Living, Healing and Dying in Cacheu

Jorge himself was a sick man, and his illness led to many of Crispina's consultations of the *djabakós*. There were two views of this in Cacheu: Crispina said she had consulted the healers in a loving attempt to cure her husband, while her enemies said that she did so with a view to keeping him laid up in bed through the *djabakós'* wicked contrivances. If he was bedridden, she could control him, and not suffer sexual jealousy when he departed on one of his trading trips.

The couple's enemies waxed lyrical on this misogynist idea. According to Domingos de Aredas, 'it was commonly said that his wife Crispina Peres kept him prisoner, in that bed, out of jealousy.' Francisco Tavares said that 'he had commonly heard that the said Crispina Peres had kept her husband bedridden by the art of witchcraft, and when she was arrested he got up out of bed and felt better.' However, the reliability of these claims is paper-thin; they really just reveal the extent to which illness and disease were currencies that could be converted into malicious gossip and entertainment throughout the town – as well as how far the general social arrangements of Cacheu challenged the ingrained misogyny of arrivals from elsewhere in the empire.[2]

Malicious gossip was at the root of the accusations that Crispina consulted the *djabakós* to keep Jorge bedridden. This was made clear by the deposition of Vaz de Pontes. The priest put a more balanced appraisal of Jorge's condition than many in his own account, confirming that:

> for many years, I have seen Captain Jorge Gonçalves Frances ... ill and usually lying in bed and living sheltered because of the many aches and pains he suffers in all his joints; some say they are due to bad humours and others [say it is] arthritis, from which he suffers dearly, and [that] he has undergone many prolonged and difficult treatments to see if he would get better, such as herbs, fumigation and ointments and many other medicines, without ever feeling any considerable improvement, which is known and public [knowledge] to everybody.[3]

The role of arthritis in Jorge's condition seems evident from his own account. There are several depositions in which Jorge describes his own conditions in his own words. In one, he notes that 'it is public and notorious that he has been sick and lying in bed for the past seven years . . . suffering infinite pain in all the joints of his body'. This suggests a chronic inflammatory condition. It becomes clear that Jorge did not suffer from the fevers which so often shortened people's lives in Cacheu: instead, he was someone who had great difficulty in moving, and who therefore tried various approaches to healing – as anyone sensible would do in his situation.[4]

Jorge described in greatest detail his condition, as well as the treatments prescribed by the herbalists, in a letter of 19 September 1659:

> I am unable to get out of bed because of my knees and feet; all the joints of the arms are stiff; I am therefore always in infinite pain. Distressed with this disease, I decided to call, I mean, to seek a Black herbalist, who gave me local treatment [made of] an infusion of straw and trampled herbs which I [should] drink, and also to tie the said herbs where I have pain; [this is] the common manner in which they cure yaws; and the said Black man came and I followed his instructions; and I thought that the said treatment that he was going to give me was done in the same manner, because he came prepared with many herbs and roots, besides a few, which he collected here in the fields [nearby], with which he prepared two pots, from which I [should] drink.[5]

Jorge's appraisal of his condition is further clarified by Crispina. In her testimony, she described his suffering from arthritis, as well as her regular and heartfelt attempts to cure him. Far from being a duplicitous spouse who connived with malicious herbalists to keep him housebound, she suffered heartache from his ailments:

> Two years before he had married me he was afflicted with arthritis . . . and when he married me he came to my house in a chair because he could not stand on his feet; and after I married him

> I had a lot of work to cure him and assist him day and night for nine continuous years, with tears every day; and nights spent seeing him suffering and feeding him many times from my own hands; for this reason I needed assistance and to make arrangements; and I could not leave the house because I was assisting him in this manner.[6]

This account makes it seem surprising that the couple married at all. However, Crispina and Jorge were a 'power couple' in Cacheu, whose union cemented their position in the town. Moreover, illness was such a commonplace that, as far as Crispina was concerned, Jorge's condition may have seemed no worse than the risk of his dying rapidly from malaria; as someone who had been born in Senegambia and weathered the childhood bouts of illness, he was at least comparatively safe from fevers, which were the main source of rapid death.

'The illnesses of Guinea' (*os achaques da Guiné*) are one of the most frequent complaints found in the imperial sources we have. This referred to the malarial fevers which could come on at any moment, especially for European outsiders who were not used to them. The common cure was to be bled, as the priest André de Faro and the Inquisitor Paulo de Lordello noted, probably by the surgeon-barbers. When Faro fell ill on the Nunes river in 1663, he was bled six times and given purgatives. Lordello described how 'on the eighth day of kings' (i.e. during the twelve days of Christmas) in early January 1663, 'as I was awake lying in bed ill and bloodletting', the Pepel from Mata de Putame had stormed the hospice of Cacheu and stolen everything he had. This sort of illness was, then, common even for someone like Lordello, who had spent several years in Senegambia and Cabo Verde by then: on his arrival in 1658 he had been sick and had been 'bled with roots', and then two years later, in a letter written in Ribeira Grande of 5 August 1660, he noted that 'after being bled six times I am now without fever'.[7]

The feverish illnesses that were rife in West Africa were associated by missionaries like Lordello with what they saw as its condition of damnation. As a place in which the devil was hard at work, it was beset by dangerous currents. In this letter of August 1660, Lordello blamed his fevers on his recent missionary activities on the mainland, noting that although he had the right materials with which to bleed himself,

> the illness has not gone, and this is something I have brought with me from the journeys I have made [to Africa]; since this land is so malignant that when you are out in it and then return, you always get ill from the pestilential airs from which it suffers.[8]

It was the work of the devil which explained why everyone was at risk from these fevers, wherever they came from and however long they had already spent in West Africa. Even people who had spent many years there were not immune. Gaspar Vogado began one letter in 1659 describing how his 'health is very weak from these fevers that have started on the first of this month and which have not stopped for fifteen days [and] with the bloodletting I had'. Other regular forms of illness included smallpox and infected wounds, which without the modern salve of antibiotics easily turned ulcerous. The routine way in which such ailments were described in the letters and in the trials that we have make it clear just how normal a part of daily life they were.[9]

Some of these accounts allow us to get a richer sense of what the workaday reality of illness meant for daily life in the town. Fairly often, the Bautista Pérez accounts describe enslaved Africans 'ill in the house', or being sick from a condition such as smallpox and then dying. The columns of profit and loss in these books are stark: they represent an evaluation of life and death in which the condition of captives, lying sick and treated by herbalists, is valued only for the economic loss that their death represents. The accounts make it clear that such events were very common, with regular descriptions as we have seen of sick captives rowed ashore to prevent the outbreaks of epidemics on the trafficking ships. People fell ill from one moment to the next: this was something that everyone knew

## Living, Healing and Dying in Cacheu

to be true, as the matter-of-factness with which Inquisitor Lordello described being sick and bled in bed in Cacheu makes clear.

Inevitably, the frequency of illness meant that death often followed. Manoel Bautista Pérez's brother, João, never made it across the Atlantic to become rich in Peru. The last we know of him is from his will, which he dictated bedridden in Cacheu, on 12 January 1617, 'lying ill in bed from the illness which God has given me'. In his will, he showed how fully immersed he was in his life in this Atlantic-trafficking town in Senegambia, for he had four children with two different Senegambian women – Susana and Victoria – both of whom were evidently enslaved by him, since he freed them on his deathbed. The conditions which João attached to their freedom also speak loudly about the vertical, violent hierarchies of life: Victoria was freed along with their sons, Manoel and Francisco, on condition that she served the boys and went with them to Portugal, to the house of João's brother-in-law Francisco de Narvaes; and Susana was freed with their daughters, Izabel and Barbara, but was not permitted to leave her house unless she took the children to Portugal.[10]

It would not have taken much for the fates of the brothers to be reversed, for Manoel to have died, and for João perhaps to have become the richest man in Peru while sending money to his own children in Cacheu, only to have been the one burnt by the Inquisition in Lima twenty-two years later. In terms of their experience of disease, those New Christians who then came to Cacheu after that 1639 auto-da-fé, like João Rodrigues Duarte, fared little better than João had done thirty years before. In 1657, João wrote a petition to the crown in which he wrote that he had 'lived in this town for many years, suffering great illnesses, which have left him most of the time bedridden' – and asking to be granted permission to travel to be with his family in Portugal. Presumably Duarte hoped that there he might be able to pass the rest of his life in the Alentejo free from the bodily pain which had been such a daily feature of his life in West Africa.[11]

The struggle for life and the battle with death were something

## The Heretic of Cacheu

that was a daily part of the lives of all – traffickers as well as the trafficked, imperial wannabes and those who came from the *tabankas* around Cacheu. Life itself was evanescent, a process of constant separation of people from that which they knew and loved, such a passing shadow that it was much easier to grab onto the afterlife than that which was before you. Describing Crispina's sacrifice of animals on the deck of Jorge's ship, the pilot Vicente Fogaça gave a sorrowful evocation of this part of the human experience. Seeing the remnants of the blood on the helm, Fogaça said:

> [he] asked what it was, they told him the above, saying that Captain Jorge Gonçalves was not guilty in this case, but rather his wife, Crispina Peres, and Manoel Pires Torres, deceased, and Sebastião Fernandes Mascarenhas, deceased, knew about this, as well as Barnabé Siqueira, absent, and Second Lieutenant Miguel Lobo, resident on the island of Santiago, and Domingos de Andrade, born in Lisbon, and absent on a Dutch ship, and João Pimenta, born in Moura, and currently absent on the Guinea coast.[12]

Absence was a form of death, since an absent person might well in fact be dead by the time they were spoken of. All the same, a person's absence could be requited through gossip and hearsay, and this might give the sense of the continuity of life even as it was ruptured, broken and torn apart by forces of economic demand and power that were beyond anyone's control. The fantasy of an objective framing – of people, of place, of matter, of time – might provide some sense of security. On the other hand, the spiritual powers of the *djabakós* might also offer the solace of continuity, if they could be found to connect with those who had departed either this world or this place.

Did Senegambians have the same approach to death and dying as the mainly mixed-heritage people who came from the Atlantic empires? As we saw with the approaches to entertainment, the people of Vila Quente saw death as a festival as much as anything. Moreover, although trade and work were important, there was not the imperative to accumulate account-book wealth over long periods of time. Historians of death in West Africa have shown very clearly that the purpose of life was not to extend it for as long as possible. It was impossible to avoid illness, or death. Instead, what mattered was to accept death as a natural part of life, to die with honour, and in so doing to honour one's ancestral lineages in the process of joining them. It was this that connected ideas of dying in Cacheu to the religious frameworks of the *djabakós*, through which communities of the living were connected to the ancestors.[13]

On Cabo Verde, the hold of African religions was less firm. This was a settlement colony which had been uninhabited prior to the mid-fifteenth century. However, Christianity offered no better protection from death, which seems to have been every bit as frequent on the islands as it was around Cacheu itself. So many officials died in 1647 that many imperial posts were vacant; there were so few candidates that those who survived, like Antonio Peres de Souto, applied for two posts at once (one being accountant). In a letter written by the town council to the Overseas (Colonial) Council in March, the officers noted that one problem was 'the shortage of people on the island, since so many of them are dead'. In fact, the present tense showed again that for many people there death was one form of parting, just as an ocean voyage could be (which could of course also easily lead to death).[14]

Both African religions and Christianity therefore gave succour to the idea of a continuum between life and death. Witnesses in Crispina's trial would often speak of people as if they were still present, only to note that they were in fact dead. One witness said that Gregório de Andrade and the carpenter Antonio Pires would be able to declare about the canon Luis Rodrigues's scandalous behaviour in Farim, 'and make more sense of the matter than he, the witness, although they have [since] died'. Another enemy of Luis Rodrigues, João Rodrigues, had also 'since died'. Meanwhile, when the governor of Cabo Verde and Luis Rodrigues's enemy Pero Ferraz Barreto tried to make further inquiries of some of the witnesses, it was a doomed enterprise, since, as he put it, 'there won't be any further news from them, since Pedro Soares has died, and also the scribe who wrote it all down, and only the teacher of the school is alive, the Vicar-General Afonso Fernandes from Tavira.'[15]

Death was so commonplace that when people wrote letters they gave instructions as to what should happen to the reply in the event that they were by then dead. Yet while death was in its way a salve from pain, there was still a sense that best of all was to be healed from the pain that prefigured it.[16] One *djabakós* said to Crispina that 'her husband Jorge Gonçalves was in much pain, [and so] she went to great lengths and procured a lot of remedies' in order to try to free him from it. Those who were, like Crispina, apparently quite free from pain thus seem to have felt a sense of responsibility to do what was in their power to cure those they loved. They also perhaps felt a sense of guilt, knowing that they were not experiencing the sufferings of their loved ones. They knew that death could follow pain, and that the power to heal came from those who had accrued power in their society. So, in Cacheu, this meant turning to the knowledge of the *djabakós*.

The *djabakós* are the most enigmatic and emblematic figures to have come down across the centuries through the records that survive. On the one hand, the power of the *djabakós* and the apparent incapacity of the imperial institutions to prevent people from consulting them bears witness to the reality we have seen in this book, that this was first and foremost an African political and cultural space. On the other hand, the trial itself reveals that this power was now under challenge from the rival imperial forces struggling for power in the Atlantic world.

From a distance of several centuries, the powers of the *djabakós* themselves appear to cross worlds. They were associated by outsiders with Islam as well as with African religions – emblematic of 'otherness' for the imperial Portuguese. This religious dimension, and the offerings that they called on their clients to perform, went hand in hand with the power to heal disease. This is very revealing, for it shows that in Cacheu the health of the body and the spirit were seen as integrated – much as was also the case for many in the Europe of the day. In the worldview of seventeenth-century Cacheu, healing the body also required healing the spirit, even if in the account books of the human traffickers it was the control of bodies alone that counted.

This explains the approach to disease so often encountered in Crispina's trial, where the physical cures recommended by the *djabakós* were connected to spiritual frameworks. As one of her most dangerous enemies, Gaspar Vogado, explained in his testimony, the *djabakós* who came to Crispina's house had told her that her household slaves had 'eaten' her daughter, and that 'this is how the heathens of this Guinea call killing heathens; they hold that nobody dies of disease, and that only those who cast spells kill them, which they call eating.' Vogado also described how a powerful *djabakós* took a piece of flesh from the belly of those who had fallen sick through spells cast on them by others. This 'eating' was confirmed by a number of other witnesses as a way in which people perceived illness: it involved consuming their life-force through a spiritual attack, appropriating their vital energy for the assailant's own purposes; and this consumption by the *djabakós* represented an attempt to repay the attack in kind.[17]

The frequency with which people fell ill is therefore significant in terms of understanding the worldview of those who lived in Cacheu. Since illness was seen by many people as caused by spiritually powerful enemies and the hatred which they bore, and since illness was so common, the malice and quarrels which ran through the town were in fact seen as a major cause of ill health. Imbalances in the community caused by greed, rivalry, fear and ideological and religious differences led to hatreds, which in turn led to the consultation of those deemed able to muster a spiritual attack on an enemy. What this tells us is that the people who lived in the town often saw it as a dangerous place, with the discord that ran through it easily capable of provoking disease.

Of course, all this was grist to the mill of the *djabakós*, since if casting spells could produce disease, only those who worked

## The Heretic of Cacheu

with the requisite supernatural forces could fight against it. The *djabakós* made much of their supernatural powers. According to Gaspar Vogado, one in particular 'had extraordinary things [said] about him, from people with much prestige, that when he wanted to he could transform himself into a lion, a leopard, or another animal, in view of those who were present'. Shapeshifting has been commonly associated with sorcery in many cultures – and was indeed also part of the witchcraft trials in Logroño in northern Spain in the early seventeenth century – and was according to this account deemed by the *djabakós* to be a significant aspect of their skills.[18]

This approach, and these elements of the art of the *djabakós*, drew from the spiritual perception of health. From the point of view of the Inquisitors, the recourse to the *djabakós* was a sign of potential heresy, because those who were their clients had also to enter into their worldview in which a herbal cure worked in part because of its curative properties of the soul of the person who had fallen sick. If it was true that 'normally in this [settlement of] Cacheu, when people are sick, they cure themselves with *djabakós* or those who cast spells', this also indicated that most people there subscribed to the West African view of life and the spirit – something that the approach of materialist account-book imperialism could not tolerate.[19]

On the other hand, while the *djabakós* asserted the power of the spirit, they deployed a range of herbal medicines in order to treat the spiritual and physical ailments of the sick. A number of witnesses in Crispina's trial provided accounts of their approach to the curing of disease. Gaspar Vogado gave a detailed description:

> she keeps these [*djabakós*] continually in her house, and sends for them in the land of heathens, and entertains them in her house, and cures [herself] her husband, and daughter with them, and orders them to prepare baths by their arts, and witchcraft; and [that she] with the said *djabakós* or [person who casts spells] in a particular location, naked and undressed, from head to toe, standing in a bowl

has herself been washed by the said *djabakós* with words and gentile ceremonies.[20]

The use of healing baths, as described here, was very common in Cacheu. The priest Vaz de Pontes said that he had been told by the former captain-general of Cacheu, Manoel de Passos, that Crispina and Jorge had 'certain healing baths on Saturdays, which were prepared by the *djabakós*'. It needs to be remembered that this itself was seen as a potentially heretical activity by some Inquisitors, since washing was associated with the old Islamic population of Iberia and in the sixteenth century had been a charge levelled at the *morisco* (converted Muslim) population of Spain, as a sign of heresy (as washing was a prerequisite for the *sala* or prayer). Although the *moriscos* had been expelled from Spain in 1609, the presence of the Jakhanké meant that similar associations between washing and Islam probably existed here in Cacheu.[21]

The scribe Pedro Pais went further than Vaz de Pontes, linking the use of healing baths to the many households in Cacheu run by women:

> All the women, white or Black, have faith in their *chinas*, which are the idols of the heathens of the land; and when their children or slaves fall ill, they send them to the heathens, to the said *chinas* to be bathed; the witness understands that this healing bath is taken with some water [with which the baths are done], which the heathens keep in pots.[22]

Here the curing baths were directly linked to the religious practice of the African peoples of Cacheu and its surroundings, for they took place at the shrines where religious observance occurred. The gendered dimension matters too: it was not only that women ran many households and were some of the most vocal participants at the funerals of Vila Quente, but, according to Pais, it was also Cacheu's women who directed the healing approaches of the members of their households. This may explain why the interactions

## The Heretic of Cacheu

with *djabakós* in Crispina and Jorge's household were blamed especially on her: in Cacheu, it was women who often directed how healing should take place, as the deponents suggested, perhaps in this way the most powerful of them like Crispina eventually directing spiritual activities and offerings as if becoming proxy-*djabakós*.

Many women in Cacheu also practised the arts of healing through smoke-cures. According to Gaspar Vogado, Crispina had done this herself to cure her own daughter on the orders of a *djabakós*, making a 'fire with which she smoke-cured her daughter'. Vogado claimed that many people in Cacheu had known about this, which suggests both that people gossiped about one another's health and also that, unsurprisingly, it was quite hard to keep a fire secret from the rest of the town.[23]

However, the best description of this was given not by Crispina's enemies such as Vogado but in her own testimony to the Inquisitors in Lisbon:

> Approximately eight years ago in the settlement of Cacheu, when her daughter Leonor was ill, Maria Mendes – who never married and of whom she has already spoken – came to the house of the confessant [i.e., Crispina] and told her that she would cure her said daughter from the evil eye which had been cast on her; and indeed she cut a piece from the clothes of each of these people who were present, also including the confessant among them, and then she threw the said pieces of cloth into a pan lit by hot coals, and with them pieces of chicken, salt, rye grass, rosemary . . . and fumigated her said daughter with the smoke of all these things. And later, finding that her said daughter had improved, the said Maria Mendes made her a bag in which she put garlic, rye grass, salt, bread of yam flour, and sewing up the said bag she threw it around her neck, saying that it was so that no one would give her the evil eye again.[24]

This description is clearly of a pouch like the 'Mandinga pouches' that became widespread in the Americas in the eighteenth century. The description is also important, since it shows the interrelationship of healing and malice in the understanding of those who lived in Cacheu. In this view, the 'evil eye' cast by enemies through spells could be mitigated through certain ritual approaches to healing. These might involve healing baths at the *chinas*, or the integration of certain plants with curative properties into a smoke-cure. Physical treatment could also heal the spirit, and women like Maria Mendes were often able to perform some of these cures. However, all the same, the more detailed and advanced knowledge of herbs and the ways that they could treat disease was held by the *djabakós* themselves.[25]

What this discussion helps to do is to place Crispina's own position in Cacheu in a different light. As we have seen in this book, it was she – not Jorge – who had commanded sacrifices to be made on the helms of his ships to provide for a good voyage. This was a statement of power which was spiritual as well as economic. She had accumulated the power of age in a setting where life was short. Her economic power, and her knowledge of the worlds of the *djabakós*, gave her the ability to declare her symbolic power in the town through the religious practice which she commanded to take place on a ship on which, even though it was her husband's property, she could determine what took place.

By making this sacrifice, Crispina was symbolizing the varied strands of her authority over the town: over men including her husband, over people, over goods and over political functionaries. She had performed a ritual associated with the spiritual power held in the town by the *djabakós*, who in Cacheu could be women as well as men. As she was symbolic of this power, and of the power of the *djabakós*, it was no wonder that her enemies would seek to destroy her.

When I first visited Guinea-Bissau, in 1995, a friend suggested that I go with him to see someone that he knew in a small town about fifteen miles from Cacheu. She was famed for her knowledge of herbs and the way that certain plants could be used to bring good fortune. At her compound, beneath the capacious shade of a mango

## The Heretic of Cacheu

tree whose fruits were still hard and green, an old woman wearing several necklaces with thick beads came to greet us. Her face was concertinaed with lines. We had brought various offerings including rice and perfumes, which she now took away. When she returned, some hours later, she provided us with bottles filled with a cloudy, sweet-smelling water: we should use this daily, she said, washing the whole body, for it would bring us good fortune.[26]

Only many years later have I realized that I had been invited to participate in a centuries-old practice of ritual healing baths, which is still widely found in the African diaspora in Brazil. In the late twentieth century, the knowledge of how to perform these baths remained the province of women. Everyone in the area round Cacheu acknowledged this then, and my friend felt very lucky to know where this woman lived: for this was, he told me, an art that was dying out, one that was being replaced with more modern, expensive and Western forms of medical treatment. Indeed, when I returned to the area a few years later, I was told by him that this woman had died shortly after our visit.

The fact that, 350 years ago, those who claimed the power to heal in Cacheu were often women is shown in one remarkable piece of evidence in Crispina's trial. This was given by Natalia Mendes, a woman from Vila Quente, who herself was one of the herbal doctors consulted by Jorge to try to cure his arthritic condition. Not only was she the one consulted, but she is the only witness in the entire trial – man or woman – who knew the names of the herbs that were used in the process of curing, saying that she 'she cured Jorge Gonçalves with a herb that is commonly called *Lacacam*, and others such as black mulberry'*.[27]

*Lacacam* was the word in Kriol for a plant commonly known in English as morning glory. It has subsequently been said by Western scientists to have strong curative properties, being anti-microbial and anti-inflammatory – a good plant to try out on Jorge, to see if it might alleviate the chronic stiffness in his joints. Black mulberry,

---

* *Pão de Leite.*

meanwhile, is also now known for its anti-rheumatoid qualities and for being a purgative with strong antioxidants. All in all, if looking for a herbal panacea for the ailments that he suffered, Jorge had done the right thing in turning to Natalia Mendes. The fact that it was women who had recognized herbal knowledge – and were consulted by some of the most powerful men in the town – was another facet confirming their authority in Cacheu.[28]

Reading Crispina's account of her own practices, it becomes clear that she generally turned to women healers first, before considering the use of a *djabakós*. In around 1656, she had been suffering from a pain in her foot and had called on a woman called Chica Mbena. Chica Mbena had cured her with herbs through these healing baths, and after three months the pain in the foot had gone. Moreover, in her own evidence, Crispina made it clear that she was the instigator of this consultation of Natalia Mendes. She had asked Mendes to find someone who could cure her daughter, and Mendes had returned with Mãe Gomes, later the mother of Ambrosio (after she had married Jorge, Crispina's enemy), who came from the Bijagós. They had come to Crispina's house with some herbs, which they had placed in two pots of boiling water, before washing her daughter with the water. They came back daily to wash the girl with the healing water, but she died after a month. It was after this that, as Crispina movingly put it, her 'heart grew small'.[29]

Moreover, when it came to the *djabakós* themselves, Crispina's experience of their powers was mixed. With her repeatedly summoning them to treat Jorge, the couple were engaged in a desperate attempt to stave off that most inevitable part of the human condition, the process of ageing and the dissipation of power with the passing of the years. What did their status in the town count for? Younger people with new concerns, connections and sharp elbows, people like Ambrosio Gomes and Bibiana Vaz, were accumulating wealth and the authority to move their elder power-holders aside – as younger people always do.

In spite of the ministrations of the *djabakós*, Jorge's condition did not improve. One time, his arthritic condition had become so bad that:

> with her husband ill in bed, as a result of which he was left paralysed, she called various times for some heathens so that they could come and cure him, and they brought with them some herbs which they trod on, and then put them on his arms and on those parts of his body where he was suffering most acutely, moaning and performing other ceremonies whose particular style she is not aware of, and [after all this] her said husband did not improve.[30]

This makes it seem likely that Crispina turned to both women and men in her efforts to cure her husband: both female and male *djabakós*. Whatever the gripes of the Inquisitors, it was inevitable that people like her turned to the *djabakós* and healers such as Natalia Mendes. By the 1660s, West African knowledge of the healing properties of plants had been noted down for almost a century in accounts of the region by those outsiders who came to live and work there. Kola nuts alleviated headaches and problems of the liver and the bladder; this was an additional use beyond their value as a stimulant, which may explain the significance of the trade in them. Some plants were known to be good for treating malarial fevers. Malaguetta chilli peppers were used in trading towns such as Cacheu to treat colds and digestive complaints. The roots of palm trees were called on as painkillers, while the leaves were thought to have purgative and diuretic qualities.[31]

All this provides a different perspective on the daily noisescape and panorama of life in Cacheu. Among the people moving around the portside and the street running to Vila Quente with their wares were women who came with sacks of dried leaves and fruits which they had collected from the forests and fields around their *tabankas*. They were treated with respect, because their knowledge of the curative properties of these herbs came from the most humane of qualities: the way that curiosity drives the discovery of knowledge, and the way that love evokes the desire to heal. With these most beautiful of human qualities confronting the most repugnant ones also on display in the town – greed, cruelty, manipulation, hatred – it was natural that this added further to the authority and power of some of the women who lived there.

The prominence of female healers and male *djabakós* in Cacheu came also because this was a town beset by disease. Western historians have often assumed that this was because of the fevers produced by malaria and other endemic conditions on the coast. However, West African societies had the curative knowledge to address many of these illnesses. Instead, disease was rife in Cacheu because this was a town at the heart of a period of crisis-driven transformation.

Historically, periods of crisis and the collapse of an existing sociopolitical structure are often accompanied by disease. This had happened in the sixteenth century when the Spanish brought new diseases such as smallpox and measles to the Americas; the epidemics that followed wiped out up to 95 per cent of the population of the continent, although the mortality may well have been exacerbated by the hunger and economic hardship produced by conquest, alongside the psychological crisis felt by many Native Americans at the brutally violent end of everything that they had known and which had brought them security. Closer to our own time, it also happened in the 1990s when the Soviet Union collapsed, triggering an epidemic of alcoholism and waves of premature mortality in Russia among people faced with the unravelling of the social structure they had known.

Waves of disease and premature death are often evidence of a crisis in the socioeconomic structure of a society. Naturally, they cause fear and panic, generating scapegoating, gossip and hatreds until a diagnosis can be made. As with the *djabakós* and the concept of the malign spiritual 'eating' of someone who is sick, historically those who diagnose the condition in the first place are generally those who then are empowered to claim the authority to heal it. Regardless of the efficacy of the cures promoted – and many readers will doubt the efficacy of some of the treatments provided by the *djabakós* – the healing act provides a therapeutic effect. Society can then try collectively to overcome the crisis which it is facing, while inevitably rendering invisible some of the root causes of that crisis in order to avoid confronting the most painful of truths. With sickness and its curing so fundamental to the human condition, healing has in the end always been accompanied by an assumption of power by medical practitioners in all parts of the world.

This pattern was also at work in Senegambia in the seventeenth century. It is notable in the documents we have that the people who seemed to suffer most from disease and rapid death were those most closely associated with the chaotic and cruel violence of the Atlantic empires: the trafficked, and the traffickers. The historical records are filled with the accounts of captives falling sick on board their floating tomb-ships (*tumbeiros/tumbaquos*) and being rowed back to shore, of captives dying in the houses of their captors and being accounted for in the columns of profit and loss – and also, as we have seen in this chapter, of countless participants in the business of the traffic falling sick and dying from one day to the next, being fingered as someone with useful evidence even though 'they are now dead', of being remembered as part of the community even when they were no longer alive.

A haunting example is in a legal case taken about fraud and the overcrowding of enslaved Africans in the ship *Santa Cruz*, which left Cacheu for Cartagena in April 1616. The case was taken by the contractor Antonio Fernandez d'Elvas, against the ship captain Jorge López de Morales. Elvas's concern was not, however, the disease and death that had overcome the Africans on board the ship but the 'fraud' that Morales had committed against his contract by taking forty-five more captives than he was entitled to. Morales was thrown into prison in Cartagena and then was asked for more details. According to him, forty Africans had died on the transatlantic transport, and he had had to throw three of them alive into the sea since they were suffering from smallpox: the economic rigours of account-book capitalism were producing fast enough a modern understanding of the spread of epidemic disease – and the threat to 'property' that could follow – even if doctors in the Iberian empires were still practising the humoral theory of medicine.[32]

When pressed as to why he had overloaded the ship in Cacheu, Morales went further in his description of how disease and the traffic were so closely connected:

> In the port of Cacheu where he had been there had been many diseases from which many [enslaved] Africans were dying on a daily basis, and [he had packed more] as it was an ordinary thing for many of them to die at sea.[33]

Morales' account indicates that the transatlantic traffic in enslaved Africans was central to this sociopolitical crisis faced in Cacheu in the seventeenth century. For it was this traffic which, as this evidence shows, was most likely to produce ill health. Social determinants were essential in the production of disease, more so than the arrival of any new pathogens. Poverty and social stress drove the risk of exposure to disease, as any number of examples from the time can show. It wasn't only the fact that illness was most closely associated with the traffic, but that health itself was clearly directly connected to coerced impoverishment and the environmental and economic conditions that produced it.

This was made clear by the residents of Cacheu in a letter to the new king of Portugal, John IV, written on 5 December 1641. Here they pointed to the devastating effects of the famine which, as we saw in Chapter 3, ripped through Senegambia in these years as a consequence of the mini Ice Age. The residents described this as 'a huge famine which has been going on for three years in this town and in the rest of Guinea'. This had made it impossible for them to feed their captives and, they said, now made it very hard for them to remain living in Cacheu. Many enslaved persons had died, and a large amount of 'property' had been lost. From the vantage point of Cacheu, the famine went along with the general sociopolitical crisis which had come with the increasing waves of economic demand from the Atlantic empires, demands that were most readily met through the increase in the traffic of the enslaved.[34]

Once these demands were met, it turns out, the Atlantic empires soon imposed others. This included a challenge to the authority to heal and the political power which went with it. The empires were playing a political long game which would lead step by step to modern colonialism in Africa by the end of the nineteenth century. There were many ways in which this took place, but the ideological arena was key. Challenging the claims to knowledge of West African healers, and their authority to heal, was an important first step, as Crispina's trial shows. For the healers challenged many aspects of the ideological underpinnings of empire. Many were women, while the *djabakós* connected disease to African religious practice. These healers, moreover, embodied the cyclical approach to time and space which also impeded the advance of empire. Crispina's trial was therefore an early attempt to interrupt this pattern, even if it would take another century or so for the consequences to become embedded: control over the bodies of others was the central paradigm of Atlantic empires, both through their enforced labour and through the ways in which sickness could be diagnosed and then treated using often experimental medicines.

The trial proved to be symbolic of much of the history that followed. In terms of healing, the assault on African paradigms of knowledge described so meticulously therein has continued ever since. As historians of medicine have shown, a more cross-cultural approach to diagnosis and treatment of disease still characterized the period before the late eighteenth century. With the rise of modern imperialism, this then faded into a top-down approach of Western science which dismissed the role of African knowledge. This paved the way for the mass medical experimentation on the bodies of African 'others' that followed in the colonial era of the twentieth century. For Africans, as Crispina's life history reveals so poignantly, Western biomedicine was not always a solution to their medical ailments; rather it was part of a broader cultural, economic and political structure of oppression.[35]

# *Conclusion*

Look at maps of West Africa today and you will find that they are generally shaped by borders. Guinea-Bissau borders only two countries, one of which is Senegal. There are not many formal border crossings between the countries, less than ten. However, in practice, most people ignore the borders. There are bush tracks which cross between the countries almost everywhere. One time, in 2011, I even saw a group of people waiting near to the village of Simbandi-Balante in Senegal for a bus which would take them across the border to Ingore in Guinea-Bissau – on a route which did not officially exist.

Borders determined in Berlin in 1884 mean little in a world in which, as we have seen in this book, cultures, histories and ideas are shared. Paper realities are – well – fine for paper. Just as World Bank operatives compile their reports in the twenty-first century, so imperial emissaries wrote their screeds in the twentieth century, in the nineteenth century and in the seventeenth century as well. But they did not shape the world as much as they so insistently claimed. A West African town like Cacheu in the seventeenth century was a threatening space for empire, however much control its emissaries pretended to exert there: women ran the show, African religions and the practice of Islam predominated, the buildings, languages and clothes that people wore were definitively African, and hardly anyone knew or cared about the dictates of the officers of empire in Lisbon, or at which particular moment in the imperial line of time they had been written down.

Meanwhile, in the *tabankas* and creeks around the town, opinion about the arrivals from the ocean was decidedly mixed. Some rulers felt they had little option but to throw in their lot with the foreign merchants and pay lip-service to their religion. Others rebelled,

## The Heretic of Cacheu

welcoming escaped captives to form new free communities in their kingdoms. Some, like the Floup, prided themselves on attacking Atlantic traffickers on their ships, killing their captain and crew and seizing the enslaved as personal dependents. Meanwhile, many of those who lived on the rivers around Cacheu opposed the traffic, and the main African merchants in the trade were outsiders: the Bijagó, Fulani and Kristón.

All this meant that the situation of the empire itself was in the balance. Therefore, a symbolic assault was needed, an attack on one of the most powerful people in the town which could also shake up the dynamics in favour of the Portuguese. The trial of Crispina Peres was a bellwether indicating the changing winds of global politics, economics and society in the 1660s. It represented what in the short term would be a failed coup attempt by European empires. On paper it was a success, as so much is; but in practice, given that her successor as the *grande dame* of Cacheu, Bibiana Vaz, imprisoned the captain-general of the town in her house for over a year two decades later, reality was more complicated – as it almost always is. Yet although Senegambian societies soon reasserted their power, the trial certainly foreshadowed the way in which ideological assaults would come to form a key part of the imperial playbook in the centuries that followed.

The worlds we have seen in this book encompass so very many layers. There was the noise of work, of the carpenters and coopers, the hawking of the market vendors, the slap of washing on the riverside just down from the busy port. And then there was the noise of life and of death, of the frog choruses in the rainy season, the shouting of women seeking the return of stolen property through a visit to the *china*, and of the funerals that came so regularly from Vila Quente. All of this stood firm against the solemnity of Catholic processions in the town, and the chanting of the students of the Jakhanké clerics as they learnt their verses from the Qur'an from the wooden *alúas* that were leant up against the walls of the dried-mud houses.

The most regular form of work was perhaps trade. People were curious. They wanted to know what the latest fashions were in Senegambian and imported textiles. They wanted the best access to

## Conclusion

the most valued commodities, be they clothing, imported foods, locally grown crops for provision stores, kola nuts, bread made by the baker – or people. This meant that they had to develop their own networks and connections and make sure that they were in the right place at the right time to cut a deal.

By night, people got drunk, went in and out of one another's houses, gossiped and formed relationships. They gambled at cards and lost, and then went around trying to slander the people they owed money to. When they had had their fill, and their bodies were sated to excess, they might fall ill – and then lie by candlelight on a mattress, waiting for the healing powers of the *djabakós*, or of the women who came by day with their sacks of dried herbs into the town, to take effect.

Cacheu was a town managed by women. They were the most powerful traders, the people with the power to heal and the purveyors of so much that was essential. They could live in their own houses, or run households in which the men were secondary. This was why the town was so threatening to the Portuguese men who came from the empire and found to their horror that even dowries weren't paid in a place which ran according to Senegambian rules of gender. In this place, those who had the right linguistic, kinship and political connections rose to the top – and that meant women like Crispina. Three centuries later, traditions of female power remained strong, which some have seen as helping in understanding the powerful role of women fighters in Guinea-Bissau's successful war of independence against Portugal.[1]

Meanwhile, the demand-side of the Atlantic economy was growing hand over fist. Cacheu was a global town, linked virtually to the four corners of the planet: it was hardly somewhere that was outside history. As the sugar plantations spread like cancers across the Caribbean, from north-eastern Brazil to Barbados and then to Jamaica – after the British had seized it from the Spanish in 1655 – the genocide of the Native Americans meant that the requirements for enslaved African labour intensified. All this meant that the numbers of enslaved Africans grew year by year in the town, led in chains through the streets as people looked away or objectified

## The Heretic of Cacheu

them violently with cruel gazes as they were led into fortified storehouses to await their transport to the Americas. The competition between the Dutch, the English, the French, the Portuguese and the Spanish grew too, and with it their attempts to promote enslavement in Africa. European empires were beginning to stake claims and seeking to deploy their institutions to do so.

These institutions prospered in keeping with their promotion of the new imperial worldview. This perspective was one that produced capital from exchanges that were all painstakingly annotated in the books of account. It was a perspective that could commodify anything and even treated (some) people as objects that could be rendered as ciphers on paper, with their measure of value and profit and loss, just as any other merchandise might possess. This objectification went too with the linearity of time, the relentless imposition of calendar- and clock-time on a world which was shaped through the experience of events. The growing importance of this worldview to success meant that its demands were ever more insistent.

All these factors came together to lead to the arrest of Crispina by the Inquisition. From the perspective of Cacheu it must have seemed impossible that such a distant institution would ever intrude. This was the business of Catholic nations and their homelands in Europe, and their colonies in the Americas. What did their funny ideas have to do with life in Africa? Inquisitorial trials must have seemed a remote prospect to Crispina when she first heard news of them.

And yet the Inquisitors came, stung by what they perceived as an assault on empire through her use of African healing and knowledge: evidence, if it was needed, that objectivity and strong institutions do not necessarily produce positive outcomes if they are imposed by greedy and violent outsiders, and – as Crispina would find out better than anyone – that these institutions were as regressive as could be for a West African woman like her.

When Luis Rodrigues was acquitted from his trial in Lisbon, he returned to Cabo Verde a ruined man. He had to pay a large sum

*Conclusion*

to the sergeant-major – none other than Manoel de Almeida, later to be Crispina's interpreter, and then captain-general of Cacheu for a couple of years until his death. But, when Almeida remitted the money to Lisbon, the ship was attacked by English pirates and the money was lost. Rodrigues declared that he was tired and wretchedly poor: 'I found my houses crumbled to the earth, my slaves dead, and that my stipend and benefice hadn't been paid for three years, all of which amounted to a loss of three thousand *Cruzados*, and everything destroyed.' In a doleful and self-pitying letter, Rodrigues asked his superiors in Lisbon, 'as for my expenses and losses that [my enemies] forced on me, who will pay them for me?'[2]

As we have seen, Rodrigues soon found solace as a religious visitor in Cacheu, through turning on his enemies there, people who had slighted him as he saw it – and perhaps who triggered him on a deeper emotional level, for how could a man like Jorge Gonçalves Frances live in a household managed so clearly by his wife, Crispina Peres? Moreover, all his enemies were in his view Jews, and so there was an Inquisitorial justification for action. Cacheu was a lethal mixed-faith setting of Islamic clerics, African *djabakós* and apostate Jewish descendants, now converted to a hybridized Catholicism and merrily dabbling in African religious practices to boot. All of them were profiting where solid Catholics like him felt that the empire and its riches were passing them by. It was time to get his revenge for all the humiliation and loss that he had suffered.[3]

The consequences were lethal for Crispina. In spite of the uproar among her Bainunk, Pepel and Floup friends, she was arrested and deported to Lisbon, where she spent three years in the Inquisitorial jail being interrogated by the Inquisitors. Eventually, she was processed. On 20 March 1668 she was summoned before the Inquisitors and given her penance:

> she should confess on the major Wednesdays through the year, that is at Christmas, Easter Resurrection, the feasts of the Holy Spirit and the Assumption of Our Lady the Virgin. And that during the same

year she should pray weekly to the said [Virgin] with the rosary and say five Our fathers and five Ave Marias every Friday.[4]

Sent back on the long sea voyage to Cacheu, Crispina arrived there on 6 June 1668. She soon fell ill, perhaps because she had become unused to the malarial fevers so common to those who lived, worked and died in the town. On 9 August, at the height of the rainy season, in the month known in Senegambia as 'the malaria month' to this day, she made a legalized deposition to the Church authorities in Cacheu that she was very sick and unable to perform her penance as demanded:

> the first day of her penance is on the day of the Assumption of Our Lady [the Virgin], and as she is very ill, suffering from a high fever, with swellings in her mouth and bleeding, and is bedridden as is confirmed by the certificate which has been presented by the surgeon of this settlement Joseph de Mendonça, which has made it impossible for her to obey and fulfil that which has been commanded by the Holy Tribunal.[5]

In September, the surgeon Mendonça confirmed that the impediments to her performing the penance were 'very severe' in an attestation certified by the priest Vaz de Pontes. He described what had happened, saying that:

> [he had been] summoned to his house by Captain Jorge Gonçalves Frances on 1 August 1668, so that I could examine his wife Crispina Peres, who is suffering from a swelling on her face which has bled four or five times . . . the said illness had lasted throughout the whole month of August, and as this appeared to me to be the truth from what I could see, as I had been with her during most of those days, and as she asked me for this [certificate] for the discharge [of her conscience], I gave her this certificate to testify faithfully to the truth. In Cacheu, on 10 October 1668.[6]

## Conclusion

In spite of the suffering meted out by their enemies through the Inquisition, and the three long years during which they had been separated, Crispina and Jorge had been reunited. But this is also the last that we know of Crispina. Hereafter, she disappears from the historical record. Most probably, Jorge was unable to find someone who could produce a cure for her illness, just as her dealings with the *djabakós* had not resolved his arthritis. It seems that shortly after her return from Lisbon, death itself came to relieve Crispina from the enduring pain which had come from her experience of the daily struggle over life in Cacheu and in the creeks and *tabankas* beyond it.

# Bibliography

## Archives / Abbreviations

ADP – Arquivo Distrital de Portoalegre.
AGI – Archivo General de las Índias, Seville.
AGNP – Archivo General de la Nación del Perú, Lima.
AHN – Archivo Histórico Nacional, Madrid.
AHU – Arquivo Histórico Ultramarino, Lisbon.
ASV – Archivio Secretto Vatticano.
BA – Biblioteca da Ajuda, Lisbon.
BL – British Library, London.
CP – *The Inquisition Trial of Crispina Peres of Cacheu, Guinea-Bissau (1646–1668)*. Toby Green, Philip J. Havik, F. Ribeiro da Silva (eds.). Oxford: Oxford University Press for the British Academy, 2021.
CU – Conselho Ultramarino; a documentary corpus within the AHU.
EM – Etiopia Menor e Descripção Geográphica da Provincia da Serra Leôa by Manoel Alvares – manuscript at the Sociedade da Geografía, Lisbon.
GAA – Gemeentearchief, Amsterdam.
IAN/TT – Instituto dos Arquivos Nacionais da Torre do Tombo, Lisbon.
IL – Inquisição de Lisboa; documents from the Lisbon Inquisition, a corpus in the IAN/TT.
LR – The trial of the priest Luis Rodrigues of Cabo Verde, held at IAN/TT, IL, Proceso 8626. A complete transcription of the Portuguese text of this trial (made by the author) is available at www.fonteshistoriaeafricanae.co.uk/additional-material.
MMA – *Monumenta Misionária Africana, Segunda Série*, ed. António Brasio.
NCAC – National Centre for Arts and Culture, The Gambia
RDD – Research and Documentation Division, section of NCAC in Bakau, The Gambia.

*Bibliography*

SO-CO – Santo Oficio-Contencioso; a documentary corpus within the AGNP.

## *Primary Sources*

Brásio, António (1958–2004): *Monumenta Misionária Africana: Segunda Série, África Ocidental*. Lisbon: Agência Geral do Ultramar/Centro de Estudos Africanos da Universidade de Lisboa; 7 vols.

Cavazzi da Montecuccolo, Antonio (1687): *Istorica Descrizione de' Tre' Regni Congo, Matamba, et Angola Situati Nelli' Etiopia Inferiore Occidentale e delle Missioni Apostoliche Esercitatevi da Religiosi Capuccini*. Bologna: Giacomo Monti.

Cultru, P. (ed.) (1913): *Premier Voyage du Sieur de la Courbe Fait à la Coste d'Afrique en 1685*. Paris: Édouard Champion et Émile Larose.

Coelho, Francisco Lemos (1953): *Duas Descrições Seiscentistas da Guiné*. Lisbon: Academia Portuguesa da Historian; ed. Damião Goes.

Giesing, Cornelia and Vydrine, Valentin (eds.) (2007): *Ta:rikh Mandinga De Bijini (Guinée-Bissau): La Mémoire des Mandinga et des Sòoninke de Kaabu*. Leiden: Brill.

Green, Toby, Havik, Philip J. and Ribeiro da Silva, F. (2021): *The Inquisition Trial of Crispina Peres of Cacheu, Guinea-Bissau (1646–1668)*. Oxford: Oxford University Press for the British Academy.

Innes, Gordon (1976): *Kaabu and Fuladu: Historical Narratives of the Gambian Mandinga*. London: School of Oriental and African Studies.

Jobson, Richard (1968): *The Golden Trade, or a Discovery of the River Gambra and the Golden Trade of the Aethiopians (1623)*. London: Dawson of Pall Mall.*

Mauny, R., Monod, Th. and Teixeira da Mota, A. (eds.) (1951): *Description de la Côte Occidentale d'Afrique (Sénégal au Cap de Monte, Archipels) par Valentim Fernandes (1506–1510)*. Bissau: Centro de Estudos da Guiné Portuguesa.

---

* As the original English in this text reads in a very antiquated style to twenty-first century readers, I have modernized the language somewhat in the quotations from this text.

*Bibliography*

Mota, Avelino Teixeira de (1974): *As Viagens do Bispo D. Frei Vitoriano Portuense a Guiné é a Cristianização dos Reis de Bissau*. Lisbon: Junta de Investigações Científicas do Ultramar.

Mota, Avelina Teixiera de and Hair, P. E. H. (eds. and trans.) (1977): *Descrição da Serra Leoa e dos Rios de Guiné de Cabo Verde (1625)*. Lisbon: Junta de Investigações Científicas do Ultramar.

Saint Lô, Alexis de (1637): *Relation du Voyage du Cap Verd*. Paris: François Targa.

Stone, Thora G. (ed.) (1924): 'The Journey of Cornelius Hodges in Senegambia, 1689–90', *English Historical Review* 39/no. 153, 89–95.

## Secondary Sources

Achebe, Nwando (2020): *Female Monarchs and Merchant Queens in Africa*. Athens: Ohio University Press.

— (2011): *The Female King of Colonial Nigeria: Ahebi Ugbabe*. Bloomington: Indiana University Press.

Afonso, Luís U. and Horta, José da Silva (2013): 'Afro-Portuguese Oliphants with Hunting Scenes (c.1490–c.1540)', *Mande Studies* 15, 79–97.

Alfani, Guido (2024): *As Gods Among Men: A History of the Rich in the West*. Princeton: Princeton University Press.

Almeida, Carlos, Horta, José da Silva and Mark, Peter (eds.) (2021): *African Ivories in the Atlantic World, 1400–1900*. Lisbon: Centro de História da Universidade de Lisboa.

Araujo, Ana Lúcia (2023): *The Gift: How Objects of Prestige Shaped the Atlantic Slave Trade and Colonialism*. Cambridge: Cambridge University Press.

— (2024): *Humans in Shackles: An Atlantic History of Slavery in the Americas*. Chicago: Chicago University Press.

Badiou, Alain (2013): *Being and Event*. London: Bloomsbury Publishing; trans. Oliver Feltham.

Barry, Boubacar (1998): *Senegambia and the Atlantic Slave Trade*. Cambridge: Cambridge University Press; trans. A. Kwei Armah.

Baum, Robert M. (1999): *Shrines of the Slave Trade: Diola Religion and Society in Precolonial Senegambia*. New York and Oxford: Oxford University Press.

# Bibliography

Benjamin, Jody (2024): *The Texture of Change: Dress, Self-Fashioning and History in Western Africa, 1700–1850*. Athens: Ohio University Press.

Bernault, Florence (2020): 'Some Lessons from the History of Epidemics in Africa', African Arguments 5 June 2020: https://africanarguments.org/2020/06/some-lessons-from-the-history-of-epidemics-in-africa/.

Bethencourt, Francisco (2024): *Strangers Within: The Rise and Fall of the New Christian Trading Elite*. Princeton: Princeton University Press.

Bethencourt, Francisco and Havik, Philip (eds.) (2004): 'Inquisição em África', *Revista Lusófona de Ciências das Religiões* 5/6.

Bowser, Frederick P. (1974): *The African Slave in Colonial Peru, 1524–1650*. Stanford: Stanford University Press.

Boxer, C. R. (1950): *Salvador de Sá and the Struggle for Brazil and Angola 1602–1686*. London: The Athlone Press.

Brooks, George E. (1993): *Landlords and Strangers: Ecology, Society, and Trade in Western Africa, 1000-1630*. Boulder: Westview Press.

— (2003): *Eurafricans in Western Africa: Commerce, Social Status, Gender, and Religious Observance from the Sixteenth to the Eighteenth Centuries*. Athens: Ohio University Press.

Brown, Vincent (2008): *The Reaper's Garden: Death and Power in the World of Atlantic Slavery*. Cambridge, MA: Harvard University Press.

Buis, Pierre (1990): *Essai Sur la Langue Manjako de la Zone de Basserel*. Bissau: Instituto Nacional de Estudos e Pesquisa.

Candido, Mariana P. (2013): *Benguela and Its Hinterland: An African Slaving Port and the Atlantic World*. Cambridge: Cambridge University Press.

Candido, Mariana P. and Jones, Adam (eds.): *African Women in the Atlantic World. Property, Vulnerability and Mobility, 1680–1880*. Woodbridge: James Currey.

Carreira, António (1947): 'Mandingas da Guiné Portuguesa', *Centro de Estudos da Guiné Portuguesa* 4.

— (1964): 'A Etnonímia dos Povos de Entre o Gâmbia e o Estuário do Geba', *Boletim Cultural da Guiné Portuguesa* 19/75, 233–76.

Carter, Miguel and Cardoso, Carlos (eds.) (2021): *Vozes do Povo: Sociedade, Política, e Opinião Pública na Guiné-Bissau*. Bissau: DEMOS.

Ceesay, Hassoum (2011): *Gambian Women: Profiles and Historical Notes*. Kanifing: Fulladu Publishers.

## Bibliography

Chabal, Patrick and Green, Toby (eds.) (2016): *Guinea-Bissau: Micro-State to 'Narco-State'*. London: C. Hurst & Co.

Costa, Joseph da (2020): *Decoloniality and Early Colonial Thought: Grammar and Cartography in the Era of Portuguese Expansion*. London: King's College London; unpublished PhD dissertation.

Curtin, Philip D. (1975): *Economic Change in Precolonial Africa: Senegambia in the Era of the Slave Trade*. Madison: University of Wisconsin Press; 2 vols.

Curto, José C. (2004): *Enslaving Spirits: The Portuguese-Brazilian Alcohol Trade at Luanda and Its Hinterland c.1550–1830*. Leiden: Brill.

Faust, Franz X. et al. (2006): 'Evidence for the Postconquest Demographic Collapse of the Americas in Historical $CO_2$ levels', *Earth Interactions* 10, paper no. 11, 1–15.

Fonseca, Domingos (1997): *Os Mancanha*. Bissau: Ku Si Mon Editora.

Friedemann, Nina S. de and Patiño Rosselli, Carlos (1983): *Lengua y Sociedad en el Palenque de San Basilio*. Bogotá: Publicaciones del Instituto Caro y Cuervo.

Fromont, Cécile (2013): 'Dancing for the King of Congo from Early Modern Central Africa to Slavery-Era Brazil', *Colonial Latin American Review* 22/2, 184–208.

— (2014): *The Art of Conversion: Christian Visual Culture in the Kingdom of Kongo*. Chapel Hill: University of North Carolina Press.

— (2020): 'Paper, Ink, Vodun, and the Inquisition: Tracing Power, Slavery and Witchcraft in the Early Modern Portuguese Atlantic', *Journal of the American Academy of Religion* 88/2, 460–504.

Furtado, Júnia Ferreira (2007): 'Tropical Empiricism: Making Medical Knowledge in Colonial Brazil', in James Delbourgo and Nicholas Dew (eds.), *Science and Empire in the Atlantic World* (London: Routledge), 127–51.

Ginzburg, Carlo (1976): *The Cheese and the Worms: The Cosmos of a Sixteenth-Century Miller*. Baltimore: Johns Hopkins University Press.

Gomez, Michael A. (2018): *African Dominion: A New History of Empire in Early and Medieval West Africa*. Princeton: Princeton University Press.

Gómez, Pablo F. (2017): *The Experiential Caribbean: Creating Knowledge and Healing in the Early Modern Atlantic*. Chapel Hill: University of North Carolina Press.

Gonçalves, Nuno da Silva (1996): *Os Jesuítas e a Missão de Cabo Verde (1604–1642)*. Lisbon: Brotería.

Green, Toby (2001): *Meeting the Invisible Man: Secrets and Magic in West Africa*. London: Weidenfeld & Nicolson.

— (2007): *Inquisition: The Reign of Fear*. London: Macmillan.

— (2009): 'Architects of Knowledge, Builders of Power: Constructing the Kaabu "Empire", 16th–17th centuries', *Journal of Mande Studies* 11, 91–112.

— (2012a): *The Rise of the Trans-Atlantic Slave Trade in Western Africa, 1300–1589*. Cambridge: Cambridge University Press.

— (2012b): 'The Emergence of a Mixed Society in Cape Verde in the 17th Century', in Toby Green (ed.), *Brokers of Change: Atlantic Commerce and Cultures in Pre-Colonial Western Africa* (Oxford: Oxford University Press for the British Academy, 2012), 215–35.

— (2018): 'Pluralism, Violence and Empire: The Portuguese New Christians in the Atlantic World', in Francisco Bethencourt (ed.), *Cosmopolitanism in the Portuguese-Speaking World* (Leiden: Brill), 40–58.

— (2019): *A Fistful of Shells: West Africa from the Rise of the Slave Trade to the Age of Revolution*. London and Chicago: Allen Lane / Chicago University Press.

— (2022): 'Africa and Capitalism: Repairing a History of Omission', *Capitalism* 3/2, 301–32.

Green, Toby and Nafafé, José Lingna (2020): 'Lusotopian or Lusophone Atlantics? The Relevance of Transnational African Diasporas to the Question of Language and Culture', in Hilary Owen and Claire Williams (eds.), *Transnational Portuguese Studies* (Liverpool: Liverpool University Press), 129–48.

Griffiths, Jay (1999): *Pip-Pip: A Sideways Look at Time*. London: Harper Press.

Havik, Philip J. (2004): *Silences and Soundbytes: The Gendered Dynamics of Trade and Brokerage in the Pre-colonial Guinea Bissau Region*. Münster/ New York: Lit Verlag/Transaction Publishers.

— (2011): 'Traders, Planters and Go-betweens: the Kriston in Portuguese Guinea', *Portuguese Studies Review* 19/1-2, 197–226.

— (2016): 'Hybridising Medicine: Illness, Healing and the Dynamics of Reciprocal Exchange on the Upper Guinea Coast (West Africa)', *Medical History* 60/2, 181–205.

*Bibliography*

Hawthorne, Walter (2003): *Planting Rice and Harvesting Slaves: Transformations Along the Guinea-Bissau Coast, 1400–1900*. Portsmouth, NH: Heinemann.

Heywood, Linda M. (2017): *Njinga: Africa's Warrior Queen*. Cambridge, MA: Harvard University Press.

Hicks, Mary E. (2021): 'Blood and Hair: Barbers, *Sangradores*, and the West African Corporeal Imagination in Salvador da Bahia, 1793–1843', in Sean Morey Smith and Christopher Willoughby (eds.), *Medicine and Healing in the Age of Slavery* (Baton Rouge: Louisiana State University Press), 61–80.

Hooper, Edward (1999): *The River: A Journey Back to the Source of HIV and AIDS*. London: Allen Lane.

Horta, José da Silva and Mark, Peter (2010): *The Forgotten Diaspora*. Cambridge and New York: Cambridge University Press.

Ipsen, Pernille (2015): *Daughters of the Trade: Atlantic Slavers and Interracial Marriage on the Gold Coast*. Philadelphia: University of Pennsylvania Press.

Ireton, Chloe (2020): 'Black Africans' Freedom Litigation Suits to Define Just War and Just Slavery in the Early Spanish Empire', *Renaissance Quarterly* 73/4, 1277–319.

Israel, Jonathan I. (2002): *Diasporas Within a Diaspora: Jews, Crypto-Jews and the World Maritime Empires (1540–1740)*. Leiden: Brill.

Jones, Hilary (2013): *The Métis of Senegal: Urban Life and Politics in French West Africa*. Bloomington: Indiana University Press.

Kananoja, Kalle (2021): *Healing Knowledge in Atlantic Africa: Medical Encounters, 1500–1850*. Cambridge: Cambridge University Press.

Kaplan, Yosef (1996): *Judíos Nuevos en Amsterdam: Estudio Sobre la Historia Social y Intelectual del Judaísmo Sefardí en el Siglo XVII*. Barcelona: Editorial Gedisa S.A.

Kobayashi, Kazuo (2019): *Indian Cotton Textiles in West Africa: African Agency, Consumer Demand and the Making of a Global Economy, 1750–1850*. London: Palgrave Macmillan.

Kriger, Colleen E. (2006): *Cloth in West African History*. Lanham: Rowman and Littlefield.

— (2017): *Making Money: Life, Death, and Early Modern Trade on Africa's Guinea Coast*. Athens: Ohio University Press.

Lachenal, Guillaume. 2014. *Le Médicament qui devait sauver l'Afrique: un scandale pharmaceutique aux colonies*. Paris: La Découverte.

Ladurie, Emmanuel Le Roy (1978): *Montaillou: Cathars and Catholics in a French Village, 1294–1324*. New York: Scolar Press; trans. Barbara Bray.

Lahon, Didier (2005): 'Black African Slaves and Freedmen in Portugal During the Renaissance: Creating a New Pattern of Reality', in K. J. P. Lowe and T. F. Earle (eds.), *Black Africans in Renaissance Europe* (Cambridge: Cambridge University Press), 261–79.

Lamp, Frederick John (2020): 'Ivory and Stone: Direct Connections between Sculptural Media along the Coast of Sierra Leone, 15th–16th Centuries', *Afrique Archéologie Arts* 16, 11–42.

Lane, Kris (2021): *Potosí: The Silver City That Changed the World*. Oakland: University of California Press.

Lara, Silva Hunold (2021): *Palmares e Cucaú: O Aprendizado da Dominação*. São Paulo: Editora da Universidade de São Paulo.

Law, Robin (2004): *Ouidah: The Social History of a West African Slaving Port*. Athens: Ohio University Press.

Laye, Camara (1970): *The African Child*. London: Collins.

Le Goff, Jacques (1980): 'Merchant's Time and Church's Time in the Middle Ages', in Jacques Le Goff (ed.), *Time, Work, and Culture in the Middles Ages* (Chicago: University of Chicago Press), 29–42; trans. Arthur Goldhammer.

Lespinay, Charles (2000): 'Un Lexique Bagnon-Floupe de la fin du XVIIe siècle: Apport à l'histoire du peuplement de la Casamance', in Gérard Gaillard, *Migrations anciennes et peuplement actuel des côtes guinéennes* (Paris: Éditions L'Harmattan), 193–213.

Lopes, Carlos (1999): *Kaabunké: Espaço, Poder, Território e Poder na Guiné-Bissau, Gâmbia e Casamance Pre-Coloniais*. Lisbon: Comissão Nacional para as Comemorações dos Descobrimentos Portugueses.

Lovejoy, Paul E. (1980): *Caravans of Kola: The Hausa Kola Trade, 1700–1900*. Zaria: Ahmadu Bello University Press.

Lüpke, Friederike (2010): 'Multilingualism and Language Contact in West Africa: Towards a Holistic Perspective', *Journal of Language Contact – THEMA* 3, 1–12.

## Bibliography

Lüpke, Friederike and Storch, Anne (2013): *Repertoires and Choices in African Languages*. New York: De Gruyter Mouton.

Malacco, Felipe Silveira de Oliveira (2023): *História Social do Comércio na Senegâmbia: Espaço e Agência Local (1580–1700)*. Belo Horizonte: Universidade Federal das Minas Gerais; unpublished PhD dissertation.

Mann, Kristin (2010): *Slavery and the Birth of an African City: Lagos, 1760–1900*. Bloomington: Indiana University Press.

Mark, Peter (2002): *Portuguese Style and Luso-African Identity: Precolonial Senegambia, Sixteenth-Nineteenth Centuries*. Bloomington and Indianapolis: Indiana University Press.

— (2021): 'The Iconography of Reading and Writing in Selected Sapi Saltcellars', in Almeida / Horta / Mark (eds.) (2021), 73–97.

Matory, J. Lorand (2018): *The Fetish Revisited: Marx, Freud, and the Gods Black People Make*. Raleigh, NC: Duke University Press.

McIntosh, Roderick J. (2005): *Ancient Middle Niger: Urbanism and the Self-Organizing Landscape*. Cambridge: Cambridge University Press.

McNaughton, Patrick (1988): *The Mande Blacksmiths: Knowledge, Power and Art in West Africa*. Bloomington: Indiana University Press.

Mendes, António de Almeida (2008): 'The Foundations of the System: A Reassessment on the Slave Trade to the Americas in the Sixteenth and Seventeenth Centuries', in David Eltis and David Richardson (eds.), *Extending the Frontiers: Essays on the New Transatlantic Slave Trade Database* (New Haven and London: Yale University Press).

Mota, Thiago Henrique (2018): *A Grande Jihad na África: História Atlântica da Islamização na Senegâmbia, Séculos XVI e XVII*. Belo Horizonte: Universidade Federal Minas Gerais; unpublished PhD dissertation.

Nadel, S. F. (1942): *A Black Byzantium: The Kingdom of Nupe in Nigeria*. London: Oxford University Press for the International Institute of African Languages and Cultures.

Nafafé, José Lingna (2007): *Colonial Encounters: Issues of Culture, Hybridity and Creolisation: Portuguese Mercantile Settlers in West Africa*. Frankfurt-am-Main: Peter Lang.

— (2012): 'African Orality in Iberian Space: Critique of Barros and Myth of Racial Discourse', *Portuguese Studies* 28 / 2, 126–42.

— (2022): *Lourenço da Silva Mendonça and the Black Abolitionist Movement in the Seventeenth Century*. Cambridge: Cambridge University Press.

Newson, Linda A. (2012): 'Africans and Luso-Africans in the Portuguese Slave Trade on the Upper Guinea Coast in the Early Seventeenth Century', *Journal of African History* 53/1, 1–24.

— (2017): *Making Medicines in Early Colonial Lima, Peru: Apothecaries, Science and Society*. Leiden: Brill.

Newson, Linda A. and Minchin, Susie (2007): *From Capture to Sale: The Portuguese Slave Trade to Spanish South America in the Seventeenth Century*. Leiden: Brill.

Nirenberg, David (2015): *Communities of Violence: Persecution of Minorities in the Middle Ages*. Princeton: Princeton University Press; 2nd updated edition.

Ogle, Vanessa (2015): *The Global Transformation of Time: 1870–1950*. Harvard: Harvard University Press.

Oliveira, Vanessa S. (2021): *Slave Trade and Abolition: Gender, Commerce and Economic Transition in Luanda*. Madison: University of Wisconsin Press.

Osborn, Emily Lynn (2011): *Our New Husbands Are Here: Households, Gender and Politics in a West African State from the Slave Trade to Colonial Rule*. Athens: Ohio University Press.

Parker, Geoffrey (2013): *Global Crisis: War, Climate Change and Catastrophe in the Seventeenth Century*. New Haven and London: Yale University Press.

Parker, John (2021): *In My Time of Dying: A History of Death and the Dead in West Africa*. Princeton: Princeton University Press.

Patterson, Orlando (1982): *Slavery as Social Death: A Comparative Study*. Cambridge, MA: Harvard University Press.

Peiretti-Courtis, Delphine. 2021. *Corps noirs et médecins blancs: la fabrique du préjugé racial, XIXe–XX Siècles*. Paris: Éditions La Découverte.

Phillott-Almeida, Ralphina A. (2011): *A Succinct History of the Kingdom of Pachesi in the Empire of Kaabu*. Brikama: University of The Gambia.

Polónia, Amélia and Capelão, Rosa (2021): 'Women and Gender in the Portuguese Overease Empire: Society, Economy and Politics', in Francisco Bethencourt (ed.), *Gendering the Portuguese -speaking World: From the Middle Ages to the Present* (Leiden: Brill), 71–101.

## Bibliography

Rarey, Matthew Francis. 2018. 'Assemblage, Occlusion, and the Art of Survival in the Black Atlantic', *African Arts* 51/4, 20–33.

Reis, João José (1993): *Slave Rebellion in Brazil: The Muslim Uprising of 1835 in Bahia*. Baltimore: Johns Hopkins University Press.

— (2003): *Death Is a Festival: Funeral Rites and Rebellion in Nineteenth-Century Brazil*. Chapel Hill: University of North Carolina Press.

Rodney, Walter (1966): 'African Slavery and Other Forms of Social Oppression on the Upper Guinea Coast in the Context of the Atlantic Slave Trade', *Journal of African History* 7/3, 431–43.

Sackur, Amanda (1999): *The Development of Creole Society and Culture in St Louis and Gorée, 1719–1817*. London: University of London; unpublished PhD dissertation.

Saho, Bala (2018): *Contours of Change: Muslim Courts, Women and Islamic Society in Colonial Bathurst, The Gambia, 1905–1965*. Lansing: Michigan State University Press.

Saidi, Christine (2010): *Women's Authority and Society in Early East-Central Africa*. Rochester: University of Rochester Press.

Sanneh, Lamin (1979): *The Jakhanke: The History of an Islamic Clerical People of the Senegambia*. London: International Africa Institute.

— (2016): *Beyond Jihad: The Pacifist Tradition in West African Islam*. Oxford: Oxford University Press.

Santos, Vaniclèia Silva (2013): 'Africans, Afro-Brazilians and Afro-Portuguese in the Iberian Inquisition in the Seventeenth and Eighteenth Centuries', in Robert Less Adams Jr (ed.), *Rewriting the African Diaspora in Latin America and the Caribbean: Beyond Disciplinary and National Boundaries* (London: Routledge), 46–60.

Santos Granero, Fernando (2009): *Vital Enemies: Slavery, Predation, and the Amerindian Political Economy of Life*. Austin: University of Texas Press.

Seck, Ibrahima (2012): 'The French Discovery of Senegal: Premises for a Selective Policy of Assimilation', in Toby Green (ed.), *Brokers of Change: Atlantic Commerce and Cultures in Precolonial Western Africa* (Oxford: Oxford University Press, for the British Academy): 147–70.

Shaw, Rosalind (2002): *Memories of the Slave Trade: Ritual and the Historical Imagination in Sierra Leone*. Chicago: University of Chicago Press.

## Bibliography

Silva, Filipa Ribeiro da (2002): *A Inquisição na Guiné, nas Ilhas de Cabo Verde e São Tomé e Príncipe (1536–1821): Contributo para o Estudo da Política do Santo Ofício nos Territórios Africanos*. Lisboa: Universidade Nova de Lisboa; 2 vols.; unpublished MA dissertation.

— (2011): *Dutch and Portuguese in Western Africa: Empires, Merchants and the Atlantic System, 1580–1674*. Leiden: Brill.

Silva Campo, Ana María (2025): *Travellers of the Half Moon Gate*. Chapel Hill: University of North Carolina Press.

Smith, M. G. (1959): 'The Hausa System of Social Status', *Africa* 29/3, 239–52.

Stewart, Charles (2018): 'Calibrating the Scholarship of Timbuktu', in Toby Green and Benedetta Rossi (eds.), *Landscapes, Sources and Intellectual Projects of the West African Past: Essays in Honour of Paulo Fernando de Moraes Farias* (Leiden: Brill): 220–38.

Swanson, Heather (1988): 'The Illusion of Economic Structure: Craft Guilds in Late Medieval English Towns', *Past and Present* 121 (November 1988), 29–48.

Sweet, James H. (2012): *Domingos Álvares, African Healing, and the Intellectual History of the Atlantic World*. Chapel Hill: University of North Carolina Press.

Thornton, John K. (1983): 'Sexual Demography: The Impact of the Slave Trade on Family Structure', in Claire C. Robertson and Martin A. Klein (eds.), *Women and Slavery in Africa* (Madison: University of Wisconsin Press), 39–48.

— (2020): *A History of West-Central Africa to 1850*. Cambridge: Cambridge University Press.

Touray, Ensa (2023): 'Islam and the Rise of Islamic States in Sub-Saharan Africa', *Journal of Philosophy, Religion and Culture* 6/2, no. 1, 1–12.

Tuck, Michael W. (2012): 'Everyday Commodities, the Rivers of Guinea, and the Atlantic World: The Beeswax Export Trade, *c*.1450–1800', in Toby Green (ed.), *Brokers of Change: Atlantic Commerce and Cultures in Precolonial Western Africa* (Oxford: Oxford University Press for the British Academy): 283–304.

Urdang, Stephanie (1979): *Fighting Two Colonialisms: Women in Guinea-Bissau*. New York: Monthly Review Press.

## Bibliography

Valerio, Miguel (2022): *Sovereign Joy: Afro-Mexican Kings and Queens, 1539–1640*. Cambridge: Cambridge University Press.

Varnhagen, Francisco Adolfo de (1842): *Noticia Historica e Descriptiva do Mosteiro de Belem, com um Glossario de Varios Termos Respectivos Principalmente a Architectura Gothica*. Lisbon: Na Typographia da Sociedade Propagadora dos Conhecimentos Uteis.

Ventura, Maria da Graça A. Mateus (2021): 'The Traffic of Raw and Carved African Ivory in the Caribbean and Lima (1555–1635)', in Almeida/Horta/Mark (eds.) (2021), 577–613.

Wachtel, Nathan (2001): *La Foi du souvenir: labyrinthes marranes*. Paris: Éditions du Seuil.

Walker, Timothy D. (2013): 'The Medicines Trade in the Portuguese Atlantic World: Acquisition and Dissemination of Healing Knowledge from Brazil (c.1580–1800)', *Social History of Medicine* 26/3: 403–31.

Wheat, David (2010): '*Nharas* and *Morenas Horras*: A Luso-African Model for the Social History of the Spanish Caribbean, c.1570–1640', *The Journal of Early Modern History* 14/1–2, 119–50.

— (2011): 'The First Great Waves: African Provenance Zones for the Transatlantic Slave Trade to Cartagena de Indias, 1570–1640', *Journal of African History* 52/1, 1–22.

Winter, Cameron (2024): 'War Canoes and Poisoned Arrows: Great Jolof and Imperial Mali Against the Fifteenth Century Portuguese Slave Raids', *Journal of African Military History* 8/1, 27–57.

# Notes

## Introduction

1. AHU, CU, Cabo Verde, Caixa 4, doc. 21 describes Castelbranco as 'hũ fidalgo pobre'. He arrived on the island probably in late May. On the Portuguese and Dutch in the South Atlantic see Boxer (1950); Silva (2011); Araujo (2023: Chapter 1).
2. AHU, CU, Cabo Verde, Caixa 4, doc. 40.
3. Ibid., for the sale of wine to the women; Achebe (2020: 25).
4. AHU, CU, Cabo Verde, Caixa 5, doc. 30.
5. Ibid., doc. 12.
6. Other histories of port cities include Candido (2013), Law (2004) and Mann (2010). For Rodrigues, see IAN/TT, IL, Proceso 8626 (hereafter LR). The first historian to look at this in detail was Silva (2002); Havik (2004) is a pioneering work drawing on Crispina Peres's inquisition trial to look at gender dynamics in the history of Guinea-Bissau; an early collection of works on the subject is in the edited collection put together by Bethencourt/Havik (2004).
7. LR, fol. 29v.
8. On the enmity between Rodrigues and Jorge Gonçalves Frances, see ibid., fols. 231v, 279v. A translation of the Crispina Peres trial has been published: see Green/Havik/Ribeiro da Silva (2021: hereafter CP). On Rodrigues embarking on the visit to Guinea, via Cacheu, on his return, see LR, fol. 296r and the first pages of CP.
9. For biographical histories of seventeenth-century Angola, see the biographies of Queen Njinga of Matamba and Dom Lourenço Silva de Mendonça, a prince of Ndongo, by Heywood (2017) and Nafafé (2022).
10. On Bautista Pérez, see Wachtel (2001); Newson/Minchin (2007); Ireton (2020). These documents are collected in AGNP, SO-CO, 18–197: for

## Notes

a detailed discussion of their provenance and utility for historical research, see Newson (2012: 5–7). For a microhistory of the Gambia river drawing on Royal Africa Accounts, see Kriger (2017).

11  Ladurie (1978); Ginzburg (1976); Sweet (2012).
12  For studies of women in later periods, see Ipsen (2015) and Oliveira (2021).
13  On the role of Cabo Verde in the sixteenth-century trade, see Green (2012a).
14  MMA, Vol. 3, 337.
15  For a recent discussion of these military encounters, see Winter (2024).
16  On the 1660s and 1670s as a turning point in the transatlantic slave trade in Western Africa, see Green (2019: Introduction). The concept of 'Greater Senegambia' was introduced in Barry (1998). On the growing spread of Islam in seventeenth-century Senegambia, see Mota (2018). On the religious competition with the Spanish Capuchins see CP, xlviii. On French missionaries in this region, see Saint Lô (1637).
17  On the suspension of the Portuguese Inquisition from 1674 to 1681, see Bethencourt (2024: 5).
18  LR, fol. 286v.
19  Santos (2013: 48); for a discussion of the elaboration, use and circulation of the *bolsas*, see Fromont (2020) and Rarey (2018).
20  On growing inequality, see Alfani (2024).
21  On ancient East-Central Africa, see Saidi (2010).
22  See for instance Wheat (2010) for these dynamics in the Spanish Caribbean world, and Green (2007: Chapter 12) for this context more broadly; I am grateful to my colleague Hannah Murphy for reminding me of this.
23  For a recent discussion of these facets of Western historiography, see Green (2022).
24  Green/Nafafé (2020: 144–5).
25  On the importance of religious brotherhoods in the lives of Africans in the Iberian empires, see Valerio (2022) and Nafafé (2022).
26  On the route from Cacheu to Bintang, see Coelho (1953: 14, 32, 36); for a more recent discussion and map, see Newson (2012: 5-7).
27  Coelho (1953: 15).

## Notes

28 Chabal/Green (2016); Green (2007).
29 AHU, CU, Cabo Verde, Caixa 5, doc. 7.
30 Ibid.
31 Ibid., Caixa 5a, doc. 114.
32 On the sodomy of which Vaz de Pontes was accused, see CP, 7, 18, 20. On the enmity described by Rodrigues in his trial, see LR, fol. 229v.

## Chapter 1: Crispina and Jorge

1 On Crispina Peres's first marriage, see CP, 183; her first husband had been Captain Francisco Nunes de Andrade.
2 Ibid., 1–109.
3 Ibid., 137.
4 Castanho's witness statement is ibid., 98ff; on his being Gonçalves Frances's brother-in-law, ibid., 16, 32; on Gonçalves Frances's own declaration, ibid., 159.
5 Ibid., 136. Rodrigues Barraza's simultaneous Islamic faith and drunkenness is surprising to modern eyes, but was more typical in the seventeenth century, when Islam coexisted with other religious practices in Senegambia. For more discussion of this, see Mota (2018).
6 On Crispina Peres never having left West Africa before her trial in Lisbon, see CP, 185. Frances made a lengthy deposition of his life history in 1664 to the Portuguese Overseas Council (Conselho Ultramarino), in which he also made clear he had never left the region – see AHU, CU, Guiné, Caixa 2, doc. 30.
7 CP, 183.
8 Ibid., 182–3; on Rodrigo Peres de Balcasar's situation in 1658, see LR, fols. 89v–90r; on Manoel de Almeida, see CP, 164, fn. 1156.
9 Ibid., 184.
10 Ibid. On the New Christian Diaspora in general, see Bethencourt (2024) and Israel (2002); on its specific texture in West Africa, see Horta/Mark (2010); on the diaspora in Amsterdam, whence many Jews came to West Africa, see Kaplan (1996).
11 CP, 185.

*Notes*

12  For examples of this kind of literature, see for instance Carreira (1947) and (1964).
13  On her dealings with peoples in West Africa, see CP, 185; for Frances's testimony on Cacheu, ibid., 138.
14  Ibid., 148.
15  On the escape see ibid., 144–5; the evidence is given by Frances, who describes the woman as his stepdaughter (i.e. Peres's daughter from her first marriage). On Crispina's son Gaspar, living in Farim in 1658, see LR, fols. 44r–v.
16  MMA, Vol. 6, 201–2.
17  On the role of hunters in political history, see Green (2019: Chapter 7).
18  AHU, CU, Guiné, Caixa 2, doc. 30.
19  CP, 167.
20  On the alleged 'Old Christian' ancestry of Jorge, see CP, 46; on Álvaro's birth in 1571, see ADP, Registos de Baptismos, Cx. 1, Maço 1B, folio 18v; on the 1594 auto-da-fé, see ASV, Secretaria di Stato di Portogallo, Vol. 9, fol. 264r; on the arrest of Álvaro in 1634 and his escape, see AHU, CU, Guiné Caixa 1, docs. 12 and 13; on his death, see idem., doc. 27, anexo 1. A good summary of the evidence on this family is in Green (2018: 42–7).
21  On Jorge's son living in Seville, see AHU, CU, Guiné, Caixa 1, doc. 52, fol. 3v; on Álvaro in Cartagena, see AGI, Santa Fé 56B, doc. 73, no. 2; on the marriage of Álvarez Prieto and Ana, see Green (2018: 46); on Ohanbú, see CP, 124; on the trial of Manuel Álvarez Prieto, see AHN, Inquisición, Legajo 1520, Expediente 15.
22  For the quotation of evidence against Crispina's alleged use of witchcraft, see CP, 103; for Jorge's testimony of his illness, see ibid., 141.
23  Ibid., 39.
24  Ibid., 112, for the quarrel over the goat sacrifice.
25  Ibid., 103.
26  Ibid., 67, for Lordello.
27  On *grumetes*, see Havik (2011).
28  CP, 53–4.
29  Ibid., 172–3; on Sara's location, see Mota/Hair (1977: 164).

30 On Barraza throwing the liquids into the river, see CP, 54; for Rodrigues Barraza's testimony, see ibid., 161–4, and esp. 162 for Aredas's theft of goods.
31 Ibid., 161–4.
32 Ibid., 163.
33 Ibid., 151.
34 On the relationship between the Gonçalves Frances and Barraza families, see Green (2018).
35 AHU, CU, Cabo Verde, Caixa 7a, doc. 133. On Gomes and Vaz, see Green (2019: 341). The most detailed study of Vaz is in Havik (2004: 162–72), and Brooks (2003).
36 CP, 52, 134–5.
37 Ibid., 142; and confirmed also in Sebastião Rodrigues Barraza's evidence, 162.
38 Ibid., 196–7.
39 Ibid., 131.
40 Ibid., 79, 90, 137.
41 On saying mass after a night out, see LR, fol. 16r; on firing off pistols at night, ibid., fol. 262v; for the party in his house in Farim, ibid., fol. 42v.
42 On his wine-drinking, see ibid., fol. 186r; on the swordfights, ibid., fols. 241r–v, 262r; on his inability to maintain friendship, ibid., fols. 242v–243r.
43 Ibid., fols. 184v–185r.
44 For Rodrigues's defence on the issue of Beatriz Monteiro's daughter, see ibid., fol. 263r.

## 2 Women and Power in Cacheu

1 On little girls dressed as nuns in Lisbon in the late seventeenth century, see BL, Add MS 23726, fol. 85r.
2 For an important study of this dynamic in a later period, see the essays in Candido/Jones (2019).
3 A number of discussions of *signares* exist. One of the best studies for St Louis and Gorée is Sackur (1999); and more recently Jones (2013).

*Notes*

See also Kriger (2017: 94–104). For the impacts of these relationships on twentieth-century histories of Gambian women, see Ceesay (2011) and Saho (2018).

4 On Inquisitorial trials as a means of revenge, see for instance Green (2007: 17–19).
5 On the initial accusation, see CP, 26.
6 Ibid., 9–10.
7 Ibid.
8 On the ways in which this represented an immense ideological challenge to the Portuguese, see Polónia/Capelão (2021).
9 Gomez (2018: 1); Phillott-Almeida (2011). On Bautista Pérez, see AGNP, SO-CO,18-197, fol. 689v.
10 IAN/TT, IL, Maço 25, no. 233; for a discussion, see Green (2012a: 162–4).
11 Havik (2011).
12 On the Bainunk–Floup dictionary, see Lespinay (2000).
13 For Ganagoga, see MMA, Vol. 3, 253. On multilingualism historically and today in this region, see Lüpke (2010) and Lüpke/Storch (2013: 13–76).
14 CP, 110, 126.
15 Kananoja (2021).
16 CP, 112.
17 Achebe (2020: 25); on the longevity of economic structures, see Green (2019).
18 Jobson (1968: 37); I have modernized the spellings of Jobson's anachronistic English in my quotations from his text in this book.
19 For João Bautista Pérez, AGNP, SO-CO, 18–197, fols. 288v, 687v, 695r (Tandakunda); fols. 689v, 700r (Tendaba); fol. 716v (Tancoaralle); fols. 719v, 723r (Cabaceira); fol. 720v (Nhamena). For Manoel, fols. 123v, 130r for Joal; and fol. 66r for Barra.
20 AGNP, SO-CO, 18–197, fol. 685v.
21 Mota/Hair (1977: 148); Coelho (1953: 17).
22 AGNP, SO-CO, 18–197, fol. 725v; on elephants and crocodiles, see Mota/Hair (1977: 144).
23 AGNP, SO-CO, 18–197, fols. 290v, 319v, 320v, 690v. The trade of horses with the king of Casamance and cloth to the king of Rufisque is

## Notes

mentioned in João Bautista Pérez's will: see AGNP, SO-CO, Caja 33, doc. 349 fols. 7r, 23r.
24 Jobson (1968: 97).
25 AGNP, SO-CO, 18–197, fol. 938v (Guiomar); fol. 948v (Domingas Lopez; fol. 953v (Esperança Vaz). For many other examples from these books, see fols. 49v (Clara Vaz); 84v (Maria Rodrigues); 288r and 697v (Antonia Fernandes); 307r (Esperança Gonçalves); 312v (Esperança Tavares); 706v (Ana Fernandes); 712v (Clara Lopes).
26 Ibid., fol. 84v (*regateiras*); ibid., fol. 442v.
27 LR, fols. 68r and 69v: Maria Mendes and Leonor Ferreira both earn their living spinning cotton in Cabo Verde; on Ferreira's time in Farim, see fol. 29r; on Bintang, see Kriger (2017: 112); on gendered patterns of textile production in Senegambia, see Curtin (1975: 213).
28 Green (2019: Chapter 2).
29 Osborn (2011).
30 CP, 69.
31 On brideprice, see Jobson (1968: 67); on the dislike of paying it, see CP, 135–6. On how this system of brideprice represented a massive shock to colonial Portuguese men, see Polónia/Capelão (2021: 82).
32 On Crispina as a 'master', ibid., 71; on Vaz de Pontes, ibid., 7. For a famous example of female political leadership in seventeenth-century West-Central Africa, see Heywood (2017); see also Achebe (2011) for an insight into how this endured into the nineteenth and twentieth centuries.
33 CP, 7, 77–8, for other accusations of his frequent visits to the house; ibid., 47, for Vaz de Pontes's own evidence; ibid., 173, for Jorge moving in with Crispina in 1655 when they married.
34 AGNP, SO-CO, 18–197, fol. 51v.
35 CP, 201.
36 LR, fol. 42v; on Afonso, fol. 21v.
37 Ibid., fol. 278v.
38 CP, 55.
39 On the preparation of food, and the colours of their clothes, see Jobson (1968: 68–9).
40 For this argument about the changes at this time, see Thornton (1983).

41 Coelho (1953: 178).
42 On rice growing, see Hawthorne (2003).

## Chapter 3 Cacheu: The Setting

1 Araujo (2024). On the early transatlantic traffic and volumes, see Green (2012a: 215). On this early trade, see also Mendes (2008), and for the Peruvian dimension, Bowser (1974).
2 On the route from Cacheu to Bichangor via Bugendo, see Mota/Hair (1977: 170).
3 For the document from 1565, see AGI, Justicia 878, no. 2. On European participation in African religious rites, see Nafafé (2007).
4 An inquisition trial of 1562 describes performance of a masquerade on Christmas Eve in Bugendo – see IAN/TT, IL, Maço 25, no. 233; on involvement in African religious practice, see Nafafé (2007)'s analysis of the word *tangomão*, used to describe Portuguese living in West Africa, as derived from the Temne name of priests in Sierra Leone; and see Green (2012a: Chapters 8 and 9) on the conflicts around Bugendo, and the migration of Caboverdeans to Cacheu.
5 On the growth in the trade from this region at this time, see Wheat (2011).
6 Parker (2013).
7 On the trees on the north bank, see Mota/Hair (1977: 170); for the provisioned canoes and names of the villages on the north bank, see Coelho (1953: 33); on the rains bringing activity to an end in Cacheu, AHU, CU, Guiné, Caixa 2, doc. 2.
8 Ibid. On Floup hostility to Atlantic trade, see Mark (2002: 35). On Floup religious practice, see Baum (1999).
9 On the small numbers of whites in Cacheu, see AHU, CU, Guiné, Caixa 1, doc. 74; on swordfights and the etiquette of hats, CP, 133–4; on clothing, EM, fol. 15r.
10 On the 1590 attack, see the description by Almada – MMA, Vol. 3, 300; for the description from the 1620s, see BA, Códice 51-VI-54, no. 37, fols. 143–4; for Magalhães, BA, Códice 51-VI-21, fol. 276v.

## Notes

11 Coelho (1953: 34); for the 1662 account, AHU, CU, Guiné, Caixa 2, doc. 22; idem., doc. 48, for the occupation of the water sources. On Coelho as Jorge's sworn enemy, CP, 144.
12 For the presence of other European empires in the region, see AHU, CU, Guiné, Caixa 2, doc. 22: 'Toda esta costa [esta] cercada de todas as nacoins do norte'.
13 On the 'loaves' (*paens*) of wax, see e.g., AGNP, SO-CO, 18/197, fols. 818r, 826v; on bringing millet from the Bijagós, see ibid., fol. 73v; on the Teles case, ibid., fol. 72v: 'dos custos de levar o fato que lhe mandei com frías e de trazer a sera a esta caza'.
14 On the *djabakòs* coming at night, see CP, 98.
15 Ibid., 99.
16 AGNP, SO-CO, 18/197, fol. 795v.
17 For Alvares, EM, fol. 15r; on the burning of the wooden houses, BA, Códice 51-IX-25, no. 26, fol. 88v; on the mix of styles by the 1630s, BA, Códice 51-VI-54, no, 37, fol. 143r.; on the fire in the church, see Coelho (1953: 35).
18 On arson, see Coelho (1953: 34), and the description of Manoel Alvares, EM, fol. 15r. On the wax in Bautista Pérez's *combete*, see AGNP, SO-CO, 18/197, fol. 84v. On *combetes* in general, see Mark (2002: 46).
19 On the two streets of Cacheu, the dock, and on the stone construction of the church, see Mark (2002: 34–5); for the 1612 description, see AGI, Contratación 800, no, 15, fol. 73r.
20 Coelho (1953: 35).
21 CP, 34.
22 On the funerals and description of Vila Quente, see CP, 10, 13.
23 Coelho (1953: 35–6). On the emergence of *tabankas* in this part of West Africa in the seventeenth century, see Hawthorne (2003: 121–3); on the arrival of the Manes in Sierra Leone, see Green (2012a: 237–40).
24 Jobson (1968: 53–4).
25 For Almada, MMA, Vol. 3, 307. We're lucky to have the analysis and detailed discussion of this made by Peter Mark – see Mark (2002: 37).
26 Again, see Peter Mark's discussion: Mark (2002: 44–5).
27 Ibid., 43–9; Jobson (1968: 55); for the benches and the wooden locks and keys, see Mota/Hair (1977: 148, 150).

## Notes

28 On Pais renting from Jorge, CP, 145; on Bautista Pérez, AGNP, SO-CO, 18/197, fol. 124r. On someone living in the house of the priest Luis Rodrigues in Farim, see LR, fol. 88r. On the way this moved from West Africa to the Americas, see Wheat (2010); on the concept of landlords and strangers, see Brooks (1993).

29 On Bonifacia, LR, fol. 85v; for Vaz de Pontes, CP, 7.

30 See LR, fols. 70r–v.

31 These details come from AGNP, SO-CO, 18/197. For mattresses, fols. 22v and 588r; for blankets, e.g., fols. 440v, 469v, 470v, and many other places.

32 For *'mantas para os negros'* (blankets for the Africans), ibid., fol. 93r; wax, e.g. fols. 441v, 467r.

33 For Chinese porcelain, ibid., fols. 10v, 11v, 14v; for Potosí silver plates, ibid., fols. 93r, 98v, 110v; for silver cups, fol. 110v; for silver spoons, ibid., fol. 22v; for the copper oven, ibid., fol. 14v; for cauldrons, see ibid., fol. 3v. On *cantareiras* in the kitchen, see CP, 112. For a new history of Potosí, see Lane (2021).

34 All the details in this paragraph from AGNP, SO-CO, 18/197: for cuscus, fols. 8v, 10v, 24v, 42v, 45v and many other places; palm oil, fol. 92v; wine is listed on virtually every folio of the account book; oil, fols. 2v, 16v, 24v; olives, fols. 6r, 8v; sugar, fols. 2v, 41v, 46r, 62v; figs, fol. 23r; almonds, fols. 11v, 18v, 26v, 27v, 75v; oranges, fol. 95r; jam, fols. 5v, 63r, 68v, 138r; cheese, fols. 6v, 18r, 44r, 163r; cured sausage, fols. 5v, 43v, 612r; chickpeas, fol. 30v; pepper, fols. 16v, 17v, 53v; Dutch cheese, fols. 608v, 612r, 623r. For a discussion of cuscus as a Senegambian grain, see Seck (2012: 162–3).

35 All the details in this paragraph from AGNP, SO-CO, 18/197: perpetuan, e.g. fols. 2r, 13v; Rouen cloth, fol 13v; Dutch cloth, fols. 16v, 46v; *picote*, fol. 8v; hats, fols. 41v, 46r.

36 For a discussion of the indigo-dyed indigo cotton textiles in Senegambia, see Kobayashi (2019). The rest of the details from this paragraph come from AGNP, SO-CO, 18/197: 'cannekins', fols. 7v, 32v, 164r, 187r, and many other places; Chinese taffeta, fols. 79v, 93r; Mexican taffeta, fols. 109r, 131r; silk socks, fols. 25v, 30v, 34r.

37 For the production of cloth currencies in Senegambia, see Kriger (2017: 110).

38 Ibid. See also AGNP, SO-CO, 18/197, fols. 739v (for João Bautista Pérez's trade in Gambia); *barafulas* are almost everywhere in the account books, e.g. fols. 2r, 29r, 35r (in this last one called 'barafulas da Gambea/from Gambia', hence the evidence they were woven there; fol. 43v (Jolof cloth, 'pano Jalofo'); 'king's cloth', e.g. fols. 13v, 14r, 14v, 30v, 32r; from Degola, fols. 9r, 30v, 48v, 59v.

39 Curtin (1975: 211–4); a new history of the textile industry and trade in Senegambia is Benjamin (2024). On the trade of *barafulas* to Cartagena, see AHN, Inquisición, Legajo 1608, expediente 27, fols. 31v–32r.

40 For the oral histories, see, e.g., NCAC, RDD, transcribed cassette 309A, pp. 27–8 and 61–2; for the denunciation of Silva, see IAN/TT, IL, Livro 205, fol. 231r.

41 For Sapi ivories in general, see Almeida/Horta/Mark (2021). On oliphants, see Afonso/Horta (2013). On the links between the traditions of ivory and stone carvings, see Lamp (2020).

42 On ivories in Lima and in Manoel Bautista Pérez's home, see Ventura (2021: 594–600); on the Sapi migration and the bringing of the ivory skills and products, see Mark (2021: 83). An example of someone descended from Sapi migrants to Cacheu of the 1550s is discussed in Ireton (2020: 18–9).

43 The Brazilian historian Thiago Mota has done the most detailed recent work on these questions: on *alúas*, see Mota (2018: 189–91); see also Santos (2013: 50).

44 On the folk tales in the Alentejo, see Nafafé (2012). On the identification of the rope motif in Manuelline architecture, see Varnhagen (1842).

45 On 1640 as a key moment defining a new period of climatic instability in Senegambia, see Brooks (1993); Parker (2013); for the resident from Ica, see AGNP, SO-CO, Caja 57, doc. 431.

46 Cavazzi (1687: 278, 443, 554).

47 AHU, CU, Guiné, Caixa 1, doc. 23, anexos 1 and 2.

48 Stone (1924: 90, 92). The most important work looking at this ecological transformation in the seventeenth century was done by George Brooks – see Brooks (1993).

49 MMA, Vol. 6, 246.

50 Faust et al. (2006).

*Notes*

## Chapter 4: Cacheu in Regional and Global Context

1 Curto (2004).
2 For the Mancaigne, see Fonseca (1997), and on the Manjako see Buis (1990); on Cobiana, see Green (2012a: 48); on Bula, see Coelho (1953: 36).
3 The foundational modern text on the relationship between migration and modern cultures of Senegambia is Barry (1998); on the origin stories of a number of these communities, see Green (2012a: 46–8).
4 Barry (1998: 7).
5 For Donelha, see Hair/Mota (1977: 118–20); Coelho (1953: 49).
6 On Geba being subject to the Farim-Bidassou, see Coelho (1953: 49).
7 For Vidigal Castanho, AHU, CU, Cabo Verde, Caixa 8, doc. 100; and see Green (2009). For *tubabodaga*, see Coelho (1953: 37); for Bautista Pérez's visit, see AGNP, SO-CO, 18/197, fol. 626v. Kriger (2017: 82–3) gives an account of trade between Cacheu and the RAC in the 1670s.
8 Coelho (1953: 38).
9 Ibid.; for sales of kola with or without their shells ('com o sem cabeça'), see AGNP, SO-CO, 18/197, fol. 694r, and for a sale of 'good-quality, selected' kolas ('boas, escolhidas'), ibid., fol. 330v. For the Fulani demand for kola, see Malacco (2023: 255).
10 The evidence in this paragraph comes from AGNP, SO-CO, 18/197: fol. 693v, for João's trading visit to Gambia in 1617; fol. 68v for the value of 5 *godenhos* of kola for an enslaved captive in Geba, where they were by far the most valuable item of trade; for the ship worth only just over a quarter of the kolas on board, see ibid., fol. 82v, where the ship is worth '8 Blacks', and the kola are worth 27; ibid., fol. 97r, for the possession of just 2 *godenhos* of kola in Geba for small-scale trade. For a general discussion of the kola trade in Senegambia, see Malacco (2023: 251–5).
11 Coelho (1953: 36) on the kingdoms; 38 for kola. On kola and its links to Islam, see Lovejoy (1980).
12 On Bujé, see CP, 48; on the sacrifices at Bugendo, see ibid., 11, 73.
13 On the trade in Baoula, see AGNP, SO-CO, 18/197, fol. 461v; for Carneiro, ibid., fol. 455v. On Bujé, Coelho (1953: 31).
14 For the African traders present on these journeys alongside Portuguese and mixed-heritage traders, see Newson (2012).

## Notes

15 CP, 4–6.
16 Barry (1998: 22). See also on Kaabu, Lopes (1999), Green (2009) and Innes (1976). On Tamba Dibi, see Green (2019: 319).
17 LR, fols. 75v, 86r.
18 CP, 173, 187; on Bissau and gifts of wine and cloth, and trade in millet, see AGNP, SO-CO, 18/197, fols. 411v, 649r; on payment of a pilot to go to Sierra Leone and back from Cacheu, see ibid., fol. 662r.
19 Coelho (1953: 49–50); for the description of Geba's settlers, see BA, Códice 51-VI-21, fol. 277r.
20 For the example of 1635, see AGI, Escribanía, 591A, Pieza 4, fols. 27r–v.
21 CP, 156.
22 On Tendaba, AGNP, SO-CO, 18/197, fol. 939v; on honey, see ibid., fol. 27v.
23 Coelho (1953: 30–32).
24 BA, Códice 51-VI-21, fol. 277r; Coelho (1953: 50).
25 Barry (1998: 18–19).
26 CP, 42–3, 49, 62, 130–31. On Leonor Ferreira, see LR, fols. 28r, 29r, 69v.
27 On Maria Mendes, ibid., fols. 68v–69r; for Viegas's testimony, see fol. 74v; another example in the trial of a woman running a household in Ribeira Grande is Susana da Cunha (fol. 33r).
28 For news of Rodrigues's fights in Cabo Verde in Cacheu, see ibid., fol. 255r; for Esperança's testimony, see ibid., fol. 71r; for the report from the 1640s, see BA, Códice 51-VI-54, fol. 143r.
29 For a case of troops from Cabo Verde being sent to protect Cacheu from a Dutch fleet in 1644, see AHU, CU, Cabo Verde, Caixa 3, doc. 30.
30 On the grain coming from Gambia to Santiago in 1609, see EM, fol. 8v. A good summary of these changes in the seventeenth century is in Green (2012b).
31 AHU, CU, Cabo Verde, Caixa 4, no. 20 – July 18th, 165; ibid., no. 46. For the division of the streets and neighbourhoods see ibid., Caixa 2, no. 37. For the responses in the trial of Rodrigues, see e.g. LR, fol. 114v.
32 LR, fols. 26v, 257v.
33 Ibid., fols. 104r, 245r, 267r, 282r.
34 Ibid., fol. 74v, fol. 102r, 105v.

35 On Rodrigues's parents, ibid., fol. 200v.
36 Ibid., fols. 121r–127r.
37 On the Jakhanké, see Sanneh (2016) and idem. (1979 ); on Dia and urbanism, see McIntosh (2005: 169–70). on their growth in the seventeenth century, see Mota (2018). For the 1620s account of Sutucó and itinerant Jakhanké preachers, see Jobson (1968: 87, 97–9); for the anonymous account, see BA, Códice 51-IX-25, fol. 89v; for the connection to Mecca, see MMA, Vol. 7, 616–7.
38 On Vaz de Pontes, see CP, 20, 187. On the wax exports of Bautista Pérez, see for Portugal, AGNP, SO-CO, 18/197, fol. 183r; for its use in Cacheu see ibid., fol. 586v; on Bautista Pérez's trade of wax from Cacheu to Lima, see ibid., fols. 908v, 909v, 910v – where he says that he brought this wax with him himself, presumably having purchased it personally in Cacheu.
39 On Cartagena's African population, see Silva Campo (2025: Chapter 3) and Gómez (2017); on the Palenque de Limón, see Friedemann/Patiño Roselli (1983).
40 On the 1651 document from Cartagena, see AHU, CU, Cabo Verde, Caixa 4, doc. 17; for Manrique's testimony, AGI, Santa Fé 56B, no. 66; for Barraza, see AGI, Contratación 5737, no. 12, Ramo 1.
41 AGI, Santa Fé 245, 18 July 1624.
42 Ibid.
43 There have been many discussions of this contraband in recent years. A good example is the ship of 1630, whose records are detailed at AHN, Inquisición, Legajo 4816, Expediente 22, fols. 4v–9r; see the discussion in Green (2007: Chapter 11); Silva Campo (2025). Some examples in the archive would be, for instance: AGI, Santa Fé 37, Ramo 4, no. 14 (1573) and Ramo 6, no. 76 (1588). For these communities of Jolofs, and the uprising of the ship from Guinea, see AGI, Santa Fé 37, Ramo 5, no. 42.

## Chapter 5: Religion, Politics and Power

1 MMA, Vol. 6, 192–3.
2 Jobson (1968: 76).

## Notes

3   MMA, Vol. 6, 194.
4   Ibid., 195–6.
5   Ibid., 196.
6   Nafafé (2022); on the Malês, see Reis (1993). On Palmares, see recently Lara (2021).
7   On the Rodrigues Duartes, see CP, 132; on Matos, see ibid., 131 and Green (2007: 226–7 and 303); see also Coelho (1953: 7). On Jorge's petition to join the *Ordem de Cristo*, see AHU, CU, Guiné, Caixa 2, doc. 30.
8   For the case from Joal, see GAA, Notarial Archive, 645A, fol. 595; for a complex view of the *Convivencia* of medieval Spain, see Nirenberg (2015).
9   For the fort at James Island, see Coelho (1953: 13).
10  Here I am following the approach of Cécile Fromont in her concept of 'spaces of correlation' in the kingdom of Kongo – see Fromont (2014).
11  CP, 95.
12  Ibid., 103.
13  For António's evidence see ibid., 96; on the description of Crispina's use of Islamic and African *djabakós*, see ibid., 101; on contemporary practice, see Green (2001); on hybridity in the Americas, see Fromont (2020: 464–5).
14  CP, 13, 16, 33, 53–4.
15  Ibid., 73.
16  Ibid., 45, 49, 51, 58.
17  Laye (1970: 1–3).
18  CP, 59.
19  Ibid., 101.
20  Ibid., 198.
21  Ibid., 198.
22  Ibid., 196–7; for the Luis Rodrigues case, see LR, fol. 27r; see also Green (2001).
23  See Mota (2018) in general – and especially, 3–6, for the seventeenth century as a key period of expansion of the social base, and 26 for its role as a popular religion.
24  Mota's analysis of Barreira's attempt to found the school is important – see ibid., 112; and MMA, Vol. 4, 58–9. On Jajolet de la Courbe, see Cultru (1913: 253). For Donelha, see Mota/Hair (1977: 120).

## Notes

25 On education, see Mota (2018: Chapter 3) and Sanneh (1979: 2, 11); for Jobson's description, see Jobson (1968: 84–7). For the madrassas, see EM, fol. 11v; see also Coelho (1953: 25).
26 Giesing/Vydrine (2007: 106–7).
27 On Vogado, CP, 3; on Jorge, ibid., 146.
28 On the school in Ribeira Grande, LR, fols. 3v, 17r, many other places; on the consecration of the host in animal hide, ibid., fols. 31r–v.
29 CP, 20, 135; for the evidence from the trial, LR, fol. 229v.
30 AGNP, SO-CO, 18/197, fols. 118r, 133v.
31 LR, fol. 18v.
32 AGNP, SO-CO, 18/197, fol. 193v: this page of the account books has the description of the costs of mounting a funeral, including digging the grave, saying mass, wax for the candles, and the procession with a cross led by the vicar. For godparent relationships, see CP, 25, 93.
33 CP, 59–60.
34 Ibid. See Fromont (2013: 185–6), Lahon (2005), and Nafafé (2022).
35 For Jorge's deposition, CP, 138; for Mendes, ibid., 68.
36 On the Jesuit mission in Cabo Verde, see Gonçalves (1996); on the conversion of the Pepel king, AHU, CU, Guiné, Caixa 2, doc. 37a.
37 For the Capuchins in Bissau and the conversion of the Bissau kings, see Mota (1974).
38 CP, 68.
39 Ibid., 118.
40 LR, fol. 78v.
41 CP, 86, 108–9, 117, 163.
42 Ibid., 117, 130.
43 For the 1630 accusation, IAN/TT, IL, Inquisição de Lisboa, Livro 222, fol. 231r; for the 1694 trial, Mota (1974: 76–7).
44 CP, 96.
45 Ibid., 70–71, 81.
46 Stewart (2018) discusses how many of the scholars from Mauritania migrated there from Timbuktu after the fall of the Songhay empire, following the Moroccan invasion of 1591.
47 On French profits in Senegal, Barry (1998: 49); Coelho (1953: 39) 'he tal Guine que dentro de hum anno recuperei a perda'.

*Notes*

48 For Barraza see CP, 163; for an attack on trading ships, see Ireton (2020: 29–30).

## 6 Slavery and Human Trafficking

1 On relative volumes from Angola and Senegambia, see Wheat (2011: 4); on the Jesuit account from 1621, see IAN/TT, Cartório dos Jesuitas, Maço 36, doc. 7; for the 1635 ship, see AHN, Inquisición, Legajo 4816, Expediente 22, fol. 75r.
2 Ireton (2020: 18–30).
3 On the accusations against Álvaro, see AGI, Escribanía 591A: *Comisión de Investigación en Fraudes de los Navios*, Cartagena, 1641. A ship of 1635 includes a list of the slaves that died on the Middle Passage, including several belonging to Gonçalves Frances (e.g. fols. 58v, 60r). On Domingos de Aredas and the Bijagós, see CP, 134–5, 143, 172.
4 EM, fol. 18v.
5 IAN/TT, IL, Livro 217, fols. 471r–v.
6 Ibid., fol. 19r.
7 AGI, Escribanía 591A, Pieza 4.
8 CP, 5, 10; LR, fol. 105v.
9 CP, 11, 49, 99, 171.
10 BA, Códice 54-XIII-15, no. 94, fols. 1v–2v – also published in Mota (1974). See also Jobson (1968: 35). On the role of the Fulani in the traffic in captives by the late seventeenth century, see Touray (2023: 9).
11 BA, Códice 54-XIII-15, no. 94, fol. 3v; Ireton (2020: 28–30).
12 Ibid., fol. 4r, for the lack of people to defend the traffic.
13 Nafafé (2022).
14 BA, Códice 54-XIII-15, no. 94, fol. 1v; and no. 94[a].
15 AGNP, SO-CO, 18/197, fol. 80v.
16 Ibid.; CP, 161–3.
17 AGNP, SO-CO, 18/197, fol. 74v.
18 For the kora origins in Kaabu, I am grateful to a personal communication from Professor Lucy Duran, SOAS, 1 April 2022.
19 Coelho (1953: 26).

## Notes

20  Mauny/Monod/Teixeira da Mota (1951: 8).
21  AGNP, SO-CO, 18/197, fols. 74v, 87v – for the 1613 purchases, they occur repeatedly down the page of the folio at 74v. The fact that he used the term also suggests that he did not entirely identify with Judaism himself, whatever the Inquisition might have determined twenty years later in Lima.
22  Ibid., fols. 133r, 133v (*tumbaquo*), 145r.
23  See also Patterson's seminal work (1982) on the relationship between slavery and social death; Vincent Brown has more recently emphasized the relationship between slavery and death itself – see Brown (2008).
24  AGNP, SO-CO, 18/197, fols. 95v–96r.
25  Ibid., fols. 31v, 32v. For a detailed discussion of this process of the financial commodification of human beings, see Green (2019: Chapter 6).
26  AGNP, SO-CO, 18/197, fol. 19v ('a barafula for millet'); fol. 68v on this 1613 list.
27  Ibid., fol. 92v for the silver to Mateus da Costa; fol. 98v for the gold transactions.
28  For the payment of a chicken for confession, CP, 6; for hides as a currency, see LR, fol. 4r, where bribes were said to be demanded in them; for the despatch of money to Sara and Bugendo, CP, 11.
29  AGNP, SO-CO, 18/197, fol. 74v for the roll of forty measures of cloth; CP, 162, for the 'Iron bar'.
30  On the fines, ibid., 2.
31  Rodney (1966).
32  BA, Códice 54-XIII-15, no. 94, fols.5r–v; Mota (1974: 130–31).
33  CP, 94, 105.
34  Ibid., 53–4, 161, 163.
35  Ibid., 54.
36  Ibid., 70.
37  Ibid., 136, and 151 on *ladino* slaves; LR, fol. 43r.
38  On the lives of the enslaved in urban Latin America, and the relationship with healing, see Campo (2025), Gómez (2017), and Sweet (2012).
39  CP, 68.

40 BA, Códice 51-IX-25, no. 26, fol. 89r.
41 On Kaabu, see BA, Códice 54-XIII-15, no. 94, fol. 3r; on the Bainunk near Sanguedogu, see Coelho (1953: 30).
42 BA, Códice 54-XIII-15, no. 94, fols. 3v–4r; CP, 163, 172
43 Coelho (1953: 31).
44 CP, 162.
45 AGNP, SO-CO, 18/197, fols. 97v, 107v, 134v, 136v; for a captive who fled and was not returned, see fol. 111v.
46 CP, 177.
47 Jobson (1968: 109).
48 Ibid., 112.
49 For a brilliant recent analysis of the relationship between Atlantic traffic in people and sexual fetishism, see Matory (2018).
50 LR, fol. 13r; AGNP, SO-CO, 18/197, fols. 3v, 49r, 74v.
51 Ibid., fol. 19r, 60r; LR, fols. 246r–v. On Rodrigues Duarte's trial in Lima, see AHN, Inquisición, Legajo 1647, Expediente 13, fol. 222v. For a recent discussion on the ways in which African captives were 'converted' into currency in the Atlantic world, see Green (2019: Chapter 6).
52 AGNP, SO-CO, Caja 2, doc. 8, fol. 714v; and on the will, fols. 988rff.
53 Ibid., fols. 1332r–1333r.
54 For the sale of captives for silver, see AGNP, SO-CO, 18/197, fols. 60r, 67r.

## Chapter 7: Work

1 EM, fol. 15r.
2 AGNP, SO-CO, 18/197, fol. 5v.
3 Ibid., fols. 9r, 37v, 933v; for the 1616 transactions, see ibid., fol. 661r. For a good study of the wax trade in Senegambia, see Tuck (2012).
4 AGNP, SO-CO, 18/197, fols. 103v, 124v, 142v.
5 Ibid., fol. 68v for the 1617 voyage to Geba.
6 Ibid., fols. 9r ('roupa da costa Baixa'); 52r ('barafulas da Gambea'); 69r ('roupa Jalofa fina', and from Casamance); 112r ('Geba cloth'). For an important discussion of the centrality of weaving to West and

## Notes

West-Central African history, see Kriger (2006) and Thornton (2020); on the role of captive labour in cotton harvesting, see also Kriger (2017: 110).

7 Coelho (1953: 8–9, 38); for 'panos brancos', AGNP, SO-CO, 18/197, fol. 8v.
8 AGNP, SO-CO, 18/197, fol. 8v.
9 Green (2022: 323–4), on 'putting-out'.
10 Mauny/Monod/Mota (1951: 54); MMA, Vol. 3, 297.
11 AGNP, SO-CO, 18/197, fols. 26r, 42r.
12 Ibid., fol. 965v.
13 Ibid., fols. 43v, 73v, 82v, 93r, 112r.
14 Ibid., fol. 19v; on the building of barricades and platforms, I am grateful to Ana Lúcia Araujo for information about similar work on the Loango coast.
15 CP, 6.
16 AGNP, SO-CO, 18/197, fols. 21v, 22v.
17 CP, 8–9, 100; see also 215, for Domingos de Goya, a pilot married to the Christian Black woman Clara Fernandes.
18 For coopers, e.g. AGNP, SO-CO, 18/197, fol. 77r; for *tortugeiros*, fols. 121v, 122v; for the 'expenses for Blacks and turtles', fol. 95r.
19 Mota/Hair (1977: 148).
20 An important work on blacksmiths in Mande societies is McNaughton (1988).
21 AGNP, SO-CO, 18/197, fols. 36v, 88v, 113v.
22 Ibid., fols. 50v, 75v, 76v, 111v, 140v. Cf Coelho (1953: 147).
23 AGNP, SO-CO, 18/197, fols. 111v, 135v (for the 1615 account of Diogo Rodrigues de Lisboa)
24 Ibid., fols. 25r, 48v.
25 For the case of Miguel Antonio, see ibid., fol. 140v 'para o barbeiro que o samgrou'. There is a wide literature on barber-surgeons in the Atlantic world: see, for instance, Furtado (2007), Hicks (2021) and Walker (2013). On the activities of barber-surgeons in twentieth-century Nupe, Nigeria – including some of the activities mentioned in this paragraph – see Nadel (1942: 298–301), and for Hausaland see Smith (1959: 248–9); on barber-guilds in late medieval Britain and early-modern Europe, see Swanson (1988: 40); I am also grateful to a

personal communication from Angelo di Cintio, on the medical role of barbers in early twentieth-century Pescara, Italy.
26 CP, 187.
27 Ibid., 95, 103.
28 Cf Havik (2016: 182): 'The extensive borrowing, adaptation and hybridisation of methods and cures for treating a wide range of diseases and health conditions shows that distinctions between African and Western knowledge were far from clear, and that boundaries were fluid.'

## Chapter 8: Entertainment and Gossip

1 CP, 54.
2 Ibid., 9–10, 34.
3 Carter/Cardoso (2021: 113).
4 Reis (2003). For an excellent recent discussion of philosophies of death and dying in West Africa, see Parker (2021); and for a potent analysis of the perspective of African religions on the 'vital force' of a human being, see Santos Granero (2009).
5 AGNP, SO-CO, 18/197, fol. 48v; for 8 swords worth 40 bolts of cloth in 1613, see ibid., fol. 77v.
6 Ibid., fols. 134v, 135v.
7 CP, 75.
8 Ibid., 76, 101.
9 Ibid., 133.
10 LR, fol. 43v.
11 On the use of *gumbe* in the 1960s, see Green (2019: 396–7); on *akontings*, ibid., 72–3.
12 LR, fols. 20r–v.
13 Ibid., fol. 26v.
14 Ibid., fol. 31v.
15 AGNP, SO-CO, 18/197, fol. 5v for the twelve crates of jam, and 25v for the one crate from Dioguo Soares; on the twelve packs of cards, fol. 27r, and on those bought from Álvaro Gonçalves Frances, fol. 31v; fol. 125v for the debt from Paulo Rodrigues d'Aguiar.

16 Jobson (1968: 48).
17 Ibid.
18 CP, 58.
19 Ibid., 60, 61.
20 Ibid., 153, 168; on Crispina's idiom, ibid., 54.
21 Ibid., 130.
22 Ibid., 131–2.
23 Ibid., 133–5; for instances of the trade in swords in Cacheu, see AGNP, SO-CO, 18/197, fols. 11v, 14v, 32v, 38v, 47v. An important discussion of the sword and knife trade in Senegambia is found in Horta/Mark (2010: 103–34).
24 CP, 60, 114.
25 Ibid., 133–4.
26 Ibid., 31.
27 LR, fols. 230v, 270v.
28 Ibid., fols. 239r, 249v, 258r.
29 Ibid., fols. 231v–232r.
30 Ibid., fols. 226r, 278r.
31 Ibid., fols. 238v–239r.
32 Ibid., fol. 230v.
33 Ibid., fol. 116v, fol. 241r.
34 Ibid.; fol. 239r, 243r.
35 Ibid., fol. 244r.
36 For Luis Rodrigues's failed pleas for mercy, see ibid., fol. 259v.

## Chapter 9: Time and Space

1 Badiou (2013).
2 Griffiths (1999: 118–38).
3 For a recent book focusing on the nineteenth century as a key moment of change, see Ogle (2015). However, Ogle herself notes that 'abstract' time was becoming hegemonic over 'concrete' time related to events by the seventeenth century – ibid., 10.
4 Griffiths (1999: 23).

## Notes

5   CP, 100.
6   Ibid., 30, 100.
7   Jobson (1968: 110, 114–5); CP, 48.
8   CP, 117; Coelho (1953: 30–31).
9   CP, 11, 94, 96.
10  Ibid., 9; LR, fol. 14r.
11  Ibid., fol. 78v.
12  Ibid., fol. 64v, on João Mascarenhas; on 10 o'clock at night, ibid., fol. 165v; on the clocks owned by the king of Kaabu, see Cultru (1913: 252).
13  LR, fol. 71v – for the receiving of written confession at dinner-time (*oras de Jantar*).
14  Ibid., fol. 20r.
15  Ibid., fol. 64v.
16  Ibid., fols. 16r (*passante de oras*), 35r (*fora de oras*).
17  Ibid., fols. 12r, 17r, 18r.
18  Ibid., fols. 13r–v.
19  CP, 121 (Mendes); LR, fol. 87v (Domingos Afonso); fol. 71r (Esperança).
20  Griffiths (1999: 137).
21  AHU, CU, Cabo Verde, Caixa 5, docs. 40–52. For a pathfinding analysis of the relationship between imperial science on the one hand and the objectivity of people, the environment and time on the other, see Costa (2020).
22  LR, fols. 13v–14v.
23  CP, 3.
24  Ibid., 100–101.
25  AGNP, SO-CO, 18/197, fol. 1r; Green (2019: xvi).
26  On sending letters via Brazil, and multiple copies being made, see e.g. CP, 82–3.
27  Cavazzi (1687: 686).
28  Griffiths (1999: 56).
29  Ibid., 126, 151, 166; for the view of the relationship between late medieval market economies and time, see Le Goff (1980).

Notes

## Chapter 10: Living, Healing and Dying in Cacheu

1 See Gómez (2017), Havik (2016) and Kananoja (2021); and see Newson (2017) for an important study of apothecaries in seventeenth-century Lima, who mainly used imported materials from Spain – which suggests that similar patterns were probably at work in Cacheu.
2 CP, 53, 103
3 Ibid., 150.
4 Ibid., 141.
5 Ibid., 152–3.
6 Ibid., 137.
7 Ibid., 81; MMA, Vol. 6, 201; LR, fols. 78r, 128r.
8 Ibid.
9 For Vogado's letter, see CP, 153; for smallpox, AGNP, SO-CO, 18/197, fols. 8v, 9r; ulcers, fol. 139v.
10 AGNP, SO-CO, Legajo 33, Cuaderno 349, fols. 6r–10r.
11 AHU, CU, Guiné, Caixa 2, doc. 10.
12 CP, 101.
13 Parker (2021).
14 AHU, CU, Cabo Verde, Caixa 3, doc. 65: *a pouca gente que nesta Ilha ha, respeito da muita que he morta'*; see also idem., docs. 70, 73.
15 CP, 5, 21; LR, fols. 5r, 154r–v.
16 LR, fols. 154r–v.
17 CP, 31–2, 38, 65; For a brilliant discussion of this approach to life and energy, see Santos Granero (2009); see also Shaw (2002).
18 CP, 31.
19 CP, 48.
20 Ibid., 38.
21 Ibid., 45; on washing, see Green (2007: 200).
22 CP, 48.
23 Ibid., 32.
24 Ibid., 199.
25 For discussion of the Mandinga pouches (*bolsas de Mandingas*), see Fromont (2020).
26 There is a longer description of this in the prologue to Green (2001).

27 CP, 92.
28 Ibid., 92, fn. 853.
29 Ibid., 187, 209.
30 Ibid., 188.
31 For an excellent summary of this knowledge, see Havik (2016: 190–93); see also Jobson (1968: 134).
32 AGI, Escribanía, 1979A, no. 8, fol. 45v.
33 Ibid., fol. 46r.
34 AHU, CU, Guiné, Caixa 1, doc. 23, Anexo 1.
35 See especially Kananoja (2021); for a discussion of Western medical imperialism in the twentieth century, see Bernault (2020), Hooper (1999), Lachenal (2014) and Peiretti-Courtis (2021).

## Conclusion

1 On this role, see Urdang (1979).
2 LR, fol. 293r.
3 Ibid.
4 CP, 230.
5 Ibid., 232.
6 Ibid.

# Index

Abreu, Acenso de 234
Achebe, Nwando 2
Afonso, Domingas 72, 117
Afonso, Domingos 245
Afonso, Luís 97, 209
Aguiar, Júlia de 74
Aguiar, Paulo Rodrigues d' 221
*akontings* 219
Alberto, Pedro 186
*alcaide* 42
Alentejo 36, 48, 93, 99, 175, 259
Alexander VII, Pope 251
Almada, André Alvares d' 8, 88, 199
Almeida, Manoel de 57, 59, 117, 279
Almeida, Ralphina Phillott de 56
*alúas* 99, 102, 148, 276
Alvarenga, João d' 244
Álvares, Domingos 6
Álvares, Manoel 85, 164
Álvarez Prieto, Manoel 37–8
Amsterdam 11, 26, 31
Andrada, Antonio Nunes de 207
Andrada, Florença de 73
Andrade, Domingos de 225, 260
Andrade, Gregório de 261
Andrade, João de 63
Andrade, Manoel 190
Angola 1, 4, 22, 77, 100, 123, 129, 137–8, 169, 197, 231
Antioquia 129
Antonio, Miguel 207, 210
Aragão, Manoel Paez de 2

Araujo, Ana Lúcia 77
Aredas, Domingos de 46, 91, 164, 184, 226–7, 255
  development of feud with Jorge Gonçalves Frances 42, 227–8
  friendship with Ambrósio Gomes and Bibiana Vaz 47–8
  hatred of Crispina Peres 41
Aredas, Mateus de 42, 47
Ayala, Gonçalo Gamboa de 119
Azores Islands 30

Badiou, Alain 237
Bafeta 110
Bahár 111
Bahelampa, Isabel 166
Bainunk 9, 17, 30–33, 57–9, 77, 109, 141, 153, 157, 165, 167–8, 170, 172, 180, 182–184, 241, 279
*balafon* 172
Balanta 76, 109, 111
Banana, Rua da (Ribeira Grande) 125
Banjul 61
Baoula 59, 106, 112, 114, 116, 156
*barafulas* 95, 164, 170, 176, 199, 206
Barbados 138, 277
Barbara 259
barbers 146, 210–11, 257
Barra kingdom 62, 188
Barraza, Dioguo 130
Barraza, Sebastião Rodrigues 43, 45, 48, 83, 156, 177, 181, 184–5, 190, 214, 223

## Index

Barraza, Sebastião Rodrigues – *cont'd*.
  desire for freedom  44, 171, 181
  hatred of Crispina Peres  29
  love of Crispina Peres's slave
    Bonifacia  180
Barreira, Baltasar  148
Barreiras Vermelhas  63
Barreto, Pero Ferraz  23, 151, 248, 261
Barros, Barbosa  126
Bartolomeo  190
Bautista Pérez, João  6, 56, 62–5, 109–10, 119, 194
  death  177, 259
Bautista Pérez, Manoel  6, 67, 70–71, 82, 85, 91–5, 100, 110, 119, 152, 176–7, 193–4, 197–8, 200, 207, 209, 216, 221, 249–50, 258–9
  daughter in Cacheu  250
  involvement in slave traffic  163, 168, 170–74, 186–7, 189
  New Christian origins  137, 152
  taste for ivory in Lima  98
Baxere  156
Belcasar, Antonio Peres  141
Benin  22, 113, 144
Bezerra, António de Barros  33
Biafada  58, 109, 165–6, 167, 170
Bidassou  109, 111–12, 114, 119
Bijagó(s)  9, 42, 47, 62, 75, 104, 112, 117, 164, 168–9, 173, 182–5, 190, 201, 222, 239, 269, 276
Bijini  149
Bintang  63, 75
  *bolon*  20, 63, 80, 118
Bissau  36, 62, 115–18, 154, 167, 169, 179
  Carnival  56, 153, 218
blacksmiths  97, 108, 177, 186, 192–3, 195, 205–6, 230
Bolivia  100
*bolons*  42, 111, 114, 118

Bonifacia, enslaved member of
  Crispina Peres's household  41, 180, 182, 226
Bosól  79
Braga, Domingas  217
Braga, Francisco de  133
Braga, Teodósia  217
Brazil  1, 6, 22, 23, 31, 37, 49, 123, 128, 138, 169, 212, 231, 250, 268, 277
Brotherhood of the Rosary  18, 126, 152, 169
Bugendo  17, 56, 77, 104, 112–13, 141–2, 167, 176, 241
  attacks by the Kassanké  78
  early settlement and trade  78
  surplus agricultural produce  201
Bujé  114, 141, 147, 185, 191, 211, 240–41
Bundu  96
Busis, King of  189

Cabaçeira  62
Cabeça de Vide  36
Cabo Verde Islands  1, 3, 17, 26, 37, 57, 67, 69, 129, 151, 199, 228, 230, 242, 250, 257, 261
  aridity of  17–18
  connections to Cacheu  120–27, 219
  droughts of the 1580s  78, 123
  elites of  22
  involvement of clergy in slaving  164
  Jesuit mission  154
Caboi  156
Cacheu  1, 3, 5, 6, 7, 8, 11, 15, 23, 24, 27, 29, 33, 36, 41–2, 45–8, 50, 56, 58–61, 63, 67, 74, 77, 101, 105, 110, 129, 143, 158, 160, 178, 188, 193, 198, 200, 216, 241, 249–50, 257–8, 262, 265, 267–8, 273, 275, 278–81
  architecture  85, 88, 193

324

# Index

attacks from Pepel 80–81, 85
borders 80, 109
Catholic practice 149–57, 207
centrality of slavery in the economy 162–5
climate change in seventeenth century 101–2, 273
condition of today 16, 83–4
connections to Cabo Verde Islands 17, 18, 23, 120–27, 219
connections to Cartagena 129–32
daily presence of slavery 8–9, 170–75, 273, 277–8
dependence on surrounding communities 18
disease 253, 259, 262–3, 271–3
escape of enslaved people 186–7
feuds 40, 45, 51, 223, 227–30
fights 73, 213, 229–30
forms of money 175–8
gambling 221–2
gossip 194, 213–14, 224–30
professions associated with Middle Passage 204
quarrels 213, 263
regional links 115–20
religious coexistence/marketplace 54–5, 147–9, 153–4, 157, 159, 215–19
ship repairs 202–4
significance of *djabakós* 142–6, 262–4
site of binge drinking 65, 71, 212–13, 219–23
slavery 9, 167–9, 180, 189–90
trade 194–6
wage labour 192–3
women's dominant role 52–5, 63, 66, 68–70
Cairo 128
Calabar 105
Calhão, Rua do 231
Canchungo 15, 84
Capei 156
Capuchins 10, 34, 100, 154, 167, 185
Cardoso, Pedro Semedo 2
Cardozo, João 202
Carneiro, Gaspar 114
Carreira, Rua da (Ribeira Grande) 125, 220
Cartagena 11, 17, 26, 96, 149, 173–4, 195, 202, 216–17, 272
cruelty of treatment of Native Americans 130–31
importance of in seventeenth century 129–30
Inquisition tribunal 37–8, 137
volume of traffic in enslaved Africans from Cacheu 162–3, 165
Carvalho, Sebastião 230
Casamance 17, 31, 56–7, 59, 63, 65, 77, 80, 97, 112, 118, 159, 184–5, 191, 196–7, 199, 201, 222
Cassão 20, 63, 73, 236
  market 64
  Queen of 56
  ship repairs 205
  *sobrados* 89
Cassilha, daughter of Crispina Peres 166
Castanho, Diogo Barraça 37
Castanho, João Nunes 28, 83, 121, 142, 214, 228
  hatred of Crispina Peres 28
Castanho, Vidigal 110
Castelbranco, Jorge Mesquita de 1, 2, 17, 247
  swindling behaviour 22
  unpopularity 21
Cavazzi, Antonio de 100, 251
Cazil 156, 180

325

# Index

Chaves, Friar Luis de 155–6
China 93–5, 100, 175
*chinas* 41, 43, 55, 65, 74, 113, 134–5, 139, 142–3, 147, 153, 167–8, 176, 180, 213–15, 276
Cidade Velha 18
Civil war between Portugal and Spain 35–6
Cobiana 107
Cocalí 109, 148
Coelho, Francisco de Lemos 21, 75, 81, 86, 109, 114, 119, 137, 149, 172, 185, 197, 207, 241
  description of Jakhanké 99
  description of kola-nut trade 110–11
  description of profits of the slave traffic 160
  feud with Jorge Gonçalves Frances 81, 229
Colombia 11, 17, 26, 37, 96, 128–9, 182
*combetes* 85, 89, 102, 192, 194–6, 200, 206
Conakry 61, 101
Constantinople 105, 129
Correa, Francisco 230
Correia, Francisco 121
Costa, Antonio da Nunes 110
Costa, Antonio Rodrigues da 174
Costa, Mateus da 176, 209
Costa, Thome Fidalgo de 221
cotton spinning 67, 121
Courbe, Jajolet de la 148

Dakar 61–2, 105
Democratic Republic of Congo 77
Dia 128
Dias, Brásia 142
Dias, Madalena 225
Dias, Nicolaça 142
Diaz Copete, Juan 165
Dioguo, Mestre 56

Direita, Rúa 86, 92, 95
*djabakós* 40–41, 47–8, 51, 57, 60, 82, 114, 138, 142–3, 146–7, 159, 176, 185, 208, 210, 212, 214, 240, 253, 260–62, 264, 269, 271–2, 274, 277, 279, 281
  contradictory understandings of by Portuguese traders 140–41
  plural religious worlds 139–40, 159, 161
  political role/influence 137, 157, 254, 262
  remedies prescribed 263–7, 270
Donelha, André 109, 148, 205
Duarte, Domingos 69, 73
Duarte, Fernão 190
Duarte, João Rodrigues 137, 189, 230, 259
Duarte, Maria Rodrigues 245
Duarte, Vicente Rodrigues 137, 140, 179, 204, 218, 229
Dutch empire 1, 10, 122–3, 138, 231, 250

Eiria, slave of Crispina Peres 28, 166, 179
Élvas, Antonio Fernandes de 272
England 46, 94
enslaved persons 29, 40, 76, 110, 117, 119, 121
  condition on Santiago island, Cabo Verde 122, 125–6
  death on ship in Casamance 160
  escape to freedom from Cacheu 186–7
  life of in Cacheu households 44–5, 180–82
  work in Cacheu 83, 192
Évora 37–8

Falabane 200
Farim 4–5, 23, 27, 31–3, 46, 48–49, 59, 67, 74–5, 109, 115–17, 132, 156, 195, 197, 205, 211, 230–31, 245

# Index

foundation 119
parties 72
rooms for rent 91
scandalous behaviour by Luis
　Rodrigues 4–5, 49, 152, 165, 181,
　203, 212, 219–20, 261
trade with Sierra Leone 110, 114,
　162, 196
Faro, André de 133–5, 152, 154, 156, 161,
　249, 257
Faroutamba 200
Fernandes, Afonso 262
Fernandes, Bastião 202
Fernandes, Domingos 170
Fernandes, Francisca 206
Ferreira, Leonor 67, 74, 121–2
Figueiredo, Rodrigo de 233
Floup 33, 57–8, 80, 106, 108–9, 114, 149,
　156–8, 167–8, 171–3, 183, 190, 223, 279
　attacks on slave-trafficking ships
　168, 185, 276
Fogaça, Vicente 217, 228, 249, 260
Fogo island 117, 121, 123, 229
Fournier, Jacques 26
Fouta Djalon 107, 167, 169, 205
Fragoso, António Mendes 28
Franca, Damião de 189
France 46
Frances, Álvaro Gonçalves 46, 221
　Inquisition trial of 37
　involvement in slave traffic 163, 168
　New Christian origins in Portugal 36
Frances, Jorge Gonçalves 5, 25, 39–40,
　47, 51, 68, 179, 184, 224, 227, 229,
　239–40, 260, 279
　attempt to calm Cacheu after
　　Crispina Peres's arrest 33, 187
　care for Crispina Peres on her
　　return from Lisbon 280–81
　Christian practice 36

feud with Domingos de Aredas 42
involvement in slave trafficking 164
life history of 35–6
mixed African-Portuguese heritage
　26, 38
New Christian ancestry 36, 137
poor health 39, 60, 211, 255–7, 262, 268
use of idioms from West African
　languages 226
year of birth, approximate 78
Frances, Manuel Luis 228
Frances, Rodrigo Gonçalves 91
Freire, João Rodrigues 234
Frique Fraque 210
Fromont, Cécile 141
Fulani 95, 107–8, 110, 159, 167–9, 173,
　197, 205, 216, 276
Fuuta Tòoro 96, 107

Gabú 205–6
Gambia river 17, 21, 56, 62, 65, 87, 96,
　101, 106–8, 110, 112, 118–19, 123, 138,
　148–9, 161, 163, 167, 178, 194–5, 197,
　199, 216
Ganagoga (João Ferreira) 58
Geba 27, 30–32, 35, 62, 74–5, 109, 119–20,
　132, 196–7, 230
　Islamic presence 148
　kola-nut trade 110–11, 118, 128, 195
Ginció 111
Ginzburg, Carlo 6
Godins, Manoel Lopes 217
gold 119, 176–8, 240
Gomes, Ambrósio 46, 50–51, 171, 224–6,
　231, 269
　hatred of Jorge Gonçalves Frances
　　47, 218
　New Christian ancestry 48, 137
　practice of African religions 47–8,
　　141, 147, 158

## Index

Gomes, Antonio 145
Gomes, Luis 181
Gomes, Mãe 269
Gomes, Teodósia 47
Gomes, Vicente 1, 21
Gomez, Michael 55
Gonçalvez, Luis 64
Gonsalves, Maria 122, 166, 245
Gorée 36, 53, 137
Griffiths, Jay 237–8, 246
*griots* 170, 172–3, 219
*gris-gris* 48, 98, 147, 149, 157, 205
*grumetes* 41–3, 64, 87, 109, 111, 121–2, 156, 167, 194–5
Guadalupe, Virgin of 134
Guinea-Bissau 1, 3, 4, 15, 20, 21, 32, 54, 57, 62, 77, 104, 106, 148–9, 159, 178, 184, 205, 219, 236, 267, 275
    egalitarian societies 108–9
    markets 61, 112–13
    rivers 8
    wars of Independence 14, 182, 219, 277
Guinea-Conakry 30, 144, 148, 197
Guinguim 20, 31, 32, 112, 118, 147, 158, 167, 184–5, 211, 241
    Capuchin missionary visit in 1663 133–5, 139, 152, 154, 161, 217–18
Gujarat 11, 95
Gulf of Urabá 131
*gumbé* 219

Havana 22
Hawthorne, Walter 76
healers and healing 15, 51, 60, 113–14, 138, 140–41, 174, 208–11, 253–4, 262, 265–7, 269–71, 274
Hegel, G. W. F. 11
Henriques, Manoel 1
Hodges, Cornelius 101, 176

honey 119, 199, 223
Horta, José da Silva 97

Ica 100
India 94–5, 105, 123
Inquisition of Portugal 4, 26, 30, 35, 86, 103
    patriarchy of 52
    procedure 28
    secrecy of trials 28
    suspension of in 1674 10
Ireton, Chloe 163
Islam 133, 137–8, 140, 154, 159, 168, 178, 262
    growth in Senegambia 147–9
Istanbul 11
ivory carvings 97–9, 102, 162–3
Izabel 259

Jakhanké 10, 58, 65, 81, 98, 137, 140, 167, 172, 199, 218, 223, 240, 265, 276
    method of teaching 99
    presence in Cacheu 147–9, 157
    regional diaspora 128
Jamaica 22, 277
James Island 110, 138
Janjangbureh 205
Jesuits 34, 148, 154, 162
Jeta Island 106
Joal 35, 62, 138
Jobson, Richard 62, 88, 149, 167, 188, 194, 223
    description of royal audience 134
    description of *tabankas* 87
    interest in gold 176, 240–41
John IV (King of Portugal) 35, 101, 273
Jola 106
Jolof 21, 33, 131, 138, 197
Jorge, Beatriz 2
Judaism 33, 133, 137–8, 140, 159, 168, 172–3, 230–31, 233, 279

## Index

Kaabu 31, 57, 74, 107, 109–12, 116, 144, 148–9, 172, 184, 197, 222, 243
   consolidation 120
   role in slave traffic 117, 119
Kansala 205
*kantong* 96
Kantora 20
Kassanké 78, 109, 156, 170
Kaur 20
   as biggest town in seventeenth-century Gambia 21
kola-nut trade 110–11, 117, 148, 162, 195, 197, 200
Kombo 149
Kriol 11, 21, 57, 59, 66, 226, 268
Kristón 167–9, 204, 209, 276

Ladurie, Emmanuel le Roy 6
Laye, Camara 144–5
Lázara 189
Lima 6, 98, 100, 129, 137, 189, 229, 250, 259
Lisboa, Diogo Rodrigues de 209, 216
Lisbon 4, 5, 11, 23, 24, 26–7, 30–1, 71, 80, 117, 139, 149, 151, 179, 194–5, 202, 210, 250, 253, 278–9
   gender relations 52
   imperial theory 89
Liste, Fracisco Alvares de 2
Lobo, Miguel 231–2, 260
Logroño 264
Lopes, Ana 71
Lopes, Baltasar 145
Lopes, Domingas 66
Lopes, Genebra 54, 142
Lopes, Isabel 54, 70–71, 142
Lopes, Susana 153, 217
Lordello, Friar Paulo de 26, 127, 150, 155–6, 158, 161, 227, 242, 249, 257
   involvement in mission to Guinguim 133–5

preparations of Crispina Peres's trial 26–7
*lumos* 112–16, 195, 198
Luz, Maria da 127

Machado, Simão 83
Madeira 1, 22, 212, 219, 227, 235
Madinah 128
Magalhães, Luis de 81
Maio island 123, 127
Makkah 128–9
Malacca 96, 104–5, 128
Malê uprising 137
Mali (Republic of) 159
Mali, Empire of 56, 87, 107, 112, 169
   decline 108–9
Mancaigne 106
Mancara, Tomane 64
Mandinga (people) 33, 58, 64, 98, 102, 109, 111–12, 123, 140–41, 170, 188, 206
Mandinga pouches (*bolsas de Mandinga*) 12, 47, 141, 266
Manes 87, 98
Manjako 15, 106
Manoel I, King of Portugal 31
Manrique, Antonio Rodrigues de San Isidro 130
Mansa Bare 200
Manuel, Maria 2
Martín, Francisco 163, 168
Mascarenhas, Canon Antonio 233
Mascarenhas, Sebastião Fernandes 224, 260
Mascarenhas, João 243
Mascarenhas, Thome Vaz 233
Mata de Putame 79–81, 154, 158, 185, 201, 257
Matamba 251
Matos, Manoel de 48, 137
Mauritania 159

Mbena, Chica 129, 269
medical colonialism 253, 274
Mendes, Domingos 239
Mendes, Ines 190
Mendes, Maria 69, 121, 146, 155, 182, 245, 266–7
Mendes, Natalia 268–70
Mendonça, Diogo Furtado de 73, 231–2, 248
Mendonça, Joseph de 280
Mendonça, Pedro Furtado de 245
Mermellada, Salvador Rodrigues 73
Mexico 77, 95, 175
Mexico City 134
mini Ice Age 79, 100–102, 273
Miranda, Izabel 71
Misericordia, Rua da 232–3
Misogyny of the Portuguese empire 51, 69–70, 73–4
Monteira, Beatriz 50
Monteiro, Belchior 234
Montemor-o-Novo 48
Morais, Pero Vaz de 193, 221
Morales, Jorge López de 272–3
Moreno, Pero 170
*moriscos* 265
Morocco 159
Moura 260
Moura, Luis de 218
Mouira, Manoel Dias de 230
Mota, Francisco 167–9

Nafafé, José Lingna 136
Nalú 173, 186
Narvaes, Francisco de 259
National Centre of Arts and Culture of The Gambia 20
Ndongo 169, 251
New Christians 31, 47, 56, 111, 129, 137, 189, 259

Newton, Isaac 251
*ngoni* 172
Nhamena 62
Nhonho creek 77
Nigeria 22, 113
*Njal's Saga* 226
Nunes, Pedro 115, 165, 171, 203, 249
Nunes river 30, 32, 34, 42, 109, 117, 199, 241
Nunez, Maria 198
*nyantios* 116, 120
Nzumbi 137

Ohanbú (daughter of Crispina Peres and Jorge Gonçalves Frances) 37, 58, 166
Oliveira, Joseph Gonçalves de 46
*Ordem de Cristo* 35, 137
Ornelas, Antonio da Fonseca de 171, 185, 218, 227
Ottoman Empire 11, 31
Ouidah 105, 144
Our Lady of Victory (Church in Cacheu) 129, 152

Pabuto 156
Pachesi 56, 73
Pais, Pedro 91, 143, 240, 265
Palenque de Limón 129
Palma, João de 189
Palmares 136–7
Panamá 129
Passos, Manoel de 265
Pecixe Island 106
Pegado, Gaspar 179
Pelegrino, Manoel 138
Peña, Angel Fuente de la 167–9
Pepel 9, 33, 37, 80, 88, 90, 102, 106, 109, 114, 153, 155, 157, 167–8, 170, 173, 183, 190, 279

# Index

attacks on Cacheu 80–82, 85, 108, 152, 156, 168, 185, 257
migrations to the coast 107
Pereira, Bernardo Rodrigues 230
Pereira, Roque 170
Peres, Crispina 3, 5, 7, 9, 13, 14, 52, 61, 68, 226, 257, 260, 277–81
   accusations of keeping a spirit-snake 145–7
   alleged 'witchcraft' to keep husband bedbound 39, 255
   ally of Bainunk and Pepel peoples 155–6
   arrest 33, 155–6, 187, 278
   Christian practice 31, 32–3
   denunciation of her enemies 28, 227
   deportation to Portugal by the Inquisition 29–30, 139
   household (with Jorge Gonçalves Frances) 27–9, 34, 40, 43, 45, 51, 90–91, 143, 174, 213, 248–9, 266, 279
   influence in Cacheu 56–61
   Inquisition trial 25–7, 46, 136, 139, 146, 185, 204, 208, 210, 218, 227, 241, 253, 276, 279–80
   involvement in slave traffic 168, 174–5
   life history and upbringing 30–32
   mixed African-Portuguese heritage 26, 38
   multilingualism 57–8
   penance and return to Cacheu 279–80
   relations with *djabakós* 47, 60, 139–43, 174 253–5, 264–7, 269–70
   sadness at daughter's death 71, 253, 269
   tensions of marriage with Jorge 39–40, 179
   use of *chinas* 142, 214, 239
   violence towards her own slaves 44, 51, 179
   year of birth, approximate 78
Peres, Francisca 2
Peres, Marina 232
Peres, Rodrigo (father of Crispina Peres) 30
   possible New Christian ancestry 31
perpetuan 94
Peru 77, 128–9, 259
Pessoa, Domingas (mother of Crispina Peres) 30, 32, 34, 57, 59
Pessoa, Florença (grandmother of Crispina Peres) 31, 32
*picote* 94
Pimenta, João 260
Pinto, Antonio 71, 176
Pires, Antonio 203, 261
Pires, Domingues 209
Pontes, Antonio Vaz de 23, 45, 71, 73, 150, 155–6, 228–9, 255, 265, 280
   sex life 70, 152, 225–6
   slave trafficker 151
   wealth 129, 155
Portugal 4, 24, 29, 35, 46, 48, 69, 86, 94, 99, 128–9, 133, 138, 146, 169, 259
Portuguese empire 10, 35–8, 41, 49–51, 53, 68–9, 74, 81–5, 89–90, 108, 110, 122, 128, 250
   decline 123–7, 138
Potosí 93, 99, 178, 191
Praia 18

Querido, Baltasar Gonçalves 190
Qur'an 98–9, 102, 147, 276

Reis, João 216
Ribeira Grande 1, 2, 3, 17, 24, 67, 121–4, 147, 153, 164, 166, 189, 243–4, 246–7, 249, 257

## Index

Ribeira Grande – *cont'd.*
  condition today 18, 125
  female traders 1, 66
  fights in streets 49, 222–3, 232–4
  Franciscan monastery 26, 150, 155, 242, 248
  urban environment 124–7
Rodney, Walter 178
Rodrigues, Agostinho 125, 220–21
Rodrigues, Bras 220, 244
Rodrigues, Diogo 187
Rodrigues, Francisco 194
Rodrigues, João 261
Rodrigues, Luis 12, 23, 52, 68, 71, 73, 92, 121–2, 124–6, 150–51, 166, 181, 189, 225, 230, 241, 243–7, 249
  acquittal by the Inquisition and return to Cabo Verde 11, 278–9
  fights involving 122, 232–4
  fomenting of Crispina Peres's trial 5, 48–9, 230–31
  fomenting of his own trial by the Archdeacon of Santiago Island 231–2
  many enemies 232–4
  sale of fake amulets 147
  scandalous behaviour 4, 49–50, 117, 125–6, 152, 165, 219–21, 230–34, 244–5
  swindling at cards 220–21
  unholy consecration of the Host 150–51
Rodrigues, Maria 66–8
Rodrigues, Nicolão 201
Rome 170
Rouen 66, 94
Royal Africa Company 101, 110, 138, 176
Rufisque 32, 35, 65
Russia 271

Safunco 79
St Anthony's Hermitage (in Vila Quente) 86
St Louis 53
Salafi reform movement 14
Salgado, Manoel Rodrigues 51, 230
Salvador da Bahía 11, 22, 113, 137
San Juan de las Palmas 130
Sanguedogu 63–4, 118, 184
Sano, Buckor 188, 240
Santiago Island (Cabo Verde) 1, 2, 3, 7, 17, 21, 80, 150, 164, 180, 243, 245, 248, 260
  connections to Cacheu 23, 245
  Creole class 123, 127
Santo António, Rua 25, 86
Santos, Vanicléia Silva 12
São Bras quarter (Ribeira Grande) 125
São Domingos (town on Santiago Island) 234
São Domingos river 4, 23, 63, 77, 79, 108, 112, 142, 168, 214, 241
São Filipe fortress (Ribeira Grande) 124
São Pedro quarter (Ribeira Grande) 125
São Sebastião quarter (Ribeira Grande) 125
São Tomé island 22, 123
São Vicente, Friar Sebastião de 70, 180
Sapis 97, 99, 163
Sara, Kingdom of 42, 51, 176, 184
Senegal 77, 159, 205, 246, 275
Senegal river 53, 96, 107, 160
Senegambia (Greater) 10, 18, 25, 33, 59, 75, 81, 88, 107–8, 112, 116, 138, 161, 170, 178, 185, 187, 190, 197, 199, 205, 208, 213, 236, 238, 252, 254, 257, 272–3, 280
Senteio, Rodrigo Anes 232–3
Serèer 33, 197, 216
Serra, Manoel da 245

## Index

Sesimbra 37
Seville 11, 26, 37, 169
Sierra Leone 32, 42, 53, 62, 87, 97–8, 101, 105, 109, 112, 115, 117–20, 161–3, 195, 197, 222, 242
*signares* 53
Silva, Lourenço Mendonça de 136, 169
Silva, Manoel da 96, 104
silver 93–4, 99, 104, 120, 176–7, 205
Simbandi-Balante 275
Siqueira, Barnabé 157
slavery 8–9, 38, 51, 126, 161, 167–9, 189–90
  and dehumanization 189
  attacks on slaving ships by Senegambians 161, 168, 184
  branding 9, 170, 174, 175, 182
  economic centrality in Cacheu 162, 175–6
  increase of in West Africa after rise of Atlantic traffic 178
  maroon community in Bujé 185
  post-1500 changes in the Senegambian institution 179, 185
  relationship to death 174
  relationship to money 175–6, 189–91
  role of demand in 9, 277
  sexual objectification through 188–9
Smith, Adam 11, 193
Snakes and religious practice 144–7
Soár 111
Soares, Dioguo 221
Soares, Pedro 262
*sobrados* 16, 84–5, 89, 93
Socorro, Maria de 2
Songhay empire 108
Sousa, Antonio Gomes de 121
Souto, Antonio Peres de 261
Soviet Union 271
Spain 4, 29, 35, 94, 128–9, 169, 264–5
  *convivência* 138

Sulayman, Mansa 56
Susana 259
Susu 109, 112
Sutucó 128, 132, 148–9, 199, 223, 240
Sweet, James 6

*tabankas* 75, 87–8, 108, 197–8, 200, 260, 270, 275, 281
Tancoaralle 62
Tandakunda 62
Tamba Dibi 117, 143, 167
Tavares, Francisco 121, 140–41, 185, 255
Tavares, João Fernandes 232–4
Tavares, Pedro Correia 229
Tavira 262
*tchon* 158
Teles, Dioguo de 82
Tendaba 62, 119
Tenguela, Koli 107
textiles 75, 104–5, 128, 176, 196–9, 276–7
  production 95–7, 162
  trade 94–6, 110
Timbuktu 159
time 4, 14, 212, 235–52
  and imperialism 237, 247–52
  clock time 237, 243, 249–51, 278
  relativity 240
  waiting 222, 235, 238, 242–3
Tinoco, Manoel Gonçalves 234
tobacco 104
*toka-churs* 215
Torres, Jeronimo de 176
Torres, Manoel Pires 260
Traoré, Tiramaghan 107
traffickers 6, 8–9, 20, 22, 38, 40, 57, 66, 72, 101, 117, 121–3, 129, 131, 159, 168, 189, 272
transatlantic slave trade 9, 59, 117, 122, 131, 162, 165, 166–70, 263

## Index

attacks on trafficking ships by
  Senegambians 161, 168, 184
connection to acquisition of capital
  175
disease on trafficking ships 173–4,
  209–10, 272–3
maroon communities in today's
  Colombia 129–31
Middle Passage 9, 165, 204, 209–10
naming as act of possession 165–6
potential impact on gender
  relations 75
role of Catholic church 151–2, 164
sexual objectification through 188–9
uprisings by the enslaved on
  trafficking ships 132
Tripoli 128
Tubabodaga 109, 116

UNESCO 18
Usól 79

Valdeveso, João de 152
Vatican 10, 169
Vaz, António 66
Vaz, Bibiana 46, 50, 52, 55, 231, 269, 276
Vaz, Esperança 66
Vaz, Sebastião 54–5, 166, 181, 204, 241
Vélingara 205
Viçoso, Manoel 231
Victoria 259
Viegas, Domingos Rodrigues 121, 126, 233

Vila Quente 25, 54, 63, 66–7, 70, 74–5,
  84, 86, 88, 92, 95, 152, 166, 200,
  206–7, 241, 251, 268, 270
defences 88, 100
Pepel quarter 86–7
religious life 54–5, 87, 142, 153–4,
  157, 174, 217–18, 223, 235, 260,
  265
Vogado, Gaspar 39, 51, 150, 229–30,
  258, 263–4, 266

*warri* 223–4
Wassu 21, 236
wax 66, 82, 92, 110, 114, 118, 120, 129,
  138, 152
stored in *combetes* 85
trade from Casamance 195–6, 199
weaving 67, 95, 108, 193, 197
Wolof 21, 33
women's households and labour 1–2,
  55, 61–2, 66–8, 70–71, 121, 142, 201–2,
  265–6, 277
World Bank 275

Xacôbraga 135, 154
Ximenes, António Fernandes 26

Yòrubá 113

Zaragoza mines 129
Ziguinchor (Bichangor) 20, 62–3, 77,
  118, 195, 241
Zurze, Manoel Rodriguez 233–4